D1526867

Psychiatric
and
Mental Health Nursing
with
Children and Adolescents

Edited by

Patricia West, MSN, RN, CS
Clinical Nurse Specialist
Psychiatric-Medical Unit
St. John Hospital
Detroit, Michigan

Christina L. Sieloff Evans, MSN, RN, CNA
Clinical Director
Psychiatric Program
Oakland General Hospital
Madison Heights, Michigan

AN ASPEN PUBLICATION®
Aspen Publishers, Inc.
Gaithersburg, Maryland
1992

Psychiatric and mental health nursing with children and adolescents /
edited by Patricia West, Christina L. Sieloff Evans.
p. cm.
Includes bibliographical references and index.
ISBN: 0-8342-0240-9
1. Child psychiatric nursing. 2. Adolescent psychiatric nursing. I. West, Patricia.
II. Evans, Christina L. S.
[DNLM: I. Psychiatric Nursing—in adolescence. 2. Psychiatric Nursing—in
infancy & childhood.   WY 160 P9713]
RJ502.3.P79   1992
610.73'68'033—dc20
DNLM/DLC
for Library of Congress
91-26125
CIP

Aspen Publishers, Inc., grants permission for photocopying for limited personal or
internal use. This consent does not extend to other kinds of copying, such as copying
for general distribution, for advertising or promotional purposes, for creating new
collective works, or for resale. For information, address Aspen Publishers, Inc.,
Permissions Department, 200 Orchard Ridge Drive, Gaithersburg, Maryland 20878.

The authors have made every effort to ensure the accuracy of the information herein,
particularly with regard to drug selection and dose. However, appropriate information
sources should be consulted, especially for new or unfamiliar drugs or procedures. It is
the responsibility of every practitioner to evaluate the appropriateness of a particular
opinion in the context of actual clinical situations and with due consideration to new
developments. Authors, editors, and the publisher cannot be held responsible for any
typographical or other errors found in this book.

Editorial Services: Barbara Priest

Library of Congress Catalog Card Number: 91-26125
ISBN: 0-8342-0240-9

Printed in the United States of America

1 2 3 4 5

To my daughters, Julie and Katie, who
have taught me about caring for children,
and to my husband, Marty,
whose patience, love, and hours of
child care made this project possible.

P.W.

To Doris and Louis, and Mildred Sieloff who were,
and are, always there.
And to Joyce Hoyt. Without her as my faculty and superb
mentor for my first psychiatric experience with children,
this book might never have been written.

C.S.E.

Contributors

Virginia Trotter Betts, MSN, JD, RN
Associate Professor
School of Nursing
Vanderbilt University
Senior Fellow
Vanderbilt Institute for Public Policy Studies
Nashville, Tennessee

Beth Bonham, MSN, RN, CS
Assistant Professor
Department of Nursing
Marian College
Associate
BDGW Counseling Associates
Indianapolis, Indiana

Kathleen Zink Bradley, MSN, RN
Psychiatric Clinical Nurse Specialist
Children's Hospital Medical Center
Cincinnati, Ohio

Ann W. Burgess, DNSc, RN, CS, FAAN
van Amerigen Professor of Psychiatric Mental
  Health Nursing
School of Nursing
University of Pennsylvania
Philadelphia, Pennsylvania

Deane L. Critchley, PhD, RN, CS, FAAN
Private Practice & Consultation
Child and Adolescent Psychiatric Nursing
Albuquerque, New Mexico

Catherine Gray Deering, PhD, RN, CS
Adjunct Assistant Professor
College of Health Sciences
Georgia State University
Atlanta, Georgia

Linda M. Finke, PhD, RN
Associate Dean of Graduate Programs
School of Nursing
Indiana University
Indianapolis, Indiana

Hertha L. Gast, PhD, RN
Assistant Professor
College of Nursing
Wayne State University
Detroit, Michigan

Lynne Goodykoontz, PhD, RN, CNA
Dean, College of Nursing
University of North Carolina at Greensboro
Greensboro, North Carolina

Carol R. Hartman, DNSc, RN, CS
Professor of Psychiatric Mental Health
  Nursing
School of Nursing
Boston College
Chestnut Hill, Massachusetts

Billie J. Hayward, MSN, RN, CS
Certified Clinical Nurse Specialist
Private Practice
Farmington Hills, Michigan

Charlotte A. Herrick, PhD, RN, CS
Acting Chairman
Department of Community Mental Health
    Nursing
College of Nursing
University of South Alabama
Mobile, Alabama

Robert H. Herrick, MD
Chief, Division of Child Psychiatry
College of Medicine
University of South Alabama
Mobile, Alabama

Madeleine M. Leininger, PhD, LHD, DS, DNS, RN, CTN, FAAN
Professor of Nursing
College of Nursing
Professor of Anthropology
Department of Anthropology
Wayne State University
Detroit, Michigan

Sharon K. Lewis, MA, RN, CNA
Assistant Administrator for Clinical Services
    and Quality Planning Kingswood Hospital
Ferndale, Michigan

Maxine E. Loomis, PhD, RN, CS, FAAN
Distinguished Professor Emeritus
College of Nursing
University of South Carolina
Columbia, South Carolina

Judith Fry McCornish, PhD, RN
Assistant Professor
College of Nursing
Wayne State University
Detroit, Michigan

Nancy D. Opie, DNS
Professor
College of Nursing and Health
University of Cincinnati
Cincinnati, Ohio

Geraldine S. Pearson, MSN, RN, CS
Nurse Clinical Specialist
RiverView Hospital for Children
Middleton, Connecticut
Assistant Clinical Professor
School of Nursing
Yale University
New Haven, Connecticut

Patricia C. Pothier, MS, RN, FAAN
Professor Emeritus
School of Nursing
University of California, San Francisco
San Francisco, California

Alyson Moore Ross, MSN, RN
Adjunct Professor
School of Nursing
Vanderbilt University
Program Coordinator
School Based Counseling Program
Department of Child Psychiatry
Vanderbilt Mental Health Center
Nashville, Tennessee

Mary Lou de Leon Siantz, PhD, RN
Assistant Professor
Director of Child and Adolescent Programs
Graduate Department of Psychiatric Mental
    Health Nursing
School of Nursing
Indiana University
Indianapolis, Indiana

Sarah Stanley, MS, RN, CS, CNA
President
Advocates for Child Psychiatric Nursing
Assistant Director
Division of Nursing Practice and Economics
American Nurses' Association
Washington, DC

Sharon M. Valente, PhD, RN, FAAN
Adjunct Assistant Professor
Clinical Specialist in Mental Health
Department of Nursing
University of Southern California
Los Angeles, California

Louise C. Waszak, PhD, RN
Assistant Professor
School of Nursing
West Virginia University
Morgantown, WV

Sandra J. Wood, MSN, RN, CS
Clinical Faculty
Department of Nursing
Marian College
Associate
BDGW Counseling Associates
Indianapolis, Indiana

Edilma Yearwood, MA, RN, CS
Nursing Care Coordinator
Child Day Hospital—Bard House
New York Hospital, Westchester Division
White Plains, New York

Susan Lea Ziegler, BSN, RN
College of Nursing and Health
University of Cincinnati
Cincinnati, Ohio

Table of Contents

Foreword

It is natural as I think about child and adolescent psychiatric nursing and the nursing literature that describes the discipline that I compare this book with what I believe was the first book published in the field—*Nursing in Child Psychiatry* (Fagin, 1972). At that time, the field was new, and nursing authors were few and far between. There was no formal group unifying the practitioners and educators, and the practice experience among the writers was more promising than fulfilled. Changes in the latter characteristic are prominently displayed in this book.

The modest number of nurses who have had graduate preparation in child psychiatric nursing creates continuing problems. Certainly, in the late 1960s and throughout the 1970s, those of us who were actively engaged in the field believed not only that we could and should strengthen the field through a primary care approach, but also that our numbers must increase sharply to meet the needs of children and adolescents. The place of the child psychiatric nurse in a vast variety of settings, including the school, demanded a supply of specialists far greater than was available then. We believed that the field offered sufficient challenge and potential to draw interested nurses who would subsequently stake a claim to a distinctive practice that would advance the entire profession. Recently, several major figures in child psychiatry and health policy shared with me their similar hopes for the present. They indicated their belief that child psychiatric nurses are the ideal health care providers for community and school interventions for children of all ages (and their families). While happy to hear such laudatory comments about my own predictions and the value of our specialty, the fact is that we are very far from an adequate supply of nurses to meet our challenges and potential. Thus, policy questions about recruitment must be examined and answered by nursing, the federal government and its funding agencies, and foundations.

Although admittedly few in number, the exciting role models who now practice in the field of child and adolescent psychiatric and mental health nursing are evident throughout this book. The authors' expertise in theory, practice, and research shows the thrilling progress that nurses have made in the past 20 years—progress brought about by nurses' own dauntless interest and commitment, and helped by federal funding for training. We can be grateful for that past support and also hopeful that current trends in research funding from the National Center for Nursing Research, the National Institutes of Health, the National Institute of Mental Health, and other agencies will continue to enable nurses to expand their knowledge base for practice.

This impressive book will be read and valued by nurses and others who want to learn about or to work with emotionally disturbed children and adolescents. The chapters cover a wide variety of theoretical and practice areas, revealing the changes in knowledge and practice over the two decades since my book was published. Particularly gratifying to me is the testimony that nurses are working in areas of great concern to the public, in the "health" side of the health-illness continuum. Work with children who are having difficulties in communicating, socializing, and learning is vitally important to the families involved and pertains to vast numbers of people. Contemporary problems, such as eating problems, substance abuse, sex offending, and legal issues, are well presented throughout the book. The discussion of early intervention with high-risk infants and children is also extremely valuable. This area holds extraordinary promise for nursing intervention. Work with infants and their families calls for nurses' multiple talents. The possibilities for making a major contribution to the science of our field are abundant here.

Finally, the chapters on evaluation and research are extremely commendable. Examining the work that nurses do and exploring the directions for the future are crucial aspects of our continuance. The compilation of knowledge presented by these nurses transcends the boundaries of child and adolescent psychiatric nursing and will be useful to all readers interested in the broad aspects of working with children and families in our contemporary world.

Claire M. Fagin, Ph.D., R.N., F.A.A.N.
Margaret Bond Simon Dean of Nursing
School of Nursing
University of Pennsylvania
Philadelphia, Pennsylvania

REFERENCE

Fagin, C. (Ed.). (1972). *Nursing in child psychiatry.* St. Louis, MO: C.V. Mosby.

Preface

This book is a comprehensive text on psychiatric and mental health nursing with children, adolescents, and their families. It was created for all nurses with an interest in the emotional, interpersonal, and behavioral needs of youngsters and their families. The specialty of child and adolescent psychiatric and mental health nursing incorporates nurses in multiple settings: (1) psychiatric settings, where multidisciplinary teams address the psychiatric problems of youngsters; (2) mental health settings, which may focus on a child's adjustment difficulties; (3) health care settings, where a youngster's reaction to hospitalization, illness, injury, or long-term disabilities requires collaboration with a nurse; and (4) other settings (e.g., schools), where health promotion, screening, and early nursing interventions facilitate the mental and emotional growth of the child.

We chose to focus the book primarily on psychiatric nurses' direct role in caring for the individual youngster and family. Furthermore, this book is based on a nursing perspective of practice rather than the application of nursing within a medical perspective. The ANA's Classification System of Human Responses guided us in selecting the human response patterns that are of primary importance to child and adolescent psychiatric and mental health nurses. Nationally and internationally recognized nursing experts contributed chapters on their areas of nursing expertise.

The nursing process provided the organizing framework of the book. The major sections open with an overview of a component of the nursing process as applied to psychiatric nursing with children and adolescents. The following chapters are more detailed considerations of specific aspects of the respective component, particular populations of youngsters, or applications to various settings of child psychiatric nursing practice. Within the intervention chapters, conceptual frameworks and nursing diagnoses are identified. The need for nursing research is recognized and addressed throughout the chapters.

Acknowledgments

We acknowledge the efforts and support of the various individuals whose contributions made this work possible. Our many psychiatric nurse colleagues and contributors provided the impetus and the content for this text, stimulated our thinking, and supported the endeavor. The doctoral students and faculty at the Wayne State University College of Nursing facilitated our conceptualization of nursing and emphasized the importance of incorporating nursing theory and research into the practice environment. Dr. Marjorie Isenberg and Dr. Madeleine Leininger deserve particular recognition for their mentoring efforts.

We are particularly grateful to Patricia Pothier for her review of the early drafts of several chapters and for her valuable critiques and suggestions. Dr. Claire Fagin not only provided the foreword for this book, but also served as a role model for our nursing practice.

We also wish to thank Darlene Como and Nancy Weisgerber, former acquisitions editors at Aspen. Their efforts were extremely helpful and enabled the manuscript to become a reality.

Finally, we acknowledge our families and friends. Without their patience and support, this project would not have been completed.

1

The Specialty of Child and Adolescent Psychiatric Nursing

Patricia West and Christina L. Sieloff Evans

After reading this chapter, the reader will be able to:

1. identify three historical trends that influenced the emergence of child psychiatric and mental health nursing
2. describe the phenomena of interest to child and adolescent psychiatric nurses
3. explain the distinctive characteristics of the specialty of child and adolescent psychiatric nursing
4. describe the types of practitioners in child and adolescent psychiatric nursing and their respective roles

Psychiatric and mental health nursing with children and adolescents is a specialty area of nursing. The goal of nurses in this specialty is to promote mental health for youngsters and their families by intervening with human responses to actual or potential health problems (American Nurses' Association [ANA], 1980). In child psychiatric nursing, the predominant focus is on selected intrapersonal, behavioral, and interpersonal human responses.

The nursing process provides a guide for nurses to address these health goals systematically. They deliver care to individuals and families through direct interventions with individual youngsters, groups of children, and families. In addition, a nurse may also provide care in an indirect role, such as in consultation.

HISTORICAL PERSPECTIVE

The emergence of child psychiatric nursing as a specialty can be traced from the later part of the 19th and through the 20th century. Pothier (1984) identified three major trends that influenced the emergence of this specialty: (1) the prevailing theories of the etiologies and treatment of psychiatric disorders, (2) the increasing public need for mental health care, and (3) a shift in the centers of care.

The various theories about emotional disorders that prevailed over the 20th century influenced psychiatric nursing considerably. The work of Sigmund Freud began to generate support early in the 1900s. Freud emphasized a psychological understanding of behavior and advocated the psychoanalytic treatment of emotional disorders. The psychoanalytic treatment of children began with such pioneers as Anna Freud and Melanie Klein. Because only those trained as analysts provided psychoanalysis, the psychoanalytic movement did not recognize a role for nurses (Pothier, 1984).

Social influences early in the 20th century led to an increasing public demand for mental health care services for children. The juvenile court system generated a major impetus for this awareness (Fagin, 1974). In the early 1900s, there were few courts for dealing with youths who were accused of crimes. Several judges began to question the reasons for the delinquent behavior of the youths who were appearing in their courts. This inquiry led to an emphasis on early intervention and prevention of emotional disturbances.

Changes were simultaneously occurring in education. The enactment of laws making education compulsory focused new attention on children, their development, and the process of learning. The education movement highlighted the potential influence of the environment outside the family on children's development and contributed to the concept of professional intervention to facilitate child development and to treat emotional difficulties. The combined forces of dynamically oriented psychiatry, the mental hygiene (prevention) movement, and compulsory education were the prime forces behind the emerging specialties of child development and child psychiatry (Fagin, 1974).

In 1909, Healy opened the first child guidance center in Chicago as a court-related project to study the precipitants of juvenile delinquent behavior (Chess & Hassibi, 1986). This center and other similar demonstration projects formed the base of the child guidance movement. By 1930, there were more than 500 child guidance centers in the United States. The professionals involved with the care of these children included psychiatrists, psychologists, and social workers, but there was no recognized role for nurses (Middleton & Pothier, 1970).

In 1930, the W.B. Saunders Company published the first book on child development (Fagin, 1974). Entitled *Growth and Development of the Young Child*, it was written by Winifred Rand, Mary Sweeney, and Lee Vincent. Fagin noted that one of the authors, Rand, was a nurse and social worker; she wrote the sections on the family and community.

The introduction of psychiatric care for children and adolescents in a hospital setting during the 1930s and the 1940s significantly influenced the emergence of child psychiatric nursing (Middleton & Pothier, 1970). The use of somatic treatments moved the center of treatment for youngsters to this setting. The first children's unit within a psychiatric facility opened in 1934 at New York's Bellevue Hospital, and a separate adolescent unit followed in 1937 (Chess & Hassibi, 1986). In the psychiatric hospital setting, nurses provided the physical care and monitored somatic treatments. Pothier (1984) noted that, through the process of monitoring the children and later administering medications to them, psychiatric nurses began establishing relationships with the youngsters. Subsequently, the nurses recognized the potential benefit of these relationships and sought additional education and experience to augment their skills.

During the 1940s and the 1950s, the growing body of available treatment interventions and the effectiveness of some somatic treatments created a public awareness of the need for more trained mental health professionals. To address this demand, Congress enacted the National Mental Health Act in 1946, establishing the National Institute of Mental Health (NIMH). The NIMH carried out this national priority by funding the education of mental health care professionals and supporting research on effective treatment interventions. Because the Mental Health Act recognized nursing as one of the four core disciplines in the provision of mental health care services, NIMH in 1948 began funding undergraduate and graduate education programs in psychiatric nursing. The first graduate program in child psychiatric nursing began in 1954 at Boston University; several other programs began shortly after. The NIMH supported an average of seven programs per year over the following 30 years (Murphy & Hoeffer, 1987).

Another significant milestone that took place during this time was the publication of the first theoretical perspective on psychiatric nursing. In 1952, Hildgard Peplau's seminal work, *Interpersonal Relations in Nursing*, was published. Her contributions focused on the dynamics and phases of the nurse-patient relationship, central to all nursing, but especially to psychiatric nursing.

The 1950s through the 1970s were decades of growth for psychiatric nursing. The NIMH awarded 20,000 undergraduate and graduate traineeships to nurses from 1947 to 1978 (Pothier, 1984). The scope of psychiatric nursing practice expanded during this time in areas of direct and indirect functions (ANA, 1976). Nurses assumed increasing responsibility for carrying out milieu management, screening high-risk populations, and providing psychotherapy. Some psychiatric nurses opened independent practices.

The ANA recognized the increasing importance of specialty nursing practice areas. In 1967, the ANA published its first Statement on Psychiatric and Mental Health Nursing Practice. The statement was revised in 1976 and described psychiatric nursing as "a specialized area of nursing practice employing theories of human behavior as its science and purposeful use of self as its art" (ANA, 1976, p. 5). Following the 1976 revision of the statement, the first Standards of Practice for

Psychiatric and Mental Health Nursing Practice were published in 1982. These standards presented the state of agreed upon levels of practice. In 1985, the ANA published the first subspecialty standards of practice—for child and adolescent psychiatric nursing practice (see Appendix A).

During the 1980s, the growth of psychiatric nursing and its subspecialties began to decline. The number of applicants to graduate programs in child psychiatric nursing decreased. Enrollment in child psychiatric nursing graduate programs went from 20% of the total nursing enrollment in 1974 to 1975, to 13.5% in 1983 to 1984 (National League for Nursing, 1985). The number of schools of nursing that received NIMH awards dropped from 140 awards in 1976 to 1977 to 20 awards at 16 institutions in 1986 to 1987 (NIMH, 1987). In 1988, the Advocates for Child Psychiatric Nursing identified 11 graduate programs in this field. Pothier (1988b) noted that most of these programs are now included in larger psychiatric nursing curricula. The programs vary in the number of child-oriented courses and the amount of supervised clinical experience.

Currently, 55,000 nurses identify themselves as psychiatric nurses. Of these, approximately 1,000 have graduate preparation in child psychiatric nursing (de Leon Siantz, 1990). Nurse generalists also work in psychiatric settings where children receive treatment, such as child or adolescent psychiatric units, residential centers, or partial hospitalization programs. The number of trained personnel needed to provide mental health care services to children and adolescents appears far greater, however. In 1986, the Office of Technology Assessment (OTA) reported that approximately 7.5 to 9.5 million children in the United States were experiencing mental health problems significant enough to require treatment. This group represented 12% to 15% of children under the age of 18. The OTA report noted that nearly 80% of the identified population of children who needed treatment had received no or inadequate care. Clearly, additional trained professionals and services are necessary to address the mental health care needs of youngsters.

Compounding this increasing need for mental health care professionals to care for youngsters is an underutilization of prepared child and adolescent psychiatric nurse specialists. Pothier, Norbeck, and Laliberte (1985) surveyed clinical nurse specialists in child psychiatric nursing and found that, although these nurses were prepared for work with children, they spent less than half of their time caring for youngsters. Pothier and colleagues concluded that there is a significant gap between the need for mental health care services for children and the use of child and adolescent nurse specialists.

As a specialty, child psychiatric nursing has received only limited recognition within nursing, by other mental health professionals, and by the public at large (McBride, 1988). The underutilization of prepared child psychiatric nurses may be related to this unawareness of the contribution and the role that child psychiatric nurses have in the care of youngsters and their families.

CHARACTERISTICS OF THE SPECIALTY

Child psychiatric nursing has three distinctive dimensions: the phenomena of interest, the perspective of the specialty, and the nature of its nursing actions. These dimensions overlap and are interdependent.

Phenomena of Interest

In 1980, the ANA defined nursing as "the diagnosis and treatment of human responses to actual or potential health problems" (p. 9). Thus, the phenomena of interest for nursing are focused on health-restoring response patterns to actual health problems and health-supporting responses to potential health problems. Human responses include biological, cognitive, affective, and motor behaviors; O'Toole and Loomis (1989) described response patterns as a "reliable sample of traits, acts or other observable features characterizing an individual" (p. 290).

The types of human response patterns of interest to psychiatric nurses have been identified as activity-related, cognitive, ecological, emotional, interpersonal, perceptual, physiological, and valuative (O'Toole & Loomis, 1989). All types of responses may be of interest in certain child psychiatric settings. Most often, however, child psychiatric nurses address responses related to the mental health care needs of the youngster and family. These selected human response patterns include alteration in emotional expression, self-care limitations, and potential self-destructive violence.

O'Toole and Loomis (1989) have introduced a classification system of the human responses of interest to psychiatric nurses (see Appendix B). Further development will lead to a consensus on definitions, descriptors, and research-based validation. The following characteristics assist in describing the phenomena of interest for child psychiatric nurses.

Health Focus. A distinguishing characteristic of the phenomena of interest for child psychiatric nurses is a focus on the total health of the child and family. As opposed to focusing on a disease or illness, child psychiatric nurses use their knowledge of general health (Lego, 1980), growth, and development to address the health goals of the child and the family. Nurses "focus on assisting individuals to attain their highest level of health possible" (Carter, 1986, p. 27).

Child psychiatric nurses assist youngsters and their families to restore, maintain, or improve a previous level of health (ANA, 1980). They view these individuals holistically, although they focus predominantly on the youngsters' mental health needs. Emphasizing a child's strengths, they help the child to develop strategies to resolve the distressing human responses. Nurses implement their health-oriented perspective through interventions that include health teaching and anticipatory guidance.

Nonverbal Communication. The child psychiatric nurse recognizes that nonverbal cues and behavior reflect another dimension of a youngster's response to health problems. A careful appraisal of a youngster's nonverbal cues and their congruence with verbalizations provides valuable clinical input. Children and adolescents may demonstrate their responses to health problems through behavioral manifestations rather than verbalizations. Youngsters who cannot identify their feelings may be hesitant to engage in the therapeutic relationship or may be guarded in sharing their intimate thoughts. Child psychiatric nurses use nonverbal expressive techniques, such as play therapy and art, with children and adolescents to facilitate the identification of their feelings, engage them in the treatment process, provide a mechanism to work through conflicts, and support a progression to verbalizations of responses.

Subjectivity. The phenomena of interest for child psychiatric nurses are often subjective in nature. Many of the human responses to health problems are intrapersonal. There may be alterations in perceptions, including body image or self-esteem, or alterations in valuation, such as helplessness. The existence of these phenomena is based on the subjective perception of the child. Through perceptual processes, the youngster interprets behavior and interactions, and determines their subjective meaning.

Intimate Nature. Child psychiatric nurses are concerned with human response patterns that are highly personal. Nursing care involves a "privileged intimacy" in which the nurse has access to the individual on both a physical and emotional basis (ANA, 1980, p. 18). The child psychiatric nurse on an inpatient unit assumes responsibility not only for physical health care, but also for activities of daily living (ADLs), such as bathing, toileting, and eating behavior. Attempts to meet these personal needs set up opportunities for unique interactions between the nurse and the child (Evans, 1968).

Other phenomena of interest for child psychiatric nurses involve intimate interactions. For example, youngsters often experience very personal human responses, such as hallucinations and suicidal thoughts, to abusive situations. The content of nurse-client interactions related to these experiences may be highly intimate. A youngster may share his or her perceptions of self-worthlessness, or a family may disclose the details of physically assaultive behavior.

Perspective of the Specialty

A unique perspective, or distinct way of viewing phenomena, distinguishes a discipline (Donaldson & Crowley, 1978). McBride (1988) succinctly described nursing's perspective.

> Nursing is the science of caring; nursing has 24-hour responsibility for patients, and thus a nonsegmented view of individuals; nursing is con-

cerned with the activities of daily living (functional ability); it is concerned with people's responses to real or potential health problems
rather than only with diseases per se. (p. 57)

Nursing's perspective can be described as a holistic view of health care with an
individual and family, focusing on their human response patterns in the context of
daily living. It is the application of nursing's unique perspective to the selected
phenomena of interest that makes an area of practice a nursing specialty. The following are several components of this unique perspective.

Holism. As a central characteristic of nursing's perspective, holism is a
nonsegmented view of people that takes into account all aspects of their responses.
Although generally viewed as a contemporary trend of nursing, the concept of
holism has long been evident in psychiatric nursing. Church (1987) noted the
work of Euphemia Jane Taylor in emphasizing the need to perceive people in a
holistic manner. In 1926, Taylor wrote:

It is imperative that all nurses have an understanding of the patient as a
whole and there is no such thing as mental nursing apart from general or
general nursing apart from mental nursing. They form a oneness and
make up the whole. From our knowledge of how the whole organism
acts, it is obvious that what affects one part affects the other and a sense
of well-being in either mind or body brings about reactions which are
not confined to one part alone but affects the whole being. (p. 133)

In the holistic perspective, children and families are viewed in the context of their
daily lives. The context includes the cultural and social backgrounds of the
youngster and family. In some cases, it may be necessary to define problematic
behavior by cultural norms.

Developmental Focus. The practice of child psychiatric nursing is based, in
part, on theories in which a child's development is viewed on a continuum from
infancy through adolescence (ANA, 1985). Development proceeds simultaneously and interactionally along several dimensions: cognitive, emotional, social, and physiological. Variations in development may occur in single or multiple
dimensions (ANA, 1985). The child psychiatric nurse recognizes that there are
individual differences in developmental patterns and considers these differences
in assessments and interventions.

The infant, child, and adolescent population includes individuals with a wide
range of skills and needs. For example, interactions with young children are characterized by: (1) concrete thought processes, (2) limited verbal skills, (3) behavioral manifestations to the human responses, (4) the use of play or activities to
express their feelings, (5) limited insight, and (6) limited judgment and knowledge
base to use in problem solving. A child psychiatric nurse incorporates develop-

mental considerations into his or her nursing approach with these children, for example, by using puppets, drawing, or mutual storytelling. With adolescents, the nurse-client interactions may be characterized by abstract thought processes, a broad range of verbal skills, and problem-solving abilities. With these individuals, therefore, a nurse may choose interventions such as journal writing, group psychotherapy, or health teaching in consideration of the developmental characteristics of teen-agers.

Activities of Daily Living. Child psychiatric nurses focus on a youngster's ability to function on a daily basis. They attend to the child's response patterns as manifested throughout his or her daily life. Nursing has traditionally addressed ADLs through hospital practice in providing 24-hour care. Their around-the-clock availability has placed nurses in the best position to help youngsters integrate the treatment goals into their daily activities. Nurses may use daily interactions and conflicts as opportunities for therapeutic interactions (Redl, 1959).

The orientation toward ADLs also lends itself to nursing's action, or doing, approach (Loomis & Horsley, 1974). Child psychiatric nurses assist youngsters and their families to "do" something to function better on a daily basis in society. This perspective is evident in nursing interventions that address mealtime behavior, sleep promotion, and leisure activities.

Social Systems. Nurses who provide psychiatric care to children recognize that youngsters are generally part of a family system and view them in this context (ANA, 1985). Children are usually dependent on family members or guardians to seek health care. The participation of family members, especially parents and other primary care-givers, fosters the success of treatment.

Child psychiatric nurses also recognize that children live within the context of larger social systems. In their interventions, they consider peer groups, other care-givers, schoolteachers, and extended family members. The child psychiatric nursing perspective on social systems becomes evident in nursing interventions such as the provision of parental guidance concerning child management or group therapy to address peer relationships. At times, treatment may be implemented indirectly through the primary care–giving adults.

Nature of Child Psychiatric Nursing Actions

Given the nature of the phenomena of interest and the perspective of the specialty, the actions of child psychiatric nurses are also distinctive. These nurses use therapeutic techniques that are similar to those used by other mental health care professionals, but the nature of their specific nursing actions differs. The following are several characteristics of child psychiatric nurses' actions.

Nurturant Nature. "One of the most distinguishing characteristics of nursing is that it involves practices which are nurturant, generative or protective in nature" (ANA, 1980, p. 18). Initially described by Blevis (1978), this characteristic pertains to the nature of nursing actions involved in meeting the health care needs of individuals. Leininger (1988) identified nurturant care as the concept that describes the essence of nursing. For example, this characteristic may be seen in the manner in which a child psychiatric nurse sets limits for children and adolescents who are unable to limit their impulses internally. A child psychiatric nurse communicates the limit in a warm and caring manner that demonstrates the nurse's concern to the youngster while establishing the needed external structure.

Preventive Interventions. In their health-supporting orientation, child psychiatric nurses take a preventive approach in their interventions.

> The child and adolescent psychiatric and mental health nurse is involved in primary, secondary and tertiary levels of preventive care. . . . The major assumption is that it is possible to reduce the incidence or decrease the effect of beginning mental disorders by offering a broad range of services necessary to support the normal growth and development of a child or adolescent, particularly one who lives in a high-risk environment. (ANA, 1985, p. 3)

Even with severely limited children, the child psychiatric nurse focuses on prevention of further disability and promotion of health.

Coordination of Client Transitions. Within child psychiatric nursing, the nurse coordinates the transitions of a youngster and family into, through, and out of treatment. A child psychiatric nurse assumes "responsibility for the continuity of care in inpatient settings and the integration of a myriad of services in outpatient settings. . . . This individual plans, monitors and executes transitions for clients among modalities, services and settings" (Smoyak, 1987, p. 180). The nurse assumes accountability for assisting a child or adolescent through the admission, transfer, and discharge processes. In fulfilling these responsibilities, a child psychiatric nurse

- orients a newly admitted child or adolescent to a unit or treatment program and its milieu
- facilitates a youngster's adjustment to the milieu and the treatment environment
- works with a child and family regarding their feelings and fears surrounding a transfer, should a transfer be warranted, and assists in the physical and emotional move to a new setting

- aids a child or adolescent in anticipating discharge, identifying responses related to discharge, and facilitates a client's ability to resolve those responses

Throughout a course of treatment, a child psychiatric nurse also serves as an advocate for a child and family.

Collaborative Care. Child psychiatric nurses view the provision of health care as a collaborative activity that they carry out with children and their families. Burgess and Burns (1973/1990) suggested that nurses view clients as "consumers" of health care, recognizing their legitimate request for care and their right to an understanding of the service to be received. Nurses more frequently refer to individuals as "clients," indicating a belief that an individual or family is employing the services of a professional. On the other hand, the use of the term *patient* may imply that one individual is acting upon another. In some child psychiatric settings, however, the term *patient* continues to be used.

Child psychiatric nurses recognize the need for the participation of a youngster and family in the treatment process. In the initial request for nursing care, a nurse and family begin to develop a treatment alliance. Through the course of their relationship, a nurse, child, and family work toward the identified health goals. Child psychiatric nurses work *with* children, adolescents, and their families. Only when children or families are unable to care for themselves does the psychiatric nurse care *for* the child and family.

In addition, the child psychiatric nurse collaborates with other mental health professionals in the delivery of care. This collaboration may occur formally through team conferences or rounds, or informally through daily interactions with other mental health professionals to coordinate the implementation of the interdisciplinary treatment plan.

APPROACH OF CHILD PSYCHIATRIC NURSES

The approach used by child psychiatric nurses in providing care with youngsters and their families includes the use of the nursing process and the nurse-client relationship. Additional considerations include theoretical applications in the specialty, the types of child psychiatric nurses, and their respective roles.

Nursing Process

The profession has recognized the nursing process as the dominant modality to address nursing's health-oriented practice. The components of the nursing process include assessment (data collection and analysis), diagnosis (naming of the phenomena of concern), planning, implementation, and evaluation.

These components are viewed as dynamic rather than distinct linear steps. Through the course of contact with a child and family, the nurse continuously assesses the individual's health status, gathering information on response patterns. Based on this appraisal, the nurse may alter the plans of care, the diagnoses, or a specific action. From the first interaction, the nurse continuously evaluates the youngster's responses to the interventions. These evaluative processes provide the continuous feedback needed to ensure that the interventions address the needs of the child and the family.

Specific actions by the nurse may serve several components of the nursing process at the same time. During the course of assessment, for example, a nurse also gathers information and clarifies the situation of a youngster and family. The process of clarification may serve as a data-gathering and validation mechanism, as well as an intervention technique with the family.

The nursing process allows child psychiatric nurses to apply their health-oriented perspective within the multidisciplinary mental health team. This approach is systematic, yet flexible enough to address individual health care needs. Although critics may say that the nursing process is the same as any problem-solving approach, no other discipline uses and documents this type of approach as consistently as does nursing.

Nurse-Client Relationship

All nursing care takes place within the context of the nurse-client relationship. In psychiatric nursing, the relationship between the nurse and the client is especially important, as it is a major vehicle for nursing interventions. Therefore, the nurse-client relationship in psychiatric nursing is often formally structured (e.g., by primary nursing assignments).

The nurse-client relationship has three phases, each with its own characteristics and objectives. Moscato (1988) described these as the orientation, working, and termination phases. During the orientation phase, the nurse's objective is to establish contact with the child and family; the tasks include clarifying the purpose of the relationship, initially addressing the distress of the child and family, and negotiating a therapeutic contract. The working phase involves maintaining and analyzing the contact by identifying the focal response patterns, facilitating self-assessment, identifying the forces resistant to change, and promoting the development of new skills. In the termination phase, in which the contact is discontinued, the therapeutic tasks include helping the child and family to evaluate the therapeutic experience and related changes, consolidating the gains, and facilitating any necessary future care (Moscato, 1988).

In child psychiatric nursing, there are specific developmental considerations in the nurse-client relationship. The "inherent nature of the adult-child relationship [presents] a perceived inequality of status and role, with the adult the dominant authority figure" (Faux, Walsh, & Deatrick, 1988, p. 84). This relationship requires a child psychiatric nurse to adopt an approach that decreases his or her dominance without relinquishing the therapeutic role of the nurse.

Theoretical Applications

The ANA has identified the role of scientific knowledge, both scholarly conceptualizations and research findings, in child psychiatric nursing practice. "The nurse applies appropriate, scientifically sound theory as a basis for nursing practice actions" (ANA, 1985, p. 7). Clearly, child psychiatric nurses are expected to integrate scientific knowledge throughout the structure, process, and outcomes of their practice.

Scientific knowledge encompasses a variety of information that can prove useful to the child psychiatric nurse. Conceptual frameworks and theories provide information that varies in abstraction and usefulness for direct application. This knowledge can be divided into nursing knowledge, and nonnursing knowledge. The former includes knowledge from such nursing theorists as King (1981), Orem (1985), Paterson and Zderad (1976), Peplau (1952) and others, while the latter may include conceptualizations from communications models, crisis theories, learning frameworks, stress theories, symbolic interactionism, and systems (ANA, 1976). Fitzpatrick, Whall, Johnston, and Floyd (1982) as well as Beard and Johnson (1988), applied selected conceptual frameworks and theories to psychiatric nursing practice. In addition, many of the intervention chapters in this book utilize a selected conceptual framework to assist the reader to further incorporate theoretical perspectives and research findings into clinical practice.

Scientific knowledge benefits a child psychiatric nurse throughout the nursing process. First, "the nurse's use of appropriate theories provides comprehensive, balanced perceptions of client characteristics or presenting conditions and ensures accurate diagnoses" (ANA, 1985, p. 7). The framework helps a nurse to structure and implement the nursing process in a systematic manner. Second, child psychiatric nurses use scientific knowledge to "direct nursing therapeutics and to evaluate outcomes of nursing interventions" (Beard & Johnson, 1988, p. 48). Scientific knowledge facilitates a nurse's ability to articulate nursing interventions and the specific outcomes of such interventions in a clear and concise manner. Third, the application of scientific knowledge and the subsequent publication of the results of the application contribute to the further advancement of nursing knowledge and provide resource materials that facilitate future nursing interventions.

Types of Child Psychiatric Nurses

Nursing may be done directly by specific nursing actions with individuals or indirectly through guidance to family members or other health care providers.

"Direct nursing care functions presume that the nurse's actions and reflections are focused on a particular client or family" (ANA, 1976, p. 15). Direct care functions in child psychiatric nursing may include: (1) community action, (2) counseling, (3) health teaching, (4) psychotherapy, (5) intake screening, (6) milieu management, and (7) medication surveillance (ANA, 1976). Indirect nursing care functions support those providing direct nursing care; these functions may include: (1) administration, (2) clinical supervision, (3) consultation, (4) education, and (5) research (ANA, 1976).

The ANA (1980) has recognized two levels of nurse practitioners: the nurse generalist and the nurse specialist. Each type of practitioner may assume both direct and indirect roles. A nurse generalist in child psychiatric nursing is "a nurse who is educated at the basic level for entry into professional practice, who practices child and adolescent psychiatric and mental health nursing, and who refines clinical skills through ongoing supervision of practice in a clinical setting" (ANA, 1985, p. 26). Such a nurse generalist may assume any of the following roles:

1. milieu therapist
2. counselor or teacher of parents
3. collaborator with other mental health professionals
4. responsible change agent providing for the mental health needs of children
5. promoter of mental health
6. participant in nursing research (ANA, 1985, p. 5)

One of the nurse generalist's primary direct care responsibilities in inpatient settings is that of milieu maintenance (Flaskerud, 1984). A nurse in child psychiatric nursing structures and maintains a living environment in which every action and activity is intended to be therapeutic for each child and adolescent. Within the milieu, the staff members assume therapeutic parental roles; they provide: (1) safety, (2) external limits as needed by an individual child or adolescent, (3) health teaching as needed by a client, and (4) an environment that facilitates growth by supporting a client's attempts to practice new behaviors.

The second type of nurse practitioner in child psychiatric nursing is the clinical nurse specialist,

> a nurse who holds a minimum of a master's degree in child and adolescent psychiatric and mental health nursing, has had supervised clinical experience at the graduate level, and demonstrates depth and breadth of knowledge, competence, and skill in the practice of child and adolescent psychiatric and mental health nursing. (ANA, 1985, p. 26)

A clinical nurse specialist in child psychiatric nursing not only may assume any of the roles of the nurse generalist, but also may choose to participate in the following functions:

1. direct care as a psychotherapist with children, adolescents and families
2. indirect care as a
   a. clinical supervisor
   b. administrator of nursing services
   c. educator
   d. consultant
   e. researcher (ANA, 1985)

The direct care role of case manager may also be appropriate for the psychiatric clinical nurse specialist. The elements of the case manager role may include efforts to ensure continuity of care, patient advocacy, coordination of care, health promotion, and resource development. The appropriate use of child psychiatric nurses in case management is to coordinate and manage services for children and adolescents (Pothier, 1988a).

The changes in psychiatric care present many challenges to child psychiatric nurses. With an increased emphasis on cost containment, the increased acuity of illness in hospitalized youngsters, and the decreased lengths of stays, child psychiatric nurses must provide more intensive care with the same or fewer resources. Child psychiatric nurses can best meet these challenges by: (1) clearly articulating and quantifying their role in the delivery of quality health care to youngsters and their families, (2) validating effective and efficient nursing interventions through research and publications, and (3) becoming more politically involved in advocating for children and their families to ensure timely access to care.

REFERENCES

Advocates for Child Psychiatric Nursing. (1988). Graduate programs in child and adolescent psychiatric and mental health nursing. *National Newsletter, 17*(1), 4.

American Nurses' Association. (1967). *Statement on psychiatric nursing practice*. New York: Author.

American Nurses' Association. (1976). *Statement on psychiatric and mental health nursing practice*. Kansas City, MO: Author.

American Nurses' Association. (1980). *Nursing: A social policy statement*. Kansas City, MO: Author.

American Nurses' Association (1982). *Standards of psychiatric and mental health nursing practice*. Kansas City, MO: Author.

American Nurses' Association. (1985). *Standards of child and adolescent psychiatric and mental health nursing practice*. Kansas City, MO: Author.

Beard, M.T., & Johnson, M.N. (1988). Nursing theorists' approaches. In C.K. Beck, R.P. Rawlins, & S.R. Williams (Eds.), *Mental health-psychiatric nursing: A holistic life-cycle approach* (pp. 48–63). St. Louis: C.V. Mosby.

Blevis, E.O. (1978). *Curriculum building in nursing: A process*. St. Louis: C.V. Mosby.

Burgess, A.C., & Burns, J. (1973/1990). Partners in care. *American Journal of Nursing, 90*(6), 73–75.

Carter, E.W. (1986). Psychiatric nursing. *Journal of Psychosocial Nursing and Mental Health Services, 24*(6), 26–30.

Chess, S., & Hassibi, M. (1986). *Principles and practice of child psychiatry* (2nd ed.). New York: Plenum Press.

Church, O.M. (1987). From custody to community in psychiatric nursing. *Nursing Research, 36*(1), 48–55.

de Leon Siantz, M.L. (1990). Issues facing child psychiatric nursing in the 1990's (Commentary). *Journal of Child and Adolescent Psychiatric Nursing, 3*(2), 65–68.

Donaldson, S.K., & Crowley, D.M. (1978). The discipline of nursing. *Nursing Outlook, 26*(2), 113–120.

Evans, F.M.C. (1968). *The role of the nurse in community mental health.* New York: Macmillan.

Fagin, C.M. (1974). Introduction. In C.M. Fagin (Ed.), *Readings in child and adolescent nursing* (pp. 1–5). St. Louis: C.V. Mosby.

Faux, S.A., Walsh, M., & Deatrick, J.A. (1988). Intensive interviewing with children and adolescents. *Western Journal of Nursing Research, 10*(2), 180–194.

Fitzpatrick, J.J., Whall, A.L., Johnston, R.L., & Floyd, J.A. (1982). *Nursing models and their psychiatric mental health applications.* Bowie, MD: Robert J. Brady Company.

Flaskerud, J.H. (1984). The distinctive character of nursing psychotherapy. *Issues in Mental Health Nursing, 6,* 1–19.

King, I.M. (1981). *A theory for nursing: Systems, concepts, process.* New York: John Wiley & Sons.

Kneisl, C.R., & Wilson, H.S. (1988). Historical perspectives. In H.S. Wilson & C.R. Kneisl (Eds.), *Psychiatric nursing* (3rd ed., pp. 10–24). Menlo Park, CA: Addison-Wesley.

Lego, S. (1980). Point/counterpoint: A psychotherapist is a psychotherapist. *Perspectives in Psychiatric Care, 28,* 38–39.

Leininger, M.M. (1988). Care: The essence of nursing and health. In M.M. Leininger (Ed.), *Care: The essence of nursing and health* (pp. 3–15). Detroit: Wayne State University Press.

Loomis, M.E., & Horsley, J.A. (1974). *Interpersonal change: A behavioral approach to nursing practice.* New York: McGraw-Hill.

McBride, A.B. (1988). Coming of age: Child psychiatric nursing. *Archives of Psychiatric Nursing, 2*(2), 57–64.

Middleton, A.B., & Pothier, P.C. (1970). The nurse in child psychiatry—An overview. *Nursing Outlook, 18*(5), 52–56.

Moscato, B. (1988). The one-to-one relationship. In H.S. Wilson & C.R. Kneisl (Eds.), *Psychiatric nursing* (3rd ed., pp. 720–760). Menlo Park, CA: Addison-Wesley.

Murphy, S.A., & Hoeffer, B. (1987). The evolution of subspecialties in psychiatric and mental health nursing. *Archives of Psychiatric Nursing, 1*(3), 145–154.

National Institute of Mental Health. (1987). *Task force in nursing: Summary report.* Washington, DC: Author.

National League for Nursing. (1985). *Nursing data review.* Washington, DC: Author.

Office of Technology Assessment. (1986). *Children's mental health: Problems and services—A background paper* (Publication No. OTA-BP-H-33). Washington, DC: U.S. Government Printing Office.

Opie, N.D. (1990). Response and recommendations (Commentary). *Journal of Child and Adolescent Psychiatric Nursing, 3*(2), 68–71.

Orem, D.E. (1985). *Nursing: Concepts of practice.* New York: McGraw-Hill.

O'Toole, A.W., & Loomis, M.E. (1989). Revision of the phenomena of concern for psychiatric mental health nursing. *Archives of Psychiatric Nursing, 3*(5), 288–299.

Paterson, J.G., & Zderad, L.T. (1976). *Humanistic nursing.* New York: John Wiley & Sons.

Peplau, H.E. (1952). *Interpersonal relations in nursing*. New York: G.P. Putnam's Sons.

Pothier, P.C. (1984). Child psychiatric nursing. *Journal of Psychosocial Nursing and Mental Health Services, 22*(3), 11–21.

Pothier, P.C. (1988a). Child mental health problems and policy. *Archives of Psychiatric Nursing, 2*(3), 165–169.

Pothier, P.C. (1988b). Graduate preparation in child and adolescent psychiatric and mental health nursing. *Archives of Psychiatric Nursing, 2*(3), 170–172.

Pothier, P.C., Norbeck, J.S., & Laliberte, M. (1985). Child psychiatric nursing: The gap between need and utilization. *Journal of Psychosocial Nursing and Mental Health Services, 23*(7), 18–23.

Pothier, P.C., Stuart, G.W., Puskar, K., & Babich, K. (1990). Dilemmas and directions for psychiatric nursing in the 1990s. *Archives of Psychiatric Nursing, 4*(5), 284–291.

Rand, W., Sweeney, M., & Vincent, L. (1930). *Growth and development of the young child*. Philadelphia: W.B. Saunders.

Redl, F. (1959). Strategy and techniques of the life-span interview. *American Journal of Orthopsychiatry, 29*, 1–18.

Smoyak, S.A. (1987). Psychiatric/mental health nursing. In Group for the Advancement of Psychiatry, *Psychiatry and the mental health professionals: New roles for changing times* (pp. 170–182). New York: Brunner/Mazel.

Taylor, E.J. (1926). Psychiatry and the nurse: Discussion of a paper by Arthur H. Ruggles, M.D. *American Journal of Nursing, 26*, 133.

2

Psychiatric Nursing Assessment with Children and Adolescents

Patricia West

After reading this chapter, the reader will be able to:

1. identify the goals and objectives of the assessment process in psychiatric nursing with children and adolescents
2. delineate two components of the psychiatric nursing assessment process
3. describe several tools available for data gathering in psychiatric nursing assessments with youngsters and their families
4. elaborate on the areas of data collection for a psychiatric nursing assessment
5. develop strategies for initiating a psychiatric nursing assessment with a child or adolescent and his or her family

Psychiatric nursing with children and adolescents begins with assessment. Since Peplau (1952) and Orlando (1961), among others, initially described it, the nursing assessment process has become a key element of the psychiatric nursing process. Assessment has been described as the initial step of a linear nursing process; however, the nursing process itself can be viewed as a dynamic process with interactive components of assessment, diagnosis, planning, intervention, and evaluation.

ASSESSMENT PROCESS

As a component of the nursing process, assessment is dynamic and continuous. It provides the nurse with a means of developing a holistic perspective of the individual. The standards for child psychiatric nursing practice published by the American Nurses' Association stated that, by thorough assessment, the nurse can "reach objective conclusions and plan appropriate interventions with and for children and adolescents" (ANA, 1985, p. 8). Therefore, assessment is the basis for the other nursing process components.

Fagin (1972) introduced several guidelines for the psychiatric nurse when assessing the mental and emotional health status of youngsters. First, the nurse has a perspective that is based on child development research and theoretical conceptualizations regarding which behaviors are normal for a given age. The nurse must be aware, however, that various social, cultural, and physiological factors may influence developmental progression. Second, there are individual differences in youngsters' response patterns that may or may not represent a true variation from the norm. Fagin suggested that the nurse observe a child on several occasions to make an adequate appraisal; single occurrences of behaviors are less important than are consistent patterns. Third, the psychiatric nurse must recall that all human responses occur within the context of social, cultural, and family life. A child's environment may determine which responses are problematic; a problematic response in one family may not be of concern in another. The nurse must carefully delineate which patterns are of concern for that particular child and family. Finally, child psychiatric nurses focus on promoting the health goals of the child and family and minimizing efforts to isolate the cause of the problematic human responses. Causal relationships are difficult to identify clearly in human relationships, and efforts to do so can deflect the nurse's energy from effective nursing care.

Goals of Assessment

The primary goal of a child psychiatric nursing assessment is to provide a holistic understanding of the human response patterns of the youngster and family. Each child and each family present a unique combination of human responses, social supports, and health care needs. A child psychiatric nurse views the youngster holistically, considering all domains of function in the context of daily living. The resultant conceptualization of the youngster guides the nurse in planning beneficial interventions. In addition, a child psychiatric nursing assessment can be an intervention. Through the collection and clarification of information, clients gain a better understanding of their human responses and a greater insight into their situation. This process is educational in nature and, therefore, characteristic of a nursing intervention.

Initial Assessment Procedures

The child psychiatric nurse should develop a plan for the initial meeting. It is advisable to have the parents or guardian accompany the youngster to the early meetings. Seeing the parents and child together initially gives the nurse an opportunity to clarify the reason for the referral and to outline a plan for the early sessions. If the parents are not available, the nurse may obtain information from the primary care-givers and other individuals who have a vested interest in the child and a knowledge of his or her daily functioning. Because some parents are initially reluctant to discuss certain topics in front of their child, it is often helpful to interview the parents or guardians separately to hear their perception of the situation. Next, the nurse should see the child individually to discuss the reasons for referral, clarify the motivation for treatment, and attempt to engage the child in the treatment process. This first meeting should end with everyone reconvened so that the nurse can outline the plan of assessment prior to determining treatment.

At this first meeting, the nurse should give specific parameters on appointments, cancellation policies, and rescheduling. The best policy is to have the family cancel by speaking with the nurse directly so that the nurse may appraise and deal with any resistance to treatment. Specific guidelines on the charges for the services should also be explained.

The psychiatric nurse should also clarify confidentiality in the nurse-client relationship, particularly as it applies to the child's sharing of information with the nurse. It is important to clarify what information would be shared with the parents and in supervision. Furthermore, the nurse must address the times when confidentiality would be broken (e.g., suicidal threat).

The nurse may take notes, if necessary, but must not let the note taking interfere with efforts to establish rapport with the child and family, and to elicit information.

Initially, the nurse should contract for three or four meetings to assess the situation thoroughly. By identifying an "assessment period," the nurse provides a focal point and time frame as to when the parents and child can expect the nurse's recommendations. During this time, the nurse should focus on developing the active participation of all family members by completing a thorough history, addressing the problematic human responses, determining what needs to be done to address them, and identifying the strengths of the child and family. The nurse should describe how interventions work, including the phases of the relationship. It helps the family understand the process and may resolve their initial ambivalence in engaging in a treatment relationship.

Nursing assessment is the systematic appraisal of an individual's patterns of human responses to health care issues in the context of his or her daily life. It is generally viewed as having two elements: data collection and data analysis (Hagerty, 1984). Data collection provides the substance of the assessment, and data analysis provides an interpretation based on the nurse's theoretical perspective. These elements are interdependent, identifying and giving meaning to the youngster's patterns of human responses.

DATA COLLECTION PROCESS

The objectives of the data collection element of the assessment process include: (1) clarification of the need for referral, (2) development of an inventory of the youngster's strengths, (3) plan for developing rapport between the nurse and the child, and (4) provision of the foundation for identifying problems and establishing the priorities of needs. The initial data collection usually includes a history-taking procedure and a review of the current problematic human responses. This sharing of information contributes to the development of a rapport with the child, parents, and other involved parties and establishes a basis for the continued mutual sharing of information. It provides the nurse with the opportunity to hear the participants' views, ask elaborating and clarifying questions, and promote an understanding of the situation.

While gathering the data, the child psychiatric nurse sets the tone of the relationship. The nurse's approach to the interview and methods of data collection are basic to his or her understanding of the youngster. The child psychiatric nurse, youngster, and family focus predominantly on data collection during the orientation phase of their relationship. The data collection process continues throughout the nurse-client relationship, however, because response patterns change during the course of treatment; the nurse appraises the situation continuously.

Techniques for Data Collection

Child psychiatric nurses gather data by using a variety of techniques, such as observation, questionnaires, and art techniques. By means of such techniques, they can develop a comprehensive and valid picture of the child and family. The following considerations are important in determining which techniques and tools are appropriate in a particular instance:

- The reason for the use of the technique or tool and the anticipated outcome of its use should be clear.
- The timeliness of using a particular technique or tool should be considered. For example, the introduction of journals to facilitate teen-agers' disclosure of their emotional responses early in psychotherapy may lead to later verbal processing of the feelings.
- The nurse needs adequate training and supervision with certain techniques. For example, the use of projective techniques requires some specialized training and skill.
- The nurse's explanation of the purpose of the technique and its expected benefit always affects the context of the nurse-client relationship.
- The tools and vocabulary used in gathering data should be age-appropriate. Nurses in child psychiatric nursing may work with youngsters from infancy through adolescence. The selection of effective assessment tools must reflect the developmental state of the youngster.

Numerous techniques are available for use by psychiatric nurses in completing assessments. The techniques of history taking, communication techniques, and observation can be used in most settings and with most age groups.

History Taking

The traditional technique for initiating psychiatric nursing data collection is the interview process of history taking. A nurse can take a history with a youngster and family in several ways, including structured or semistructured interviews, or questionnaires. Once the nurse is adept at interviewing, it is advisable to use the semistructured interview; it provides some structure to the initial meeting, but allows the nurse to request details while the youngster and family provide information in their own, unique way.

Barry (1989) suggested a semistructured technique described as the "tree" assessment approach. Using a loosely structured format, the nurse takes cues from the child and parent about the areas to investigate. By asking open-ended questions, the nurse encourages the child to relate his or her perceptions in his or her own way. The nurse follows the youngster's lead (down the branch), striving to understand the situation thoroughly—not leaping from topic to topic (or branch to branch), but reconnecting the information to perceive the whole person.

Communication Techniques

By using effective communication techniques to gather data, the child psychiatric nurse encourages the child and family to share information and clarify their feelings. These techniques need to be congruent with the youngster's stage of development. Specific communication techniques that may be used include open-ended sentences, validation, clarification, confrontation, and reflection. Child psychiatric nurses also use nonverbal techniques, such as establishing eye contact, putting themselves at the same level as the child, and maintaining a therapeutic distance. It is advisable for the nurse to begin by asking easier questions and to move into more difficult areas when rapport has been established.

Observation

Another important technique for child psychiatric nurses is clinical observation of the youngster and family. The nurse observes the behavioral manifestations, affective responses, and patterns of interaction in the child and family. It is particularly important to note the congruence of behavior with verbal interchange and nonverbal communication patterns. The nurse may want to observe a very young child in an unstructured play environment, as play is a natural setting for children where they can be more at ease. By observing a child at play, a child psychiatric nurse may learn much about the youngster's response patterns and interpersonal relationships.

Areas of Data Collection

The standards of practice for child psychiatric nursing (ANA, 1985) call for the nurse to gather information about the youngster's developmental stage, strengths, individual differences in behavioral patterns, social support systems, and daily activities, among other factors. The nurse uses clinical judgment in determining which areas need further inquiry.

Several tools are available to facilitate the collection of information regarding several response patterns simultaneously. The tools may be varied according to the developmental age of the child.

Presenting Problem(s)

A good starting point is to clarify the reason for the child's referral. Teachers may refer children because of academic or behavioral problems, or parents may seek treatment for their child because of certain behavioral or emotional responses. Older youngsters may request treatment because of feelings or behaviors that they have not yet shared with family members. Burgess and Gosselin (1985) stressed that the nurse should especially attend to the client's first sentence or description of the reason that he or she is seeking treatment, as it often gives significant cues to the underlying dynamics of the situation.

Reasons for referral may include the need for control, safety, or intervention regarding a specific human response. Clarifying the reasons for referral gives the nurse an indication of the focal response patterns that need initial intervention and may also reveal the family's anticipated outcomes of treatment. The psychiatric nurse addresses the reasons for referral and the child's felt need (Peplau, 1952) early in treatment to engage the family in the treatment process.

The information collected should include a history of the duration and intensity of the human responses, as well as possible precipitating or contributing factors. A chronological description of the contributing factors is especially helpful. The nurse should also inquire about recent changes in life style, losses, and alterations in coping patterns.

Information regarding the presenting problem is usually gathered through the initial interview process. The extent to which the child is involved in the interview depends on his or her willingness to participate and communication skills. Questionnaires, such as the Child Behavior Check List (Achenbach & Edelbrock, 1983) and the Pediatric Symptom Checklist (Jellinek & Murphy, 1988), may also be helpful in clarifying some situations.

Family History

All children are part of a family or extended care system. To appraise a child's response patterns adequately, the nurse should evaluate the child's position in the family or system, the child's relationship with members, predominant roles of members, the patterns of communication among members, and disciplinary practices. This area of inquiry also includes information about those who reside in the home, other significant family members, and the social support systems available. Additional information about the family members' psychiatric and medical histories is helpful. It is important to note any recent change in the family constellation or significant stress.

Various tools are available to guide the nurse in gathering information about the families at the onset and during the course of treatment. The majority of these facilitate the accumulation and organization of information to clarify the patterns of behavior and dynamics of the family unit (e.g., Barbee, 1982; Delaney, 1982; Morgen & Macey, 1978). A genogram may also be quite beneficial, as all family members can be involved in providing their own information. A genogram is a technique in which the extended family consultation is diagramed with significant background data. Smoyak (1982) developed a nursing adaptation of this technique through the Rutgers Community Mental Health Center.

Developmental History and Status

A psychiatric nursing assessment of a youngster includes a history of the child's growth, developmental milestones (e.g., walking, talking, toilet training), and current level of functioning. This should begin with the prenatal history and birth of the child. The nurse should also consider the progression of development and parental expectations. Apparent lags in the developmental progression must be carefully appraised to identify potential contributing factors, such as organic damage, neglect, or prenatal toxin exposure. In the case of an adolescent, the nurse should obtain information on pubertal development, cognitive processes, and progression toward emancipation.

The nurse usually gathers information regarding the child's developmental history and status through history taking with the parents and observation of the youngster. An alternative is the use of questionnaires completed by family members. Checklists may make the data gathering more systematic and less time-consuming. The Minnesota Child Development Inventory (Ireton & Thwing, 1974) is useful with children 6 years of age and younger. The Assessment of Child and Adolescent Functioning Instrument (MacNair, 1983) focuses on nine areas of social functioning and may be quite helpful, as it can measure functioning prior to and following treatment.

History of Previous Treatment

It is important to obtain past records and inquire about any previous treatment, including the course, duration, reasons for referral, correlation with therapist's goals, progress, and status at termination. When previous therapy was unsuccessful, the child psychiatric nurse tries to determine the reason for the failure. This information provides a basis to determine openness to current interventions and some cues as to effective interventions.

Human Response Patterns

Data collection about the child's cognitive, affective, motor, and physiological response patterns is the core substance of the child psychiatric nursing assessment. The nurse is concerned with the responses of the child and family to health problems. The following is a brief description of the response patterns, reflecting the Classification System of Human Responses that was developed by the ANA Phenomena Task Force (O'Toole and Loomis, 1989; Appendix B).

Activity Patterns. A child's motor behavior, recreational trends, and self-care practices make up activity patterns. A child psychiatric nurse is concerned with such motor behaviors as hyperactivity, hypoactivity, and psychomotor retardation. These responses may be related to psychological stimuli, organic problems, or toxic reactions. Patterns of solitary and associative play are of particular interest. Recreational patterns, including participation in sports and extracurricular activities and use of leisure time, are especially important for the adolescent. The age-appropriateness of recreational activities is a consideration. Activities such as taking turns and sharing reflect the child's developmental level.

The child's sleep habits are also important. Sleep problems may reflect the child's depression, manipulation of the parents, or organic problems. The nurse gathers detailed information if there is concern about a child's sleep habits.

The self-care practices of the child or adolescent reveal the youngster's ability to meet the basic needs of eating, elimination, and hygiene. These behaviors are of particular concern with children admitted to inpatient psychiatric units. Denyes' (1980) Self-Care Practice Instrument, a self-report questionnaire for adolescents designed to measure specific self-care behaviors and general health practices, may be helpful in collecting this information.

Cognitive Patterns. The child psychiatric nurse must also assess the child's ability to make decisions and to exercise judgment, as well as the child's level of knowledge. In addition, the psychiatric nurse is concerned about orientation, memory, problem-solving abilities, and concentration. The nurse needs to determine what is developmentally and culturally expected of the child. For example, magical thinking in very young children is quite common, but may be a matter of some concern in older youngsters.

It is also important to investigate the child's ability to learn. Difficulties in learning may be related to specific cognitive processes that interfere with the child's ability to function in the classroom. The nurse also identifies the child's dominant modes of thinking, such as concrete thought processes. The appraisal of these processes is essential to plan the teaching approaches to be used in nursing interventions.

The child's history should include previous academic performance and participation in nursery and school programs. Of particular concern are the areas of
achievement and the areas of limited performance, which may suggest possible
learning disabilities. Information about the child's school experience should also
include behavioral elements, such as the child's relationship with teachers, the
principal, and peers.

In gathering information regarding a child's cognitive processes, the psychiatric nurse may use the techniques of interviewing, observation, and a formalized
mental status evaluation. Burgess and Gosselin (1985) noted that "the purpose of
the mental status examination is to objectively determine and record observable
aspects of the patient's psychological functioning" (p. 143). Such an evaluation
determines the youngster's level of functioning at the time of the interview and
includes data gathering about the child's cognitive, perceptual, and emotional
functioning (Critchley, 1979). Through the course of history taking, the nurse can
gather a great deal of general information; the nurse then uses specific tasks to
gather information about particular areas. The components of a mental status
evaluation with youngsters may include the following:

- *general appearance:* age, appropriate dress, hygiene, size, stature, handicaps
- *speech pattern:* developmentally appropriate
- *motor activity:* alterations related to context of discussion
- *mood/affect:* predominant themes, range of variation, quality
- *anxiety level:* predominant theme and variation
- *defense mechanisms:* predominant mechanism, variations, avoidance
- *thought processes:* problem-solving abilities, predominant modes
- *thought content:* ease of expression, age-appropriate conversation, self-concept, body image, suicidal and homicidal thoughts
- *intellectual functions:* orientation, memory, concentration, ability to abstract, insight, language skills
- *judgment*
- *attitude:* cooperative or guarded toward treatment, toward parents, toward
  presenting human responses
- *sensory-motor:* right, left, gross, and fine motor
- *coping abilities:* initiative, patterns of control, support systems
- *fantasy:* capability, creativity

Psychologists have developed numerous instruments to assist in assessing various cognitive functions, including verbal skills and problem-solving abilities
(Siegel, 1987; Wodrich, 1984). Psychiatric nurses should have a working knowledge of these instruments and should be able to interpret the relevant results.

Ecological Patterns. Given the dependent position of young children on their environment, nurses should consider ecological patterns carefully. Of primary concern are the potential hazards, such as access to weapons, drugs, and alcohol. Home safety and the provision of a stimulating environment are particular concerns for families of toddlers and infants.

A tool that can be helpful in assessing the ecological patterns of a family is the Home Observation for Measurement of the Environment Inventory (HOME; Caldwell & Bradley, 1979). A clinician-completed questionnaire used to appraise the level of stimulation in the home environment, this instrument has been developed for three age groupings (infancy through childhood). It has six subscales, including organization of the environment, provision of appropriate play materials, avoidance of restriction and punishment, maternal emotional and verbal responsiveness, and opportunities for variety in daily stimulation.

Emotional Processes. Psychiatric nursing assessments always involve an appraisal of the child's emotional responses and development, including predominant moods and range of emotions. The nurse specifies current and past patterns which may identify resources available to the child. The exploration of family members' patterns of emotional expression is also helpful, as this may indicate acceptable, reinforced patterns and pathology.

This information is gathered through interviewing the youngster, mental status evaluations, and observation for affective responses and congruence with verbalizations. Many children, however, have significant difficulty recognizing their emotions and verbalizing their thoughts and feelings. With these children, art techniques are helpful tools (Siemon, 1982). Elementary school-aged children have basic skills in drawing and often respond positively to requests to draw a picture. Other art forms, such as collages, may be useful with older children and adolescents. The Children's Depression Inventory (CDI; Kovacs, 1985), a 27-item self-report questionnaire designed for school-aged children and adolescents, is a useful instrument in assessing potential emotional responses to depression.

Interpersonal Processes. Problems in the child's interactions with other people are frequently the reason for referral. Because communication patterns are an essential element of the interpersonal process, the psychiatric nurse collects information about the child's usual patterns of communication. Problematic behaviors often include stuttering, inappropriate nonverbal communication, and inability to express thoughts and feelings.

Conduct and impulse processes encompass the youngster's capability for self-control. Acting out behaviors are another common reason for referral; such behaviors may include truancy, running away, and substance abuse. A careful appraisal of the substance abuse history of youngsters is always indicated. Open-ended questions presented in a nonthreatening manner are most likely to produce accurate information. The nurse should request specific details as to the type of substance used, the amounts consumed, and the frequency of use. The Adolescent Addiction Assessment Form may be helpful in collecting pertinent information regarding substance use (Marlow & Redding, 1988). Another area of impulse control is self-destructive behavior; the psychiatric nurse must specifically inquire about suicidal intent, plans, and past attempts.

In addition to the family history, the psychiatric nurse inquires about the dynamics of the family. This includes information about the family's decision-making capabilities, the roles of various members, family values, and goals. Significant patterns of concern may include scapegoating or enmeshment. It is important to appraise both the strengths and the limitations of the family unit. Several of the tools used for gathering the family history also provide information regarding family dynamics.

Children have numerous roles in which they must function every day, such as family member, student, and playmate. The psychiatric nurse gathers information about the youngster's functioning in each of these roles. Peer relationships are also of interest, as they are indicative of a child's social capabilities of sharing, compromising, and competing. When behavioral problems are identified, careful assessment may clarify patterns (e.g., initiation or destructiveness).

Children's play and activity patterns indicate their developmental level. Youngsters often express themselves nonverbally through such activities. It is essential to note patterns, such as parallel (side-by-side) play, and interactive tendencies. This area of assessment may reveal psychosocial strengths and interests of the child that may direct the choice of treatment interventions.

Adolescent sexual development often creates increasing anxiety for both the child and parents. In this area of assessment, the nurse should ask about the timeliness of pubertal development, the experience of the youngster, and the birth control practices of the sexually active adolescent. The nurse should also elicit information about the values of the child and parents regarding sexual activity.

Perceptual Processes. The way in which a child perceives his or her world is a significant concern for the psychiatric nurse. These perceptual patterns include levels of comfort and attention. Variations in the child's perceptions may result in illusions or hallucinations, both indicators of a significant disturbance. If a child has hallucinations, the nurse needs to clarify the nature of the hallucinations, as well as their duration and frequency. Command hallucinations are of particular concern if the child is hearing destructive voices.

The child's self-perception is another concern. A child's low self-esteem often precipitates a referral, may accompany other problems, or may be the underlying cause of acting out behaviors. Because this area is difficult for many children to discuss at first, nonverbal or projective techniques, such as drawings or journals, may be helpful. Several instruments to measure self-esteem are available (e.g., Coopersmith, 1967).

Information about a youngster's perceptual processes can be gathered through a variety of methods. Direct questions may elicit important information from older children and adolescents. In addition, observation of the youngster is essential for significant perceptual alterations, such as hallucinations. With children who are unable to share this information directly, nonverbal tools may be more helpful. For example, art techniques such as asking the child to draw a person reveal a child's body image or perceived role in the family.

Physiological Processes. A thorough psychiatric nursing assessment requires a history and appraisal of the youngster's physical health, including a history of physical disabilities, illnesses, operations, and immunizations. With adolescents, a careful appraisal of growth and sexual development, including menses, is necessary.

A physical examination of the youngster may be helpful in completing a psychiatric nursing assessment. The use of the physical examination as a data-gathering tool for the psychiatric nurse requires authorization from the child's guardian, however. Depending on the needs and the nurses' level of expertise, and the context of the nurse-client relationship, the nurse may either perform the physical examination or refer the child to a pediatric practitioner for a complete examination. The child's particular response patterns may indicate the need for a complete or partial examination; for example, if neurological deficits are suspected, a more thorough examination is indicated.

Many children have developed problematic nutritional patterns, such as overeating, significant weight loss, or consumption of unusual substances (i.e., pica). Other children have particular nutritional needs as a result of injury, medical illnesses, poverty, or lack of parental knowledge. The nurse gathers information about the child's patterns of weight loss or gain, the types of foods usually eaten, and specific dietary requirements (Murphy, 1984).

Valuation Processes. The psychiatric nurse gathers information about the child's values and feelings of meaningfulness. Youngsters frequently feel powerless, hopeless, and helpless. The religious beliefs of the child and family are clarified, including church participation and the integration of spiritual and religious beliefs into the family's daily life. Potential conflict of an adolescent's beliefs or behaviors with family, society, or culture values may need careful appraisal.

ANALYSIS OF ASSESSMENT DATA

Like data collection, data analysis is an ongoing process that begins when the nurse first meets the youngster and family. The nurse seeks to validate all information related to the child and to obtain a comprehensive understanding of the situation. The nurse organizes the information into behavioral, emotional, and cognitive patterns to facilitate the determination of nursing diagnoses. The objectives of the analysis include: (1) organization of the collected data, (2) framing of the problem, and (3) identification of the human response patterns of concern.

Validation occurs while the nurse collects the data. The nurse looks for cues or indications of congruence, as well as inconsistencies in the collected data. Carnevali (1983) described cues as units of information that are obtained through the senses. They contribute to the development of inferences or the determination of the subjective meanings of observed or experienced stimuli. The psychiatric nurse validates the information obtained from one source with other sources, such as the youngster, the parent, an extended family member, the physician, or a teacher. By validating the information, the nurse gains confidence that the information collected, inferences made, and problematic human responses identified are accurate.

To treat a youngster effectively, a child psychiatric nurse must have a working hypothesis of the situation. A comprehensive data analysis that leads to an understanding of the child and family is essential to develop this hypothesis and focus treatment efforts. The nurse and family develop the working hypothesis by exploring possible contributing factors to the problematic situation and identifying areas of needed change.

The development of a working hypothesis is related to the framing of the problem or situation. The process was initially described for nurses by deChesnay (1983), who stated that "problem framing is a way of conceptualizing a problem either as an individual or system problem" (p. 8). Problems may be first-order (i.e., individually focused) or second-order (i.e., system-based). The system may be the family, the group, or the community, rather than the single individual. Because children have dependent positions in family systems, it may be best to frame a child's problematic behavior within the context of the family system. Family members often hesitate to frame the problem as a system-based one, and it may be necessary to address this hesitancy early in treatment.

The way in which a situation is framed influences which human responses the nurse identifies, the nursing diagnoses, and the nursing care plans. For example, a nurse may perceive a youngster's fire-setting behavior as an individual's pattern of destructive behavior and use individually focused intervention, such as individual psychotherapy. On the other hand, a nurse may view the youngster's fire-setting as attention-seeking behavior directed toward the parents and implement system-based interventions, such as parental guidance and family therapy.

The psychiatric nurse analyzes the assessment data by applying scientifically sound theories, including scholarly conceptualizations and research findings, to explain developmental and behavioral phenomena (ANA, 1985). The use of multiple theoretical perspectives, such as those derived from nursing, developmental, systems, cultural, psychopathology, social, and learning theories, augments nurses' holistic focus. The nurse's theoretical perspective markedly influences the type of information collected and its analysis.

The clinical formulation is the working hypothesis and initial analysis of the child's situation. The nurse highlights the most pertinent human responses, and identifies the areas that require nursing intervention. This formulation also includes the apparent motivation for treatment, the rapport between the participants, and the child's ability to engage in the therapeutic relationship. The nurse then proceeds to identify the nursing diagnoses and delineate a plan of care.

REFERENCES

Achenbach, T.M., & Edelbrock, C.S. (1983). *Manual for the C.B.C.L. and revised child behavior profile.* Burlington, VT: University of Vermont.

American Nurses' Association. (1985). *Standards of child and adolescent psychiatric and mental health nursing practice.* Kansas City, MO: Author.

Barbee, M.A. (1982). A practical guide to family assessment. In K. Babisch (Ed.), *Assessing the mental health needs of children* (Monograph 2C126, pp. 47–58). Boulder, CO: Western Interstate Council of Higher Education.

Barry, P.D. (1989). *Psychosocial nursing: Assessment and intervention* (2nd ed.). Philadelphia: J.B. Lippincott.

Burgess, A.W., & Gosselin, J.M. (1985). The process of assessing in psychiatric mental health nursing practice. In A.W. Burgess (Ed.), *Psychiatric nursing in the hospital and the community* (4th ed., pp. 128–162). Englewood Cliffs, NJ: Prentice-Hall.

Caldwell, B.M., & Bradley, R.H. (1979). *Home Observation for Measurement of the Environment.* Little Rock: University of Arkansas Press.

Carnevali, D.L. (1983). *Nursing care planning: Diagnosis and management* (3rd ed.). Philadelphia: J.B. Lippincott.

Coopersmith, S. (1967). *The antecedents of self-esteem.* San Francisco: W.H. Freeman.

Critchley, D.L. (1979). Mental status examinations with children and adolescents. *Nursing Clinics of North America, 14*(3), 429–441.

deChesnay, M. (1983). Problem solving in nursing. *Image: The Journal of Nursing Scholarship, 15*(1), 8–11.

Delaney, L.L. (1982). Nursing assessment: Data collection of the family unit. In J.W. Griffith & P.J. Christenson (Eds.), *Nursing process: Application of theories, frameworks and models* (pp. 54–65). St. Louis: C.V. Mosby.

Denyes, M.J. (1980). Development of an instrument to measure self-care agency in adolescents (unpublished doctoral dissertation, University of Michigan). *Dissertation Abstracts International, 41,* 171-B (University Microfilm No. 80-25 672).

Fagin, C.M. (Ed.). (1972). *Nursing in child psychiatry.* St. Louis: C.V. Mosby.

Hagerty, B.K. (1984). *Psychiatric–mental health assessment.* St. Louis: C.V. Mosby.

Ireton, H., & Thwing, E. (1974). *Manual for the Minnesota Child Development Inventory.* Minneapolis: Behavior Science System.

Jellinek, M.S., & Murphy, J.M. (1988). Screening for psychological disorders in pediatric practice. *American Journal of Diseases of Children, 142,* 1153–1157.

Kovacs, M. (1985). The children's depression inventory (CDI). *Psychopharmacology Bulletin, 21*(4), 995–998.

MacNair, R.H. (1983). *Assessment of Child and Adolescent Functioning: A practitioner's instrument for assessing clients*. Athens, GA: Institute of Community and Area Development, University of Georgia.

Marlow, D.R., & Redding, B.A. (1988). *Textbook of pediatric nursing* (6th ed.). Philadelphia: W.B. Saunders.

Morgen, S.A., & Macey, J. (1978). Three assessment tools for family therapy. *Journal of Psychosocial Nursing and Mental Health Services, 16*(3), 39–42.

Murphy, C.M. (1984). *Quick reference to pediatric nursing*. Philadelphia: J.B. Lippincott.

Orlando, I. (1961). *The dynamic nurse-patient relationship*. New York: G.P. Putnam's Sons.

O'Toole, A.W., & Loomis, M.E. (1989). Revision of the phenomena of concern for psychiatric mental health nursing. *Archives of Psychiatric Nursing, 3*(5), 288–299.

Peplau, H.E. (1952). *Interpersonal relations in nursing*. New York: G.P. Putnam.

Siegel, M.G. (1987). *Psychological testing from early childhood through adolescence: A developmental and psychodynamic approach*. Madison, CT: International Universities.

Siemon, M.K. (1982). Using Di Leo's and Koppitz's models for assessing children's drawings. In K. Babisch (Ed.), *Assessing the mental health needs of children* (Monograph 2C126, pp. 95–104). Boulder, CO: Western Interstate Council of Higher Education.

Smoyak, S. (1982). Family systems: Use of genograms as an assessment tool. In I.W. Clements & D.M. Bruchanan (Eds.), *Family therapy: A nursing perspective* (pp. 245–250). New York: Wiley & Sons.

Wodrich, D.L. (1984). *Children's psychological testing: A guide for nonpsychologists*. Baltimore: Paul H. Brookes.

3

Role of Developmental Theory in Child and Adolescent Mental Health Assessment

Deane L. Critchley

After reading this chapter, the reader will be able to:

1. identify major approaches to assessing human development
2. describe recent significant findings in human development
3. examine important issues for the child psychiatric nurse in assessing the development of children and adolescents

Developmental theory has changed markedly within the last 25 years because of the explosion of new knowledge and ideas in the biological, behavioral, and social sciences. Evolving ideas and research from neurochemistry, neurophysiology, psychology, psychiatry, epidemiology, sociology, and several other disciplines have modified perceptions of the developmental process and its patterns. In addition, longitudinal behavioral studies have contributed important information about individual developmental patterns.

There are several important issues in the field of human development. It is no longer automatically assumed, for example, that an individual's reactions to a situation are the culmination of a long history of events. Currently available knowledge makes it clear that, while past experience makes a significant contribution to present functioning, the role of the uniquely human cognitive abilities and temperamental qualities, as well as the possibilities for discontinuity in development, must be recognized. These issues influence the clinical process in terms of the philosophical approach taken in assessment and treatment.

Developmental phenomena are integrally related to human health and functioning. An understanding of the processes of development is critical to nursing interpretations of the behaviors and health needs of clients at different developmental levels. A developmental framework establishes criteria for some of the unique human characteristics that psychiatric nurses can use to guide their assessments and interventions with clients.

Because of nursing's holistic perspective, a psychiatric nursing assessment goes beyond the functioning in any one dimension. Furthermore, the psychiatric nurse looks not only at the total functioning of the individual, but also at the individual-environment interactions. Thus, a psychiatric nursing assessment with a child or adolescent focuses on the learning and growth experiences of the youngster, as well as on ways to foster the ability of the youngster to learn and grow. An inherent value of a nursing assessment is that it determines the individual's level of developmental functioning and focuses on his or her strengths, as well as limitations.

As nursing has increased its knowledge base, it has moved from intuitive decision making to more objective judgments based on theoretical and clinical data. There is a critical need for valid and reliable nursing assessments, and such nursing assessments must be based on a sound theoretical framework. Assessment can then provide guidelines for treatment planning and intervention, evaluation of progress, and follow-up care.

TRADITIONAL DEVELOPMENTAL FORMULATIONS

Although psychoanalysis and behaviorism have provided contrasting conceptual frameworks for developmental theory, they have certain features in common. Both theories emphasize the interaction of biological and environmental factors in the formation of behavior patterns. Both theories take into account the ways in which life experience transforms simple patterns into more complex patterns. Both theories have provided methods of studying human development that have generated enormous amounts of knowledge.

In his theory of psychoanalysis, Freud identified the meaning and purpose to be found even in behavior that appears accidental or trivial. He demonstrated that motivations outside of awareness determine much of behavior and that anxiety, conflict, and defense mechanisms influence and shape human actions, goals, feelings, and thoughts. Freud also developed a system of treatment for a multitude of psychological disorders through the use of free association, dream interpretation, and analysis of transference.

Pavlov's behavioral theory made a valuable contribution to knowledge by showing that the formation, modification, and extinction of the neurophysiological mechanism of the conditioned reflex is the basis of simple learning (Pavlov, 1960). The physiological laws of conditioning have proved useful in developmental psychology, learning theory, and in certain psychopathological conditions. Pavlov's discovery of the mechanism of the conditioned reflex provided a conceptual basis for behavior therapy.

Despite their contributions to knowledge, there has been increasing dissatisfaction with both psychoanalysis and behaviorism in explaining human development. Genetically predetermined instinctual patterns diminish in their influence as organisms become more complex. It is now well understood that the more complex the organism, the greater its capacity for learning through experience and modifying genetically given behavior patterns. In addition, the human conditioned reflex is not the same as that in lower animals. Once established in lower animals, the conditioned reflex remains basically unchanged over time. It may become linked with other reflexes, it may be weakened or strengthened, but the association with the original environmental stimulus remains essentially unchanged. This is not so in the human, however.

For example, a preschool child may develop a fear of water as a simple conditioned reflex after a frightening experience at the beach. Very quickly, the child's anxious behavior elicits reactions in parents, siblings, and other adults and children. These reactions modify the original conditioned behavior and give it symbolic meaning. A sequential interaction process develops. By the time the child is 10 years old, the same phobia has developed new aspects, new meanings, and new influences on the child's functioning and social interactions. The phobia may remain throughout adulthood, but its significance for the individual, for the family, and for friends will be different at any given point in time.

Limitations of Traditional Developmental Models

Although the ideas and research of the modern psychoanalytic and social learning theorists have stimulated important studies into sociocultural influences on human development, they have not overcome two basic limitations of the original models: (1) the use of animal models for the biological aspect of development and (2) the use of an interactional approach in conceptualizing the interplay among biological, psychological, and social factors at all levels.

Animal Models

In recent years, theorists in both ethology (i.e., the comparative study of animal behavior) and sociobiology have used animal models to explain human developmental processes. Ethologists have developed hypotheses that are very compatible with instinct theory. They have emphasized the decisive and permanent role of early life experience through the concept of "imprinting," the theory that early learning from one experience results in permanent and irreversible effects, and the concept of "critical period," the theory that the young organism must be exposed to a given learning experience at a specific age or forever suffer some degree of deficit. Both concepts have been challenged, however. There is no evidence to support the idea of imprinting in human infants (Hess, 1972). There are undoubtedly optimal periods in life for different kinds of learning, but development itself shows that there are multiple paths to learning, both in time and situations (Wolff, 1970).

Lorenz (1966) dealt with human aggression by analogy with animal behavior and stated that human social behavior is governed by the laws prevailing in all phylogenetically adapted instinctive behavior. Tinbergen (1968) went even further and stated that it is necessary to study animal behavior in order to clarify human behavior problems such as aggression. Others have justifiably criticized the idea of a fundamental destructive aggressive instinct in humans. Marmor (1974) pointed out that war is not merely the sum of countless human aggressions, but is itself a complicated social institution. Like all social institutions, it is subject to evolution and change as a result of complex social, economic, political, and psychological factors.

Sociobiologists assert that various aspects of social behavior are genetically rather than culturally transmitted through randomly produced genetic variations in social behavior that have superior adaptive value; they derive supportive data for this belief chiefly from animal studies. The sociobiological approach does make it possible to explain the newborn's capacity for social behavior. This capacity rests on the newborn's ability to form conditioned reflexes, to perceive certain stimuli, to communicate, and to learn. Such behavior is an asset in cementing a bond with the care-giver and in communicating needs. It is plausible that the behavior arose randomly through genetic variation that was then favored by natural selection.

The issue is considerably different once experience and learning take place and social functioning becomes increasingly elaborate. To ascribe such complex behaviors to genetic inheritance is questionable, and to reason by analogy with the behavior of animal communities is both hazardous and likely to be highly unreliable. Many authorities have attacked sociobiology as being merely a more sophisticated version of biological determinism (Sahlins, 1976).

Interactional Approach to Development

Linear, static models in which biology and culture are dichotomized have proven increasingly inadequate for developmental theory. Although the theory of an interactional, more holistic model has existed for years, it has become overwhelmingly accepted only within the last 20 years.

Central to interactional theory is the belief that the child is neither *tabula rasa* nor *homunculus*. Tabula rasa describes the child as a blank slate on which the environment would etch its influence until the adult personality emerged. Homunculus refers to the child being an adult in miniature who already possesses all the attributes that will characterize the adult. The human infant is an active agent from birth in interactions with the environment. The infant's capacity for learning and for flexibility in development permits changes in developmental patterns in response to new life experiences. In human development, the most important interaction of the organism is that with the social environment. Thomas and Chess (1977), in their longitudinal study of human temperament, found that a child's temperament significantly influences the attitudes and behaviors of peers, older children, parents, and teachers. At the same time, the child's specific temperamental attributes mediates the effect that these significant individuals' behaviors and attitudes have on the child.

Characteristics of an Ideal Human Developmental Model

In a human developmental model, it is necessary to emphasize the structural and functional characteristics that are special, even unique, to human behavior—those attributes that make learning, language, the use of tools, and abstract thought possible. A human developmental model must also emphasize the inheritance of culture through human social institutions. Human development occurs in a biopsychosocial matrix through a continuous dynamic interaction of the biological, psychological, and social variables.

BIOLOGICAL AND EXPERIENTIAL FACTORS IN DEVELOPMENT

Developmental theory includes two contrasting views of the child: one focused on the relative influence of inherited, biological abilities on the individual's developmental potential and one focused on the impact of life experience.

Biological Capacity

The most important biological influences on development are those that regulate the maturation of the central nervous system and, thus, permit motor and cognitive abilities to appear at regular times. It was previously thought that newborns are not capable of processing information from the external world, that their immature development makes them psychologically incompetent, confused, and disorganized. Now, that view is known to be totally erroneous. Careful, naturalistic observations, combined with new experimental techniques, have provided overwhelming evidence that newborns begin life as extremely competent learning and perceiving organisms. They can recognize visual patterns and show a preference for those with greater complexity, movement, and three dimensionality over plain visual stimuli. Neonates are also responsive to sound, can localize its direction, and show a capacity for a functional interaction between what they see and hear. The Neonatal Behavioral Assessment Scale is based on a range of neonatal behavioral integrative processes that give clear evidence of cortical control (Brazelton, 1984).

It has been demonstrated that learning begins actively at birth, if not before. Learning by imitation begins within the first week of life. Thus, biological perceptual and learning capacities allow the infant to respond to and to integrate information from the environment that has both cultural and sensory-motor significance.

Early Life Experience

Theorists with diverse backgrounds have agreed that early life experiences have a decisive influence on subsequent development. Some theorists see this influence as all powerful. Some believe that family pathology and dynamics determine whether the young child will develop schizophrenia and other forms of psychopathology. Early malnutrition has been considered the cause of irreversible psychological effects. Adverse socioeconomic circumstances, commonly described as "cultural deprivation," have been presumed to have serious, permanent behavioral and cognitive consequences.

In the past 10 years, there has been a shift in thinking about the significance of early life experiences. Clarke and Clarke (1984) compiled an impressive number of reports to document the fact that poor care in early life does not necessarily cause permanent damage to the child. The studies that they cited consistently demonstrated children's amazing resilience and a dramatic improvement in their later functioning when there was a positive change in care and in the environment. Other studies have confirmed the concept of malleability in older children and adults (e.g., Winick, Meyer, & Harris, 1975).

CONTINUITY AND PREDICTABILITY IN HUMAN DEVELOPMENT

Both continuity and change occur over time at all stages of the life cycle. Continuity emerges from change, but can itself become an agent for further change. For example, a kindergartner may learn to accept help easily from parents, siblings, and teachers. This ability leads consistently to task achievement, which enhances the child's self-confidence in approaching new demands and challenges. It also contributes to the child's becoming a responsible leader among peers and one to whom others turn for help.

In developmental theory, it has been tempting to seek invariant sequences of development in which subsequent stages follow preceding ones in a fixed order. Such sequencing would provide a basic structure of continuity and stability in the process of change from one period to another. In his work on the development of cognitive thinking, Piaget (1963) hypothesized that sequential periods of cognitive growth occur in an invariant sequence, although the ages at which the sequences occur may vary.

Flavell (1972) seriously questioned Piaget's formulation of a "linear, sequential, unidirectional conception of cognition, behavior and development" (p. 341). Flavell's research convinced him that most cognitive behavior and development occur in a spiral rather than a linear fashion, are cyclical rather than unidirectional, and do not necessarily take place in fixed sequences. He pointed out that these characteristics resemble those of reciprocal interaction, which is prevalent in other developmental processes. Reciprocal interaction is the concept that, as learning occurs, what is being learned mutually shapes and regulates other learning that occurs concurrently or subsequently. Learning is a continuous, interactive process.

Erikson (1963) based his psychosocial developmental framework on the invariant sequential stages of psychosexual development proposed by Freud (1949), in which progress to the next stage depends on mastery of the tasks of the earlier stage. Erikson's scheme goes beyond the traditional psychoanalytic framework by including adult developmental stages. Some have criticized Erikson's system, however, for the personality attributes used and for the close connection to psychoanalysis with its emphasis on shifts in libido or sexual energy as the basis for the different developmental stages (Hess, 1970; Lidz, 1968).

Two more recent formulations based on fixed sequential stages include Loevinger's model of ego development (Loevinger, 1976) and Kohlberg's model of moral development (Kohlberg, 1964). Both of these models have been criticized because of their content and the methodology used (Hauser, 1976; Vaillant, 1977).

Development does proceed sequentially. Learning, maturation, and ongoing genetic variables interact to produce new and increasingly complex behaviors throughout the life cycle. The concept of sequential developmental stages can provide important insights into the laws governing developmental processes from the simple to the complex. There are great individual differences in the quality, timing, and transition from stage to stage, however. More significantly, given the individual variation in biological capacities, genetic influences, maturation, temperament, environmental pressures, life experiences, and social and cultural expectations, as well as the quantity and complexity of the interactions among these variables, there simply cannot be an invariant, linear developmental sequence for any behavior pattern. There may be group trends for a given population of similar backgrounds, but marked individual variation always occurs.

In addition, the idea of fixed sequential stages of development leads to the pervasive belief that the characteristics of the child foretell the personality of the adult. Parents fear that their shy and timid preschooler will become a lonely adolescent or anticipate that their active, outgoing 6-year-old will become the high school class president. Long-term developmental studies have consistently indicated that early behavior and life experiences do not presage functioning in later life (Murphy & Moriarity, 1976; Vaillant, 1977). Simple linear prediction from early childhood to later developmental stages is impossible (Thomas & Chess, 1977; Kagan, 1986). The human being's unique capacity for learning and flexibility in development would be wasted if the individual's potential for mastery and adaptation were arrested or even severely limited by early life experiences. Emde (1978) made the point that the variability and range of their behavior provide infants with greater opportunities to adapt to their care-giving environments, which are to a large extent unpredictable. Emde noted that perhaps the vulnerable infant is the one who has a narrow range of behavioral variability that limits his or her adaptability to the environment.

The decreasing belief in the overwhelming importance of early life experiences has had a positive practical effect. Parents, particularly mothers, are less likely to be accused of being responsible for their child's problems. As a result, there has been a reduction in parental guilt, anxiety, and self-blame.

IDEOLOGICAL ISSUES

In a review of the voluminous literature on development throughout the life cycle, certain basic ideological questions stand out as controversial.

Development as Crisis

Crisis is an emotional state that represents a significant disruption in an individual's psychological equilibrium. Originally, the construct was applied to the adolescent period by Hall (1904), and it is still widely used in describing this stage. Many theorists see crises in other developmental periods as well. Some investigators state unequivocally that individuals who say that they are not experiencing turmoil or crisis are either denying it or losing an opportunity for personal growth (Levinson, Darrow, Klein, Levinson, & McKee, 1978).

When discussing crisis, theorists must outline the behavioral consequences of their particular theory of crisis. Not all normal adolescents exhibit the behaviors that many theorists ascribe to adolescents in crisis (Rutter, Graham, Chadwick, & Yule, 1976), such as dramatic shifts in affect, cognition, interpersonal relationships, and behavior. Individuals without these characteristics are not likely to be experiencing crisis.

Coleman (1978) sought to reconcile the contradiction between those who speak of adolescence as a period of crisis and those who see it as relatively harmonious. He proposed a "focal" theory of adolescence, suggesting that particular relationship patterns and issues become most prominent at different ages, but that no pattern is specific to only one age. Thus, patterns overlap and different issues come into focus at different times. Individuals are likely to face certain issues, such as anxiety over heterosexual relationships, at an earlier point in adolescence than others, such as fear of rejection by their peer group. According to Coleman, his theory provides for more flexibility and individuality in the expression of the individual's developmental pattern.

Fitzpatrick (1982) attempted to reformulate the crisis perspective with Rogers' nursing model (Rogers, 1970). Within her reformulation, the crisis experience is conceptualized as the turning point in a developmental phase. She identified holistic manifestations not only of the developmental phase, but also of the crisis experience itself, such as temporality or perceptual experiences. This nursing crisis reformulation has yet to be tested.

Variations in Normal Developmental Patterns

Human development is marked by a capacity for learning that is linked to an attribute of great significance—plasticity. The source of developmental plasticity lies in the biological characteristics of the brain as expressed in interaction with the opportunities and expectations that the environment provides. The development of children with severe handicaps, such as congenital deafness or blindness, illustrates the significance of developmental plasticity. These children are deprived from birth of a major sensory modality, which contributes to a major alteration in their developmental pattern. Such a handicap delays their achievement of many developmental landmarks in the use of verbal or visual cues, in the use of language, and in social interactions. As these children mature neurologically and physically, however, they begin to adapt to their own particular handicap by using alternative sensory modalities. These children can then move forward rapidly in their cognitive and adaptive functioning (Chess, 1978; Jan, Freeman, & Scott, 1977).

The plasticity of the human brain allows a host of alternative adaptive developmental pathways to be used, depending on the characteristics of the child and the nature of the environment. Normal development in such children contradicts Fraiberg's idea that there is only one path of normal development and that any deviations from this path are always unsatisfactory and inferior (Fraiberg, 1977).

Adaptation and Development

Much of current developmental theory emphasizes adaptation. The premise is that individuals' successful adaptation to external reality ensures a smoothly running society. According to these theories, the adaptation process begins early and continues throughout life.

When adaptation becomes a therapeutic goal, however, the obvious question is, to what should the client adapt? What is a healthy environment? By definition, successful adaptation to the environment results in individual adjustment, but it may not result in desirable personal experiences. Neurosis is an adaptation to reality, but no one suggests that it is healthy (Hartman, 1958). How does one decide what reality is best for healthy adaptation? Only by studying widely diverse groups of normal and disturbed individuals and their interactions with society will it be possible to understand fully the role of adaptation in human development.

Family's Role in the Developmental Process

The development of the individual cannot be understood outside the context of the family, as it obviously shapes the functions of individual family members. The family is more than a passive conduit for cultural norms. Within the family, interactions help some members to grow and inhibit the growth of others. Developmental processes within the family are continuously being influenced and influencing multiple complex biopsychosocial variables over time.

Families with disturbed children and adolescents have been described as disturbed social systems. Dysfunctional communication patterns that make it impossible to communicate basic values, beliefs, and affect within the family are considered conducive to mental illness and deviant behavior in the family members

(Lewis, Beavers, Gossett, & Phillips, 1976). Most of the research about family functioning has involved disturbed families. The assumption has been that well functioning families are the opposite of those with overt psychopathology. Recently, however, systematic efforts to study the "normal" family have begun. Clearly, an understanding of normal family processes is critical to the understanding of disturbed family functioning. It is essential to develop appropriate methodologies to explore the ways in which the normal family affects its members and the development of a normal individual within a deviant family; efforts in this direction are continuing (Cohen, Weissman, & Cohler, 1984; Lewis, Beavers, Gossett, & Phillips, 1976; Walsh, 1982).

ISSUES IN ASSESSING DEVELOPMENT

The child psychiatric nurse does not need special techniques to assess development, but rather needs a knowledge of the range of normal development, as well as its pathological manifestations, in order to place clinical observations and other data into a coherent framework. The fact that child psychiatric nurses focus on children and adolescents who are disturbed or who have emotional problems may skew these nurses' perspective of all children and adolescents.

Mentally healthy children and adolescents see the world as a place where they are secure and can trust others. They have a realistic and positive self-concept and self-image that contributes to their positive sense of identity. They are able to learn and master knowledge and skills, and they can maintain satisfying and satisfactory interpersonal relationships. They have the capacity to cope with stress and anxiety, as well as to perceive the world accurately and realistically in relation to their developmental level.

Thus, in order to assess the mental and emotional status of a child or adolescent accurately, the nurse must understand the developmental needs and tasks for a given age group, the behaviors characteristic of particular developmental levels, and the possible maturational concerns that may occur during a particular developmental period. Most important, the nurse needs to keep an open mind and to realize that the child or adolescent may or may not meet all the developmental expectations for a particular period in the accustomed ways and yet still be a well-adjusted and competent individual.

Both traditional interviewing and projective techniques are helpful with children and adolescents. Such techniques include human person drawings, family drawing, puppet and doll house play, and board games. These types of play help clarify questions about the behavior of the child or adolescent and confirm data obtained from other sources. Standardized measures and inventories can provide additional information (see Appendix 3-A).

In obtaining data through interviews with the child or adolescent, the parents, and other significant adults, the child psychiatric nurse has an opportunity to explore in detail those aspects that appear most relevant to the presenting problem or problems. Face-to-face contact permits the identification of attitudes, feelings, and ideas that expand the data base. Contradictions may be identified and clarified, and any confusions or misunderstandings can be explored.

Need for Assessment

An understanding of the possible sources of stress and the accompanying coping responses is critical in evaluating the unique developmental pattern of a child or adolescent. Eggert (1978) stressed that, in assessing the developmental status of adolescents, nurses must be sensitive to their own reactions to the youth, the impact of the environment on the situation, and, of course, the adolescent's responses.

Bumbalo and Siemon (1983) identified three broad potential risk areas for children: the environment, parental characteristics, and innate factors in the child that increase his or her vulnerability. Many emotional problems of children and adolescents result from the stresses experienced either within or among these areas (Sahin, 1979). Developmental transition points are cases in point. The birth of a sibling or accelerated sexual development with its internal, interpersonal, and environmental ramifications sometimes, although not always, produces stress or conflict for the youngster. Any factor that limits the flexibility of the child or adolescent in coping with such events increases his or her vulnerability in development. Increased vulnerability does not automatically result in deviant developmental progress, however.

Framework for Assessment

In working with children and adolescents, child psychiatric nurses need a theoretical framework for assessment, treatment, and evaluation that differentiates between (1) psychopathological and medical diagnoses and (2) the human responses of concern to nursing. The framework used requires a developmental focus so that nurses can identify strengths, as well as needs, and potential intervention methods. Several of nursing's conceptual models emphasize the significance of developmental phenomena or use developmental concepts in their formulations.

Rogers (1970) proposed that development is characterized by an increasing complexity and diversity of pattern and organization in both the human and environmental fields. The model's principle of helicy portrays development as a continuously innovative process. The principle of helicy is the continuous, innovative, probabilistic, increasing diversity of human and environmental field patterns characterized by non-repeating rhythmicities. Thus, the life process is viewed as a constantly evolving series of changes which incorporate the past and out of which new patterns emerge (Rogers, 1970). Rogers' model of unitary human beings is not congruent with the traditional models of human development, but is more consistent with current approaches to human development, such as life span developmental views. Rogers defines unitary human beings as four-dimensional, negentropic energy fields identified by pattern and organization and manifesting characteristics and behaviors that are "different from those of the parts and which cannot be predicted from knowledge of the parts" (1970, p. 332). Rogers' model would require changes in nursing attitudes and practices in order to accommodate greater individuality in the expression of the developmental process and to assist clients in enhancing their responses to their own developmental patterns.

Parsé's theory of nursing, which is derived from Rogers' model, incorporates the concept of health as a process of development toward greater complexity and diversity (Parsé, 1981). Several principles in Parsé's theory reflect developmental concepts, including the abilities to individuate and achieve identity; to use abstractions and symbols increasingly to incorporate new experiences into previous ones in order to give life meaning; and to evaluate current perceptions and perspectives as a means of finding alternative, more useful beliefs and behavior.

The interpersonal relations nursing theory of Peplau (1952) is based on the idea of growth and change in both the client and the nurse. Peplau perceived the individual as someone who has the ability to learn and develop problem-solving skills to meet his or her own needs. Peplau also viewed the goal of nursing intervention as the further development of personality toward a more creative and productive life. Through their relationship, the client and the nurse both move forward in their development.

Regardless of the framework used, certain general principles help determine which developmental characteristics may be important in the etiology and evolution of a youngster's behavior patterns. Significant developmental characteristics are likely to be at the extremes of the spectrum rather than at intermediate levels. Furthermore, the identification of behavior patterns usually requires information about the individual's behavior in a wide variety of situations. Assessing a youngster's developmental functioning as part of the evaluation gives the child psychiatric nurse a clearer sense of the youngster's strengths, limitations, and characteristic behavioral repertoire. Such information helps to indicate where and how to begin helping the child. Simultaneously assessing family relationships gives the nurse a sense of any previous relationship problems and the resulting coping behaviors. With an understanding of the unachieved developmental goals, the nurse can determine the best way to enhance the client's sense of effectiveness and the efforts needed to help in the achievement of the next developmental tasks.

Objectives of Mental Health Assessment

The assessment of a youngster's functioning and mental health status has several objectives, including

- evaluating the strengths and needs of the youngster and family from the perspective of the youngster, the family, and the nurse
- determining in which areas and to what degree the youngster's behavior is similar to and differs from that of his or her age mates
- developing hypotheses regarding past and present contributing factors and their relationship to the youngster's present behavior
- assessing the adaptive and maladaptive nature of the youngster's coping responses
- identifying and setting priorities for goals in promoting the achievement of developmental tasks and adaptive coping

In order to meet these objectives, a nursing assessment must take into account the total child or adolescent. Assessment should include the client's health and developmental history; the current patterns of biophysical, cognitive, and psychosocial functioning; and the patterns of coping (Critchley, 1979). A number of systems interact with and contribute to the youngster's strengths, resources, and problems; all need to be identified. An assessment of the family's perception of the child or adolescent, of the family's needs and resources, and of their interaction patterns is crucial. Other systems that contribute significantly to the youngster's mental health include school, extended family and other significant adults, peer group, and those associated with other activities and interests. In the final analysis, it is necessary to determine how comfortable and happy are the individual, the family, and significant others with the attitudes and behaviors exhibited.

Use of Assessment Data

By analyzing the information obtained in the assessment, the child psychiatric nurse is able to develop a diagnosis and plan for intervention. During this process, the nurse identifies areas of strength, areas of concern, and possible contributing factors to problems.

In addition to knowing whether a youngster's behavior is typical or expected for a given developmental level, the nurse needs to be able to determine if the behavior is adaptive or maladaptive for the youngster. Certain general questions can be explored in order to make this determination.

- Is the behavior "in" or "out" of tune for the developmental level?
- Is the behavior age-appropriate, immature, or precocious?
- How isolated or pervasive are the areas of difficulty/problem behaviors? Do they occur chiefly in a single area of functioning (e.g., cognitive, affective), or do they cover a number of areas?
- How frequently does the difficulty occur?

- How aware and concerned is the child or adolescent of the difficulties? How intense are the difficulties for the individual? For others? How much suffering and unhappiness is the child or adolescent experiencing?
- How has the problem been dealt with previously?
- What is the pattern of the difficulty/problem behavior?
- What are the support systems available to the youngster?
- Has the behavior diminished the availability of support systems?

Finally, any nursing diagnosis must take into account the client's potential for healthy responses. The child psychiatric nurse needs to identify for the youngster and the family the maturational and developmental factors that are operating in an adaptive way. The nurse can then help them identify ways to support and strengthen the healthy developmental growth that is occurring. Helping the youngster and family to recognize and strengthen the youngster's communication skills, interpersonal techniques, or athletic ability, for example, builds on existing strengths and enhances competence and self-confidence.

NURSING RESEARCH RELATED TO DEVELOPMENT

Children and adolescents are interesting research subjects because they are learning about themselves, their social environment, their parents, and significant others. The nursing research literature contains several developmental studies of infants and a few of children and adolescents. Few of the studies dealt with problem identification, strategy utilization or risk prediction of future problems.

Research Related to Infants and Toddlers

Kramer, Chamorro, Green, and Knudtson (1975) found that gentle, nonrhythmic daily stroking of the preterm infant's body while the infant was hospitalized improved the rate of social development, although it had no effect on physical, motor, or cognitive development. In a related study, Rice (1979) found that systematic massaging of preterm infants during the first 4 months after hospitalization stimulated neurological development, weight gain, and mental development.

Barnard and Douglas (1974) identified early factors in the child and his or her environment that were related to later development. They found that measures of perinatal or infant physical status were very weak predictors of IQ or language ability at age 4; assessments of child performance before 2 years of age were poor predictors, but after 2 years of age were excellent predictors of later performance; measures of levels of stress, social support, maternal education, and parent perception of the child were highly correlated to IQ and language ability for children of mothers with a high-school education or less; and mother-infant interaction and general quality of environment assessments were among the best predictors at each age tested and were as good as child performance measures at 2 and 3 years of age in predicting IQ and language ability.

Research Related to Preschool Children

Hammond, Bee, Barnard, and Eyres (1983) identified early assessments of a child's performance, environment, and family situation as predictors of the child's later functioning in school. The findings suggest that the later the measure of the child's performance or environment, the more accurate the prediction of second-grade performance. In the family environment measures, however, predictions derived from prenatal or perinatal measures were most accurate.

In a study of temperament, Palisin (1983) found that self-concept was related inversely to emotionality. The age of self-help was related to mood, distractibility, and approach-withdrawal, whereas self-concept was related to intensity, mood, persistence, and approach-withdrawal. The study findings support a relationship between preschool temperament and later academic performance. Moller (1983) studied the relationship between temperament and development and found that children who were mildly active, adaptable, rhythmic, persistent, and approachable, and who had a positive mood tended to attain higher developmental status. Both the Palisin and Moller studies are consistent with the work of Thomas & Chess (1980) on temperament and development. Thomas & Chess found that temperament plays a significant role in the individual-environment interactional process at sequential age-stages of development. Temperament, motivation and cognitive characteristics enter into a mutually reciprocal interactional process in helping to shape development at each age period.

Research Related to School-Aged Children and Adolescents

Porter (1974), Quiggin (1977), and Williams (1978) studied children's perceptions of their internal body systems. All three studies indicated that children's knowledge of their bodies is fairly extensive and accurate in terms of structure, position, and function. The quality and extent of knowledge varied with age, however (Porter, 1974). Boys at all ages identified more body parts than did girls (Porter, 1974; Quiggin, 1977).

In her study of children aged 2 through 16, Swain (1979) found that concepts of death differed by age with respect to finality, inevitability, and acknowledgment of death as a personal event. Yeaworth, York, Hussey, Ingle, and Goodwin (1980) developed and refined an instrument to measure the amount of stress that adolescents perceive in association with each of a series of life change events. Regardless of age, adolescents rated death and separation as most painful.

Areas for Future Research

A number of areas require further nursing developmental research. For example, it is important to identify the characteristics of environments that exert either a positive or negative impact on development, as well as to identify the nursing interventions necessary to develop nurturing environments that are conducive to optimal development. Research is needed on the impact of alternative care settings on the development of children and adolescents. Nurses' sensitivity to children's experiences and the way in which they communicate their feelings needs to be studied further. The knowledge base for nursing practice with children and adolescents will become increasingly sound if research in areas related to development is continued.

REFERENCES

Barnard, K.E., & Douglas, H.B. (Eds.). (1974). *Child health assessment. Part 1: A literature review* (DHEW Publication No. HRA-75-30, Stock No. 1741-00081). Washington, DC: U.S. Government Printing Office.

Brazelton, T. (1984). Neonatal behavioral assessment scale (2nd ed.). *Clinics in Developmental Medicine, 88,* 1–115.

Bumbalo, J.A., & Siemon, M.K. (1983). Nursing assessment and diagnosis: Mental health problems of children. *Topics in Clinical Nursing, 5,* 41–54.

Chess, S. (1978). The plasticity of human development. *Journal of the American Academy of Child Psychiatry, 17,* 80–91.

Clarke, A.M., & Clarke, A.D.B. (1984). Constancy and change in the growth of human characteristics. *Journal of Child Psychology and Psychiatry, 25,* 191–210.

Cohen, R., Weissman, S., & Cohler, B.J. (Eds.). (1984). *Parenthood as an adult experience.* New York: Guilford Press.

Coleman, J.C. (1978). Current contradictions in adolescent theory. *Journal of Youth and Adolescence, 7,* 1–11.

Critchley, D.L. (1979). Mental status examinations with children and adolescents: A developmental approach. *Nursing Clinics of North America, 14,* 429–441.

Eggert, L.L. (1978). The therapeutic process with adolescents experiencing psychosocial stress. In D.C. Longo & R.A. Williams (Eds.), *Clinical practice in psychosocial nursing: Assessment and intervention* (pp. 257–288). New York: Appleton-Century-Crofts.

Emde, R. (1978). Commentary. In Organization and stability of newborn behavior, A. Sameroff (Ed.). *Monograph on Social Research on Child Development, 43,* 5–6.

Erikson, E. (1963). *Childhood and society* (2nd ed.). New York: W.W. Norton.

Fitzpatrick, J.J. (1982). The crisis perspective: Relationship to nursing. In J.J. Fitzpatrick, A.L. Whall, R.L. Johnston, & J. A. Floyd (Eds.), *Nursing models and their psychiatric-mental health applications* (pp. 19–35). Bowie, MD: Robert J. Brady.

Flavell, J. (1972). An analysis of cognitive-developmental sequences. *Genetic Psychology Monograph, 86,* 279–350.

Fraiberg, S. (1977). *Insights from the blind.* New York: Basic Books.

Freud, S. (1949). *An outline of psychoanalysis.* New York: W.W. Norton.

Hall, G.S. (1904). *Adolescence.* New York: Appleton.

Hammond, M., Bee, H., Barnard, K., & Eyres, S. (1983). *Child health assessment: Part IV. Follow-up at second grade* (pp. 1–64). Seattle: University of Washington, School of Nursing.

Hartman, H. (1958). *Ego psychology and the problem of adaptation.* New York: International Universities Press.

Hauser, S. (1976). Loevinger's model and measure of ego development: A critical review. *Psychological Bulletin, 83*:928–955.

Hess, E. (1972). Imprinting in a natural laboratory. *Scientific American, 227,* 24–31.

Hess, R. (1970). Social class and ethnic influences on socialization. In P. Mussen (Ed.), *Carmichael's manual of child psychology* (pp. 457–557). New York: John Wiley.

Jan, J., Freeman, R., & Scott, E. (1977). *Visual impairment in children and adolescents.* New York: Grune & Stratton.

Kagan, J. (1986). Continuity and discontinuity in development. In J. Noshpitz (Editor-in-Chief), *Basic handbook of child psychiatry* (Vol. 5, pp. 33–37). New York: Basic Books.

Kohlberg, L. (1964). Development of moral character and moral ideology. In M. Hoffman & L. Hoffman (Eds.), *Review of child development research* (Vol. 1, pp. 383–431). New York: Russell Sage Foundation.

Kramer, M., Chamorro, I., Green, D., & Knudtson, F. (1975). Extratactile stimulation of the premature infant. *Nursing Research, 24,* 324–334.

Lewis, J.M., Beavers, W.R., Gossett, J.T., & Phillips, V.A. (1976). *No single thread: Psychological health in family systems.* New York: Brunner/Mazel.

Levinson, D., Darrow, C.N., Klein, E.B., Levinson, M.H., & McKee, B. (1978). *The seasons of a man's life.* New York: Alfred A. Knopf.

Lidz, T. (1968). *The person.* New York: Basic Books.

Loevinger, J. (1976). *Ego development: Conceptions and theories.* San Francisco: Jossey-Bass.

Lorenz, K. (1966). *On aggression.* New York: Harcourt Brace.

Marmor, J. (1974). *Psychiatry in transition.* New York: Brunner/Mazel.

Moller, J.M. (1983). Relationships between temperament and development in preschool children. *Research in Nursing and Health, 6,* 25–32.

Murphy, L., & Moriarity, A. (1976). *Vulnerability, coping and growth.* New Haven, CT: Yale University Press.

Palisin, H. (1983). Two studies on temperament. *Child health assessment: Part IV* (pp. 72–96). Seattle: University of Washington, School of Nursing.

Parse, R.R. (1981). *Man-being-health: A theory of nursing.* New York: John Wiley & Sons.

Pavlov, I.P. (1960). Conditioned reflexes. (G.V. Anrep, Trans. and Ed.). New York: Dover Publications.

Peplau, H.E. (1952). *Interpersonal relations in nursing.* New York: G.P. Putnam's Sons.

Piaget, J. (1963). *The origins of intelligence in children.* New York: International Universities Press.

Porter, C.S. (1974). Grade school children's perceptions of their internal body parts. *Nursing Research, 23,* 384–391.

Quiggin, V. (1977). Children's knowledge of their internal body parts. *Nursing Times, 73,* 1146–1151.

Rice, R. (1979). The effects of the Rice infant sensorimotor stimulation treatment on the development of high-risk infants. In G.C. Anderson & B. Raff (Eds.), *Newborn behavioral organizations: Nursing research and implications* (Vol. 15, pp. 131–143). New York: Alan R. Liss.

Rogers, M.E. (1970). *An introduction to the theoretical basis of nursing.* Philadelphia: F.A. Davis.

Rutter, M., Graham, P., Chadwick, O., & Yule, W. (1976). Adolescent turmoil: Fact or fiction. *Journal of Child Psychology and Psychiatry, 17,* 35–56.

Sahin, S.T. (1979). The nurse and the early identification of young children at risk. *International Journal of Nursing Studies, 16*(2), 141–149.

Sahlins, M. (1976). *The use and abuse of biology.* Ann Arbor, MI: University of Michigan Press.

Swain, H.L. (1979). Childhood views of death. *Death Education, 2,* 341–358.

Thomas, A., & Chess, S. (1977). *Temperament and development.* New York: Brunner/Mazel.

Thomas, A., & Chess, S. (1980). *The dynamics of psychological development.* New York: Brunner/Mazel.

Tinbergen, N. (1968). On war and peace in animals and man. *Science, 160,* 1411–1418.

Vaillant, G.E. (1977). *Adaptation to life.* Boston: Little, Brown.

Walsh, F. (Ed.). (1982). *Normal family process.* New York: Guilford Press.

Williams, P.D. (1978). A comparison of Philippine and American children's concepts of body organs and illness in relation to five variables. *International Journal of Nursing Studies, 15,* 193–202.

Winick, M., Meyer, K., & Harris, R. (1975). Malnutrition and environmental enrichment by early adaptation. *Science, 190,* 1173–1175.

Wolff, P. (1970). Critical periods in human cognitive development. *Hospital Practice, 11,* 77–87.

Yeaworth, R.C., York, J.A., Hussey, M.A., Ingle, E., & Goodwin, T. (1980). The development of an adolescent life change event scale. *Adolescence, 15,* 91–97.

Appendix 3-A

Suggested Reading for Assessment Tools

Achenbach, T. (1979). The child behavior profile: An empirically based system for assessing children's behavioral problems and competencies. *International Journal of Mental Health, 3/4,* 4–23.

Bayley, N. (1969). *Bayley scales of infant development.* New York: Psychological Corporation.

Bayley, N. (1969). *Manual for the Bayley scales of infant development.* New York: Psychological Corporation.

Burn, R.C., & Kaufman, S.F. (1970). *Kinetic family drawings.* New York: Brunner/Mazel.

Coopersmith, S. (1981). *Self-esteem inventories.* Palo Alto, CA: Consulting Psychological Press.

Di Leo, J.H. (1973). *Children's drawings as diagnostic aids.* New York: Brunner/Mazel.

Doll, E. (1953). *The measurement of social competence: A manual for the Vineland social maturity scale.* Circle Pines, MN: American Guidance Service.

Dunn, L. (1965). *Expanded manual for the Peabody picture vocabulary test.* Circle Pines, MN: American Guidance Service.

Fagin, C.M. (1972). Tools and tasks. In C.M. Fagin (Ed.), *Nursing in child psychiatry* (pp. 13–27). St. Louis, MO: C.V. Mosby.

Frankenburg, W.K., Dodds, J., & Fandal, A. (1973). *Denver developmental screening test: Manual workbook for nursing and paramedical personnel.* Denver: University of Colorado Medical Center.

Goodenough, E. (1926). *Measurement of intelligence by drawings* (Goodenough Draw-A-Person test). New York: World Book.

Koppitz, E. (1968). *Psychological evaluation of children's human figure drawings.* New York: Grune & Stratton.

McCarthy, D. (1970). *Manual: McCarthy scales of children's abilities.* New York: Psychological Corporation.

McDevitt, S.C., & Carey, W.B. (1978). Stability of ratings versus perception of temperament from early infancy to 1–3 years (Behavioral Style Questionnaire). *American Journal of Orthopsychiatry, 17,* 342–345.

McLeavey, K. (1979). Children's art as an assessment tool. *Pediatric Nursing, 5,* 9–14.

Plomin, R., & Roe, D.C. (1977). A twin study of temperament in young children (Colorado Childhood Temperament Inventory). *Journal of Psychology, 97,* 107–113.

Pothier, P.C. (1982). Sensory motor development, dysfunction and assessment. In K. Babich (Ed.), *A workbook: Assessing the mental health of children* (pp. 71–94). Boulder, CO: Western Interstate Commission for Higher Education.

Rose, M.H., Kelly, M.E., Knapp, M.B., & Bohanna, D.K. (1985). *The preschool behavior inventory.* Kent, WA: Early Learning Associates.

Thomas, A., & Chess, S. (1977). *Temperament and development* (Parent Questionnaire). New York: Brunner/Mazel.

Winnicott, D.W. (1971). *Therapeutic consultations in child psychiatry* (The Squiggle Game). New York: Basic Books.

4

Transcultural Mental Health Nursing Assessment of Children and Adolescents

Madeleine Leininger

After reading this chapter, the reader will be able to:

1. identify the key factors in and the importance of a culurological assessment with children and adolescents
2. discuss specific cultural concepts, principles, and guidelines for an emically based culture assessment
3. present an overview of the Leininger theory of culture care with the sunrise model as a conceptual guide for mental health nursing appraisals and care
4. discuss specific Western and non-Western examples of cultural factors that influence mental health assessments of children and adolescents
5. identify pertinent concepts and reference sources to guide the thinking and actions of transcultural mental health nurses in child and adolescent human care appraisals

Inextricably linked together, culture, mental health, and environment influence the way in which an individual or group responds to life events or conditions. It is a major challenge for mental health personnel to consider this fact as they advance their knowledge and skills in the care of children and adolescents. Mental health personnel should know and use transcultural nursing and health care concepts, principles, and research in all aspects of humanistic and scientific nursing practices.

In a major cultural movement during the past three decades, transcultural nurses have developed and incorporated knowledge related to cultural factors into client health care services (e.g., Boyle & Andrews, 1989; Hautman, 1979; Leininger, 1970, 1978, 1984b, 1984d, 1989). Medical anthropologists have also contributed to this cultural movement (e.g., Foster & Andersen, 1978; Kaplan, 1961; Kennedy, 1961; Kleinman & Lin, 1981; Kluckhohn, 1962; Marsella, 1979; Pederson, Sartorius, & Marsella, 1984). Understanding people of diverse cultures and being able to care for them in meaningful and appropriate ways is one of the greatest challenges today for mental health providers, and it will be even more important in the next century as multiculturalism increases in all aspects of life.

NEED FOR "CULTUROLOGICAL" CARE ASSESSMENTS

Several significant factors have made it necessary to incorporate transcultural nursing and anthropological concepts and research findings into the mental health care of children and adolescents. For example, there is the societal reality that cultural norms, beliefs, and lifeways have a significant impact on all aspects of human behavior (Leininger, 1970, 1978). Children and adolescents are greatly influenced by cultural values and norms through daily family life, school, television, and everyday encounters.

Children and adolescents today come to mental health facilities from many different cultures and subcultures. This reality has posed a critical problem for mental health nurses who must care for clients whose behavior, patterns of thinking, acting, and functioning are markedly different from their own. The culturally different child or adolescent speaks a different language, responds to daily life experiences differently, and has different nursing care and medical treatment expectations. Most mental health nurses have not been prepared in transcultural nursing, and they often experience cultural shock and related stress problems in caring for clients of diverse cultures (Leininger, 1970, 1978, 1979).

Children and adolescents of different cultures have a right to expect that their cultural values, beliefs, and lifeways will be understood, respected, and responded to in appropriate and congruent ways, however, and professional mental health nurses must be keenly aware of this expectation. Modern mental health nurses need to be knowledgeable and skilled to care for clients of many different cultures in our growing multicultural world.

Mental health nurses are beginning to realize that cultural expressions, forms, and patterns of human behavior require different nursing care and treatment approaches (Leininger, 1981a, 1984a, 1988a). No longer can nurses treat all children or adolescents alike; they must recognize and respond to cultural variabilities. The mental health nurse who does not understand the client's cultural expressions can be greatly handicapped when doing a mental health assessment or trying to change the "deviant" behavior patterns of children and adolescents.

For these reasons, transcultural nursing knowledge and skills have become of major importance to mental health nurses as they work with clients of diverse cultural backgrounds. It is especially important as nurses assess the mental health of children and adolescents, who express their cultural behavior and needs in a very open, often uninhibited, and naturalistic way. Mental health nurses who have transcultural insights are in a key position to understand and make appropriate decisions to help these clients in the hospital, clinic, home, school, or other contexts.

The definition of "normal" or "deviant" behavior of children and adolescents is largely culturally based and must be screened through a cultural perspective. Cultural beliefs, values, and behavior are complex, however. They require that mental health nurses know different cultural values and practices as a basis for therapeutic and congruent care interventions. Fortunately, mental health nurses have available today a body of transcultural nursing knowledge to guide their practices.

The above realities became apparent to me while developing the child psychiatric mental health clinical specialist program at the University of Cincinnati in the mid 1950s (Leininger, 1970, 1978). Through cultural shock experiences, I realized the critical importance of culture on the child and adolescent's behavior, and of the need to understand cultural variabilities in order to be therapeutic with clients. More specifically, I discovered that there were obvious differences in the ways the Jewish, Afro-American, German-American, and Appalachian and other children and adolescents from different cultures wanted to be cared for and treated by mental health personnel. These children had definite and different expectations in daily care such as the choice of foods they would eat, their play patterns, their ways of interacting with adults, going to bed, and many other daily activities. While I could have overlooked these obvious differences and not taken them into account, I would have been seriously avoiding their behavior and neglecting their cultural needs and human rights. This discovery of the need to understand cultural differences led me to pursue graduate study in anthropology and to develop the field of transcultural nursing in the early 1960s. (Leininger, 1970, 1978). Since then the field of transcultural nursing has been growing worldwide and nurses are valuing its vital importance in professional care practices (Leininger, 1981a, 1984b).

TRANSCULTURAL NURSING: AN AREA OF STUDY & PRACTICE TO ADVANCE MENTAL HEALTH NURSING

The field of transcultural nursing is now well established as a formal area of study and practice in nursing, and mental health nurses and nurses in other areas of nursing can benefit from the knowledge developed about transcultural differences and similarities, and other important concepts, theories and principles to improve care to clients. I have defined transcultural nursing as an area of study and practice focused on comparative cultural care and health values, beliefs, and practices, with the goal to use this knowledge to provide culture-specific and culturally congruent nursing care to people. (Leininger, 1978, 1981b, 1984a, 1989). Transcultural nursing provides one of the broadest means to know and understand people because it is focused on culture which is the total lifeway of particular individuals or groups with a culture's values, beliefs, and norms. Culture is a powerful, practical and abstract concept which includes the learned and transmitted ways of human groups that guide their daily decisions and actions. All humans are born into a culture and they live, become ill, and die within a cultural frame of reference. The meaning of life experiences are culturally and intergenerationally based. Hence culture must be an integral part of all aspects of nursing and health care practices. To ignore cultural beliefs, values and practices leads to unfavorable and often nontherapeutic ways of helping children and adolescents with their mental health problems. More and more, there is growing evidence that mental illnesses or deviations are closely linked with the client's cultural values and lifeways, and their behavior can only be accurately and reliably understood with cultural interpretations (Leininger, 1970, 1984a, 1988a, Marsella, 1979, Pederson et al., 1984). Moreover, mental illnesses are often culture-bound, which means that cultural factors mainly define and determine mental illnesses.

MAJOR TRANSCULTURAL CONCEPTS FOR CULTUROLOGICAL ASSESSMENTS

In its simplest definition, culture refers to the learned and transmitted values, beliefs, material and nonmaterial expressive lifeways that are usually passed on intergenerationally and that guide human actions and decisions. Cultures are complex and dynamic, although its members tend to preserve that which they value most over time. When doing a culturological assessment, the mental health nurse explores ideas with the client related to kinship, religion, world views, politics, economics, technologies, education, gender differences, and the meanings of symbols and nonverbal expressions. The nurse becomes aware of differences between Western and non-Western cultures and does not assess all children and adolescents from a Western viewpoint (Leininger, 1984c).

In this regard, the concepts of emic and etic, which were originally identified by Pike (1954) in his study of cultures and language uses, recognize an important distinction in transcultural nursing. The term *emic* refers to the local or internal ideas, expressions, and practices of a culture. In contrast, the term *etic* refers to an outsider's or external viewpoint that is viewed as more universal (Leininger, 1978, 1985a, 1988b). These terms have been most useful in distinguishing a client's world view and beliefs from etic views.

Cultural variability refers to slight or major changes in the beliefs, values, and lifeways with respect to certain ideas or practices within the culture under study (Leininger, 1978, 1979, 1984c). Cultures vary with respect of being more *traditionally* or *non-traditionally* oriented in values, beliefs, and practices. The mental health status of children and adolescents must be assessed with respect to these cultural dimensions, and with an awareness of the possibility of intergenerational variability. Hence, the child or adolescent may not follow exactly their parents' values and beliefs; which is often evident with many Anglo-Americans, but is less evident with Mexican-Americans, for example, or members of non-Western cultures. Subtle and variable changes in values, beliefs, and lifeways must be assessed along with traditional and nontraditional variabilities in such areas as dress, care patterns, behavior expressions, values, religions, and kinship beliefs. It may be necessary to talk to parents or the children's guardians in order to assess cultural variabilities accurately. Most important, the behavior of a child or adolescent should not be viewed as "deviant," "altered," or "underdeveloped" unless assessed within the youngster's cultural framework and values. The client's emic expression may vary considerably from the professional nurse's etic norms and values.

A strange physical environment, such as a hospital or clinic, and unfamiliar health care personnel can leave the child or adolescent not knowing how best to act or survive in the new setting. Any signs of cultural resistance, uncooperativeness, and cultural shock need to be recognized in initial and ongoing assessments. Cultural shock often leaves the child or adolescent greatly disoriented, which may be manifested by hyperactive or withdrawal behavior, depending on the client's culture. Although culturological assessments begin immediately when the child is admitted, the nurse assesses subsequent behavior and watches the youngster over time as he or she becomes familiar with the setting. The nurse should document cultural variability, resistance, and the length of time required to overcome cultural resistance or shock. Such data are important indicators of the client's efforts to cope with a strange cultural context and provides a guide for nursing care decisions and actions.

Mental health nurses must also understand the concept of ethnocentrism when they are doing a cultural assessment. Ethnocentrism refers to the belief that one's ways of thinking and doing are the best, preferred, or superior way of behaving (Leininger, 1970, 1978, 1984c). All nurses and health care personnel have potential ethnocentric values and beliefs that can seriously interfere with their ability to help clients. A nurse whose ethnocentric tendencies are completely rigid, however, may never fully understand the client's emic viewpoints. Nurses must acknowledge that there are different ways of communicating, seeing the world, acting toward others, learning, eating, sleeping, or playing. Listening to, observing, and letting children behave as naturally as possible provides valuable clues to understand *their* cultural behavior. To achieve an emic assessment, nurses must first know their own ethnocentric tendencies and must be prepared to keep them reasonably under control or neutral during the assessment. Encouraging youngsters to interpret or explain their thinking and behavior is important. Indirect, "tell me about" approaches are helpful ways to get to emic data.

Closely related to ethnocentrism is cultural imposition, the unintended or intended actions to impose one's own values, beliefs, and practices on another person or group (Leininger, 1970, 1973, 1978). Cultural imposition remains a serious problem in the health care field, largely because of a lack of transcultural knowledge, an inability to make accommodations, or a failure to consider the cultural values and differences of others. Cultural imposition tends to occur almost immediately when individuals, particularly those in authority positions, encounter a viewpoint that is markedly different from their own and when they want to change a situation according to their own values or expectations. It is often done without the full awareness of health care personnel, but clients who experience cultural imposition are quite aware of this practice. Clients may perceive it as a violation of their human rights, a cultural bias, or sometimes discrimination. Cultural imposition practices can hinder an effective interview in obtaining an accurate assessment of behavior.

Many cultures and subcultures in the world define normal and abnormal behaviors in different ways, and some cultures never use these terms (Kaplan, 1961; Kennedy, 1961; Kleinman & Lin, 1981; Leininger, 1979). Such attributes must be understood in the context of a particular culture (i.e., the emic viewpoint) rather than assuming they are universal concepts. The emic and etic viewpoints are valuable for comparative purposes to identify differences and similarities in "normal" and "abnormal" behaviors. Hallowell (1934) stated that the cultural investigators must

> have an intimate knowledge of the culture as a whole, he [the investigator] must also be aware of the normal range of individual behavior within the cultural pattern and likewise understand what the people themselves consider to be extreme deviations from this norm. In short, he must develop a standard of normality with reference to the culture itself, as a means of controlling an uncritical application of the criteria that he brings with him from our civilization. (p. 2)

Clearly, it is necessary to avoid labeling and diagnosing mental disorders according to the mental health assessor's etic culture. The assessor must know the culture of the child or adolescent and then carefully assess the extent of cultural variability. Transcultural nursing education and anthropological insights are essential to do accurate assessments.

The nurse who is culturally sensitive is able to enter the world of a client as a cultural stranger, to understand cultural symbols and grasp their meanings to the client, identify subtle cues during the assessment, interpret cultural expressions and comments accurately, and use the data in culture-specific ways. Children and adolescents are usually quick to "test" the nurse in picking up their behaviors and understanding them. Knowledge and reflective assessment of the client's cultural background helps to ensure that the nurse will be able to respond to the client in a culturally sensitive way. Most important, mental health assessments must be highly reflective of the youngster's world. This approach leads to client-centered emic data, which provides fresh new insights about the youngster and ways to provide culturally congruent mental health and holistic care.

USE OF TRANSCULTURAL CONCEPTS

The following are two examples of the application of transcultural nursing concepts in assessing children and adolescents.

> An Anglo-American Caucasian nurse who had been taught the etic professional values of cleanliness and orderliness in her nursing education was working with an Appalachian adolescent in a psychiatric unit. The Appalachian client was resistant to the nurse's requests to tidy his bed and his room in the morning and to help with any cleaning on the unit. The adolescent also refused to take a shower after playing volleyball. The nurse found the adolescent's behavior strange, especially the refusal to shower after exercising. The adolescent's behavior had cultural meanings, however, in that cleanliness and orderliness were not valued in the "hollows" where he lived in Appalachia.
>
> As the nurse insisted on the showers, the client screamed at her, "In our hollows back home, we don't have to wash ourselves all the time and do things the way you want me to do here. I don't like this place, and I want out of here." The nurse firmly replied, "While you are here, you must follow our rules if you want to go home. You must show that you can keep your room clean and in order and keep yourself clean. These are important things for you to learn." This made the Appalachian adolescent very angry and determined to leave. He finally left and found his way back home.

In this situation, the client's (emic) world and the nurse's (etic) world were very different, which created cultural conflicts. The nurse had strong professional ethnocentric values of cleanliness and order, whereas the adolescent did not value cleanliness and order. As a result, gross misunderstandings occurred between the client and nurse. The client resisted the nurse's cultural imposition practices and became uncooperative, which led to his return to the Appalachian hills. The nurse was unaware of the Appalachian culture and "had never met a client so resistant to common nursing care expectations of cleanliness and orderliness." She expected this adolescent to be like all other adolescents on the unit. The nurse was unable to grasp the client's cultural world in which the values of kindness and family were far more important than cleanliness and tidiness.

> A public health nurse referred a 5-year-old North American Cree Indian boy to a psychiatric children's unit because "the child is hyperactive and needs some medicine or some kind of treatment to calm him down." When the nurse had initially visited the Cree child in his home, she found he was running about the house, climbing stairs, tossing small objects, and talking constantly to his parents and older siblings. The

nurse was struck by the child's activity and by the fact that he was the "center of attention." The parents did not seem at all upset about the child's behavior. The nurse documented in her notes that the child was "running the household and no one seemed concerned." The child's active behavior was most disturbing to the nurse, and she tried to stop the child's behavior. She was also upset because the parents did not try to control the child or discipline him. Diagnosing the child's condition as "hyperactive" and as a "grossly altered state of activity," the nurse strongly advised the parents to seek psychiatric treatments for the child to deal with his "hyperactive behavior." The parents looked puzzled and did not understand the nurse's recommendation, nor did they comply with her request.

In this situation, the nurse did not understand Cree Indian culture, family values, and child-rearing practices. In the Cree culture, the child's behavior was quite acceptable, even important in his socialization. The parents were not upset with the child's behavior, and hence did not understand the nurse's comments and insistence to take their child for psychiatric treatment. It was an insult to the parents. Cree parents highly value active children, as their behavior reflects supernatural activity, special wisdom, and insights given to children. Because they are endowed with spirit messages and special insights, Cree children are expected to give advice to their parents. Cree Indian parents treat their children as "sacred," being very permissive and indulgent. The Indian family viewed the nurse's visit and advice as confusing and insulting. Their emic cultural values were in marked contrast with the Anglo-American public health nurse's etic learned professional values to keep "children in their place." For this nurse, the Cree child's behavior was not acceptable and needed to be regulated by medications and therapy. Hence, the nurse's etic and ethnocentric view of children conflicted with the Cree Indian family values and practices. Such cultural conflicts and misunderstandings can be reasons why people are reluctant to use mental health services.

CULTURAL CARE THEORY IN ASSESSMENT

The theory of cultural care diversity and universality and the use of the sunrise model can be extremely helpful in mental health assessments of children and adolescents (Leininger, 1978, 1984a, 1984c, 1984d, 1985a, 1985b, 1988a, 1988b). The theory is based on the central premise that care is the essence of nursing. Care is critical to the health and well-being of individuals and groups. There are universal and diverse structural forms, patterns, meanings, and expressions of human care in Western and non-Western cultures that must be documented as the basis for making assessments and for research to contribute to culturally congruent care. Lay and professional care patterns and practices vary transculturally, and the purpose of the theory is to discover cultural care universals (or commonalities) and diversity patterns among different cultures in the world and, thus, to establish a distinctive body of nursing knowledge. Not only is care the distinctive component of nursing, but also it can make the difference in recovery from illness or the ability to cope with life stresses (including mental), death, or disabilities. The ultimate goal of the theory is to ensure culturally congruent care to individuals, families, groups, and communities that will support the health or well-being of clients (Leininger, 1985a, 1988b). This knowledge is also used for culturological assessments. The major assumptions or tenets of the theory help the nurse reflect while doing a cultural assessment and are as follows (Leininger, 1978, 1981, 1985a, 1988b):

- Care is the essence and distinctive feature of nursing.
- Care is essential for human growth, well-being, survival, and the ability to face death or disabilities.
- Culture care is the broadest and most important concept to know, understand, explain, and predict human care because culture encompasses the total lifeways and values of people.
- There are diverse forms, patterns, expressions, and structures of care transculturally.
- Culture care knowledge is derived from the world view, religion, kinship, politics, cultural values, economic factors, technology, language, and environmental context, as well as from folk (or lay) and professional health care sources.
- Human beings seek care that fits with their lifeways and values to aid them in recovery or to prevent illness patterns.

An awareness of the theory helps the nurse to make a culturological assessment, along with the use of the sunrise model. The model helps to identify the different dimensions to be assessed (Figure 4-1). The upper part of the model depicts the world view and social structure dimensions; the lower part, the folk (lay) and professional care systems. These different dimensions are assessed by using open-ended inquiry modes and by following leads from the clients to discover emic or etic knowledge (Leininger, 1984c, 1985a; Spradley, 1979, 1980).

In assessing the mental health of small children, nurses often involve the parents; they may interview adolescents alone. It is important to discover what children and adolescents know about care or treatments and how they receive care. The folk or lay care beliefs and practices include the use of home remedies, treatments, and general activities related to human caring. Clients do not usually discuss folk practices openly with professional staff, because they fear being demeaned or ridiculed for their use of home or nonprofessional remedies. Parents and grandparents are especially good informants in several cultures for folk treatments, especially for young children, who often receive folk remedies as first-line

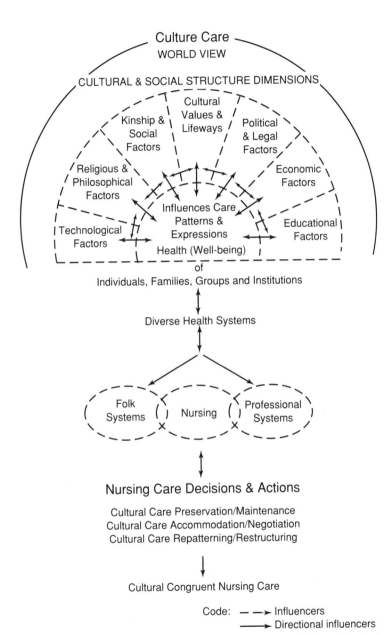

Figure 4-1 Leininger's Sunrise Model To Depict Dimensions of Cultural Care Diversity and Universality: A Theory of Nursing. *Source:* From "Leininger's Theory of Cultural Care Diversity and Universality" by M. Leininger, 1988, *Nursing Science Quarterly, 1(4),* pp. 152–160. Copyright 1988 by Chestnut House Publishers. Reprinted by permission.

treatments. Information shared about folk medicines and care is extremely valuable to help the nurse grasp the patterns, and other ways of care in the client's culture. It is wise for mental health care nurses to learn about frequently used cultural medicines and care practices before interviewing children and adolescents so that they can be alert to culture-specific language terms and different folk remedies for mental health, wellness, or illnesses (see, e.g., Foster & Andersen, 1978; Hautman, 1979; Leininger, 1970, 1984b, 1984c).

In a cultural assessment, it is important to explore the past experiences of children and adolescents with professional nurses and medical staff within and outside the hospital context. Sometimes these previous experiences greatly influence the way the child or adolescent responds during the assessment and care. Negative past experiences in a mental hospital can lead to open resistance and difficulty communicating with the client. Nonverbal expressions may be the important assessment focus when the client refuses to talk.

Using the sunrise model to assess different influences on behavior, the nurse listens for clues to cultural patterns that health care personnel should know about in order to provide culturally congruent care. These data are important in order to make culture-specific decisions in relation to three modes of action identified in the theory (Leininger, 1985b, 1988b): (1) cultural care preservation and/or maintenance, (2) cultural care accommodation and/or negotiation, and (3) cultural care repatterning and/or restructuring. The assessment will generate several ideas to guide the nurse in using one or all of these modes of care for nursing care plans. This approach ensures the incorporation of cultural and holistic care to the client, with a special focus on mental health needs and concerns.

SPECIFIC PRINCIPLES FOR CULTUROLOGICAL ASSESSMENT

The *first* principle to keep in mind is that culture plays a powerful and central role in mental health, and so nurses are challenged to learn as much as possible about clients of diverse cultures, especially those who frequently come to the hospital, who represent the community at large, or who may seek care at any time. Taking transcultural nursing courses and reading about different cultures are essential means to expand nurses' knowledge about diverse cultures. Moreover, nurses usually find the reading highly informative and stimulating. Mental health nurses need to be aware, for example, that different verbal statements and nonverbal expressions by the nurse can have different meanings to clients of diverse cultures. "Put the patient on the second floor" may be interpreted literally and create fear in the child. The nurse who stares at a Mexican child may aggravate the illness, as the child may fear that the nurse has cast an evil eye on the child by staring. In contrast, an Anglo-American child may not fear the staring, but may interpret a look with a frown as punishment. Clearly, mental health nurses cannot assume that all children and adolescents view experiences or actions in a similar way, because culture influences meanings.

A *second* principle is that many culture-bound expressions do not fit within the American Psychiatric Association nor the American Nurse's Association's diagnostic classification systems. Mental behaviors vary with expressions and forms of illness and wellness in a culture. For example, some cultures, such as the Gadsup in New Guinea, do not have schizophrenic behavior (Leininger, 1978). Adolescents and adults in some cultures do not have psychotic depression, but may have short periods of sadness, profound grief, or ritual grief due to loss of a family member. Individuals have culture-specific expressions of mental states that need to be known by mental health personnel rather than classifying child and adolescent behaviors to fit Western psychiatric nomenclature. Thus, the client's behavior should always be evaluated with respect to the cultural context and culture-specific values, beliefs, and lifeways of the client in order to get an accurate and dependable cultural assessment.

The *third* principle is that the client's culture largely determines whether a particular behavior is "normal" or "deviant." Some cultural behavior that is considered abnormal or pathological in Western cultures is quite normal in non-Western cultures (Kaplan, 1961; Kennedy, 1961; Kleinman & Lin, 1981; Leininger, 1979; Marsella, 1979; Pederson et al., 1984). Moreover, when children or adolescents come to the hospital, they are exposed to another culture, which they may view as strange, frightening, and even disturbing to them. Behavior "taken out of cultural context" can be easily misinterpreted, possibly leading to some very unfortunate problems for the client. For example,

> a Vietnamese adolescent girl who was taught never to openly complain about a serious physical or mental injury was brought to the hospital. The girl's stoic behavior was viewed as "abnormal" and "masochistic." She was given pain medications and received psychotherapy. This 19-year-old teen-ager had been enculturated by the Vietnamese norms or rules of behavior to accept pain without overt verbal complaints. Her religious beliefs and cultural values helped to support her calm acceptance of pain. Thus, she and her family considered her quiet and noncomplaining behavior as normal. However, the Anglo-American psychiatric staff viewed her behavior as abnormal. The staff imposed their etic cultural views on the client and administered pain medications because they believed "she had to have a lot of physical and psychological pain." This imposition of the staff's cultural values to the client was most disturbing to the client and her family and led to nontherapeutic practices and the girl's departure from the health care facility.

A *fourth* major principle to guide the nurse in doing a culturological assessment is that the nurse should reflect on his or her own cultural background with its specific values, beliefs, and lifeways in order to prevent ethnocentric values from interfering in the accurate interpretation of the client's cultural information. The saying "know thyself" or "self-awareness" is extremely important to prevent cultural imposition, ethnocentric and biased interpretations, and inability to work within the client's frame of reference.

Similarly, Japanese and Chinese adolescents may find that psychiatric staff are often too probing and too assertive with their questions, especially on private matters. One adolescent commented, "Americans dig after all the facts in a one-two-three forceful way without any cultural etiquette." Japanese adolescents may become extremely quiet and will not usually share their ideas in an assessment or treatment when nurses become too assertive. Thus, the nurse must know the client's cultural rules and their patterns of behavior in order to avoid infringing on cultural norms and values during the interview and total assessment.

A nurse's cultural awareness can make a great difference in clients' willingness to cooperate and share their values and beliefs with the nurse and others who are cultural strangers to them. The nurse should remember that many clients from different cultures often view the hospital and medical regimens as high-risk, strange experiences. Children will be even more cautious to share ideas with nurses unless they have their parents or other family members with them. Indirect and low-key inquiry modes are usually more helpful to those from other cultures than are the usual American direct, fact-searching, and assertive fact-gathering approaches.

A *fifth* principle to guide a cultural assessment for children and adolescents is that the nurse must learn to be an active listener, observer, recorder, and interpreter of themes of behavior almost simultaneously to obtain a holistic and accurate picture of the client from a different culture. Focusing on fragmented bits and pieces of behavior can result in a sketchy and incomplete view and can lead to misinterpretations. The nurse who can be an active listener, observer, and recorder will gain a better total view of the client. This ability, however, requires considerable skill and some mentor guidance.

In order to facilitate a successful culturological assessment, the psychiatric nurse should try to do the assessment in the youngster's *natural setting* whenever possible, such as the home, school, or community environment. If this is not possible, the nurse should try to find a quiet and reasonably naturalistic environment to the client in the hospital or clinic. Recreating a naturalistic or familiar environmental approach is essential to make the cultural stranger feel reasonably "at home" and facilitates the sharing of ideas with the nurse. Parents or extended family members are usually present during assessment procedures with non-Western children and adolescents, not only to make them feel comfortable, but also to help overcome potential language difficulties. In contrast, Western youngsters may not want their parents with them, and the interview environment is often familiar to them.

In conducting a culturological assessment, the nurse should plan for approximately two or three 30-minute time spans to assess different aspects of the sunrise model. Cultures are complex and so cultural assessments are also somewhat complex, and they differ from physical or routine psychological assessments in that cultural values, norms, beliefs, and lifeways are explored. The nurse needs to rely heavily upon observations, on participation with the child or adolescent in diverse activities, and on the youngster's response to daily living and family or other people. Informal interviews are used with open-ended inquiries rather than asking a series of direct and structured questions (Leininger, 1979, 1984c; Spradley, 1980).

The assessment must move with the client's line of thinking and experience rather than solely with the nurse's interests. "Moving with the client" means using verbal and nonverbal cues to enter the client's cultural world. The nurse must be willing to try to experience vicariously the client's world view and some of his or her life experiences. When the nurse becomes too directive to a child or adolescent by verbal or nonverbal comments, the child or adolescent will usually remain silent, and the assessment will not be productive. Whenever the client's line of thinking or action patterns are suppressed, the amount of emic data obtained is decreased or modified. A reflective and indirect inquiry approach is far more helpful to clients of unknown or strange cultures to the nurse. Letting the client spontaneously share, interpret, or explain his or her behavior is desirable, no matter how bizarre it may seem to the nurse. It takes time to master this approach, but it is essential to obtain meaningful cultural data from the client, and to facilitate transcultural mental health nursing care practices.

Language difficulties can be a major and serious problem in obtaining accurate data, especially in unfamiliar surroundings such as a hospital. The assessment should be done in the client's own language, but if this is not possible, an interpreter will be needed. Interpreters or translators must be carefully selected, as they can facilitate or hinder a cultural assessment, and lead to inaccurate data. Interpreters from the same culture are usually more effective than those of another culture because of subtle differences in cultural meanings, gestures, and interpretations of key symbols and expressions (Kennedy, 1961; Kluckhohn, 1962; Leininger, 1970, 1978). Cultural gestures and symbols are also important. Sometimes countertransference and cultural resistance problems may occur because of age, sex, or similar cultural origins. The mental health nurse must be alert to such problems.

The nurse who listens with genuine interest to what the client says or does is likely to learn culture-specific terms such as *susto, mal ojo, bewitched, black evil, running amok, ataques, spirit-helpers, curandero, machismo,* and many other cultural terms with mental health relevance. These terms help the nurse to gain insight into the client's behavior. For example, *ataques* is a hysteria-like expression with hyperkinetic seizures due to acute tension and anxiety that may occur in

Puerto Rican youth, but it is not a serious mental disorder; it is a culturally accept-able reaction to situations of extreme stress. Each of the other terms cited above also have special cultural meanings.

At all times, the nurse should maintain an attitude and position of learning from the client during an assessment—not the attitude of a clinical and all-knowing expert. If the nurse maintains the learner's role, the client becomes the active par-ticipant, account teller, or informant. Being a humble and open-minded learner is extremely important and helpful in doing a culturological assessment in order to develop cultural care plans for the client. Seeking the meaning of cultural expres-sions, cultural patterns, and lived through experiences is important.

During the assessment, the nurse tries to learn the cultural strengths or assets that the client may use in a positive way to regain his or her health. The nurse should focus less on the deficits and shortcomings of the client and more on the ways that the client and family cope with life's problems or stresses and resolve them. For example, Southern Afro-American adolescents rely on their "brothers and sisters" when in crisis by having the family members with them, petitioning to Jesus to help them, and by relying on family concerns as the dominant care values (Leininger, 1984a). Praying is an extremely important means to relieve mental troubles and to face life crises for the Southern African-Americans. From the author's research, Greek-American adolescents viewed culture care as "being re-sponsible for one's kin and church members" and "making sacrifices for them" to relieve tension or to be healed (Leininger, 1986). These two examples reveal dif-ferences in cultural care values that require different nursing care practices.

Some children and adolescents live in two or more conflicting value systems, and they may need help to discover how to live in two or more cultural worlds. The nurse first identifies these different sets of values and then tries to clarify with the client or family members how best to meet their needs. In this way, the nurse can do culture care repatterning or maintenance, depending on the value needs and the problem. The nurse should also consult with a transcultural nurse expert pre-pared in specific culture areas to assess accurately the complex and different world views to provide culturally relevant care (Leininger, 1989).

In this chapter, the author has provided several transcultural nursing concepts, principles, and guidelines to help nurses do mental health culturological assess-ment of children and adolescents using culture care theory and the sunrise model. The powerful role of culture beliefs, values and practices that influence behavior was discussed as well as ways to enter the client's world. Today, the greatest challenge of mental health nurses is to become transculturally knowledgeable and skilled to assess, understand, and care for people of diverse cultures. The rich clinical experiences and genuine interest of nurses to care for people is important to achieve this goal. Transcultural nursing is the new frontier for mental health nurses that must become an integral part of nursing to serve people of diverse cultures effectively.

REFERENCES

Boyle, J., & Andrews, M. (1989). *Transcultural concepts in nursing care.* Boston: Scott, Foresman, Little, Brown College Division.

Foster, G.M., & Andersen, B.G. (1978). *Medical anthropology.* New York: John Wiley & Sons.

Hallowell, A. (1934). Cultural and mental disease. *Journal of Abnormal and Social Psychology, 29*(6), 2.

Hautman, M. (1979). Folk health and illness beliefs. *Nurse Practitioner,* July-August, 23–24.

Kaplan, B. (Ed.). (1961). *Studying personality cross-culturally.* New York: Harper & Row.

Kennedy, D. (1961). Key issues in the cross-cultural study of mental disorders. In B. Kaplan (Ed.), *Studying personality cross-culturally* (pp. 1–20). New York: Harper & Row.

Kleinman, A., & Lin, T.Y. (Eds.). (1981). *Normal and deviant behavior in Chinese culture.* Hingham, MA: Reidel.

Kluckhohn, C. (1962). *Culture and behavior.* New York: The Free Press.

Leininger, M. (1970). *Nursing and anthropology: Two worlds to blend.* New York: John Wiley & Sons.

Leininger, M. (1973). Becoming aware of types of health practitioners and cultural imposition. In American Nurses' Association, 48th convention report (pp. 9–15). Kansas City, MO: American Nurses' Association.

Leininger, M. (1978). *Transcultural nursing: Concepts, theories and practices.* New York: John Wiley & Sons.

Leininger, M. (Ed.). (1979). *Transcultural nursing.* New York: Masson International Press.

Leininger, M. (Ed.) (1981a). *Care: An essential human need.* Thorofare, NJ: Charles B. Slack.

Leininger, M. (1981b). Transcultural nursing: Its progress and its future. *Nursing and Health Care, 2*(7), 366–371.

Leininger, M. (1984a). *Care: The essence of nursing and health.* Thorofare, NJ: Charles B. Slack.

Leininger, M. (1984b). Cultural care: An essential goal for nursing and health and health care. *EDTNA Journal III,* June, 1984, 7–20.

Leininger, M. (1984c). Transcultural interviewing and health assessment. In P. Pederson, N. Sartorius, & A.J. Marsella (Eds.), *Mental health services: The cross-cultural context* (pp. 107–117). Beverly Hills, CA: Sage Publications.

Leininger, M. (1984d). Transcultural nursing: An essential knowledge and practice field for today. *Canadian Nurse, 80*(11), 41–45.

Leininger, M. (1985a). *Qualitative research methods in nursing.* Orlando, FL: Grune & Stratton.

Leininger, M. (1985b). Transcultural nursing care diversity and universality: A theory of nursing. *Nursing and Health Care,* (4), 209–212.

Leininger, M. (1986). *Ethnonursing and ethnocare study of Greek-Americans in urban community.* Detroit: Wayne State University Press.

Leininger, M. (1988a). *Care: Discovery and uses in clinical and community nursing.* Detroit: MI: Wayne State University Press.

Leininger, M. (1988b). Leininger's theory of cultural care diversity and universality. *Nursing Science Quarterly, 1*(4), 152–160.

Leininger, M. (1989). Transcultural nurse specialists and generalists: New practitioners in nursing. *Journal of Transcultural Nursing, 1*(1), 4–17.

Marsella, A.J. (1979). Cross-cultural studies of mental disorders. In A.J. Marsella, R.G. Tharp, & T.J. Cibrowski (Eds.), *Perspectives on cross-cultural psychology*. New York: Academic Press.

Pederson, P., Sartorius, N., & Marsella, A.J. (1984). *Mental health services: The cross-cultural context*. Beverly Hills, CA: Sage Publications.

Pike, K. (1954). Language in relation to a unified theory of the structure of human behavior. Glendale California Summer Institute. 1.

Spradley, J. (1979). *The ethnographic interview*. New York: Holt, Rinehart & Winston.

Spradley, J. (1980). *Participant-Observation*. New York: Holt, Rinehart & Winston.

5

The Relationship between Psychopathology and Nursing Problems

Maxine E. Loomis

After reading this chapter, the reader will be able to:

1. identify the importance of health and illness/psychopathology in the practice of psychiatric and mental health nursing with children and/or adolescents
2. examine the most recent efforts by the American Nurses' Association and the North American Nursing Diagnosis Association to develop classification systems for identifying human responses to actual or potential health problems
3. identify and describe the relationship between nursing diagnosis, medical diagnosis, and etiology in the practice of psychiatric and mental health nursing with children and/or adolescents

THE PRACTICE OF PSYCHIATRIC AND MENTAL HEALTH NURSING

Definitions of Nursing

From the time of Florence Nightingale to the present, professional nurses have been attempting to define their practice domain. Nightingale (1860) wrote about acts that put the patient in the best position for nature to heal. Henderson (1960) defined nursing in terms of a goal: "to assist the individual, sick or well, in the performance of those activities contributing to health or its recovery (or to a peaceful death) that he would perform unaided if he had the necessary strength, will or knowledge. And to do this in such a way as to help him gain independence as rapidly as possible" (p. 3). Both of these definitions address what nurses do, but not why or how they do it.

The American Nurses' Association (ANA, 1980) defined nursing as "the diagnosis and treatment of human responses to actual or potential health problems" (p.

9). Despite its inadequacies in addressing health promotion and illness prevention, the ANA focus on human responses has provided an essential direction for nursing practice, education, research, and theory development. Yet there is still concern within the psychiatric and mental health nursing specialty that there is too much emphasis on psychopathology.

The recent professional literature contains a number of challenges to develop a new definition of nursing—one that focuses attention on health and holism. Hall and Allen (1986) proposed a separation of the science of health and the science of illness. They defined nursing as a process "concerned with the phenomena of human responses to health and illness" (p. 319), and they criticized the reductionistic, illness orientation of the medical model (1988). Schlotfeldt (1987) took the issue one step further and asserted that "nursing is the appraisal and the enhancement of the health status, health assets, and health potentials of human beings" (p. 67).

This type of debate is healthy for the nursing profession as long as it does not lead to unproductive polarities that force nurses to focus on either health or illness, or worse, to consider one approach "good" and the other "bad." Rather, both perspectives should be considered within their contexts. With some people and in some settings, health may occupy the foreground while illness fades into the background. This is the case with many chronic health problems, such as mental retardation and pervasive developmental disorders. Because there is no way to reverse the chronic problem, the nurse must focus on enhancing the client's functional abilities, developing wholeness with the family system, and facilitating the ability of the client and family to deal with the acute episodes that are an inevitable correlate of chronic health problems.

In other situations, illness must be the primary concern, with issues of health promotion temporarily in the background. The nature of many acute health problems, such as conduct disorders or anxiety disorders, forces those in the youngster's environment to focus their attentions on relieving the distress and discomfort of the immediate problem before they can begin to plan for long-range movement toward health. In the best of all possible therapies, the immediate intervention in the illness situation is accomplished with an eye toward the healthiest overall outcome for all involved.

It is also necessary to confront the political and economic realities of licensure, state practice acts, and reimbursement when attempting to define nursing practice. There are times when it appears that the definitions of nursing, social work, medicine, and psychology are determined by power, money, and legislative influence. For example, the federal government and the insurance industry determine who will be reimbursed for providing mental health care, what mental health therapies are reimbursable, and exactly how long therapy (no matter how essential) for a particular problem should take. In the face of these political and economic constraints, it is foolish to search for "the" definition of nursing without considering the environment in which nursing must be marketed.

Although nursing may be described as the science of health and the delivery of health care, the current reality is that people and organizations pay for health in terms of the treatment, and sometimes the prevention, of disease. The profession must develop a way to organize and explain the care that nurses deliver. Nurses *do* diagnose and treat human responses to actual and potential health problems.

The Nursing Process

Perhaps the best way to place psychopathology in proper perspective is to examine the use of the nursing process in the practice of psychiatric and mental health nursing with children and adolescents. Although there is indeed a relationship between psychopathology and nursing problems, the scope of psychiatric and mental health nursing practice with children and adolescents encompasses and extends beyond attention to a specific psychopathology.

The nursing process is basically a problem-solving process that includes the collection of data, the analysis of that data into the formulation of a diagnosis, or statement of the problem, systematic planning for correction of the problem, the implementation of treatments or nursing interventions, and evaluation of targeted outcomes. Regardless of the terminology or number of steps included, there is nothing unique about the process itself. Millions of professionals, technicians, housewives, and children across the world use this problem-solving process daily.

The focus of the problem-solving activity makes nursing unique. The definition of nursing practice followed influences the type of data collected, the diagnostic formulations that will direct interventions, and the evaluation of selected outcomes. Whether the definition focuses on health or illness, information about a diagnosis of psychopathology is likely to be important in formulating the nursing diagnosis or assessment. The following case example illustrates the general relationship between nursing problems and psychopathology.

Data Collection

Carol was dragged by the police onto the adolescent behavioral medicine unit of a large city hospital at midnight, the week before spring break. She was swearing, screaming, kicking, and struggling to free herself in a hysterical frenzy, and she was unable to respond to external attempts to calm her. Police told the admitting resident that Carol had been incoherent and hysterical for the past 2 hours and that her mother had finally called the police when Carol began throwing lamps, books, and furniture around their suburban home. Because Carol continued to lash out and was a threat to herself and others, she was restrained in a private room and tranquilized until she fell into an exhausted sleep under the careful monitoring of the nursing staff.

The psychiatric and mental health clinical specialist, Pat, met with Carol's mother, Julia, the next morning when Julia brought Carol some clothes and cosmetics on her way to work. She informed the nurse that Carol had always been a problem child; that Carol was willful and defiant of her parents; and that Carol was very unlike her older brother, aged 19, and her younger sister, aged 9. Things had become much worse during the past year when Carol turned 16 and began driving. She started "running around with a bad crowd" that was known for drinking, rowdy parties, and possible drug use. In addition Julia discovered about this time that her husband, Bobby Joe, had been seeing another woman and threw him out of the house. Their marriage had been in question ever since, although there had been brief periods of reconciliation during the past several months.

Julia said that she thought Carol's most recent upset had begun two nights earlier when Bobby Joe had denied her permission to drive to Daytona Beach with her friends over spring break. Carol had argued with her father, skipped school, and spent the day drinking beer with her friends. She came home very late that evening, drunk and abusive. When Carol's behavior became dangerous, Julia had called the police.

Julia appeared moderately concerned about Carol's current status, but did not want to see her, did not have time to talk longer or she would be late for work, and just wanted to leave some items for her daughter. Yes, she would be willing to stop tomorrow morning to talk again—perhaps with Carol present. She did leave her work number in case there were any problems.

In morning team rounds, Pat learned from the nursing staff that Carol was still sleeping. They had carefully monitored Carol's condition for possible interaction between alcohol, unknown drug use, and tranquilizers; however, it appeared that Carol's physiological status was stable. No one knew what to expect when she awakened fully. There were few data available, but the team did need to formulate an initial assessment and plan of care.

Assessment/Diagnosis and Planning

Pat talked with the nursing staff about the immediate nursing problems that they might anticipate. Their immediate concerns were Carol's potential for physical aggression toward herself and others, and her verbal aggression toward others. Although the immediate need was for protection and safety, the staff also talked about Carol's pattern of defiant and oppositional behavior and the need to view the current situation as the first step in helping Carol and her family move toward a more functional method of conflict resolution. Altered conduct/impulse processes was the nursing diagnosis of highest priority.

The next two nursing diagnoses, Altered Feeling Processes and Potential for Alteration in Self-care, were determined to be of equal importance. Although many data had yet to be collected, it was evident to Pat and the nursing staff that Carol was experiencing a great deal of difficulty in dealing with and expressing her feelings. Anger was her current problem, but there was a strong possibility that sadness, fear, or guilt was hiding just below the surface of her aggressive exterior. The staff would begin immediately to help Carol deal more directly and constructively with her feelings. They would also work with those in Carol's environment to be reactive and responsive to their own and Carol's feelings.

Because of her recent turmoil and rebellious posture, Carol was at risk for Alterations in Self-care. The nursing staff would need to assess further her nutritional status and other self-care activities in order to determine the need for intervention. Such interventions might range from assuming responsibility for Carol's diet, hygiene, and grooming to providing information regarding self-care activities.

Finally, the nursing diagnosis of Ineffective Family Coping would require that Pat, as clinical specialist, spend time with all family members, both individually and collectively. Without more information regarding the entire family system, it was impossible to determine the reasons for the current crisis. What was the relationship between Julia and Bobby Joe, and how had their marital problems affected the children, especially Carol? Was there some family system problem that Carol was acting out? What was the family's individual and collective commitment to change? What were the strengths of this family, and how could problems for Carol's 9-year-old sister be prevented?

In addition to the above nursing assessment data and beginning diagnoses, the psychiatrist had proposed an initial diagnosis of Oppositional Defiant Disorder (American Psychiatric Association [APA], 1987), based on Carol's behavior of the past year. This diagnosis of psychopathology provided confirmation of the nursing staff's primary concern regarding conduct/impulse problems. According to the criteria for Oppositional Defiant Disorder, the nursing staff could anticipate that Carol might lose her temper, argue with adults, defy ward rules and policies, and deliberately do things to annoy the staff and other patients. Her swearing and abusive language was bound to upset the positive treatment milieu that the staff had worked to develop, and they would need to assess her impact on her peers in the daily community meeting of patients and staff.

Discussion

The Standards of Child and Adolescent Psychiatric and Mental Health Nursing Practice (ANA, 1985) provide a set of clear guidelines for practice within the specialty and use of the nursing process. Standard IX, Interdisciplinary Collaboration, asserts the need for a collaborative process in the treatment of children, adolescents, and their families. All members of the treatment team collect assessment data about the human responses of the client and family to actual or potential health problems. These data do not belong to any one discipline; in fact, they belong to the patient. Nurses, however, bring a unique perspective to their synthesis of the data in the diagnostic process.

In the case of Carol, the nursing staff quickly focused their attention on her altered conduct/impulse processes, which could potentially lead to aggression toward herself or others. Carol's altered feeling processes and potential for altered self-care would require immediate attention, and the clinical specialist was making plans for dealing with the entire family system. Even though the nursing staff would initially focus on the acute mental health problems that Carol presented, they would also be attempting to prevent potential health problems by promoting health for the entire family.

The acts of diagnosis and treatment are based on the assumption that there is a problem. By definition, the diagnostic process involves determining the cause and nature of a disease or problematic situation. Most definitions of disease are fairly reductionistic, indicating that disease is a condition of an organ, part, structure, or system of the body. Psychopathology, as one form of disease, also presents a limited picture of the person and does not usually address persons within their family, social, or cultural contexts.

By contrast, nursing diagnoses tend to describe patterns of human responses within a system. For example, even though Carol was the identified patient with a psychopathological diagnosis of Oppositional Defiant Disorder, the clinical nurse specialist was attempting to place Carol's responses within the context of her family and social systems. She was also concerned about the impact of any family system problems on Carol's 9-year-old sister and the prevention of potential mental health problems.

This broader health perspective has several beneficial outcomes when working with children and adolescents. First, nurses and other health care professionals who view the identified patient within a family, social, and cultural context are much less likely to label or blame the victim for the problem. Although not always the case, traditional psychotherapists have a tendency to focus on a child's psychopathology and then send the child back to a sick family or social system as the ambassador for mental health. In essence, the most vulnerable member of the system is expected to change the complex relationships with which he or she has already been unable to cope. With a more holistic approach, change in the identified patient requires change in the entire system, and change must be individually and collectively negotiated.

The second benefit of a broader health perspective is that nursing diagnoses and treatments can include care, cure, and healing. Standard V of the Standards of Child and Adolescent Psychiatric and Mental Health Nursing Practice (ANA, 1985), Intervention, states, "The nurse intervenes as guided by the nursing care plan to implement actions that promote, maintain, or restore physical and mental health, prevent illness, effect rehabilitation in childhood and adolescence, and restore developmental progression" (p. 11). Nursing *care* activities are required by persons who are unable to manage some aspect of their lives and may be delivered in inpatient, community, or home settings. The activity is of a protective nature and requires that the nurse temporarily take charge. In the case of Carol, the nursing staff was responsible for protecting her from physical harm and ensuring that her nutritional and self-care needs were met. *Cure* for Carol would require psychotherapy for her and her family. While the clinical specialist worked with Carol and her family to change their communication and relationship patterns, the nursing staff would be helping Carol apply what she was learning in therapy to her everyday life and relationships within the treatment milieu.

The object of treatment for Carol would be restoration of health. The word *health* has often been defined as the absence of disease, but most nursing texts now define health much more holistically. Terms such as *soundness, vitality,* and *vigor* of mind and body are used to convey a general sense of completeness and comfort of the person in the environment. With children and adolescents health is also judged in terms of normative growth and development, and age-appropriate behaviors, thoughts, and feelings.

The case example of Carol and her family illustrates several important points. First, any member of the treatment team can use assessment data. Second, the psychopathological diagnosis is one useful piece of information in the data base used by psychiatric and mental health nurses. Third, the phenomena of concern for psychiatric and mental health nursing practice are human responses to actual or potential health problems. Therefore, it is extremely important that psychiatric and mental health nurses develop a system for the diagnosis and labeling of human responses and for discussing their relationship to actual or potential health problems.

IDENTIFICATION AND CLASSIFICATION OF HUMAN RESPONSES

There is currently no one universally accepted classification system that describes the nursing practice elements of assessment, diagnosis, interventions, and outcomes. Because such a system does not exist, there are no empirical data to describe nursing practice consistently across clinical settings, client populations, diagnosis-related groups, medical diagnoses, patient acuity levels, geographical areas, or time. Therefore, it is not possible to know with any accuracy how or to what extent the dimensions and characteristics of nursing practice vary according to these and other factors. In a very real sense, if the question is posed as to what professional nurses do and how they do it, the answer depends on which nurse answers the question.

The need to explicate and classify the basic elements of nursing practice has been recognized for a number of years. In 1973, the ANA published its generic standards for nursing practice and acknowledged the elements of the nursing process as data collection, diagnosis, planning, treatment, and outcomes. In that same year, the North American Nursing Diagnosis Association (NANDA) began its pioneering work on the identification and categorization of nursing diagnoses. Since that time, the ANA and NANDA have maintained a collaborative relationship regarding the development of standards, nursing diagnoses, and the classification of elements of the nursing process.

The Council of Specialists in Psychiatric and Mental Health Nursing was the first ANA structural unit to attempt to classify the phenomena of concern for a specialty nursing practice (Loomis et al., 1987; O'Toole & Loomis, 1989; West & Pothier, 1989; Wilson, 1989), and its work created considerable interest and controversy within the profession. The degree of interest on the part of psychiatric and mental health nurses in clinical settings has underscored the need for the development of specialty diagnoses. Some of the controversy has been political, relating to concerns about the extent to which the ANA should be involved in the development of diagnostic classification systems; some of the controversy has centered around the diagnosis and treatment of human responses to actual or potential problems that is clearly reflected in the classification system.

The Psychiatric and Mental Health Nursing Classification System (Appendix B) is organized by human response patterns in eight processes: activity, cognition, ecological, emotional, interpersonal, perception, physiological, and valuation. Specific human responses (i.e., biological, cognitive, affective, and motor behaviors) or human response patterns (i.e., reliable samples of traits, acts, or other observable features characterizing an individual) are then included under each process (Exhibit 5-1).

A great deal of effort has been made to ensure that the psychiatric and mental health nursing specialty diagnoses are compatible with the diagnoses approved by the NANDA. Even though there are still differences in the major headings, all of the approved NANDA diagnoses are now included in the Psychiatric and Mental Health Nursing Classification System.

To use this system in Carol's care, nurses would focus on Conduct/Impulse Processes (Exhibit 5-2) and Self–Care (Exhibit 5-3). Based on the information available on admission, Carol's specific human response patterns were 5.3.1.1 Potential for Violence, 5.3.2.2 Aggressive/Violent Behavior Toward Environment, 5.3.2.5 Physical Aggression Toward Others, and 5.3.2.12 Verbal Aggression Toward Others. The clinical specialist was aware that delinquency, promiscuity, and substance abuse were other possible problems that would need to be confirmed or disconfirmed once Carol and her family were able to engage in therapy.

As mentioned earlier, Carol's emotional state alerted the nursing staff to her Potential for Alteration in Self-care. Further assessment would be required to determine whether she would need specific nursing care in the areas of eating, health maintenance, and hygiene. Carol's need for nursing care would also relate to her need for ongoing tranquilization.

As it is currently structured, the classification system includes a code for potential patterns "not otherwise specified." This latter designation should allow psychiatric and mental health nurses to record diagnoses not currently on the list and contribute to the ongoing development of the system.

Exhibit 5-1 Psychiatric and Mental Health Nursing Structure for Classification of Human
Responses

Human Response Patterns In:
Activity Processes
  1. Motor Behavior
  2. Recreation Patterns
  3. Self–Care
  4. Sleep/Arousal Patterns
Cognition Processes
  1. Decision Making
  2. Judgment
  3. Knowledge
  4. Learning
  5. Memory
  6. Thought Processes
Ecological Processes
  1. Community Maintenance
  2. Environmental Integrity
  3. Home Maintenance
Emotional Processes
  1. Feeling States
  2. Feeling Processes
Interpersonal Processes
  1. Abuse Response Patterns
  2. Communication Processes
  3. Conduct/Impulse Processes
  4. Family Processes
  5. Role Performance
  6. Sexuality
  7. Social Interaction

Perception Processes
  1. Attention
  2. Comfort
  3. Self–Concept
  4. Sensory Perception
Physiological Processes
  1. Circulation
  2. Elimination
  3. Endocrine/Metabolic Processes
  4. Gastrointestinal Processes
  5. Musculoskeletal Processes
  6. Neuro/Sensory Processes
  7. Nutrition
  8. Oxygenation
  9. Physical Integrity
 10. Physical Regulation Processes
Valuation Processes
  1. Meaningfulness
  2. Spirituality
  3. Values

The future development and refinement of the classification system will involve several activities. First, content experts in subspecialty areas of psychiatric and mental health nursing must expand the content of the system and establish construct validity. For example, specialists in child, adolescent, and family psychiatric and mental health nursing will need to develop more specific diagnoses under the categories of child abuse, substance abuse, and family interaction patterns, to name only a few. Once these diagnoses have been tested in clinical practice, they will be ready for submission to NANDA's Diagnosis Review Committee for official consideration and potential membership approval. This process will take not only time, but also the commitment of numerous psychiatric and mental health nurses who are interested in developing a uniform classification system for the specialty.

Exhibit 5-2 Human Response Patterns in Interpersonal Processes

```
5.3   Conduct/Impulse Processes
      5.3.1   Potential for Alteration
              *5.3.1.1   Potential for Violence (Carol)
              5.3.1.2    Suicidal Ideation
      5.3.2   Altered Conduct/Impulse Processes
              5.3.2.1    Accident Prone
              5.3.2.2    Aggressive/Violent Behavior Toward Environment (Carol)
              5.3.2.3    Delinquency (Carol ?)
              5.3.2.4    Lying
              5.3.2.5    Physical Aggression Toward Others (Carol)
              5.3.2.6    Promiscuity (Carol ?)
              5.3.2.7    Running Away
              5.3.2.8    Substance Abuse (Carol ?)
              5.3.2.9    Suicide Attempt(s)
              5.3.2.10   Truancy
              5.3.2.11   Vandalism
              5.3.2.12   Verbal Aggression Toward Others (Carol)
      5.3.99  Conduct/Impulse Processes Not Otherwise Specified

*Approved NANDA Diagnosis
```

HUMAN RESPONSES AND HEALTH PROBLEMS

The development of a classification system of human responses, unfortunately, will not solve all the conceptual problems within the psychiatric and mental health nursing specialty. The process of making a diagnosis is more than labeling a condition; it includes determining the cause or nature of a problem or situation. It is the statement of etiology or causation that contains the elements of either reductionism or holism. The health problem was either caused by a microorganism or a stressful work environment—or could it be both? The treatment depends on the conceptualization of the etiology.

To complicate matters even more, human responses do not lend themselves well to linear statements of cause and effect. This diagnostic dilemma is illustrated in the four health care prototypes of the relationship between human responses and health problems developed by Loomis and Wood (1983).

Prototype 1: Health Problem(s) Precede Human Response(s).

In a medical model perspective, a disease, accident, or genetic defect affects a person, and treatment efforts are mobilized to deter the invasive organism or repair the damage caused by trauma. The phenomena of concern to the nurse working in the general hospital are the emotional, family, and social human responses

Exhibit 5-3 Human Response Patterns in Activity Processes

1.3   Self–Care
    1.3.1   Potential for Alteration in Self–Care
    *1.3.2   Potential for Altered Health Maintenance (Carol)
    1.3.3   Altered Self–Care
        *1.3.3.1   Altered Eating (Carol ?)
            1.3.3.1.1   Binge-Purge Syndrome
            1.3.3.1.2   Non-nutritive Ingestion
            1.3.3.1.3   Pica
            1.3.3.1.4   Unusual Food Ingestion
            1.3.3.1.5   Refusal to Eat
            1.3.3.1.6   Rumination
        *1.3.3.2   Altered Feeding
            1.3.3.2.1   Ineffective Breast Feeding
        *1.3.3.3   Altered Grooming
        *1.3.3.4   Altered Health Maintenance (Carol ?)
        *1.3.3.5   Altered Health Seeking Behaviors
        *1.3.3.6   Altered Hygiene (Carol ?)
        1.3.3.7   Altered Participation in Health Care
        *1.3.3.8   Altered Toileting
    *1.3.4   Impaired Adjustment
    *1.3.5   Knowledge Deficit
    *1.3.6   Noncompliance
    1.3.99 Self–Care Patterns Not Otherwise Specified

*Approved NANDA Diagnosis

---

to illness or injury. These responses may include anxiety, fear, alterations in family processes, and noncompliance, to list only a few possibilities. Good emotional care may facilitate the physical healing process. The augmentation of individual and family strategies for coping with acute or chronic health problems will certainly prevent further disability and may even enhance future coping.

Prototype 2: Human Response(s) Precede Health Problem(s).

Developmental life changes and cultural/environmental stress are often precursors of physical or mental illness. For example, some adolescents respond to the developmental expectation of going away to college with anxiety, disturbance in self-concept, ineffective individual coping, or social isolation. For others, the unfamiliar university environment engenders a response of powerlessness, fear, sleep pattern disturbance, or an alteration in family processes. Any or all of these human responses may precede a case of mononucleosis, for example, or an accident that interferes with final examinations. Other distraught, unhappy students may resort to drug use, promiscuity, or suicide in an attempt to relieve their distress. The phenomena of concern to nurses in these situations are the human responses that can precede health problems. Support groups for college students, unemployed autoworkers, and professionals approaching retirement are all efforts to help people deal with the human responses associated with stressful life changes and prevent health problems.

Prototype 3: Health Problem(s) Are Defined by Human Response(s).

Acute or chronic health deviations or problems are sometimes defined by their symptoms or human responses. Upon closer examination, it becomes apparent that the human responses listed as diagnostic criteria in the *Diagnostic and Statistical Manual of Mental Disorders* (DSM III-R; APA, 1987) are merely more specific statements of accepted nursing diagnoses. For example, the DSM III-R diagnosis of Conduct Disorder includes a number of specific behaviors, such as stealing, lying, running away from home, firesetting, truancy, and cruelty to animals. Although not all these behaviors are currently included in the psychiatric and mental health nursing classification system, they are in keeping with the nursing diagnosis format; with increased input from psychiatric and mental health nurses, NANDA will undoubtedly develop and accept these diagnostic categories.

Prototype 4: Health Problem(s) Interact with Human Response(s).

Some health problems cannot be cured. Chronic health deviations, such as respiratory disease, diabetes, mental retardation, and organic mental disorders, must be treated symptomatically. When the damage to the human organism has already been done, the focus of intervention is on maintaining existing functional abilities and preventing further deterioration.

Other health problems that were once thought to be incurable can now be controlled or reversed through self-regulation. Exercise, biofeedback, mental imagery, and meditation are only a few of the techniques available for conscious control and regulation of the autonomic nervous system or various disease processes. Cousins (1979) claimed to have cured himself of ankylosing spondylitis by laughing. Simonton and Simonton (1978) reported extended life expectancy and remission in cancer patients who used relaxation and mental imagery techniques. All these techniques take into account the interaction between health problems and human responses. Green and Green (1977) stated that "every change in the physiological state is accompanied by an appropriate change in the mental-emotional state, conscious or unconscious, and conversely, every change in the mental-emotional state, conscious or unconscious is accompanied by an appropriate change in the physiological state" (p. 33).

Whether or not the health problem is capable of cure, psychiatric and mental health nurses should focus on human responses. Whether the health problem (disease) causes the human response (behavior) or whether the human response causes the disease remains an unanswered question. In the meantime, many individuals seek treatment to ease their intrapersonal and interpersonal discomfort.

FUTURE DIRECTIONS

The future of psychiatric and mental health nursing clinical practice with children and adolescents depends on the development of classification systems that clearly identify the assessments, diagnoses, interventions, and outcomes for which the specialty practice is responsible. Nurses must be able to articulate the essential elements of their practice to consumers, administrators, politicians, and reimbursement agencies. The NANDA nursing diagnoses and the ANA classification of the human responses of concern for psychiatric and mental health nursing practice are two beginning attempts to specify the domain of nursing practice that have generated excitement and realistic clinical interest among practicing nurses.

The task force that developed the existing psychiatric and mental health classification system defined human responses as cognitive, affective, and motor behaviors, and did not concern itself with specific nursing, medical, psychological, or social theories about the etiology or context of actual or potential mental health problems. Because of this process, the classification system contained in Appendix B focuses on behavior that is only one aspect of the holistic human phenomena with which nurses should be concerned. Future work in clinical practice settings *must* attend to the complex ways in which children, adolescents, their families, and social systems define their realities and their positions within them, however. For example, there is no mental health "problem" of infancy, childhood, or adolescence that can be defined without the inclusion of relationship and environmental variables, even though nurses can specify the discrete behavioral indicators that are observed. Although the medical diagnosis is one piece of information available in making a nursing diagnosis, it is often patient- and disease/illness-specific and does not account for all of the variance in each situation. Nursing practice is holistic and that practice should be reflected in its classification systems.

Nursing Theory Development

To date, the major nurse theorists have not had a uniform or major impact on nursing practice. Although there are geographical pockets of emphasis on self-care, humanistic nursing, adaptation, transcultural nursing, homeostasis, unitary human beings, and goal attainment/contract-centered nursing practice, none of the extant classification systems is based on a specific theory of nursing practice. There are two major reasons for this incongruity.

First, the disease care system in which nursing is practiced rewards and reimburses the diagnosis and treatment of medical/illness problems. Therefore, nurses have been educated and rewarded primarily for functioning in medical specialty areas (such as psychiatric and mental health nursing), and their concern for and attention to the holistic nature of human health is either secondary or acquired at the graduate level. Rewards within the majority of nursing practice settings are given for medical care and cure, not holistic nursing care. Care implies the existence of a problem; nursing cure has yet to be defined. For example, if nurses are concerned with "assisting others in more fully understanding their realities and their positions within them," as Moccia (1988) has proposed, what is the relevance of cure? Nurses must value and control their own practice if they are truly to practice nursing. Then the medical diagnosis would become one additional piece of data (identifying the patient's limitations) in managing the patient's total care.

Second, there is minimal consensus regarding the definition(s) of nursing, the goals and outcomes of clinical practice, and the phenomena of concern for nursing practice. This situation is not surprising in view of the current stage of the professional and scholarly development of nursing as a clinical and scientific discipline; however, the lack of consensus creates educational dilemmas for nursing faculty and practice difficulties for nurse clinicians. For example, if the goal of nursing care is to help patients adapt to actual health care problems, the assessment data, nursing diagnosis, and interventions will focus on the client's strengths and weaknesses. If the goal is to facilitate self-care, however, self-care agencies, self-care deficits, and resources guide the nursing process.

This conceptual confusion is compounded by the lack of clarity in defining *when* a human response becomes problematic. In the majority of situations, people do not seek help until a specific human response becomes a problem. When a child is truant from school or an adolescent is arrested for drunk driving, the family or social system is forced to acknowledge the immediate behavioral problem. Those individuals within the illness care system may have no interest in viewing the immediate problem within an adaptation, stress, or coping framework.

The answer to nursing's current difficulties will become apparent when the nursing profession identifies its phenomena of concern. In an interview by Smith (1988), seven nurse theorists expressed opinions about nursing diagnoses that ranged from the pragmatic statement of Peplau (p. 83) that nursing diagnoses are essential for reimbursement for nursing practice to the statements of Rogers (p. 84) and Schlotfeldt (p. 83) that nursing diagnosis is either inappropriate or not linked to their holistic definitions of nursing. All appeared to agree that identifying and defining nursing practice requires identification and definition of the phenomena of concern, however. Therefore, it is essential to identify, define, and classify the unique dimensions by which nurses define and develop knowledge about their phenomena of concern.

Clinical Research

Psychiatric and mental health nursing research with children and adolescents is in its infancy. Researchers have a responsibility to approach the clinical situation with sensitivity and from a holistic perspective. It is necessary first to identify and name the phenomena of concern for psychiatric and mental health nursing practice in terms that describe the experience for clients, their families, social networks, and nurses. This research will be factor isolating or naming (Dickoff, James, & Wiedenbach, 1968) and probably be qualitative in nature. For example, what is the lived experience of a family with an autistic child? a retarded child? an adolescent on drugs? a hyperactive youngster? an exceptionally bright or talented child? How do different family members define normal, sick, or exceptional behavior? What is the experience of families in which one member has a chronic health problem? These and other questions must be raised by clinicians and studied by collaborative clinician/researcher teams. The answers to these and similar questions will increase clinical sensitivity and promote additional research. For example, are exceptionally bright youngsters more likely to have drug or sexual problems? Will the presence of a female role model enhance the practice of safe sex among adolescent girls who are sexually active?

Clinical psychiatric and mental health nursing research is also required to assist in the identification of "problematic" human responses. For example, when and why do children and adolescents come for help? Who defines the problem? In what terms is the problem defined? Does this definition differ from that of the nurse? If so, how is it different? When there is a difference, what is the process for negotiating a change/treatment contract?

A great deal of theoretical and clinical work is required to clarify the problems that have been addressed in this chapter. Although there have been several creditable attempts at developing assessment (Morrison et al., 1985) and diagnostic (Coler & Vincent, 1987) classification systems, there is an urgent need to develop data-based systems to describe and direct psychiatric and mental health nursing practice. Such systems must be validated in clinical practice and tested in the field to establish generalizability across settings and patient populations. A structure and process for ongoing feedback, revision, and dissemination is essential for the maintenance of a relevant classification system. Finally, any psychiatric and mental health nursing classification system should provide for linkages with both the NANDA nursing diagnostic system and the DSM III-R system (APA, 1987) of diagnosing psychopathology. This work has begun and will continue as psychiatric and mental health nurses continue in their role as pacesetters for the profession.

REFERENCES

American Nurses' Association. (1973). *Standards for nursing practice*. Kansas City, MO: Author.

American Nurses' Association. (1980). *Nursing: A social policy statement*. Kansas City, MO: Author.

American Nurses' Association. (1985). *Standards of child and adolescent psychiatric and mental health nursing practice*. Kansas City, MO: Author.

American Psychiatric Association. (1987). *Diagnostic and statistical manual of mental disorders* (3rd ed., rev.). Washington, DC: Author.

Coler, M., & Vincent, K. (1987). Coded nursing diagnoses on axes: A prioritized, computer-ready diagnostic system for psychiatric/mental health nurses. *Archives of Psychiatric Nursing, 1*(2), 125–131.

Cousins, N. (1979). *The anatomy of an illness*. New York: W.W. Norton.

Dickoff, J., James, P., & Wiedenbach, E. (1968). Theory in a practice discipline: Practice oriented theory (Part I). *Nursing Research, 17*(5), 415–435.

Green, E., & Green, A. (1977). *Beyond biofeedback*. New York: Delta.

Hall, B.A., & Allen, J.D. (1986). Sharpening nursing's focus by focusing on health. *Nursing and Health Care, 7*, 315–320.

Hall, B.A., & Allen, J.D. (1988). Challenging the focus on technology: A critique of the medical model in a changing health care system. *Advances in Nursing Science, 10*(3), 22–34.

Henderson, V. (1960). *Basic principles of nursing care*. London: International Council of Nurses.

Loomis, M.E., O'Toole, A.W., Brown, M.S., Pothier, P., West, P., & Wilson, H.S. (1987). Development of a classification system for psychiatric/mental health nursing: Individual response class. *Archives of Psychiatric Nursing, 1*, 16–24.

Loomis, M.E., & Wood, D.J. (1983). Cure: The potential outcomes of nursing care. *Image: The Journal of Nursing Scholarship, 15*(1), 4–7.

Moccia, P. (1988). A critique of compromise: Beyond the methods debate. *Advances in Nursing Science, 10*(4), 1–8.

Morrison, E., Fisher, L.Y., Wilson, H.S., & Underwood, P. (1985). The NSGAE. *Journal of Psychosocial Nursing, 23*(8), 10–13.

Nightingale, F. (1860). *Notes on Nursing*. London: Harrison.

O'Toole, A.W., & Loomis, M.E. (1989). Revision of the Phenomena of Concern for psychiatric/mental health nursing. *Archives of Psychiatric Nursing, 3*, 288–299.

Schlotfeldt, R. (1987). Defining nursing: A historic controversy. *36*(1), 64–67.

Simonton, O., & Simonton, S. (1978). *Getting well again*. Los Angeles: J.P. Tarcher.

Smith, M.J. (1988). Perspectives on nursing science. *Nursing Science Quarterly, 1*(2), 80–85.

West, P.P., & Pothier, P.C. (1989). Clinical application of Human Resources Classification System: Child example. *Archives of Psychiatric Nursing, 3*, 300–304.

Wilson, H.S. (1989). Field trials of the Phenomena of Concern for psychiatric/mental health nursing: Proposed methodology. *Archives of Psychiatric Nursing, 3*, 305–308.

6

Nursing Diagnoses and Planning of Psychiatric Nursing with Children and Adolescents

Patricia West

After reading this chapter, the reader will be able to:

1. describe the goal of psychiatric nursing diagnoses
2. identify relevant psychiatric nursing diagnoses for children and adolescents
3. elaborate on the elements of the planning process for psychiatric nurses working with children and adolescents
4. describe several tools available to the psychiatric nurse in diagnosing and planning care with youngsters and their families

After the initial assessment data have been collected and analyzed, a psychiatric nurse uses the information to develop nursing diagnoses and a plan for care with the child and family. Developing nursing diagnoses and planning are participatory components of the nursing process in that they actively engage the youngster and family in a therapeutic relationship. Nursing diagnoses and plans provide direction for nursing interventions by focusing on the human response patterns of the child or adolescent and family.

THE DIAGNOSTIC PROCESS

The goal of the nursing diagnostic process is to name the focal human responses that have been identified through assessment. To reach this goal, the psychiatric nurse, client, and family go through an initial phase of orientation during which they become acquainted and identify the problematic responses. The nurse's theoretical perspective focuses the assessment process on the phenomena of concern. The nurse then synthesizes the collected data; develops a clinical formulation of the client's situation; and, with the family, determines the relevant nursing diagnoses.

Nursing diagnoses (1) identify need for nursing care, (2) set a priority of a client's needs, (3) focus nursing interventions, and (4) serve as a professionally recognized means for naming a client's needs for nursing care. These functions exemplify the way in which nursing diagnoses link assessment and planning of nursing care. Data collection provides the substantive information about an individual, and the analysis provides a theoretical and clinical understanding of these data. The diagnoses name the response patterns of concern. Then, by developing a nursing care plan based on the diagnoses, a nurse focuses nursing interventions on the identified human responses. The processes that nurses use to identify and formulate pertinent diagnoses are best described by Carnevali (1984, 1988) and Gordon (1987). As Carnevali (1984) stated,

> The diagnostic reasoning process is a complex observation-critical, thinking-data gathering process used to identify and classify phenomena that are encountered in presenting clinical situations. This classification with associated labeling is not an end in itself, but a means to an end. It provides the foundation of recognition and knowledge of the nature of the phenomena being observed. This classification and the knowledge associated with it, in turn, shape the decisions on treatment regimens that can be undertaken to produce a desired outcome in patient/family response. (p. 26)

Central to this view of the diagnostic reasoning process are the concepts of cues and inferences. Cues are the signs and symptoms presented by a client and family. A nurse attempts to clarify a relationship between the cues and the client's subjective or internal state by an inference. Diagnosing is the process of inferring the internal state of a client from the observed cues and, therefore, suggesting a probabilistic relationship. Because of the "probabilistic" nature of the inference, diagnosing is a complex process (Carnevali, 1984). Gordon (1987) described this process as the development and testing of hypotheses. A nurse develops a hypothesis about a client's situation and then tests it through validation and other interventions.

Carnevali (1984) described the diagnostic reasoning process as being composed of diagnostic elements, a pattern or sequence, and other influencing factors. The elements and sequence of the diagnostic process may fall into patterns or steps (Figure 6-1). In applied clinical situations, the sequence and particular elements are difficult to delineate, may overlap, and may vary with the course of treatment. Influencing factors include: (1) the education and experience of the nurse, (2) the nature of the clinical setting, and (3) the nature of the diagnostic process. For example, the conceptual frame of reference of the nurse influences the type of questions asked, the phenomena of interest, and the patterns of human responses identified.

In applying these diagnostic reasoning processes with children and adolescents, a psychiatric nurse has several special considerations. First, the cues (signs and symptoms) of a child may be subtle and difficult to detect, particularly in a young child whose cognitive and communication capabilities are still developing. Sec-

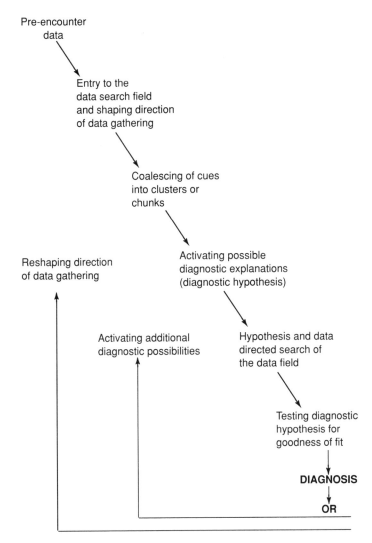

Figure 6-1 *Source:* From *Diagnostic Reasoning in Nursing,* (p. 28) by D.L. Carnevali (Ed.), 1984, Philadelphia, PA: J.B. Lippincott Company. Copyright 1984 by J.B. Lippincott Company. Reprinted by permission.

ond, individual differences in development make identification of problematic responses a complex process and require a nurse to look for recurrent patterns of behavior, the family's definitions of areas of concern, and clarification of environmental determinants. Third, a child psychiatric nurse must often use multiple sources of information (e.g., other informants, such as extended family members and teachers) and alternate ways of collecting information (e.g., verbal exchange, art, storytelling, and play techniques) to determine the probabilistic relationship of pertinent cues and inferences. Finally, a nurse working with children should consider the impact of multiple contributing factors in developing diagnoses for children. Developmental processes, family influences, and other factors not readily identifiable may contribute to the problematic human responses.

PSYCHIATRIC NURSING DIAGNOSES

Like other types of nursing diagnoses, psychiatric nursing diagnoses name the pertinent phenomena toward which nurses direct their plans and interventions. The diagnoses add clarity to the focus of nursing interventions. The focal response patterns are identified as the planning of nursing care is initiated. Furthermore, the nursing diagnoses focus nursing interventions toward the identified human responses.

In using psychiatric nursing diagnoses with children and adolescents, a nurse develops problem statements that include the three components of the diagnosis. Gordon (1976) identified these three components referred to as the PES format: (1) P, the health problem; (2) E, the etiology or related factors; and (3) S, the clustered signs and symptoms of defining characteristics. In psychiatric and mental health situations, the causes of the human responses are often speculative. Therefore, etiology is frequently omitted from the diagnosis.

The nurse focuses on formulating three or four key diagnoses. This number of diagnoses is reasonable to manage in treatment and should reflect the most significant human responses as determined by all involved in setting priorities.

Tools for Psychiatric Nursing Diagnoses

The tools available to psychiatric nurses in formulating psychiatric nursing diagnoses include not only their own diagnostic skills, but also the diagnostic classification systems.

Diagnostic Skills

Tanner (1984) described a number of factors related to the characteristics of the diagnostician that influence the diagnostic process. Several of these characteristics reflect diagnostic skills, and they are differentiated in the novice and the expert nurse. An expert nurse diagnostician: (1) seeks multiple cues in making inferences, (2) recognizes patterns of cues, (3) starts with systematic inquiry to avoid premature closure, (4) looks for information that differs from pre-encounter expectations, and (5) uses patterns of cues in developing working hypotheses. With youngsters and their families, the psychiatric nurse also uses a knowledge base of normal development, family dynamics, and cultural variations to formulate nursing diagnoses.

Diagnostic Classification Systems

Classification System of Human Responses. This classification system was developed by a panel of experts from ANA. It provides the most comprehensive identification of the phenomena of interest for psychiatric nurses and a foundation for further development of psychiatric nursing diagnoses (See O'Toole & Loomis, 1989, Appendix B, and Chapter 5 for a detailed discussion).

The North American Nursing Diagnosis Association (NANDA). The clearing house organization for nursing diagnoses, NANDA began classifying its list of nursing diagnoses into a taxonomy of nine human response patterns in 1986. The taxonomy, which was revised in 1988, functions as an organizing framework for the currently recognized nursing diagnoses (Carroll-Johnson, 1989). In the most recent taxonomy, those recognized diagnoses pertinent to psychiatric practice include Anxiety, Fear, Powerlessness, Self-esteem Disturbance, Hopelessness, Personal Identity Disturbance, and Potential for Violence (either self-directed or directed at others).

Critics of the taxonomy claim that there is little evidence of valid relationships between the diagnoses and the response patterns (Coler, 1989), and that the categories overlap considerably (Kritek, 1986). The identification of diagnoses for nursing is a recent pursuit of the discipline, however, and extensive development and research will be necessary for clarification of a comprehensive taxonomy.

University of Washington Psychiatric Nursing Diagnosis Project. Using the conceptual framework of Carnevali (1984, 1988), members of the University of Washington Psychiatric Nursing Diagnosis Project have begun developing psychiatric nursing diagnoses. Carnevali identified two major categories of the phenomena of interest for nursing, daily living and health status, as one way of conceptualizing nursing's unique domain of knowledge and proposed a dual-directional model of these variables. The model results in five categories of nursing diagnoses:

a) a functional health status that interferes with effective management of daily living;

b) daily living that contributes to health problems or dysfunction;

c) daily living that is affected by functional health status associated with age-related psychological status, developmental task status and pathology plus medical diagnostic or treatment activities;

d) difficulties in integrating health care or medical treatment regimens into daily living effectively and with satisfaction, and

e) inadequate or inappropriate external resources that interfere with effective management of daily living, given the presenting health situation. (Carnevali, 1988, p. 333).

Sanger, Thomas, and Whitney (1988) also used Carnevali's conceptual framework to develop a guide for the nursing assessment of psychiatric inpatients. The guide has been used in two research studies, one with adults who were depressed (Thomas, Sanger, & Whitney, 1986) and the second with adults who were experiencing thought disorders and manic symptoms (Thomas, Sanger, Wolf-Wilets, & Whitney, 1988). Although not yet adapted for children, this guide has usefulness in identifying nursing diagnoses among adult inpatients.

Diagnostic and Statistical Manual of Mental Disorders. The American Psychiatric Association's *Diagnostic and Statistical Manual of Mental Disorders,* third edition, revised (DSM-III-R; APA, 1987) is an interdisciplinary approach to psychiatric diagnoses. The current format is a multi-axial system that addresses

1. identifiable mental disorders (Axis I)
2. personality and developmental disorders (Axis II)
3. physical disorders (Axis III)
4. severity of psychosocial stressors (Axis IV)
5. level of functioning (Axis V)

The DSM-III-R permits an atheoretical, comprehensive appraisal of an individual's status, resulting in diagnoses associated with specific criteria. It has been useful for psychiatric nurses (Williams & Wilson, 1982).

There are several important benefits to be obtained from using the DSM-III-R in psychiatric nursing care with children and adolescents. First, the DSM-III-R is widely recognized, as it is currently used in most settings where youngsters receive psychiatric care. Second, because the diagnostic categories have undergone extensive field trials, they are reliable and valid (Williams & Wilson, 1982). Third, there may be a relationship between the defining characteristics of the specific diagnoses and the human responses identified in the Classification of Human Responses (see Appendix B). Loomis, O'Toole, Brown, Pothier, West, & Wilson (1987) suggested that the symptoms of a DSM-III-R diagnosis may include human responses of concern to psychiatric nurses.

Changes in the DSM-III-R currently being discussed would clarify ways in which the multi-axial system can better designate severity and the course of psychiatric disorders and modify several diagnoses that need clarification (Frances, First, Pincus, Widiger, & Davis, 1990).

THE PLANNING PROCESS

Planning nursing interventions includes the following activities: (1) setting priorities, (2) establishing goals and expected outcomes, (3) determining nursing interventions, and (4) documenting the plan (Alfaro, 1990). These components are interrelated and continuously change as a family and nurse work through the treatment of the problematic human responses.

Setting Priorities

In setting priorities, the child psychiatric nurse responds to the priorities for care of the child and family. These priorities are initially addressed if a child and family are to engage in treatment. The health and the safety of the child are always priorities. For example, a risk of abuse or self-destructive tendencies mandate immediate nursing intervention and require a high priority.

Gordon (1987) specified that "priorities for treatment depend on (1) the urgency of the problem, (2) the nature of the treatment indicated, and (3) the interaction among diagnoses" (p. 315). The economics of health care also influence priorities in planning psychiatric nursing care. Limitations of financial resources and insurance coverages require a nurse to set effective priorities for nursing interventions. Alfaro (1990) commented that priorities of nursing interventions are influenced by (1) the child and family's perception of the problem, (2) the overall treatment plan, (3) the overall health status of the youngster, and (4) the presence of potential or compounding difficulties.

Establishing Goals and Expected Outcomes of Care

"Goals are statements that reflect a client outcome, leading to alleviation of the concern indicated by the [nursing] diagnosis" (Christensen, 1986, pp. 172–173). In child psychiatric nursing, goals are mutually determined by the child, the parents/legal guardians, and the nurse. Other health care professionals, family members, or other involved individuals (e.g., teachers and clergy) may also participate in goal setting.

Nurses differentiate nursing goals, which they themselves are to meet, from client goals, which are directed toward the child and family. Nurses currently document their interventions as related to the client-centered goals and objectives, as well as nursing interventions that will assist the youngster. The goals of nursing interventions may be short-term, requiring a month or less to achieve, or long-term, requiring an extended length of time to achieve, depending on the setting, frequency of contact with the family, and nature of the presenting response patterns.

Objectives are the incremental steps toward treatment goals. They are short-term, realistic, and measurable (Parsons, 1986). In determining the parameters of "short-term," the child psychiatric nurse considers the problematic human responses, the overall goals, and the resources of the child and family. Objectives are realistically achievable for the particular child or adolescent. They are also measurable or comparable to a standard. The standard can be included in the written description of the objective, providing the nurse with a basis for comparison. Christensen (1986) suggested that there are four ways to state a standard in nursing objectives: speed, accuracy, quality, or criterion. For example, "Janet will describe three relaxation techniques by 4/7" is a speed objective.

Outcomes reflect demonstrated improvement or resolution of the focal human responses. They should be concrete, measurable, and time-oriented. There are three types of expected outcomes: affective, cognitive, and psychomotor (Bloom, 1956). Affective outcomes address changes in feelings, values, and attitudes, including the sharing or expressing of emotions. Cognitive outcomes refer to the acquisition of knowledge, such as the side-effects of medications. Psychomotor outcomes are behaviorally based and are generally related to motor skills. These outcomes may include demonstrating relaxation techniques or participating in a group activity for a designated period of time. It is important for the nurse to address all types of outcomes with the youngster and family to implement comprehensive, effective nursing interventions.

Gordon (1987) described the relationship between a nursing diagnosis and the desired outcome of nursing care. By reversing the focal human response identified by the nursing diagnosis, the nurse can specify the anticipated outcome of care. For example, the nursing diagnosis for a young adolescent who has experienced a significant loss may be hopelessness. By reversing the diagnosis, the nurse can identify an anticipated outcome of hopefulness. The specified outcome would meet the individual situation of the youngster.

Alfaro (1990) suggested several guidelines in determining the goals and outcomes of nursing interventions. Child psychiatric nurses should:

- be realistic, considering growth and development, health status, behavior patterns, available resources, time frame, and other treatment factors
- develop the goals mutually with the child and family
- use measurable, observable verbs in describing desired outcomes
- be sure that the goals are client-centered, for example, "a child will . . ."
- identify goals and outcomes that are consistent with the Standards of Practice (ANA, 1985), state laws, and work setting

Determining Nursing Interventions

In planning the interventions for a child or adolescent, a psychiatric nurse determines the most appropriate therapeutic techniques for that particular youngster and family. Schaefer and Millman (1977) stated,

Rather than attempting to force a child into one "all purpose" therapeutic mold . . . therapists are now trying to individualize, to fit the remedies or techniques to the needs of the individual child. Ideally, the prescriptive approach will result in maximum therapeutic effectiveness in the briefest possible time period. (pp. 1–2)

Child psychiatric nurses carefully select appropriate interventions to meet the needs of the child and family within the education and experience of the nurse and the available environmental and financial resources. Furthermore, the choice of interventions should be in the context of the least restrictive setting for a child.

Documenting the Plan

The final step in the planning process is the documentation of the nursing care plan. According to Alfaro (1990), written nursing care plans serve three purposes; they (1) direct nursing interventions, (2) focus nursing documentation, and (3) provide a written, individualized record of care for the family on which evaluation of progress can be based. The format of the nursing care plan may vary. Most, however, include at least the following:

1. nursing diagnosis (including problem statement; etiology, if known or hypothesized; and defining characteristics)
2. goals and expected outcomes (short- and long-term)
3. nursing interventions
4. time factors, such as dates of initiation and expected dates of achievement

Interdisciplinary treatment plans are frequently used in psychiatric settings. They present a comprehensive plan for the child and family. The involved professionals either specify their interventions on the master plan or develop their own discipline-specific plan.

PLANNING OF PSYCHIATRIC NURSING CARE

In planning psychiatric care for children and adolescents, nurses use their own planning skills, standardized care plans and guides, computerized planning tools, and the nursing case conference.

Planning Skills

Not only do nurses' therapeutic communication skills facilitate the planning process, but also their specific skills can enhance the planning process. These skills correspond to the elements of planning; that is, setting priorities, establishing goals and expected outcomes, determining nursing interventions, and documenting a plan of care (Alfaro, 1990). As nurses develop a knowledge base and gain experience in these areas, their planning skills increase.

An additional planning skill is the ability to engage the youngster and family in the therapeutic process. The active participation of the youngster and family members greatly enhances the success of psychiatric nursing interventions. A psychiatric nurse's skill in engaging these individuals: (1) addresses their initial resistance to treatment, (2) gives them a sense of shared responsibility in dealing with the focal human responses, and (3) establishes a commitment to working together to reach an agreed upon goal.

Standardized Care Plans and Guides

In an effort to systematize the development and documentation of nursing care plans, numerous attempts have been made to develop standardized plans. All need some modification to meet the needs of a particular child and family. Furthermore, many of these guides do not specifically address psychiatric nursing care of children and adolescents. With some modification by the clinician, however, these plans may streamline the development of psychiatric nursing care plans.

McFarland and Wasli (1986) presented a plan based on NANDA's approved nursing diagnoses and included additional diagnoses. Their framework for each nursing diagnosis included: (1) diagnostic definitions, (2) possible causes, (3) defining characteristics, (4) areas of assessment, (5) goals, (6) nursing interventions, (7) health education-prevention, and (8) evaluation. Although they did not include developmentally specific diagnoses for children and adolescents, it is possible to modify their suggested plans and interventions for youngsters.

Townstend (1988) presented a guide to developing psychiatric care plans specifically for children and adolescents. This guide is organized according to the DSM-III-R diagnoses and includes frequently related nursing diagnoses. Each nursing diagnosis has a definition; possible causes; defining characteristics; a goal; and possible nursing interventions, which are described with selected rationale. These plans guide a nurse in developing an individualized plan for a client. For example, the DSM-III-R diagnosis of Pervasive Developmental Disability is given with the following nursing diagnoses: Potential for Self-directed Violence, Impaired Social Interaction, Impaired Verbal Communication, and Disturbance in Self-concept (personal identity).

Other planning guides specifically address children and adolescents who are experiencing emotional, social, and perceptual problematic human responses. Greenberg (1988) presented guidelines for developing care plans for youngsters who are experiencing depression, separation anxiety, difficulty with body image, and anxiety, and those who are at risk of adolescent suicide. They identified nursing diagnoses, goals, interventions, and expected outcomes. Doenges, Moorhouse, and Townstend (1989) used selected DSM-III-R diagnoses to organize their guide; then, they identified NANDA-approved nursing diagnoses with a nursing approach, including pertinent data base information, nursing interventions, and discharge criteria.

Computerized Care Plans

With increasing frequency, nurses are using computers to develop nursing care plans. Although some of these plans are standardized, computerization allows a nurse to develop an individualized plan within a structured format. Bailey (1988) described a computer system based on the accepted NANDA nursing diagnoses in which a nurse first validates the nursing diagnosis by noting the etiology and defining characteristics from the NANDA-accepted diagnoses and then chooses nursing interventions from: (1) a list of actions frequently used with individuals with that diagnosis, (2) a pool of additional actions, or (3) those actions individually specified by the nurse. Bailey noted a significant reduction in the time that nurses needed to initiate a nursing care plan—from 50 to 15 minutes. Throughout the process, the care plan can be individualized for the client and his or her response patterns.

Ormiston, Barrett, Binder, and Molyneux (1989) described a partially computerized treatment planning process for psychiatric settings. This model provides computer assistance at various phases in the development of interdisciplinary treatment plans. The health care personnel who treat the client are able to individualize the plan throughout the process. Although these authors did not report the use of this system with children and adolescents, partially computerized plans would be beneficial with this population.

Nursing Case Conference

Case conferences with nursing staff members can be a valuable tool in planning interventions for a particular youngster and family. The collective effort often generates innovative approaches and better staff communication on the designated plan. Reed (1987) identified three basic steps in the conference process to improve planning of care: (1) planning ahead by identifying nursing diagnoses, goals, and anticipated actions; (2) involving clients in the planning process to individualize their unique needs and encourage their participation in therapy; and (3) frequently reviewing and monitoring progress so that the plan can be adjusted as needed.

RESEARCH

Research related to nursing diagnoses and planning has occurred in numerous areas. For example, Larson (1989) studied female adolescents and young adults who had been admitted to an inpatient unit for anorexia nervosa and found that the defining characteristics previously identified with the nursing diagnosis of Disturbance in Self-esteem occurred with varying frequency.

Wilson (1989) outlined methodological directions for the field testing of the Classification of Human Responses. The testing would focus on (1) interrater reliability of the system of psychiatric nursing diagnoses when applied in the clinical setting and (2) its practical utility for nurses. The results of this field testing not only would provide direction for revisions of the classification system and adaptation for computerization, but also would promote dissemination of the system and development of continuing educational programs.

Research in the area of psychiatric nursing care planning is sparse; there have been few investigations with any population. In one study, however, Ferguson, Hildman, and Nichols (1987) compared three types of planning systems in relation to the outcomes of nursing interventions, such as length of stay, recidivism, and client satisfaction. The planning types varied in the extent to which nursing diagnoses and nursing orders were used. No evidence was found that one type of planning system resulted in more improved outcomes, but this study had numerous limitations, including a lack of random assignment.

Nursing research is needed on nursing diagnoses and planning psychiatric nursing care with children, adolescents, and their families. Investigations should explore the apparent benefits of participatory planning with a child and family, of computerized care planning, and of standardized care plans. Further studies are indicated to address the integration and utility of nursing diagnoses in the planning process.

REFERENCES

Alfaro, R. (1990). *Applying nursing diagnosis and nursing process: A step-by-step guide* (2nd ed.). Philadelphia: J.B. Lippincott.

American Nurses' Association. (1985). *Standards of child and adolescent psychiatric and mental health nursing practice.* Kansas City, MO: Author.

American Psychiatric Association. (1987). *Diagnostic and statistical manual of mental disorders* (3rd ed., rev.). Washington, DC: Author.

Bailey, D.R. (1988). Computer applications in nursing. *Computers in Nursing, 6*(5), 199–203.

Bloom, B. (Ed.). (1956). *Taxonomy of educational objectives: The classification of educational goals. Handbook I: Cognitive domain.* New York: David McKay.

Carnevali, D.L. (1984). The diagnostic reasoning process. In D.L. Carnevali, P.H. Mitchell, N.F. Woods, & C.A. Tanner (Eds.), *Diagnostic reasoning in nursing* (pp. 25–56). Philadelphia: J.B. Lippincott.

Carnevali, D.L. (1988). Daily living and functional health status: A perspective for nursing diagnosis and treatment. *Archives of Psychiatric Nursing, 2*(6), 330–333.

Carroll-Johnson, R.M. (Ed.). (1989). *Classification of nursing diagnoses: Proceedings of the eighth conference of the North American Nursing Diagnosis Association.* Philadelphia: J.B. Lippincott.

Christensen, P.J. (1986). Planning: Priorities, goals, and objectives. In J.W. Griffith-Kenney & P.J. Christensen (Eds.), *Nursing process: Application of theories, frameworks and models* (2nd ed., pp. 169–182). St. Louis: C.V. Mosby.

Coler, M.S. (1989). Diagnoses for child and adolescent psychiatric nursing: Combining NANDA and the DSM-III-R. *Journal of Child and Adolescent Psychiatric Mental Health Nursing, 2*(3), 115–119.

Doenges, M.E., Moorhouse, M.F., & Townstend, M.C. (Eds.). (1989). *Psychiatric care plans: Guidelines for client care* (2nd ed.). Philadelphia: J.B. Lippincott.

Ferguson, G.H., Hildman, T., & Nichols, B. (1987). The effect of nursing care planning systems on patient outcomes. *Journal of Nursing Administration, 17*(9), 30–36.

Frances, A., First, M., Pincus, H.A., Widiger, T., & Davis, W. (1990). An introduction to DSM-IV. *Hospital and Community Psychiatry, 41*(5), 493–494.

Gordon, M. (1976). Nursing diagnosis and the diagnostic process. *American Journal of Nursing, 76,* 1298–1300.

Gordon, M. (1987). *Nursing diagnosis: Process and application* (2nd ed.). New York: McGraw-Hill.

Greenberg, C.S. (1988). *Nursing care planning guides for children.* Baltimore: Williams & Wilkins.

Kritek, P. (1986). The struggle to classify our diagnoses. *American Journal of Nursing, 86,* 722–723.

Larson, J. (1989). Validation of the defining characteristics of disturbance in self-esteem in patients with anorexia nervosa. In R.M. Carroll-Johnson (Ed.), *Classification of nursing diagnoses: Proceedings of the eighth conference of the North American Nursing Diagnosis Association* (pp. 307–312). Philadelphia: J.B. Lippincott.

Loomis, M.E., O'Toole, A.W., Brown, M.S., Pothier, P., West, P., & Wilson, H.S. (1987). Development of a classification system for psychiatric-mental health nursing: Individual responses class. *Archives of Psychiatric Nursing, 1*(1), 16–24.

McFarland, G.K., & Wasli, E.L. (1986). *Nursing diagnoses and process in psychiatric mental health nursing.* Philadelphia: J.B. Lippincott.

Ormiston, S., Barrett, N., Binder, R., & Molyneux, V. (1989). A partially computerized treatment plan. *Hospital and Community Psychiatry, 40*(5), 531–533.

O'Toole, A.W., & Loomis, M.E. (1989). Revision of the phenomena of concern for psychiatric-mental health nursing. *Archives of Psychiatric Nursing, 3*(5), 288–309.

Parsons, P.J. (1986). Building better treatment plans. *Journal of Psychosocial Nursing, 24*(4), 8–14.

Reed, C. (1987). Patient care conferences: 3 fast steps to better patient care plans. *Nursing 87, 17*(3), 66.

Sanger, E., Thomas, M.D., & Whitney, J.D. (1988). A guide for nursing assessment of psychiatric inpatients. *Archives of Psychiatric Nursing, 2*(6), 334–338.

Schaefer, C.E., & Millman, H.L. (1977). *Therapies for children.* San Francisco: Jossey-Bass.

Tanner, C.A. (1984). Diagnostic problem-solving strategies. In D.L. Carnevali, P.H. Mitchell, N.F. Woods, & C.A. Tanner (Eds.), *Diagnostic reasoning in nursing* (pp. 83–104). Philadelphia: J.B. Lippincott.

Thomas, M.D., Sanger, E., & Whitney, J.D. (1986). Nursing diagnosis of depression: Clinical identification on an inpatient unit. *Journal of Psychosocial Nursing, 24*(8), 6–12.

Thomas, M.D., Sanger, E., Wolf-Wilets, V., & Whitney, J.D. (1988). Nursing diagnoses of patients with manic and thought disorders. *Archives of Psychiatric Nursing, 2*(6), 339–344.

Townstend, M.C. (1988). *Nursing diagnoses in psychiatric nursing: A pocket guide for care plan construction.* Philadelphia: F.A. Davis.

Williams, J.B.W., & Wilson, H.S. (1982). A psychiatric nursing perspective of DSM-III. *Journal of Psychosocial Nursing, 20*(4), 14–20.

Wilson, H.S. (1989). Field trials of the phenomena of concern for psychiatric-mental health nursing: Proposed methodology. *Archives of Psychiatric Nursing, 3*(5), 305–308.

7

Selection of Treatment Modalities

Charlotte A. Herrick, Lynne Goodykoontz, and Robert H. Herrick

After reading this chapter, the reader will be able to:

1. explain the use of Neuman's systems model as a guide in the selection of various treatment modalities when planning a continuum of care for disturbed children and their families
2. identify stressors and three levels of responses to the stressors
3. select appropriate settings based on the level of responses to stressors
4. describe the criteria for the selection of different group, family, and individual treatment modalities
5. identify the indications, contraindications, and selection criteria for strategies within modalities
6. describe current research and its clinical implications for selecting treatment modalities

A major goal of health care planning for children and adolescents with mental disorders is to select the most appropriate and least intrusive treatment modality within the least restrictive setting. The sociocultural aspects of treatment and the economic resources available also require consideration. A systems model for nursing provides a conceptual framework for assessing and planning to meet the mental health care needs of emotionally disturbed children and their families.

NEUMAN'S NURSING SYSTEMS MODEL

In the nursing systems model developed by Neuman (1989), which is based on systems theory, individuals, families, groups, and communities are viewed as open systems within which internal and external environmental factors interact. Individual family members are interdependent, and each one's problems affect other family members and the family as a whole. A child's symptom may be the presenting problem; however, interpersonal factors are also considered in the analysis. In addition, although a child's symptom may be a reflection of family problems, a child may have some intrapsychic problems that also must be addressed.

Neuman's model has been successfully used as a guide for nursing assessment and intervention for a dysfunctional family (Herrick & Goodykoontz, 1989). In the model, each system has a center core that contains the resources and energy to drive the system to obtain a "steady state" for self-regulation, homeostasis, and growth and development (Neuman, 1989; Figure 7-1). The flexible line of defense defines the outer boundary of the system and constantly expands or contracts in response to internal and external biopsychosocial and developmental stressors. The normal line of defense maintains the system's state of wellness by developing, over time, coping mechanisms that provide resources for self-regulation. The lines of resistance serve to stabilize and return the system to health if the line of defense (e.g., the immune system) has been penetrated.

Health and illness are viewed along a continuum and are dependent on the stressors encountered and an individual's or system's responses. Health results from the stability of the normal line of defense, and illness is the reaction of stressors with the lines of resistance (Neuman, 1989). Nursing's goal is to assist individuals, families, groups, and communities to achieve and maintain wellness by purposeful interventions intended to reduce the impact of stressors that threaten optimal functioning (Cross, 1985).

SELECTION OF MODALITY USING NEUMAN'S MODEL

In planning a continuum of care for children and adolescents, nurses may select a treatment modality by using the systems model developed by Neuman (1989). The components of Neuman's model are: (1) identifying the source and type of stressors, (2) determining the level of response and selecting the setting, and (3) identifying the system of focus to select the treatment modality and strategies within a modality (Table 7-1).

A nurse bases a treatment plan on the assessment data, including: (1) the system targeted for change (i.e., the individual, family, group, or community), (2) stressors and the response components, (3) resources, (4) goals, and (5) anticipated outcomes. The term *system*, unless otherwise specified, reflects both the child and the family.

Jimmy, a 9-year-old, was referred because of destructive and impulsive behaviors. Adopted as a baby, he was the youngest of four adopted children. The adoptive parents knew very little of his prenatal history, although they knew that the delivery had been normal. His mother, a homemaker, suspected that Jimmy was different from the other children just prior to his entering school, but assumed that the hyperactivity was a result of the added stimulation of the older children. Subsequently, it

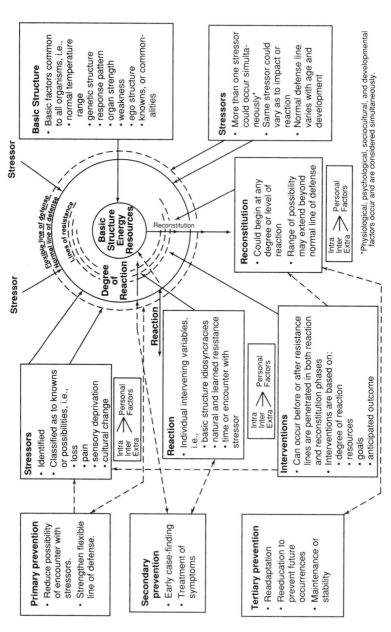

Figure 7-1 The Neuman Systems Model. *Source:* From *The Neuman Systems Model*, 2nd ed., (p. 31) by B. Neuman (Ed.), 1989, Norwalk, CT: Appleton and Lange. Copyright 1989 by Appleton and Lange. Reprinted by permission.

Table 7-1 Components of Neuman's Systems Model for Selection of Treatment Modalities

Component One

Identify the source of stressors:
  Extrasystem
  Intersystem
  Intrasystem
	Identify the type of stressors:
	  Psychological
	  Sociocultural
	  Physiological

Component Two

Identify the level of response:
  Primary
  Secondary
  Tertiary
	Select the setting:
	  Community
	  Outpatient
	  Partial hospitalization
	  Hospitalization
	  Residential care

Component Three

Identify the system of focus to
select the treatment modality:
  Group
  Family
  Individual
	Select strategies within the
	modality:
	  Individual counseling
	  Play therapy
	  Behavior therapy

was determined that Jimmy was not only hyperactive, but also learning-disabled. Jimmy's father, a businessman, moved the family to another town in order to invest in a new venture that was failing. The boy's hyperactivity escalated after the move. The mother felt that Jimmy's impulsiveness was beyond her control. Daily, the neighbors complained that Jimmy had committed some act of vandalism. He ran his bike into cars and set fires in the neighborhood. In fact, he was fascinated by fire. His parents were concerned about his safety and also the safety of the neighborhood.

The financial stress of the new venture necessitated the father's working extra hours away from home on weekends. Although he was a loving spouse and father, he was unavailable to meet his family's emotional needs. The mother, who was chronically depressed, had been self-medicated on antidepressants since Jimmy had been identified as learning-disabled, 4 years previously.

Component One: Stressors (Source and Type)

Stressors, which may be internal, external, universal, or specific to the individual, have the potential to disrupt homeostasis. The assessment of the stressor component includes the determination of the type, number, strength, and length of time with the encountering stressor. Stressors may be

1. extrasystem or extrapersonal. For example, a child's symptoms may reflect a father's job loss due to a failing economy.
2. intersystem or interpersonal. For example, a child's symptoms may result from conflicts between persons or systems. Parent-child conflicts that reinforce maladaptive behaviors are intersystem problems.
3. intrasystem or intrapersonal. For example, psychological, sociocultural, or biological forces within the individual may cause temper tantrums, oppositional behavior, and hyperactivity.

All three types of stressors—extrasystem, intersystem, and intrasystem —were identified in the case of Jimmy and his family. Extrasystem stressors were the financial stress and the recent move. Intersystem stressors developed between the mother and child, as her depression and his hyperactivity affected each other in a dynamic way. The mother's depression and the child's hyperactivity also represented intrasystem stressors. It was evident that the type, number, and severity of stressors penetrated the family's line of defense and resistance, resulting in the family's disequilibrium. The nursing diagnosis developed for the mother was Ineffective Individual Coping Related to Depression, as evidenced by chronic fatigue, tearfulness, inability to set limits with her children, and hostility toward educators and health care providers; for the child, Disturbance in Self-esteem Related to Learning Disability and Overactivity, as evidenced by poor impulse control; for the father, Ineffective Family Coping Related to Inadequate Understanding of Family Members' Needs and the Paternal Role Required to Meet Their Needs.

Component Two: Level of Response and Setting

The assessment of the response includes the: (1) symptoms, (2) targeted subsystem or organ involvement, and (3) severity of the response. Responses to stress may occur at the primary, secondary, or tertiary levels. At the primary level, there is total resistance to the penetration of the normal line of defense. Consequently, no symptoms occur (Cross, 1985). Secondary level responses occur when the line of defense has been penetrated, and they require interventions to strengthen the defenses. Tertiary level responses require multiple interventions to reconstitute and stabilize the child or adolescent and family.

When planning a continuum of care, the selection of a setting for treatment follows the assessment of the impact of a stressful event and the severity of the response. Each setting has an overall goal: (1) at the primary level, prevention; (2) at the secondary level, early intervention; and (3) at the tertiary level, cure and/or care for those who are unable to care for themselves.

Primary Level of Response: Community

The nursing goal at the primary level of response is to identify populations at risk, such as people who have experienced a recent trauma, single poor mothers, or teen-aged parents of firstborn children. Community-focused strategies directed at healthy populations include consultation-liaison to agencies, personnel who serve children and families, and community education focused on parents and community leaders. Primary level strategies deal with those at risk for mental illness before expensive treatments are necessary and facilitate self-care.

At this level of response, nurses act to strengthen the flexible and normal lines of defense in order to reduce the impact of a stressful event. Nursing care at the primary level can be provided in a community setting and is intended to prevent mental illness and promote mental health.

Secondary Level of Response: Outpatient Services and Partial
* Hospitalization*

When nursing care has failed to strengthen the flexible and normal lines of defense adequately, symptoms occur. The goal of interventions for responses at the secondary level is to reestablish homeostasis. Discomfort stimulates patients to seek mental health care in secondary level agencies. Early signs of distress in children and adolescents include poor peer relationships, poor school performance, a variety of somatic complaints, sadness, listlessness, timidity, withdrawn behavior, distractibility, hyperactivity, restlessness, sleeplessness, irritability, and temper tantrums. A child's discomfort may be a reflection of family distress and/or may spread to other family members.

Settings in which secondary levels of responses are treated include community-based treatment centers that provide an array of mental health services (e.g., outpatient services, partial hospitalization or day treatment). Nursing care at the secondary level of response does not require the patient's removal from the family or community. Along a continuum of care, these services are the "least restrictive," the patient voluntarily seeks care, and family and community relationships continue.

The goals of outpatient services are to provide access to care during the acute phase of a crisis in order to prevent hospitalization or to facilitate the patient's reentry into the community after discharge from an inpatient setting. Partial hospitalization provides a structured milieu in the least restrictive setting. Outcome research has demonstrated that partial hospitalization is superior to inpatient care for those who do not need a protective environment (Frances, Clarkin, & Perry, 1984).

Because outpatient services allow the child or adolescent to remain both at home and in school, they require the least adjustment. The focus of treatment remains on the family and the community rather than solely on the child or adolescent. Outpatient care does not take away the family's responsibility for the child, however, family members' involvement is expected.

Tertiary Level of Response: Hospitalization and Residential Care

When symptoms are severe or persistent enough to warrant placement in a more protective environment or if the family is too dysfunctional to support the youngster, a setting appropriate to this tertiary level of response is required. Intensive therapeutic regimens in an acute care setting may be short-term and crisis-oriented, while treatment in a residential program may extend over a long time. In either case, the youngster is separated from the family and the community.

The residential setting is generally associated with long-term treatment. The goal is to restructure the personality so that the highest level of wellness can be achieved; this goal is accomplished by means of a psychosocial framework, with the medical model as an adjunct. The residential setting provides a refuge for disturbed children whose families are too dysfunctional to care for them or for children whose behaviors are too difficult to be cared for in foster homes (Harper & Geraty, 1986; Harren, 1964). The nursing model of care in these settings focuses on management of the milieu.

Inpatient settings integrate the expertise of the various disciplines, as they involve several treatment modalities that culminate in a higher intensity of treatment. Consequently, some patients respond more quickly to treatment in a inpatient setting. A secure, protective environment intervenes in destructive behaviors. Separation from the family disrupts destructive family interactions, allowing time for healing. Close observations by the nursing staff provide monitoring of the patient's responses to treatment.

> It was determined during the intake examination that, because of her depression, Jimmy's mother was not capable of providing the consistent limits that Jimmy required to intervene in his potentially dangerous behaviors. She needed time to recover from her own depression. His father was not available to set limits or to assist the mother. Because Jimmy needed a more protective and structured environment, he was hospitalized in a psychiatric short-term care facility for children. This environment protected both Jimmy and the neighborhood from his dangerous fire setting. When protection was no longer needed, he was transferred to an outpatient program to facilitate his reentry into school and the neighborhood.

Component Three: System of Focus and Treatment Modality

The source of the stressor determines the system of focus for treatment. The three foci are extrasystem (group), intersystem (family), and intrasystem (individual). The appropriate treatment modality is dependent not only on the source of the stressors, but also on the needs of each child or adolescent and on several other considerations (Table 7-2). Developmental issues and the motivation of the parents to participate in therapy are also important.

Extrasystem Focus: Group Therapy

If the source of the youngster's stressors are extrasystem, the treatment modality should include the community and peer groups. An examination of the youngster's environment may point to the need for some kind of environmental manipulation, such as removing the youngster from the home or changing school classrooms. The assessment may also reveal poor peer relationships that may require a change in the youngster's interpersonal behaviors. In this case, a group modality is appropriate if the goals of the group match the therapeutic goals for the child or adolescent.

Group therapy focuses on relationships and is effective for specific problems, particularly for adolescents who are impaired because of alcohol or drug abuse (Bingham & Barger, 1985; Critchley, 1982; Gilbert, 1988). Group therapy for children mostly takes the form of parallel play therapy; for older, grade school children, a combination of play and talking therapy; for adolescents, activity and talking therapies (MacLennon, 1986). For children and adolescents, group therapy improves their social and communication skills through role modeling, feedback, and practice. For example, small children learn the social skills of taking turns, sharing, and participating in cooperative play.

The biggest disadvantage of a children's group is the contagious effect that the children may have on one another. Aggressive and impulsive behaviors may spread throughout the group, creating chaos that is destructive for the group and for each member. Furthermore, a group may provoke extreme anxiety in some children, which may stimulate acting out behaviors.

Intersystem Focus: Family Therapy

Children often carry the family's anxiety or act out family conflicts. If the child's problems result from parental or intergenerational conflicts that have led to a breakdown in communication, the source of the stressors is intersystem and the focus of treatment should be the family. For example, a nursing diagnosis of Ineffective Child and Family Coping Related to Dysfunctional Communication Patterns, as evidenced by anorexia, delinquent behavior, or phobias, requires family therapy (Gurman & Kniskern, 1981). The major goal is to change family interactions rather than to change an individual's behavior. Other goals include helping family members to achieve autonomy while belonging to the family and improving communication within the family.

The advantages of family therapy are that it strengthens family ties, improves communication, and reduces scapegoating of the child (labeling him or her as

Table 7-2 System of Focus Considerations for Selecting a Treatment Modality

Indications	Other Selection Criteria	Contraindications
Modality: Group Therapy (Extrasystem)		
Timid, withdrawn children who need multiple relationship experiences	Source of the stressors: extrasystem	Children with fragile egos
Adolescents with authority conflicts who need confrontation and peer support	Timing: the working phase where rapport has been established	Extremely anxious children
Adolescents' denial of reality, which requires confrontation and peer support	Child responsive to verbal limits	Extremely agitated children
Need for role models for identification	Availability of a group that is the same developmentally with similar goals	Undersocialized and sociopathic children
Need to learn social and communication skills	Balance between aggressive and timid children	Acutely psychotic children
Socially isolated children	Parental compliance	Extremely aggressive children
	Least costly format	Hyperactive children who are extremely disruptive and have poor impulse control
		Conflict between therapeutic goals of the child and those of the group
Modality: Family Therapy (Intersystem)		
Structural problems (e.g., symbiotic relationship between the identified child/patient and the mother)	Source of the stressors: intersystem	Family members so disengaged that there is no commitment to the family or one spouse has already decided to separate from the family
Dysfunctional family communication patterns	Family commitment to improving family functioning	Family climate so noxious that separation of the child from the family is required for the health of the child
Developmental stalls	Family willingness to examine alternate perceptions and life styles	Poverty of family coping skills or extreme resistance to therapeutic interventions
More than one symptomatic member	Family climate hostile, but not lethal	Adolescent ready developmentally to leave home
Identified member is scapegoated	Family capable of learning to listen and convey respect to each other	Refusal of some members to cooperate with therapeutic prescriptions, including regular attendance
Development of symptoms in one member after another member becomes asymptomatic	Willing participation of all members	
Conflictual interpersonal relationships	Individual format unsuccessful	
Enmeshed family	Cost-effective if more than one family member is symptomatic	

Modality: Individual Therapy (Intrasystem)

Children who are in need of undivided attention

Children who do not tolerate groups of people (e.g., disruptive, impulsive, distractible, highly anxious, aggressive, and/or psychotic children)

Severity of symptoms requiring a 1:1 format

Source of the stressors: intrasystem

Timing: initial phase during the assessment process, which may continue as indicated

Parents who are unavailable and/or resistive to family-focused interventions

Most costly of all formats

Family, school, peer and community involvements in problems

Dependent children, enmeshed in family dynamics or scapegoated by the family

Children who have poor interpersonal skills, are social isolated and in need of peer support, requiring group therapy "bad" or "sick"). The participation of several generations provides a historical perspective that increases insight. The family's climate improves when problems are reframed without blame, but with shared responsibility.

The pitfalls of family therapy include the loss of privacy if intimate secrets are revealed. As Napier and Whitaker (1978) pointed out, however, the impact of this problem may be minimal, because it appears that families work hard to keep secrets that every family member knows anyway. In addition, children under the age of 3 may be distracting in a family session, and volatile families may be destructive to the process.

Family therapy is preferred for working with children whose symptoms reflect family pathology. This type of therapy depends not only on specific selection criteria, however, but also on the cooperation of family members and the availability of professionals interested in providing family therapy. If a family is resistive, an individual focus may be necessary even if the family's functioning is pathological.

Intrasystem Focus: Individual Therapy

If, during the assessment phase of the nursing process, the problematic responses are found to be intrasystem (i.e., intrapsychic, behavioral, physiological or developmental), the focus of the intervention should be on the individual. Work with the family can be done conjointly or with the child and family together after the acute symptoms subside.

In nursing, the individual focus takes place in the one-to-one relationship (Doona, 1979). The one-to-one relationship takes many forms, depending on the orientation of the nurse, the needs of the client, and the client's stage of growth and development. Strategies that are useful within the context of the one-to-one relationship are play therapy, talking therapy, behavior modification, cognitive therapy, and puppet therapy. Within the therapeutic relationship, the child receives, often for the first time, concentrated attention. Herein lies the power of the therapeutic relationship to heal.

> For Jimmy and his family, the altered individual and family processes necessitated a combination of individual, family, and group treatment modalities to reduce the impact of the extrasystem stressors (the financial stress and the recent move) and to intervene in the intersystem stressors between mother and child, as well as the individual stressors. The mother's depression and Jimmy's hyperactivity were pathologically intertwined, and both received individual therapy.
>
> Besides hospitalization for Jimmy, therapy was needed for the family to interrupt the vicious cycle between mother and child, and to re-involve the father emotionally. Although the mother's depression was an intrasystem problem that required individual psychotherapy, her resentment of the father's continual absence from the family augmented her depressed state. Once the mother could mobilize enough energy to be-

come an active participant in the family business and the father became an active participant at home, the mother's symptoms began to subside. Jimmy, who felt emotionally isolated from the family, needed an opportunity to belong; family therapy provided this opportunity. The family met other selection criteria for family therapy as well: there was more than one symptomatic member; the child was the scapegoat; and the family was committed to solving its problems and willing to learn to convey respect even to Jimmy, the scapegoat. Structural problems revolved around the father's total authority even when absent, which contributed to the mother's sense of helplessness.

Group therapy for mothers of learning-disabled children provided Jimmy's mother with badly needed social support in a new community, and the inpatient group offered Jimmy an opportunity to establish healthy peer relationships.

Selection of Strategies

Nurses' roles are related to strategies within a modality, which may include individual counseling, play therapy, and behavior therapy. In play therapy and counseling, the nurse provides a supportive therapeutic relationship to enable the patient to express thoughts and feelings. In behavior modification, the nurse provides reinforcers to change behavior. A strategy is selected based on the youngster's specific needs (Table 7-3) and may be provided within the context of group, family or individual treatment modalities.

Individual Play/Talking Strategy

Psychodynamic strategies such as individual counseling/talking strategies and play therapy are directed at intrapsychic problems. Among the nursing diagnoses related to intrapsychic conflicts in children are Ineffective Individual Coping Related to Anxiety, Adjustment Disorders, and/or Depression, as evidenced by symptoms that may range from hyperactivity to underactivity. Play or talking strategies allow the nurse to give the child or adolescent undivided attention and to meet the youngster's needs without concern for others. The one-to-one relationship provides a model for intimacy that may be generalized to other relationships. This asset is especially valuable for children who have never formed a trusting relationship with an adult. The trusting relationship provides freedom for the youngster to express feelings without censure and, thus, to work through emotional conflicts. Younger children who do not have the verbal skills to talk about their feelings may play out their feelings through art or other play activities (MacLennon, 1986; Wilkinson, 1983).

Play or talking strategies are selected on the basis of the youngster's age or stage of growth and development. Whether play or talking therapy, whether con-

Table 7-3 Strategies within Modalities

Indications	Other Selection Criteria	Contraindications
Talking Therapies: Counseling/Psychotherapy		
Intrapsychic symptoms	Children who need the opportunity for catharsis	Symptoms that require more appropriate treatment
Children motivated to overcome resistance and to participate in therapy	Children who need the opportunity to experience a trusting 1:1 relationship with an adult	Regressive behaviors
Fairly strong ego skills		Poor impulse control, exhibited by acting out behaviors
Good verbal skills	Appropriate stage of growth and development	Poor cognitive skills
Intellectual ability to gain insight	Least intrusive treatment modality	Poor communication skills
		Exhibition of sociopathic behaviors
Play Therapy		
All of the above *except*: good ego, verbal and intellectual skills	All of the above	Symptoms that require more appropriate treatment ONLY
	All preschool and latency age children, even regressed, developmentally delayed and autistic children	
Behavior Therapy		
Symptoms that are observable and measurable	Behavior that is dangerous, requiring immediate intervention (e.g., head banging)	Inability to apply the plan consistently
Problem under environmental control as contingencies	Good communication among change agents	Lack of motivation and/or cooperation among change agents
Problem that is a result of faculty learning	Availability of a leader to coordinate the plan	Problem that is intrapsychic so that the child and therapist need to understand the underlying intrapsychic conflicts
Failure of other therapies	Level of cooperation and motivation	Problem that is somatic, requiring medications
Limited cognitive abilities	Appropriate adjunct to other therapies in a treatment program	Need for children to emote or to express feelings
Limited ability to communicate to a therapist	Direction in structuring the milieu	Family problems or lack of skills that make them poor change agents
Agreement of child/family to the therapeutic plan with informed consent	Parental guidelines for discipline; good parental motivation	

centrated for a specific time in a therapy session or provided as needed on an inpatient unit, individualized one-to-one therapy is often initiated as an assessment tool; it is also frequently used in conjunction with other treatment strategies, such as behavior modification strategies (Critchley, 1985).

Behavior Modification Strategy

Nurses may use behavior modification or behavioral strategies to change learned maladaptive behavior. The critical assumption is that learned behavior can be unlearned (Closurdo, 1975). If persons in the child's environment, including nurses, parents, and teachers, act as change agents by consistently reinforcing the desired behavior, the child will replace maladaptive behavior with more appropriate behavior. Changing the environment may include removing the child from the home to a more structured environment, such as a hospital, or it may focus on teaching the parents and teachers to be change agents.

Outcome research indicates that behavior modification is effective for the relief of observable and measurable symptoms (Berni & Fordyce, 1977). In fact, it often relieves some symptoms faster than does talking therapy. Behavior modification has been successful with behaviors that have not responded to other therapies and with populations that have cognitive and communication deficits. The less complex the behavior, the easier it is to modify. Behavior modification strategies may either increase or decrease a behavior, however, and requires close observation and documentation to select appropriate reinforcers. It can be used effectively with groups of children or individually.

Behavior modification strategies may require additional parental informed consent and, if possible, informed consent from the youngster. In behavioral strategies, the nurse is largely responsible for the intervention and its application. Ideally, the primary care nurse facilitates cooperation of change agents, which include the nursing staff, parents, teachers, therapists, and physicians. Because consistency is required, it is often easier to implement a behavior modification program by means of primary nursing in the hospital (Berni & Fordyce, 1977). Patient education about techniques and expected outcomes promotes an informed choice.

Upon his hospitalization, Jimmy was examined by a neurologist, who found soft neurological signs typical of an attention deficit disorder with hyperactivity. The nursing diagnosis was Impaired Motor Activity Related to Hyperactivity, as evidenced by poor coordination and overactivity. Methylphenidate (Ritalin) was prescribed. Because of the complexity of the symptoms and the family system, a combination of strategies was selected.

Jimmy responded well to play therapy and behavior modification. At first, the hyperactivity was clearly evident, as Jimmy literally scaled the walls and randomly threw toys everywhere. After limits were set around destructive behaviors, he could finally focus on a task; he adjusted to the predictability of the milieu, and the medication reduced the hyperactivity. Then, he used the toys as a means of expression. He played with a toy hospital, locked a doll in it, and threw away the key. The feelings of abandonment and rejection by his family were identified. Jimmy gradually progressed from playing with toys to playing and talking simultaneously. He drew a picture of a family of spotted dogs with one all black puppy placed away from the rest of the family. The feelings of being "left out" and "no good" were discussed. As time progressed, the play became incidental to talking as he played ball with the therapist while discussing thoughts and feelings. Jimmy received play therapy twice a week and family therapy once a week. Group and behavior modification were part of the daily structure of the inpatient milieu. He was discharged 2 months later.

The continuing care outpatient plan included special education for emotionally conflicted and learning-disabled children, occupational therapy to enhance his poor coordination, and play and family therapy at a local mental health center provided by a clinical nurse specialist who was able to follow him from the inpatient setting to an outpatient program. Jimmy's mother continued to participate in a psychoeducational group focused on helping mothers manage their own stress and cope with their challenging children.

The father's business improved so that he was no longer away every weekend and, therefore, contributed emotionally to the care of the children. The mother's depression improved to the point that she no longer needed an antidepressant and happily worked in the father's business. Jimmy's behaviors improved, but he continued to require Ritalin with intermittent drug holidays and a small classroom setting to deal with the hyperactivity and learning disabilities.

Issues Related to Selecting a Modality and Strategy

Nurses should consider clients' coping skills and prior levels of functioning, as well as their previous responses to treatment modalities and strategies, in selecting a treatment modality for a youngster who needs psychiatric care. Strategies that are least intrusive in the least restrictive setting are preferred. Interacting variables include the developmental age of the youngster; for example, the younger the age, the more likely the treatment setting will be in the community—especially if the family is intact and cooperative. Other considerations are the availability of services, the financial resources of the family, and the expertise of the health care professionals.

Child psychiatric nurses may encounter ethical dilemmas when selecting a modality or strategy. For example, a nurse may consider family therapy the modality of choice, but it may be necessary to use individual strategies if all the family members will not participate in therapy. A child may benefit most from a behavior modification approach, but the nurse may not be knowledgeable about this approach. Does the nurse refer the patient to another colleague or use the intervention that may be less helpful? The solution is not clear, as is true of all ethical dilemmas.

Because of their holistic orientation, nurses often select a combination of modalities and strategies during the planning process. A combination of modalities may have an additive effect, or one treatment may prepare the patient for another. Planning a combination of modalities enlarges the focus from the individual to the individual within a system. Nurses participate in many different treatment modalities in a variety of settings and perform a variety of professional roles.

RESEARCH

There is a paucity of research on the selection of treatment modalities in the field of child/adolescent psychiatric nursing. Problems often arise in studying the relationship of specific strategies to treatment outcomes because of ethical constraints, as well as because of the diversity of strategies and variations among children. The lack of agreement on therapeutic success or failure also complicates research. For example, for one patient, hospitalization represents relapse; for another, however, it represents prevention of relapse (Baier, 1988). The fact that few nurses in child/adolescent psychiatric nursing conduct research may be attributed to the scarcity of literature in the area or to poor utilization of prepared nurses in positions that serve children/adolescents (Pothier, Norbeck, & Laliberte, 1985).

There have been some outcome studies to identify program strategies that enhance behavioral and academic change. Outcome research has provided evidence to support the usefulness of primary prevention (Beard, 1980; Panzarine & Elster, 1982) and brief hospitalization followed by day treatment (Baenen, Stephens, & Glenwick, 1986; Frances, Clarkin, & Perry, 1984). Barack (1986) studied 92 children who had been admitted to an inpatient setting in order to determine the differences between hospitalized children and their peers who received care in an outpatient setting. Hospitalized children tended to be older, and their conditions were more often diagnosed as "conduct disorders" or Impaired Individual Coping Related to Ineffective Parenting, as exhibited by impulsive and destructive behaviors. Each of these hospitalized children had experienced a critical event within a month prior to admission.

Studies in the nursing literature usually focus on the group, family, and the one-to-one nurse/client relationship within the inpatient setting. Hinds (1988) found a correlation between the "caring behaviors" of nurses and "hopefulness" among adolescent substance abusers, which supported nurses' use of caring interpersonal skills to enhance adolescents' positive view of themselves.

Studies related to nursing interventions are often more concerned with nursing issues than with specific strategies. When interactions were examined between nurses and a group of hospitalized, behaviorally disordered children who had been sexually abused, for example, the specific issues identified included: (1) difficult child behaviors, (2) parent-related problems, (3) the maintenance of a therapeutic milieu, and (4) countertransference issues (Kohan, Pothier, & Norbeck, 1987).

In spite of some limitations in terms of scientific merit, research findings for clinical practice have merit in terms of clinical relevance (Fawcett, 1982). The information provided by research guides a practitioner in selecting appropriate interventions. A case study, such as the study of an autistic child who was more desirous of human interaction on a different level after confinement to a sensory impaired environment (Schecter & Primeaux, 1971), can have an impact on a nursing care plan, for example. The results are the antithesis of many nurses' assumption that autistic children need human stimulation. In a review of more than 400 outcome studies, however, Smith, Glass, and Miller (1980) concluded that, even with a large data base, the data are insufficient to determine which technique is best for which patient. They noted that "clinical wisdom must still prevail" (p. 143). In planning a continuum of care, each clinical situation is unique, and choices must be tailored to the individual.

REFERENCES

Baenen, R.S., Stephens, M.A., & Glenwick, D.S. (1986). Outcome in psychoeducational day school programs: A review. *American Journal of Orthopsychiatry, 56,* 263–270.

Baier, M. (1988). Why research doesn't yield treatment. *Journal of Psychosocial Nursing and Mental Health Services, 26*(5), 29–33.

Barack, R.S. (1986). Hospitalization of emotionally disturbed children: Who gets hospitalized and why. *American Journal of Orthopsychiatry, 56,* 317–319.

Beard, M.T. (1980). Interpersonal trust, life events and coping in an ethnic adolescent population. *Journal of Psychosocial Nursing and Mental Health Services, 18*(11), 12–20.

Berni, R., & Fordyce, W.E. (1977). *Behavior modification and the nursing process.* St. Louis: C.V. Mosby.

Bingham, A., & Barger, J. (1985). Children of alcoholic families: A group treatment approach for latency age children. *Journal of Psychosocial Nursing, 23*(12), 13–15.

Closurdo, J.S. (1975). Behavior modification and the nursing process. *Perspectives in Psychiatric Care, 13*(1), 25–36.

Critchley, D.L. (1982). Therapeutic group work with abused preschool children. *Perspectives in Psychiatric Care, 20,* 70–85.

Critchley, D.L. (1985). Individual and group play therapy. In D.L. Critchley & J.T. Maurin (Eds.), *The clinical specialist in psychiatric mental health nursing* (pp. 229–510). New York: John Wiley & Sons.

Cross, J.R. (1985). Betty Neuman. In J.G. George (Ed.), *Nursing theories: The base for professional nursing* (2nd ed., pp. 258–286). Englewood Cliffs, NJ: Prentice-Hall.

Doona, M.E. (1979). *Travelbee's intervention in psychiatric nursing.* Philadelphia: F.A. Davis.

Fawcett, J. (1982). Utilization of nursing research findings. *Image, 14,* 57–59.

Frances, A., Clarkin, J., & Perry, S. (1984). *Differential therapeutics in psychiatry: The art and science of treatment selection.* New York: Brunner/Mazel.

Gilbert, C.M. (1988). Sexual abuse and group therapy. *Journal of Psychosocial Nursing, 26*(5), 19–23.

Gurman, A.S., & Kniskern, D.P. (1981). *Handbook of family therapy* (3rd ed.). New York: Brunner/Mazel.

Harper, G., & Geraty, R. (1986). Hospital and residential treatment. In A.J. Solnit, D.J. Cohen, & J.E. Schowalter (Eds.), *Child psychiatry* (Vol. 6, pp. 477–496). New York: Basic Books.

Harren, M.C. (1964). Residential treatment for the emotionally disturbed child. *Journal of Psychiatric Nursing, 2,* 112–115.

Herrick, C.A., & Goodykoontz, L. (1989). Neuman's systems model for nursing practice as a conceptual framework for a family assessment. *Journal of Child and Adolescent Psychiatric Nursing, 2,* 61–67.

Hinds, P.S. (1988). The relationship of nurses' caring behaviors with hopefulness and health care outcomes in adolescents. *Archives of Psychiatric Nursing, 2*(1), 21–29.

Kohan, M.J., Pothier, P., & Norbeck, J.S. (1987). Hospitalized children with history of sexual abuse. *American Journal of Orthopsychiatry, 57,* 258–264.

MacLennon, B.W. (1986). Child group psychotherapy in special settings. In I. E. Riester & I.A. Kraft (Eds.), *Child group psychotherapy* (pp. 83–103). Norwalk, CT: International Universities Press.

Napier, A.Y., & Whitaker, C.A. (1978). *The family crucible.* New York: Harper & Row.

Neuman, B. (1989). *Neuman's systems model.* Norwalk, CT: Appleton-Century-Crofts.

Panzarine, S., & Elster, A.B. (1982). Prospective adolescent fathers: Stresses during pregnancy and implications for nursing interventions. *Journal of Psychosocial Nursing and Mental Health Services, 20*(7), 21–23.

Pothier, P.C., Norbeck, J.S., & Laliberte, M. (1985). Child psychiatric nursing: The gap between need and utilization. *Journal of Psychosocial Nursing and Mental Health Services, 23*(7), 18–23.

Schecter, M.D., & Primeaux, M. (1971). The utilization of nursing staff in a psychiatric research project. *Journal of Psychosocial Nursing and Mental Health Services, 9*(1), 7–10.

Smith, M.L., Glass, G.V., & Miller, T.L. (1980). *The benefits of psychotherapy.* Baltimore: Johns Hopkins University Press.

Wilkinson, T.R. (1983). *Child and adolescent psychiatric nursing.* London: Blackwell Scientific Publications.

8

Legal Issues in Child and Adolescent Mental Health Nursing

Alyson Moore Ross and Virginia Trotter Betts

After reading this chapter, the reader will be able to:

1. explain society's changing views of children and mental health over time
2. name and define key terms inherent in mental health law specific to the care of children and adolescents
3. identify and apply to the child/adolescent client the implications of the broad constitutional and statutory rights in mental health care
4. identify appropriate approaches to confidentiality and privileged communication
5. synthesize approaches to the daily nursing care of children and adolescents with enhanced awareness of legal parameters

No study of nursing is complete without careful attention to the legal parameters of professional practice. In no specialty of nursing is this more true than in psychiatric and mental health nursing. Because of the special needs and vulnerabilities of their clients, as well as the unique and intimate nature of the care that they provide, psychiatric and mental health nurses require a fundamental knowledge of and attention to the legal aspects of their practice.

An added element for legal concern arises when the mental health care client is a child or adolescent. The peculiarities in the law concerning minors and the special treatment in the law of parent-child relationships complicate the already difficult issues inherent in mental health treatment.

HISTORICAL PERSPECTIVE

Society's View of the Child

The current U.S. view of the child and the rights of children is based on the import of English common law values. Children in 17th century England were perceived as property or "chattels" of their parents. Although parents had a duty to support, protect, and educate their children, there were no legal mechanisms to ensure that parents performed these duties (Blackstone, 1859). This notion of parental sovereignty was deeply engrained in the minds of the first settlers in Puritan New England. This is evidenced by the Massachusetts Stubborn Child Law of 1646, which authorized the death penalty for children whom their parents considered disobedient or "stubborn and rebellious" (Shurtleff, 1854). There is no evidence that this law was ever actually enforced, but it exemplifies the absolute authority and autonomy colonial parents held over their children.

The Industrial Revolution of the early 19th century prompted many changes in U.S. society. With the rapid influx of immigrants and the shift from rural to urban living, many poor children were forced to work long hours under inhumane conditions (de Leon Siantz, 1988). Concerned that children were being exposed to dangerous and exploitative work, social reformers advocated the enactment of child labor and compulsory education laws.

Despite the enactment of laws that legislated parental conduct, it was not until the late 19th century that the courts began actively to intervene when parental behavior did not meet acceptable standards. Illinois established the first juvenile court system in 1899. By 1930, all but two states had enacted such a system (Horowitz & Davidson, 1984).

Historical View of Mental Health Care and Mental Illness

The concepts of mental illness and mental health care have undergone a transformation similar to the evolution of the rights of children. Early beliefs about mental illness were based on superstition and supernatural forces. During the first three centuries A.D., the Greek and Roman cultures partially accepted the medical model of illness that is based on natural rather than supernatural causes. Nevertheless, the general public continued to view mental illness as a punishment from the angry gods (Mora, 1975).

The Middle Ages (500 to 1400 A.D.) marked a very dark period in the treatment of the mentally ill. During this time, few advances were made in the understanding and treatment of mental illnesses. The mentally ill were cared for in a neglectful and/or punitive fashion. This treatment of the mentally ill was carried over to Puritan New England in the early 16th century. The insane were cast out by their families and placed in jails or poorhouses where, shackled with handcuffs and leg irons, they were exhibited to the public for a fee.

The 19th century was a period of reform in the care of the mentally ill that corresponded with the advancement of children's rights. During this period, the Quakers were influential in humanizing the care of the mentally ill, and the first public mental hospitals were established.

In 1896, a psychologist, Lightner Witmer, established the first psychological clinic for emotionally disturbed children. During the next 30 years, the same period in which the juvenile justice systems were evolving across the United States, psychiatrists and psychologists were beginning to identify and describe psychopathologies specific to children. It was not until 1953, however, that the American Academy of Child Psychiatry was established.

Legal Status of Children and Adolescents in the 1990s

The age of majority is defined as the age at which the disabilities of childhood are removed and the individual legally becomes an adult. Majority or minority is not considered an inherent right. Rather, it is a legal concept subject to statutory limitations and exceptions. In recent years, many states have used this concept to allow minors more autonomy and authority over certain decisions.

On reaching majority status, the individual becomes free from parental control and authority (Horowitz & Davidson, 1984). Since the enactment of the Twenty-Sixth Amendment, giving all 18-year-olds the right to vote in federal elections, all but a few states have lowered the age of majority from 21 to 18 years. An individual who has attained the age of majority does not necessarily gain all the rights afforded to adults, however. For example, most states today continue to withhold the right to purchase alcoholic beverages until the age of 21.

Over the past several decades, the courts have recognized the increasing independence of adolescents and have developed by case law what is known as the "mature minor rule." In several states, minors as young as 14 have the right to consent to sexual intercourse, seek contraception and abortions, and consent to their own medical treatment for venereal disease and some types of psychiatric and mental health care (Guggenheim & Sussman, 1985).

Emancipation is a legal term used to describe the condition whereby a child, before reaching the age of majority, is considered free from parental authority and is regarded as an adult for some purposes. Emancipation may also release the parents from their rights and duties of child-rearing. A minor may become emancipated in one of two ways: first, a court may grant emancipation; second, a minor may become emancipated by getting married, by living separate and apart from the parents in a self-supporting manner, by entering the military, or by reaching an express agreement with the parents.

COMMITMENT

An individual is admitted to a mental health care institution under one of two methods: involuntary admission through commitment or voluntary admission. The method of admission directly determines the extent of liberty that the individual retains while a patient.

Involuntary Commitment

Civil commitment statutes for involuntary admissions to mental health care facilities allow the state to detain and treat an individual without the consent of the individual or the individual's family or guardian. Such an involuntary commitment is a judicial decision that is made by a judge, jury, or commission, depending on the legal requirements of the state. To be civilly committed, individuals must pose a threat to themselves or to society, or be unable to survive outside the institution alone or with the aid of family and friends (*O'Connor v. Donaldson*, 1975).

In addition to establishing the dangerousness of the individual, the state is required to show a specific standard of proof that the individual should be committed. In order to comply with the due process requirements of the Fourteenth Amendment, the state must establish the need for the involuntary commitment of an individual by "clear and convincing" evidence (*Addington v. Texas*, 1979). In the *Addington* ruling, the Supreme Court required the state to apply a standard of proof more substantial than "preponderance of the evidence," required in civil cases, and less substantial than "beyond reasonable doubt," required in criminal cases. This standard of proof is the minimum required, and many states have since adopted the stricter criminal standard of proof in their commitment statutes.

Although state laws vary significantly regarding commitment policies and procedures, most civil commitment statutes contain provisions for emergency hospitalization and treatment until a hearing can be held to determine the need for continued treatment. An emergency commitment is necessary when a mentally ill individual poses an immediate threat to self or others. The emergency commitment differs from the involuntary commitment in that it is time-limited and can range from a few hours to several days. For example, the state of Tennessee allows a patient to be held on an emergency commitment for a period of not more than 5 days, after which the patient must be released or given a probable cause hearing to determine whether a general involuntary commitment is necessary. (Tenn. Code Ann. §33-6-103, 1990).

Voluntary Admission

Nearly every state has adopted voluntary commitment statutes that enable competent individuals to admit themselves to a psychiatric facility. These statutes also allow the parent or guardian of a minor or incompetent adult to consent to the voluntary admission of the minor or ward. Under these voluntary commitment statutes, the individual who initially consented to the admission may release the patient from the institution at any time, as long as the facility receives adequate notification.

The issue of voluntary commitment becomes very complicated when it involves children and adolescents, as evidenced by the widely disparate mental health treatment statutes applicable to minors across the states. In addition, the mature and emancipated minor laws create many exceptions by which individuals who have not yet reached the age of majority may voluntarily admit themselves to a psychiatric care facility. Despite the complexity and fluidity of the laws, child and adolescent psychiatric nurses must be knowledgeable about their state's specific legal requirements regarding mature and emancipated minors, involuntary and voluntary commitment procedures, and both inpatient and outpatient mental health care.

Probably the most difficult commitment dilemma in child and adolescent psychiatry arises when a parent or guardian seeks to admit a minor child against the wishes of the child. In what is probably the most important case that affects child and adolescent psychiatry, the Supreme Court ruled on this issue in the case of *Parham v. J.R.* (1979). The plaintiffs in *Parham* were minors under the age of 18 who had been hospitalized in a Georgia state mental institution. The plaintiffs argued that the Georgia voluntary admission statute (Ga. Code Ann. §88-503.1, 1979), which authorized the superintendent or chief medical officer of a mental health care facility to admit a child on request of the parent or guardian, deprived them of their liberty without due process. Although the parent or guardian was free to discharge the patient at any time after the initial 5-day observation period, the patient had no voice in either the admission or the discharge process.

The Supreme Court upheld the constitutionality of the Georgia statute. The Court recognized the necessity of procedural safeguards to protect the interests of minors, but it concluded that most parents generally act in the best interests of their children. The Court held that, although the risk of error inherent in parental judgment justifies the necessity of an independent "neutral fact finder" to determine whether the statutory requirements of admission have been met, a more formal judicial (and adversarial) hearing is not necessary. In addition, the Court mandated a "periodic review" of the child's condition, although this review was not defined.

The requirements set forth in *Parham* are the minimum necessary to voluntarily commit a child. Several states, such as New Mexico, Texas, South Dakota, and Wisconsin, also require minors to be informed of their right to object to their commitment and to have an opportunity for a hearing (Morrisey, Hoffman, & Thrope, 1986).

Child and adolescent psychiatric nurses must become familiar with the voluntary and involuntary commitment statutes of the state in which they are practicing. In addition, a nurse should know that, although a child has been voluntarily admitted to a psychiatric care facility, there are mechanisms to ensure that the child will not be removed from the facility prematurely. Most institutions require written notice of the intent to remove a child from care. If the care-givers find that a child is in need of continued treatment, a judicial commitment may be obtained to keep the child in the institution.

LEGAL PRINCIPLES BASIC TO MENTAL HEALTH CARE

Informed Consent

The doctrine of informed consent is based on the principle that an individual has the basic and fundamental right to exercise control over his or her body (Morrisey,

Hoffman, & Thrope, 1986). Health care professionals who treat patients without their consent can be sued for the tort of assault and battery. Twenty-eight states have statutes governing informed consent to treatment, with the legal requirements remaining fairly uniform.

The consent process consists of an express understanding and agreement between the health care provider and the patient about what is and what is not to be done during treatment. The basic requirements include competence, information, and voluntariness (Simon, 1987). Competence is determined by the courts and is defined as the mental capacity to make choices and understand their consequences. This requirement has posed the greatest obstacle to the advocates of children's rights, as the courts have traditionally considered children incompetent.

The health care provider has a duty to disclose all information that the patient may need in order to make a knowledgeable decision about treatment (*Cantebury v. Spence*, 1972). Rosoff (1981) thoroughly analyzed the legislative and judicial activity regarding informed consent and determined that the patient requires the following information in order to make a knowledgeable treatment decision: the diagnosis or identified problem, the nature and purpose of the treatment, the risks and consequences of the treatment, the probability that the treatment will be successful, the reasonable alternatives to treatment, and the prognosis without treatment.

The legal requirement of voluntariness ensures that the patient is free to make treatment decisions without coercion or fear of reprisal. The patient should be explicitly told that his or her consent is completely voluntary and that he or she is free to withdraw that consent at any time.

The law does not require a written consent form, but almost every health care facility uses one as written evidence that the requirements of informed consent were met (Hogue, 1986). An audio or video recording may also be used as validation. Regardless of the medium used for documentation, specific details of the information that was given to the patient, as well as those of the agreement between the patient and the health care provider about the treatment, should be included.

The consent process is nearly always witnessed as an additional safeguard that the requirements of informed consent have been met. The psychiatric nurse is frequently called on as an objective outsider to witness either the patient's signature on the consent form or the consent process itself. Whether the nurse witnesses only the signature or the entire consent process depends on the policy of the institution; for this reason, the child and adolescent psychiatric nurse must become familiar with and act in accordance with the policies of the institution in which he or she is working. Regardless of institutional policy, the nurse should act as the patient's advocate by observing for continued consent, knowledge, and voluntariness.

Unless designated a mature minor, or emancipated, a minor is generally considered incompetent, and informed consent must be obtained from the parent or legal guardian. There are several exceptions on a state-by-state basis, however. For example, nearly every state has a statute that allows minors to consent to treatment for substance abuse and sexually transmitted diseases. In addition, many states have specific statutes. Arizona, Connecticut, Idaho, Kansas, Kentucky, and Pennsylvania allow a minor 14 years of age or older to consent to inpatient mental health care with parental notification, Alabama and Vermont allow 14-year-olds to consent to inpatient treatment without the requirement of parental notification. Georgia allows minors 12 years of age and older to consent to inpatient treatment, and the states of Virginia and Nevada extend the right to individuals of any age (Morrisey, Hoffman, & Thrope, 1986). Because specific conditions and requirements vary from state to state and are subject to frequent amendments, nurses should consult their state's particular mental health laws to determine at what age and under what conditions minors may consent to mental health treatment.

Research and the Protection of Human Subjects

In 1983, the Department of Health and Human Services (DHHS) issued specific regulations regarding the use of human subjects in federally funded research projects (Protection of Human Subjects, 45 C.F.R. 46, 1983). These regulations are generally recognized as standard, although, legally, they apply only to institutions and organizations that receive federal funding. The DHHS regulations call for all institutions engaging in research that involves human subjects to have an institutional review board to review such research projects and approve only those that meet DHHS regulations.

The DHHS requires that research subjects be given the following information in writing before they agree to participate:

1. a description of the research, its purposes, its possible risks and benefits
2. alternative treatments
3. the ways in which confidentiality will be maintained
4. if the research involves more than minimal risk, a statement pertaining to compensation should injury occur
5. the name of the person to contact should the subject be injured or need more information
6. a statement that participation is voluntary and that nonparticipation will not affect the quality of care received
7. a statement that the subject may withdraw at any time

As a general rule, parental consent is required when the research subject is a minor. In addition, the institutional review board may require the researcher to obtain the minor's "assent" to treatment. Assent is defined as the child's agreement to participate in the research and should be obtained in addition to, not in place of, parental consent (Morrisey, Hoffman, & Thrope, 1986).

RIGHTS

State-Parent-Child Triad

Although parents in the past were generally free to raise their children as they saw fit, this tradition has changed dramatically during the 20th century. When enacting legislation or rendering judicial decisions, the legislature and courts began to consider interests other than those of the parent. Specifically, the legislature and courts began to recognize the additional interests of both the state and the child. Ideally, the interests of these three parties are congruent; in reality, however, they are frequently in conflict, and striking a balance among them is sometimes difficult.

The state's interests are based on the principle of *parens patriae*, which gives the state the power to protect members of society who cannot protect themselves. Specifically, the state has the authority and responsibility to care for and protect from harm those children whose parents are unable or unwilling to do so themselves. The *parens patriae* power of the state was first used when 19th century reformers pushed for child labor and compulsory education laws. It was this power that led to the conception of the juvenile court movement at the turn of the century. The Supreme Court upheld this *parens patriae* power in the case of *Prince v. Massachusetts* (1944), when the Court ruled that neither freedom of religion nor parental authority is absolute and that "the state as *parens patriae* may restrict the parents' control by requiring school attendance, regulating or prohibiting the child's labor, and in many other ways." (p. 166) This case had far-reaching implications, as it broadened *parens patriae* to include areas outside of compulsory education and child labor.

Despite the state's *parens patriae* power and the children's rights movement of the early 20th century, the English common law view of the supremacy of parental rights continues to draw support. Those who adhere to the parental rights position, known as "family libertarianism," espouse the belief that parents should be allowed to raise their children as they desire, with outside intervention appropriate only in the most extreme instances.

The Supreme Court upheld this view in the 1972 case *Wisconsin v. Yoder*, which concerned the rights of Amish parents who defied compulsory education laws and refused to send their children to school beyond the eighth grade. The Court ruled that the parents' authority, plus their right to religious freedom, outweighed the state's substantial interest in having an educated citizenry (Davis & Schwartz, 1987).

The children's rights position opposes the parental rights position that children's "best interests" are isomorphic with parents' best interests. Although the children's rights movement began near the turn of the century with the social reformation, it was not until the 1960s that the child advocacy movement began to flourish. This movement is based on the premise that the interests of children merit consideration equal to that given the interests of the state and the parents. The children's rights movement has generated both widespread support and substantial criticism. Despite the controversy, the Supreme Court has upheld a position of parity of children through several landmark rulings.

One of the first such rulings was the 1967 case *In re Gault*, in which the Supreme Court ruled that minors charged with delinquency must be afforded most of the due process safeguards afforded adults. The Supreme Court subsequently upheld the rights of minors to free speech (*Tinker v. Des Moines Independent School District*, 1969) and to privacy (*Carey v. Population Services International*, 1977). There continues to be a great deal of controversy concerning the rights of minors to free speech and privacy, and these issues will be the basis for many future court cases.

Patients' Rights in Health and Mental Health Care

All patients in mental health care facilities retain a variety of rights based on federal and state law. These rights are derived primarily from the constitutional rights to freedom of speech, freedom from illegal search and seizure, freedom from cruel and unusual punishment, and the rights to due process and equal protection (Simon, 1987). Most federal court decisions concerning the rights of institutionalized persons deal with adults, but these decisions also apply to children (Horowitz & Davidson, 1984).

Mental health care codes vary from state to state, but all contain a section on the rights of patients in institutions. Most states agree on certain basic rights. For example, hospitalized patients, including juveniles, possess the absolute right to consult with counsel. In addition, their communications with courts or counsel should remain confidential. Most states grant patients the rights of visitation and uncensored communication by telephone or mail, although these rights can be restricted for proper cause relating to the patient's care and treatment.

Hospitalized patients retain their civil rights to dispose of property, execute instruments such as a will, make purchases, give informed consent to treatment, and vote, unless they have been adjudicated incompetent. In addition, most states require that patients—and the parents or legal guardians of patients who are minors—receive advance notice if they are to be transferred from one institution to another.

Every institution should have written policies that define patients' rights. Mental health care professionals should be well versed in the policies of their institution and should ensure that these policies are posted and explained both to the hospitalized minor and to the parents or guardian on admission.

Right To Refuse Treatment

Voluntarily committed patients have an absolute right to refuse treatment, unless they have been adjudicated incompetent, in which case their guardian makes treatment decisions. Although competent adults have the absolute right to refuse treatment for themselves, they do not have the same right to refuse treatment for their children. Parental refusal to obtain adequate care for a child is considered child neglect in all states. Should a parent refuse to seek the medical or mental health care deemed necessary for a child, a court order can be obtained to treat the child despite the parent's refusal.

The right of an involuntarily committed patient to refuse treatment, including antipsychotic medications and invasive procedures, is one of the most hotly debated issues in mental health care today. The Supreme Court has refused to rule that involuntarily committed patients possess an absolute right to refuse treatment and has remanded the issue to the states to decide (*Mills v. Rogers,* 1982).

Through legislation and litigation, several states have developed further requirements for the review of treatment in an attempt to balance the interests of the individual and the state. Thus, the patient's right to refuse treatment varies from state to state and is subject to constant revision by the courts. Child and adolescent psychiatric nurses should be aware that their state's mental health care laws apply to children and adolescents, unless otherwise stated, and should stay attuned to amendments in their state's statutes on the right to refuse treatment and related court rulings.

Least Restrictive Alternative

The courts have held that individuals have the right to receive mental health treatment through the least restrictive modality that will meet their mental health care needs (*Lake v. Cameron,* 1966; *Covington v. Harris,* 1969; *Lessard v. Schmidt,* 1972). This principle assumes a hierarchy of treatment, with open wards less restrictive than closed wards and outpatient treatment less restrictive than inpatient treatment. The child and adolescent psychiatric nurse acts as the patient's advocate by assessing the patient's condition and ensuring that the patient receives the least restrictive form of treatment necessary to achieve beneficial results. There is a great deal of controversy and attention in the United States today regarding the overuse of inpatient psychiatric care for children and adolescents, which not only may be unnecessary, but also may have long-term negative effects (Darnton, 1989).

The least restrictive alternative principle also applies to procedures and treatments that may be invasive or restrict the liberty of the patient, such as the use of seclusion and restraints. The child and adolescent psychiatric nurse should become familiar with the state laws and regulations governing patients' rights related to the use of these procedures, as their use is widespread in child and adolescent psychiatry. Although the laws and regulations vary in different states, most agree on three main indications for seclusion and restraint (Simon, 1987).

1. to prevent clear and imminent harm to the patient or others
2. to protect the treatment program or therapeutic environment from disruption or damage
3. to assist in behavioral therapy

The use of seclusion or restraints as a form of punishment or to ease the workload on a unit by confining a troublesome, but nondangerous patient is absolutely contraindicated.

Hospital policies also vary from institution to institution, but most follow the guidelines set by the Joint Commission on Accreditation of Healthcare Organizations (Joint Commission, 1988). The standards on seclusion and restraints require that members of the nursing staff observe the patient every 15 minutes. In addition, the patient should receive regular meals and fluid intake, and should be allowed to use the toilet at least every 4 hours. Although the nurse practicing in child and adolescent psychiatry can place a patient in seclusion or restraints during an emergency, the nurse should notify the patient's psychiatrist immediately and obtain an order within 1 hour. The Joint Commission does not allow "as needed" orders for seclusion and restraint.

The child and adolescent psychiatric nurse should carefully record the reasons that seclusion or restraints were necessary and should document the less restrictive forms of management that were used prior to the use of seclusion or restraints. Also, the nurse should carefully document observations of the patient, as well as the need for continued seclusion or restraints. The removal from seclusion and restraints should occur as soon as the patient no longer poses a threat to others or self and the therapeutic environment is safe from disruption.

CONFIDENTIALITY AND PRIVILEGED COMMUNICATION

While confidentiality is crucial for nursing in general, in no other specialty is it such a basic component of practice as in the specialty of psychiatric nursing. Confidentiality is the ethical duty of the nurse not to disclose information obtained in the course of nursing care to any other individual or party without the express permission of the patient. A nurse's failure to abide by this ethical obligation, which is included in the American Nurses' Association Code of Ethics (1985), would destroy the patient's trust and, thus, undermine the therapeutic nurse-patient relationship that is the foundation for treatment in the field of psychiatric nursing. In addition to the nurse's ethical responsibility to maintain confidentiality, most states have statutes that prohibit the unauthorized disclosure of information about the patient from the patient's medical record (Simon, 1987). If the psychiatric nurse releases information without the express permission of the patient or the parent or legal guardian of a minor patient and the information proves to be damaging to the patient, the nurse can be sued for breach of confidentiality.

Unlike confidentiality, privilege is not considered a duty, but rather the right of an individual (the patient) to keep the information shared in a professional relationship confidential. Privilege prevents the professional from being forced to testify in court about confidential communications, unless the patient or client waives the privilege. Established by statute, privilege is granted only to specific professionals. Nearly every state recognizes a physician-patient and an attorney-client privilege, and several states now recognize a nurse-patient privilege (Knapp & VandeCreek, 1987). These statutes vary considerably from state to state, however, and nurses should consult their state privileged communications statute to determine which professionals are granted privilege and its limitations. In states that do not recognize a nurse-patient privilege, a nurse should tell the patient that confidential information shared with the nurse is not protected by a privileged communications statute, and the nurse may at some point be required to reveal the information in a court of law.

In cases regarding minors who are not designated mature or emancipated, the states have granted the control of the privilege and the right of its waiver to the parent or the legal guardian. Although this aspect of privileged communications statutes has been the basis for much controversy, with advocates of children's rights arguing that it is an invasion of the minor's constitutional right to privacy, the Supreme Court has yet to decide who controls the privilege when a minor is hospitalized. Therefore, the prudent nurse attempts to obtain the consent of both the patient and the parent or legal guardian before disclosing any confidential information to interested third parties.

There are many exceptions to privilege, and these vary significantly from state to state. Nevertheless, two exceptions remain uniform across the United States: the duty to warn third parties and the duty to report child abuse. The duty to warn third parties mandates that the therapist has a duty to protect identifiable victims from harm threatened or planned by the patient. The precedent for this arises from *Tarasoff v. Regents of the University of California* (1976). In Tarasoff the therapist failed to appropriately notify Titiani Tarasoff of a significant threat of bodily harm from the therapist's client. Ms. Tarasoff was subsequently murdered. The therapist's employer was found liable for a failure to meet a newly evolving professional "duty to warn." Although Tarasoff was not a supreme court case, it has been followed in many jurisdictions and is probably applicable to a variety of mental health workers.

Nearly every state has a statute that requires health care providers to report any suspicions of possible child abuse to the proper authority, usually the local child welfare agency. These mandatory reporting laws provide protection against civil suits to the person who reports in good faith. In addition, legal penalties can be imposed on those who fail to report suspected abuse (Knapp & VandeCreek, 1987).

The child and adolescent psychiatric nurse is often faced with a difficult dilemma when trying to balance the interests of the minor patient and the parent. The nurse's ethical duty to maintain the confidentiality of the patient is often in conflict with the rights of the parent as the child's legal guardian. This issue will most likely be an area of future litigation, and it underscores the importance of family therapy, as opposed to the exclusive treatment of the child.

Nursing has long espoused its role as the client advocate. Advocacy by the child and adolescent psychiatric and mental health nurse in the 1990s will mean not only protecting the legal rights of the client, but also addressing numerous public policy implications for children's health care. The health care system is currently troubled in terms of both access and quality of services, and in no area is this more true than in mental health care. Nursing's knowledge of what "should be" must be blended with the more practical political reality of what "can be." This will require organized and energetic political behavior by nurses. Running for office, campaigning for "pro–mental health" candidates, lobbying for monies for mental health care programs, and other such activities will be necessary for the nurses of the 1990s in order to fulfill their professional and advocacy responsibilities. Positive outcomes for child and adolescent mental health care are possible through the committed and focused activity of nurses in organized health policy processes.

REFERENCES

Addington v. Texas, 441 U.S. 418 (1979).

American Nurses' Association. (1985). *The code for nurses with imperative statements*. Kansas City, MO: Author.

Blackstone, W. (1859). *Commentaries on the laws of England, 2, 447*.

Cantebury v. Spence, 464 F.2d 617 (1972).

Carey v. Population Services International, 431 U.S. 678 (1977).

Covington v. Harris, 419 F.2d 617 (1969).

Darnton, N. (1989, July 31). Committed youth. *Newsweek*, pp. 66–72.

Davis, S.M., & Schwartz, M.D. (1987). *Children's rights and the law*. Lexington, MA: Lexington Books.

de Leon Siantz, M.C. (1988). Children's rights and parental rights: A historical and legal perspective. *Journal of Child and Adolescent Psychiatric Nursing, 1*(1), 14–17.

Georgia Code Ann: §88-503.1 (1979).

Guggenheim, M., & Sussman, A. (1985). *The rights of young people*. New York: Bantam Books.

Hogue, E. (1986). What you should know about informed consent. *Nursing 1986, 16*(6), 44–47.

Horowitz, R.M., & Davidson, H.A. (1984). *Legal rights of children*. New York: McGraw-Hill.

In re Gault, 387 U.S. 1 (1967).

Joint Commission on Accreditation of Healthcare Organizations. (1988). *Consolidated standards manual for mental health, substance abuse facilities, and facilities serving the mentally retarded/developmentally disabled.* Chicago: Author.

Knapp, S., & VandeCreek, L. (1987). *Privileged communications in the mental health professions.* New York: Van Nostrand Reinhold.

Lake v. Cameron, 364 F.2d 657 (1966).

Lessard v. Schmidt, 349 F.Supp. 1078 (E.D. Wisc. 1972).

Mills v. Rogers, 457 U.S. 291 (1982).

Mora, G. (1975). Historical and theoretical trends in psychiatry. In A. Freedman, H. Kaplan, & B. Sadock (Eds.), *Comprehensive textbook of psychiatry.* Baltimore: Williams & Wilkins.

Morrisey, J.M., Hoffman, A.D., & Thrope, J.C. (1986). *Consent and confidentiality in the health care of children and adolescents.* New York: The Free Press.

O'Connor v. Donaldson, 422 U.S. 563, 576 (1975).

Parham v. J.R., 442 U.S. 584 (1979).

Prince v. Massachusetts, 321 U.S. 158 (1944).

Protection of Human Subjects, 45 C.F.R. 46 (1983).

Rosoff, A.J. (1981). *Informed consent: A guide for health care providers.* Rockville, MD: Aspen Publishers.

Shurtleff, N. (1854). *Records of the governor and company of the Massachusetts Bay in New England, 101,* 1628–1686.

Simon, R.I. (1987). *Clinical psychiatry and the law.* Washington, DC: American Psychiatric Press.

Tarasoff v. Regents of the University of California, 17 Cal. 3d 425 (1976).

Tennessee Code Ann. §33-6-103 (1990).

Tinker v. Des Moines Independent School District, 393 U.S. 503 (1969).

Wisconsin v. Yoder, 406 U.S. 205 (1972).

9

The Physical Environment for Child and Adolescent Psychiatric Nursing

Sharon K. Lewis

After reading this chapter, the reader will be able to:

1. identify the relationship between the therapeutic needs and the design of space for both child and adolescent psychiatric and mental health nursing programs
2. describe a process for the systematic planning of space for both the child and adolescent units
3. develop strategies to provide an environment that is safe for children and adolescents
4. identify the special needs of both the child and the adolescent that require consideration in planning the physical environment

The development of the physical environment for a child or adolescent psychiatric nursing program is a complex process. The type of program, the ages and diagnoses of clients, and the philosophy of care all contribute to the nursing model envisioned. The model of care, safety issues, special needs of the client population, and financial feasibility must all be considered in the design of the physical environment. The collaboration of the nursing staff with a hospital project planning committee, architects, and interior designers will result in a physical environment with the qualities that best promote the therapeutic process and use staff in the most efficient and effective manner.

STRATEGIC PLANNING PROCESS

The development of the physical environment for child and adolescent psychiatric nursing units requires careful and thorough planning. The strategic planning process establishes direction, and the clinical program begins to take shape. Because the development of such programs requires the expertise of a myriad of individuals, the use of a committee or task force in the planning process is often helpful to obtain the valuable insights and expertise of those in nursing, medicine, architecture, engineering, finance, and administration (Rowland & Rowland, 1980). During this planning process, the nursing staff also formulates ideas or concepts of the physical environment and therapeutic program.

Role of Key Personnel

The key nursing personnel in planning a psychiatric unit include the psychiatric nurse administrator, who is on the hospital planning committee; the child and adolescent clinical specialist; and selected nurse managers and staff. During planning meetings, issues such as space requirements to support the program; safety; bed size; and codes, regulations, and standards can be explored in detail. The pros and cons of various models can be discussed. Issues such as visibility, distance of the nurses' station from client rooms, interview rooms, and space for team conferences can be addressed. The nursing planning committee is also valuable in determining equipment needs, selecting furnishings, and collaborating in the plans for construction and opening of the new program. Anticipating problems with traffic flow, noise, construction work, and safety during renovation projects can prevent or reduce the negative impact of construction on existing nursing programs. A well established plan for handling these changes can be developed and shared with staff to prepare everyone for the project.

Visits to Other Programs

Taking the time to contact other facilities with child or adolescent psychiatric programs can be very helpful. Physically seeing the layout and interior design of several programs and talking with their staffs can give nurses a better idea of the positive and negative aspects of designs. Sharing these observations and comments with the architect can eliminate certain design concepts before any plans are drawn. The experience gained in other programs can also be helpful in making selections of furniture and finishes.

Meetings with Architects and Designers

As a member of the hospital planning team, the psychiatric nurse administrator should be involved in the initial design development for any proposed psychiatric nursing program. Before creating any design, the architect must be aware of the function of the proposed program and the population that it will serve. By sharing ideas, the nurse administrator helps the architect conceptualize a design that addresses the issues of importance to nursing.

After the initial design plans have been drawn, the nursing planning committee reviews them in detail with the architect. Dialogue between the committee and the architect will resolve any questions about the design. At this point, the architect draws a schematic that details the nursing area room by room and to scale. In addition, the schematic shows the relationship of the area to other departments on the same floor and the flow of traffic. After the review of the schematic, the floor plan is fixed, and the project moves into the construction phase. The key is to be closely involved in the planning of the unit from the beginning to its conclusion.

The psychiatric care facility must meet the existing requirements of local fire and life safety codes, building codes, and public health regulations. In many states, the department of mental health has additional space, safety, or building requirements. Plans for a construction project usually require the approval of one or more offices or programs within the state. In some states, a formal certificate of need is required before the state will issue building permits; if so, the hospital must meet the established criteria and follow the established review process. After receiving the certificate of need, the project can move forward.

After the schematic has been finalized, the nurse administrator can begin the selection of furnishings and equipment in consultation with an interior designer. The interior designer must have knowledge and experience in hospital designs, preferably with psychiatric environments for children and adolescents. According to Hardy and Lammers (1986), the following should be included in interior design:

> 1) space planning—that is, planning as to how a given room will be arranged, divided and furnished in order to achieve both aesthetic appeal and functionality; 2) color coordination of furnishing, floor and walls, as well as medical equipment and other design features, including fabrics, draperies, woods, vinyls, and carpets; 3) graphic design, usually including both a signage program and wall graphics. (p. 239)

In developing an interior design, choices can be made from recommendations given by the designer. Like the architect, the interior designer can prepare a better design if aware of the basics about the environment's purpose, the client population, and anticipated problems or concerns.

Recommendations to Hospital Administrator

An ongoing dialogue between hospital and psychiatric nursing administrators is necessary throughout all phases of the project planning process. The hospital administration, charged with the responsibility of approving the project, cannot make informed decisions if the psychiatric nurse administrator does not have any voice in the planning process. In the project planning committee, the nurse administrator has an opportunity to articulate needs, concerns, and ideas for discussion.

With psychiatric nursing care at the core of the treatment programs for children and adolescents, it is important that plans for environmental designs take into account the day-to-day experience and expertise of psychiatric nursing staff. Without appropriate program and physical plant design, nursing care cannot be rendered in the most therapeutic and efficient manner.

PROGRAM DESCRIPTION

The development of architectural plans for either renovation of existing facilities or new construction requires a clear understanding of the services to be provided and the approach to be used in providing them. Therefore, an important initial step is a comprehensive program description. Although program descriptions may vary with each facility, they should include the following: (1) general program description, (2) referral mechanisms, (3) admission criteria, (4) overview of treatment components, and (5) discharge planning.

The program description is based on the philosophy of care held by the nursing department. This philosophy drives the entire project, giving the program the foundation from which treatment modalities are selected, space and equipment requirements are determined, and staffing decisions are made. The philosophy and the statement of mission (i.e., purpose) articulate the department's values and beliefs. According to Evans and Lewis (1985), the beliefs contained in the department philosophy "include the type of care required by specific client populations and the academic and clinical preparation needed by the providers of care" (p. 3). With the philosophy and mission statement as guides, the nursing program can be systematically designed for the most effective and efficient utilization of staff, space, and other resources.

The program of care must be carefully reviewed and mutually agreed upon by members of all clinical disciplines involved in the care of a child or adolescent included in the program. The nursing unit, although the central focus of care provided by the nursing staff, is also used by other care-givers. Therefore, centralization of the majority of therapeutic activities in a nursing area may be necessary or desirable. In some situations, however, a more decentralized approach may be required. The following considerations must be addressed: (1) noise level of children and adolescents and the program's proximity to other general hospital units; (2) access to playfield, gymnasium, or other recreational therapy areas; (3) classroom space; (4) dining room, lounges, and library/study space; (5) flow of traffic to limit ingress and egress; (6) potential security and safety problems; (7) combining/separating of male and female clients in the same area; (8) designation of age-appropriate groups and facilities; (9) observation and visibility of rooms; (10) on-unit interview rooms; and (11) on-unit therapy rooms (e.g., occupational therapy groups).

The configuration of the facility and the accessibility of the various areas (e.g., the dining room) must be considered in determining the floor plan. In the general hospital, it is usually prudent to maintain the inpatient psychiatric unit and all related clinical services either directly on, or adjacent to, the nursing unit. This allows for the delivery of care to these clients in a limited area of the hospital and reduces the risk of their elopements, their acquisition of contraband, and distracting noise in other client care areas; it also helps to control traffic. Furthermore, crisis situations can be handled more quickly and with a minimum of disturbance to other clients, staff, or visitors.

The use of a therapeutic community approach with an emphasis on developing social skills through the larger group necessitates fewer, but larger rooms. Multi-purpose rooms can be designed for a variety of activities, thus maximizing their usefulness. In a children's program, for example, a large lounge adjacent to a kitchenette can have an area with small tables and chairs for meals, snacks, table crafts, therapeutic games; built-in cabinets for occupational therapy supplies, games, and other items; and a sink and counter top. This room could then serve as dining room, occupational therapy room, and nursing activities room. When it is necessary to separate youngsters for short periods of time, small "timeout" or quiet rooms are needed.

The age of the population to be served is another factor in planning. Children, pre-adolescents, and adolescents require different furnishings, different unit layouts, and different interior decoration and design, all of which must aid communication. Each client needs to feel a certain level of comfort, self-expression, and identification with the environment. Furnishings and wall graphics designed for 7-year-olds are not only nontherapeutic for 15-year-olds, but also may reinforce childishness and deny the adolescent struggle for emancipation. It is usually possible to manage pre-adolescents and adolescents in the same area, but it is best if younger children have their own space.

The diagnostic mix of clients also requires consideration in designing the physical environment. Conduct disorders and behavior problems often associated with attention deficit, for instance, necessitate careful selection of furnishings for durability, ease of repair or replacement, potential for being thrown, and injury or property damage that may result from their being thrown. Clients who demonstrate depression, suicide ideation, or impulsive behavior and those who are at risk for elopement all require a physically safe, secure environment that allows the staff to maintain visual contact with them.

THERAPEUTIC MILIEU

The amount of space needed for a child and adolescent psychiatric unit is established through assessment of the type of therapeutic program to be provided, projected utilization, bed requirements (for inpatient units), staffing projections, statutory requirements, and financial feasibility.

Economies of Scale

Regardless of their size, psychiatric nursing programs require certain core rooms. For example, each nursing unit needs at least a nursing station or equivalent, medication room, clean and soiled utility rooms, pantry or kitchenette, and lounge—whether the program has 1 bed or 50 beds, 1 day patient or 50 day patients. The cost of constructing these core rooms and any other rooms required by state law is a fixed cost that depends on the size of the rooms. A program for a very small number of clients has a much higher square footage of floor space per client than does a program for a large number of clients. Consequently, the cost to construct and maintain a small program is proportionately higher. The cost of a psychiatric intensive care unit, which should be small, may be offset somewhat by charging a higher rate because of the highly specialized nature of the unit and the acuity of the conditions of the clients that it serves.

It is also generally more costly to staff small programs than to staff large ones. The combination of a high census and a large percentage of clients with acute illness may decrease the therapeutic aspects of the milieu, and an increase in staff may be necessary to ensure a therapeutic environment and to provide the structure and one-to-one contact that acutely ill young clients so greatly need. In this instance, the smaller unit, while costing more to maintain, may be more economical to run.

Unless it is possible to justify the cost of a very small nursing program, economies of scale require a larger number of clients for the most cost-effective approach. With the assistance of the finance department, pro forma financial models can be used to determine the most feasible census complement and staff assignment. If the program cannot support itself, the hospital management must decide if the service can be allowed to operate at a projected loss.

Impact of Census on the Therapeutic Milieu

Adult psychiatric nursing programs may be able to have 30 patients and remain therapeutic, but such a large number of children or adolescents in a program can become unmanageable. Once clients on an adolescent unit begin to lose control, acting out behavior can easily become contagious. The milieu can rapidly deteriorate into crisis management, leaving staff with little or no time or energy to focus on more therapeutic interventions.

Not only the number of clients, but also the mix of diagnostic problems can create challenges for staff in maintaining a therapeutic environment. High numbers of adolescents with conduct disorders, antisocial behavior, and aggression can cause massive disruption. Admission policies can be instituted to help maintain a mix that will promote the therapeutic qualities of the milieu.

Staff need to be visible within a structure that can provide these children with a sense of security and individual worth. Young children in small groups of 4 to 6 patients can usually be given adequate attention to meet their needs and maintain the therapeutic aspects of the group. Very young children may require nearly one-to-one staff attention, however. Because of the small staff-to-client ratios required to care for this age group, there must be sufficient space to accommodate several small group activities at any given time.

Utilization of Psychiatric Nursing Staff

The experience of established child or adolescent psychiatric nursing programs can be very useful in predicting the staffing needs of a program being planned. Contacts with hospitals with similar programs can provide insight into known and anticipated problems and bring unforeseen or unexpected pitfalls to light. Using the expertise of others who have encountered the same questions can save time and other resources.

A limited supply of staffing resources, increased competition within the hospital for funds, and fluctuating census all contribute to the need for an accurate prediction of staffing needs and for flexibility in responding to those needs (Evans & Lewis, 1985). The use of a client acuity classification system validates the number of nursing care hours required. In the past several years, psychiatric client classification systems have brought many positive results to nursing administration. Rowland and Rowland (1980) noted the cost savings that can be achieved through the more accurate staffing budgets made possible by effective patient classification systems.

Projections for staffing must take into account not only the anticipated acuity of clients' conditions, but also the mix of staff necessary to provide care. Streamlining the roles of direct care psychiatric nursing staff and eliminating nonnursing functions more effectively utilizes the staff.

ENVIRONMENTAL SAFETY

The safety and well-being of the children and adolescents who will be receiving care is a concern that should be conscientiously addressed in the planning phase of any psychiatric nursing program. Seemingly harmless objects may be used in elopement or self-injury attempts. The environment cannot be designed to eliminate all dangers, but the risks can be reduced. The key is to visualize the potential for harm that furnishings, appliances, unit materials, decoration, finishes, doors, windows, and walls can have. For example, the following should be considered in designing a program:

- nonbreakable, shatter-proof windows and/or security screening that clients cannot open
- collapsible shower heads, curtain rods, and clothes rods that will not support body weight
- limited and locked access to toxic chemicals (e.g., cleaning fluids, craft liquids, medications, shampoos, and other self-care/beauty products)
- locked storage for sharp or potentially harmful personal items with policies and procedures detailing exclusive items, supervision of use, and security of sharp items
- high-impact nonbreakable wall- or ceiling-mounted light fixtures

- molded or contoured edges of counters and furniture
- curtains or window shades with no cords, chains, or exposed rods
- nonreversible screws in switchplates and heat registers
- nonbreakable mirrors
- durable furniture that cannot be disassembled and that, if broken, can be readily repaired or replaced
- nonremovable drawers in dressers/cabinets in client areas
- nontoxic wall finishes
- durable wall coverings to protect against banging, hitting, or picking at walls
- limited and supervised use of any tools, with tool check mechanisms before and after use
- protected electrical sockets
- nonremovable, nontoxic caulking
- no plastic bags

Children need furniture that is sized appropriately for their height and weight. Very small children may fall from standard size chairs or hospital beds.

Because throwing furniture; pounding/kicking walls, furnishings, windows; obstructing toilets and sinks, and writing graffiti on walls and furniture are common acting out behaviors, it is very important to use nondestructive and durable materials. When property damage has occurred, repair work should be done as soon as possible. The area can very quickly deteriorate once property damage begins. As the physical appearance of the facility deteriorates, the milieu becomes less therapeutic. The failure to keep the facility in good condition gives a message to the young clients about their value as persons and the value of taking pride in maintaining a pleasant environment. It is easy to overlook small areas of damage and become accustomed to the shabby, chaotic appearance of a unit over time. Nursing rounds should be instituted to locate any new property damage and repair orders initiated.

Physical Access to the Program

The less traffic in and out of the child or adolescent psychiatric nursing unit, the better. Unnecessary traffic creates confusion that is upsetting to clients and disrupts the therapeutic program. Traffic patterns that circumvent the area, along with the use of locked entrances, provide greater security and confidentiality. Fire drills that include the child and adolescent clients should be carried out in conjunction with the hospital fire safety program. All staff must be prepared to respond in a real fire emergency.

Elopement is common among children and adolescents in a psychiatric unit. Ready access to the area can make it easy for clients to run out the door behind another person. Having the entry door clearly visible from the nursing station, keeping it locked, and distributing keys only to personnel with ongoing business in the area reduce the risk of elopement. Where entry to the unit is directly from an elevator, there should be key access onto the elevator. A sign near the elevator to alert passengers to be aware of children can also be helpful.

Control of Contagion

When children and adolescents begin to lose control, they need a quiet place away from the mainstream of activity where nursing interventions such as wrapping and holding can be done. Having a room with minimal furnishings (such as a chair, floor mat, or mattress) can provide a space that is free from visual stimulation, yet has some comfort for the youngster. The timeout room should be close to the nursing station so that a youngster there is within sight.

The timeout room can be used for other purposes; for example, the child or adolescent who wants a place to go to be quiet may use it. Based on the individual needs and time agreed upon, a youngster may be allowed to do schoolwork or other solitary activities while in the timeout room. This approach is especially useful with children who have difficulty maintaining attention, are hyperactive, or create minor disruptions on the unit.

The seclusion room should be located close to the nursing station and should be fitted with closed circuit television monitoring to provide constant surveillance of the client there. The camera should be mounted behind a protective, nonbreakable cover and recessed, if possible, in the wall so that there are no edges or projections into the room. If there is a bed in the room, it should be bolted to the floor and have no springs, bolts, or other items that can be removed and used for self-inflicted injury or property damage. The use of a solitary mattress directly on the floor eliminates the hazards associated with a bed. Light fixtures should be recessed with nonbreakable covers. There should be door knobs only on the exterior of the door, and light switches should be accessed only from outside the room. The floor covering should be padded to lessen impact and seamless to make it difficult to remove the covering from the floor. Walls should be constructed of material that can withstand repeated hitting, yet not cause extensive abrasions to hands, feet, or head. A nonbreakable, double paned window to the outdoors encased in curtains or blinds between panes helps to orient the patient to time. The soft light filtered through the window also has a calming effect and reduces the feeling of incarceration. Bathroom facilities should be immediately adjacent to the seclusion area to keep the client from the flow of unit activity. The use of subdued colors helps to reduce stimulation and the institutional feeling of the seclusion room.

Physical Needs of the Child and Adolescent

Children and adolescents who need psychiatric nursing experience the same physical problems that all youngsters have. Most units are designed with the physically well child and adolescent in mind, and major medical equipment and call systems are not necessary. If the program is designed for youngsters with physical handicaps or long-term illnesses, however, the physical design for the nursing unit must incorporate hospital style beds and other needed equipment.

Childhood illnesses, such as measles, mumps, and chicken pox, as well as pediculosis, upper respiratory infections, and influenza, are common on a child or adolescent psychiatric inpatient nursing unit. Highly contagious illnesses that require bed rest for several days are the greatest challenge. Policies should be established regarding the admission of youngsters with measles, mumps, and chicken pox; if at all possible, they should not be admitted until the risk of contagion has passed. A youngster who becomes physically ill while in the hospital should have a medical assessment, and staff should institute infection control measures immediately. Having one or two hospital style beds in a room close to the nursing station designated for this eventuality facilitates care and control of infection. Contact with an infection control specialist can be invaluable in managing specific illnesses. If the youngster is very highly contagious and requires specialized nursing care, there should be policies about removing the youngster from the unit, either through discharge or transfer to an infectious disease unit, until the period of contagion is over.

With respiratory or gastrointestinal illnesses of short duration, the separation of ill youngsters and the provision of alternative treatment and dining facilities may be effective in controlling contagion, particularly if the patient is febrile. Close monitoring and frequent staff contacts provide the attention that an ill youngster needs.

As more children and adolescents become infected with human immunodeficiency virus (HIV) and develop acquired immunodeficiency syndrome (AIDS), an increasing number of those on psychiatric care units will have these conditions. These clients present new concerns and challenges for staff, other clients, and families. Universal precautions, as well as policies and procedures based on the guidelines established by the Centers for Disease Control, should be instituted in all psychiatric nursing programs. Reducing stigma, maintaining confidentiality, and enhancing individual feelings of self-worth are important for the effective treatment and integration of this minority population of children. Ongoing education and support of staff is essential in providing care to clients who may be feared, shunned, and derided. Attention must be given to ensure a caring and humane environment for the client, as well as for the care-givers, other clients, and families.

SPECIAL NEEDS OF THE CHILD AND ADOLESCENT

Social and Individual Development

The physical appearance of the nursing area can hinder or enhance the psychiatric nursing care of the child and adolescent. The physical environment plays a very important role in facilitating group process, establishing a sense of well-being and calm, and promoting the therapeutic process (Hardy & Lammers, 1986). The layout and interior design can promote the socialization process. Both children and adolescents need some spacious areas with seating arranged to attract small groups for group-related activities. Space that the individual can decorate to his or her own taste is important for self-expression. Wall space with appropriate wall covering or bulletin boards may be set aside to allow youngsters a designated spot to hang papers without damaging paint or walls. Where possible, letting clients move furniture to their own specifications also promotes individual self-expression and ego development.

Minimization of the Institutional Feeling

The selection of bedroom and lounge furniture that is functional, yet resembles home furnishings, provides a warm and caring atmosphere. Keeping signage to a minimum and contemporary in style also indicates a less institutional tone. Through lighting, color, and window treatments, rooms can seem light and airy. The nursing station should have a minimum of barriers to eliminate the feeling of separation, allow greater visibility, and promote interaction between staff and clients.

Physical Activity and Play

An important outlet for children and adolescents is physical activity and play. This kind of activity develops not only gross and fine motor coordination, but also self-image. For young children, play areas can be separated into areas for individual or small group quiet play (e.g., with blocks, puzzles, coloring and drawing) and areas for physical play (e.g., running, jumping rope, and sports). Adolescents also need areas for individual diversional activity, such as table games, and larger areas for team sports and physical exercise. The more difficult area to plan is that for large and noisy physical activity. It is best to have a gymnasium and an outdoor playfield. Scheduled, supervised activities several times a day for both children and adolescents will reduce physical altercations. Adolescents may enjoy using punching bags and body-building equipment. Recreational equipment requires secure storage and only supervised use. Clients and staff who wear glasses should use safety goggles and eyeglass straps when they are engaged in physically active sports.

Nutritional Needs

Activities around food and eating can be fun and therapeutic. Youngsters enjoy baking, fixing special treats, and planning parties.

With the assistance of a dietitian, the psychiatric nursing staff and activities therapy staff can plan nutritious and fun food activities for children and adolescents. A kitchen is a wonderful tool to engage youngsters and promote healthy food habits. A kitchenette or pantry should have beverages and snacks for children and adolescents as supplements between meals. Soda pop should be restricted, but juices and milk should be readily available. Creative ideas modeled after fast food restaurants, such as meals made up of all finger foods or meals served in decorative theme boxes, can make food more acceptable to children and mealtime a pleasant experience. Seating in small groups promotes socialization and conforms to traditional family eating patterns. Dining and kitchenette/pantry areas should be planned with all these ideas in mind.

RESEARCH

Nursing research focusing on the design of inpatient units for child and adolescent psychiatric and mental health clients is very limited. Research is needed, however, to determine more scientifically the relationship and influence of design, finishes, and furnishings of the child and adolescent nursing unit on such aspects of care as: (1) integration of the young client into the treatment program, (2) promotion of client and family acceptance of hospitalization, (3) impulse control, (4) physical safety, (5) length of stay, and (6) treatment outcomes.

REFERENCES

Evans, C.L.S., & Lewis, S.K.L. (1985). *Nursing administration of psychiatric-mental health care.* Gaithersburg, MD: Aspen Publishers.

Hardy, O.B., & Lammers, L.P. (1986). *Hospitals: The planning and design process.* Gaithersburg, MD: Aspen Publishers.

Rowland, H.S., & Rowland, B.L. (1980). *Nursing administration handbook.* Gaithersburg, MD: Aspen Publishers.

10

Implementation of Psychiatric Nursing Interventions with Children and Adolescents

Patricia West

After reading this chapter, the reader will be able to:

1. identify the role of implementation in the process of psychiatric nursing with children, adolescents, and their families
2. examine the ways in which the implementation of psychiatric nursing interventions makes it possible to meet the objectives of the working phase of the nurse-client relationship with children and adolescents
3. describe several psychiatric nursing interventions used with children, adolescents, and their families
4. discuss the importance of nurses' therapeutic use of self in psychiatric nursing with youngsters
5. identify an area of needed nursing research related to the implementation of psychiatric nursing interventions

The implementation of nursing interventions is the core of psychiatric nursing with children and adolescents. Through this component of the nursing process, a psychiatric nurse helps youngsters who are experiencing distressing human responses. The anticipated outcome of these interventions is an improved state of mental health and well-being for the child and family.

Nurses at either the generalist or the specialist level of practice can implement a psychiatric nursing care plan (American Nurses' Association [ANA], 1980, 1985). Although nurse generalists may use many psychiatric nursing interventions, they more often use techniques such as milieu management, teaching, and psychotherapeutic interventions. The clinical nurse specialist in child and adolescent psychiatric nursing may formally contract with a family to provide more in-depth care through the modalities of individual, family, and group psychotherapy. The specialist may also provide consultation-liaison services to children and other health care professionals. The appropriate application of nursing interventions depends on the individual nurse's educational preparation, clinical supervision, and role in the treatment of a particular child and family.

ROLE OF IMPLEMENTATION IN PSYCHIATRIC NURSING

"Implementation refers to the actual delivery of nursing care to the client and the client's response to the care that is given" (Sundeen, Stuart, Rankin, & Cohen, 1989, p. 20). As an element of the nursing process, implementation integrates the other elements: (1) the assessment process, which provides an understanding of the child through the collection and analysis of data; (2) the diagnostic process, which clarifies the needs for nursing care (the focal human response patterns); and (3) the planning process, which delineates a plan of care to treat the focal human responses. The plan of care gives direction to nursing interventions, but the nurse determines when, and if, to implement those actions based on ongoing assessment (Alfaro, 1990). The collected data, diagnoses, plan, and interventions are evaluated simultaneously throughout the nurse-client contact and may result in alteration of the nursing approach.

As a result of nursing interventions, the client's human responses change, altering the substantive content of the nurse-client relationship. These changes require the nurse to evaluate the treatment approach. The nurse may modify: (1) his or her perception of the child's situation (assessment formulation), (2) diagnoses of human response patterns, (3) plans of care, or (4) specific interventions. The implementation of psychiatric nursing involves continuous modifications of nursing interventions to ensure the best care for the youngster and family.

All nursing occurs within the context of the nurse-client relationship. The working phase of this relationship is generally focused on accomplishing the needed changes. Moscato (1988) identified the goals of the working phase as: (1) the analysis of the dynamics related to the client's behavioral patterns and (2) the initiation of change of the focal behavioral patterns. According to Moscato, the therapeutic tasks and nursing approaches of this phase are related to these two objectives. In initiating change, for example, a therapeutic task may be to address the forces that are working against the desired change. The related nursing approaches include using problem-solving strategies, promoting active decision making, and encouraging the client to assert his or her own needs. The implementation of these psychiatric nursing interventions then focuses on meeting the objectives of the working phase of the nurse-client relationship.

Sundeen and colleagues (1989) described a major aspect of the nurse's role in the working phase of the relationship as using various communication techniques and interventions to facilitate the client's expression of feelings. They cited Carkhuff (1969), who identified the activities of confrontation, immediacy, and self-disclosure in facilitating expressions of emotions. Carkhuff elaborated on three types of inconsistencies that confrontation uncovers: (1) those between the child's verbal and nonverbal communication, (2) those between the nurse's perception of the youngster and the child's own perception, and (3) those between the child's desired state and current self-perception. Clarification of these inconsistencies is a major objective for the psychiatric nurse.

"Immediacy refers to the focusing of the interaction on the present situation between the nurse and the client in the relationship" (Sundeen et al., 1989, p. 189). An underlying assumption is that the nurse-client contact reflects the relationships that the youngster has with others. Constructive resolution of immediate conflicts should promote development of the child's problem-solving abilities.

Sundeen and colleagues (1989) described self-disclosure as the nurse's revelation of his or her own feelings and attitudes in the context of the relationship with a youngster (client). The purpose of self-disclosure is to provide the client with a model of effective coping patterns and realistic responses to interactions. The use of self-disclosure by nurses in treatment situations is controversial (Young, 1988), but many psychiatric nurses view self-disclosure as the nurse's sharing of thoughts and feelings in response to treatment interactions and find it helpful. The sharing of experiences or personal information is rarely advisable, however, and may even be detrimental to the child's progress in treatment.

DIMENSIONS OF IMPLEMENTATION

The implementation of psychiatric nursing interventions can be examined by considering three elements: the selection of nursing interventions, the types of nursing interventions, and the documentation of the implementation.

Selection of Nursing Interventions

Although effective nursing care requires an ongoing assessment of the child's needs and subsequent modification of specific interventions, the nurse initially outlines an approach in the nursing care plan, makes decisions about the treatment modality, and decides on techniques to be used. Nursing interventions are selected by a complex decision-making process, including consideration of factors related to the child, the nurse, the treatment relationship, treatment goals, and the treatment environment.

Factors Related to the Child

The child's response patterns, priorities for care, basic human capabilities, and current ability to engage in the treatment process all affect the selection of nursing interventions. The response patterns of a youngster vary by type, duration, and severity. The specific type of response may reflect varying priorities and require particular nursing interventions. For example, response patterns of active suicidal behavior dictate nursing actions to ensure safety. The duration and severity of responses may also influence decisions about the appropriate type of nursing interventions.

In describing the child's basic human capabilities, Orem (1991) included perceptual abilities, memory, cognitive skills, and social skills. These capabilities reflect the youngster's current interests, strengths, and development. A child's particular interest, such as drawing, may then suggest certain nursing interventions, such as art techniques.

The child's ability to engage in the treatment process at a given time also influences the selection of nursing interventions. Orem (1991) referred to this ability as an individual's self-care agency. It reflects the motivation and skills available to the child to participate in self-care activities. Depending on the youngster's self-care agency at a given time, a nurse may choose various interventions.

The types of nursing interventions that are appropriate for young children vary from those that are appropriate for adolescents. Psychiatric nursing interventions with infants and toddlers may include parental education and anticipatory guidance. Elementary school–aged children may respond to interventions such as drawing and games that build on their emerging fine motor skills and capability for cooperative activities. Teen-agers may be more receptive to nursing interventions that take into account their increasing independence, social skills, and abstract thought processes. Such interventions may include journal writing, group therapy, and health teaching.

Factors Related to the Nurse

The nurse's conceptual frame of reference, experience, role in the treatment process, and personality are all important factors in the selection of nursing interventions. All nurses practice within a theoretical perspective, be it that of a nurse theorist, an eclectic approach, or their own perspective. A nurse who practices from a psychological model may focus on conditioning learning or cognitive processes, subsequently choosing interventions such as behavior modification or cognitive retraining. Alternatively, a nurse who practices from a self-care perspective (e.g., Orem, 1991) may choose nursing interventions to meet a youngster's self-care needs and enhance development of the child's self-care agency.

The types of caring activities adapted by a nurse may also influence the selection of nursing interventions. Leininger (1985) and others who work in transcultural nursing have identified numerous modes of caring, including support, presence, and reciprocity. The modes adapted by the nurse reflect cultural values of health caring, as determined by cultural congruence between the nurse, the child, and the family.

Factors Related to the Treatment Relationship

Factors such as the degree of formality in the treatment relationship of the nurse, the child, and the family affect the selection of nursing actions. Moscato (1988) characterized treatment relationships on a continuum from informal to formal. The relationship is informal when a nurse and a youngster have minimal contact, for example, when a staff nurse covers for a colleague during a dinner break. The relationship is more formal when a nurse and a child meet on a regular basis for a specified period of time and their interaction is specifically goal-directed (e.g., primary nursing or psychotherapy). The youngster and nurse have a vested commitment to meet and work toward several identifiable goals. Depending on the level of formality of the relationship, certain nursing interventions may be more applicable.

Factors Related to the Goals of Treatment

Ideally, the goals of treatment are mutually agreed upon by the child, the family, and the nurse. Nurses generally focus on the health-related goals of health restoration, health maintenance, and health promotion. The determination of the priorities of these goals in the care of the child is a process that affects the selection of nursing actions. In health promotion, for example, the goal of improving the child's level of health and functioning suggests interventions such as teaching and role modeling.

Factors Related to the Treatment Environment

In selecting nursing interventions, it is necessary to consider the treatment environment in a very broad context. The physical surroundings, values, attitudes, and economic trends are all part of the greater environment and can significantly influence the selection process. For example, a psychiatric nurse working in a treatment program based on a behavior modification approach chooses nursing actions consistent with that approach. Nurses are adapting modalities such as crisis intervention and brief psychotherapy in response to the environmental factors of health care reimbursement with limited lengths of stay. Overriding concerns for the safety and well-being of the child are at times modified by the realities of economic factors and the family's motivation.

Types of Nursing Interventions

Because professionals who work with children and adolescents experiencing distressing human responses are creative and innovative therapists, they use a wide variety of treatment interventions: journal writing, behavior modification, pet therapy, seclusion, diet management, relaxation techniques, psychotropic medication, and various types of psychotherapy (Schaefer & Millman, 1977). The specialty's standards of practice (ANA, 1985) specified, "The nurse intervenes as guided by the nursing care plan to implement nursing actions that promote, maintain, or restore physical and mental health, prevent illness, effect rehabilitation in childhood and adolescence, and restore developmental progression" (p. 11). Associated with this standard are six types of interventions: (1) therapeutic environment, (2) activities of daily living, (3) psychotherapeutic interventions, (4) psychotherapy, (5) health teaching and anticipatory guidance, and (6) somatic therapies.

Therapeutic Environment

Psychiatric nurses play an important role in establishing an environment that facilitates development and promotes mental health.

Milieu Management. The management of the inpatient treatment milieu has long been recognized as a critical role of psychiatric nurses. Inpatient units are generally staffed with nurses who provide continuous client care and supervise the support staff. Therefore, nursing's involvement is critical to milieu therapy. Nurses structure the living environment for safety and provide a caring atmosphere that significantly supports the development of therapeutic communities (Jones, 1968).

Using the attachment theory developed by Bowlby (1979), Rowe (1988) described several aspects of nurses' role in the therapeutic milieu of hospital treatment of children: (1) support of a primary nursing model; (2) need for consistent limit setting in the context of a sensitive, responsive nurse-client relationship; and (3) increased family involvement in the daily treatment program. Rowe introduced the concept of the "good enough nurse," derived from the concept of the "good enough mother" (Winnicott, 1965). "The 'good enough nurse' encourages patients to use the [nurse-client] relationship as a secure base from which to explore behaviors and social relationships" (Rowe, 1988, p. 70).

Parental Education. Parents not only significantly influence the environment of the home, but also greatly affect a child's adaptation to a treatment program. Therefore, psychiatric nurses frequently intervene by parental education. Nurses instruct parents on the side-effects of medications, limit-setting techniques, and the development of age-appropriate expectations. Helmer and Laliberte (1987) described a parents' group focused on the children's needs as one component of their assessment program of preschool children. They stated, "A problem-solving and child guidance approach is used to help parents learn to function more successfully and to become more sensitive to their child's developmental needs" (Helmer & Laliberte, 1987, p. 338). Parental education is an effective nursing intervention that can alter the home environment and support the youngster's development.

Activities of Daily Living

The standards of psychiatric nursing developed by the ANA (1985) state, "The nurse uses the activities of daily living in a goal-directed way to foster the physical and mental well-being of the child or adolescent and family" (p. 13). Various common activities can be used: (1) to assess skills, (2) to provide teaching opportunities, and (3) to integrate the gains from the treatment programs into the child's daily life. Schulman and Irwin (1982) commented that morning routines, mealtimes, activities, rest periods, and bedtime can all be therapeutically useful.

McGinnis (1989) noted that gardening activities have been shown to be very beneficial for children on a small inpatient unit. The therapeutic program described by McGinnis included group discussion and hands-on gardening. The group discussion covered planning, feelings related to beginning new projects, plant reproduction, loss, and decision making. The actual hands-on activities included laying out of the garden, planting, weeding, watering, and harvesting. McGinnis cited the therapeutic benefits as the children's feelings of accomplishment, experiences in team work, practice in math and problem-solving skills, physical activity, and communal sharing.

Psychotherapeutic Interventions

The ANA standards for child and adolescent psychiatric nursing state, "The nurse uses psychotherapeutic interventions to assist children or adolescents and families to develop, improve, or regain their adaptive functioning, to promote health, prevent illness, and facilitate rehabilitation" (1985, p. 14). This description differentiates these interventions from those of psychotherapy, which is characterized by a formal, contractual relationship. The techniques characteristic of psychotherapeutic interventions may also be used in more formal relationships, however.

Communication Techniques. Nurses can use verbal techniques in a variety of treatment settings. These interventions can be especially beneficial in dealing with behavioral and emotional responses as they occur. Redl (1959) developed this concept as the "life-space interview." When a child acts inappropriately or becomes upset, the nurse converts the situation to a therapeutic interaction, exploring precipitants, consequences, and alternative expressions. These interactions gain their therapeutic value through the nurse's recognition of patterned behavior, as the nurse focuses on the "immediacy" of the situation (Sundeen et al., 1989) and effectively uses communication techniques. The techniques used with adults require modification in order to be developmentally appropriate for use with youngsters, however (Arnold & Boggs, 1989).

Games. The use of games with children and adolescents has become increasingly popular in therapeutic settings. Nickerson and O'Laughlin (1983) noted that: (1) games are a natural medium for children's learning and self-expression; (2) youngsters feel comfortable with games, readily participating; and (3) the game format facilitates communication among participants. Games are effective techniques for engaging resistant children in a therapeutic relationship or involving the uncooperative child in the group activities of sharing, taking turns, and competing.

Before selecting the game, the nurse should clearly understand the therapeutic intent of the activity. Furthermore, the games should be age-appropriate and either familiar or easily learned. The Talking, Feeling and Doing Game (Gardner, 1986), for example, is a board game designed to enhance the youngster's ability to verbalize various feelings, thoughts, and actions. This board game is organized so that both the therapist and the child participate in discussions of affect-related topics.

Therapeutic Holding. On inpatient units, psychiatric nurses often work with overly aggressive children who periodically lose control. Therapeutic holding is a technique to assist such a youngster in regaining self-control. Barlow (1989) defined therapeutic holding as "the physical restraint of an aggressive child by at least two nursing personnel, as soon as safely feasible after an aggressive act" (p. 10). Dougherty (1982) noted the advantages of therapeutic holding as providing safety when the child loses self-control, and supporting the child until ready to reintegrate into the milieu. Related interventions include having the youngster address his or her feelings about being held following the incident to facilitate this emotional expression and support verbal adaptation (Barlow, 1989).

Psychotherapy

The ANA has described psychotherapy as

> all generally accepted and respected methods of treatment, specifically including individual therapy; play; brief, goal-oriented therapy; behavioral therapy; group therapy; and family therapy. It is a structured, contractual relationship between the therapist and client for the exclusive purpose of effecting changes in the client. This modality attempts to alleviate emotional disturbance, to reverse or change maladaptive behavior, and to facilitate personality growth and development. (1985, p. 27)

Advanced educational preparation in nursing is required to practice psychotherapy (ANA, 1985). The following are examples of psychotherapy techniques.

Art. Some of the art techniques discussed as tools for assessment (see Chapter 2) may also function as therapeutic interventions. Several nurses have found the Color Your Life art strategy for children, which was developed by O'Connor (1983), to be helpful (e.g., Raynor & Manderino, 1989). O'Connor noted that the goals of the technique are to enhance the child's awareness of affective states, encourage the child to discuss events related to these feelings, and to help the child verbalize these feelings more directly. The child is engaged in the process of pairing an emotion with a color (e.g., red with anger). When the format has been established, the child is encouraged to fill up a piece of blank paper with the colors and to describe them. This technique focuses on the "process" of sharing emotional responses, not on the "product" of art (O'Connor, 1983).

Bibliotherapy. The use of books in the treatment of children and adolescents has received little attention in the literature, but being read to and reading are very common activities for youngsters and may have significant therapeutic benefit. Cohen (1987) noted that "the goals of bibliotherapy are to help the person express feelings and give insight while providing a supportive environment for coping with emotional stress" (p. 20). Using books as a therapeutic technique is helpful in addressing concerns such as fears, death, divorce, separation, and sleep difficulties.

Play Techniques. The value of play techniques is widely recognized in psychotherapy with younger children. According to Schaefer and O'Connor (1983), play techniques have several developmental, intrapersonal, interpersonal, and sociocultural functions. They may help youngsters develop social and communication skills or to identify and work through disturbing emotional responses to traumas, separation, or conflicts. In fact, nurses in several specialty areas have found play techniques to be effective in nursing assessments, health teaching, and psychotherapy with young children.

Irwin (1983) noted that, because puppets "provide safe, vicarious outlets for impulses and fantasies, puppets have been used in a variety of clinical settings" (p. 159). The ease of manipulation, physical safety, and symbolic potential make the use of puppets attractive for even the very young child. Nurses in multiple settings have found puppets to be useful for teaching, conducting assessments, and intervening with children.

Storytelling Techniques. Gardner (1971) developed a mutual storytelling technique for young children. The child starts by telling a story of his or her own creation. The nurse determines the underlying dynamic meaning of the story and then tells a related tale that has basically the same format, setting, and characters, but introduces a healthier resolution of the conflicts presented in the child's story. A strength of the technique is the shared referent of the story and the use of similar language without anxiety-provoking confrontation. The child's story can easily be recorded, which enhances the child's interest in participating and may facilitate assessment for the nurse.

Health Teaching and Anticipatory Guidance

The ANA standards state, "The nurse assists the child or adolescent and family to achieve more satisfying and productive patterns of living through health teaching and anticipatory guidance" (ANA, 1985, p. 17). Nurse psychotherapists identify education as their most frequently used nursing intervention (Spunt, Durham, & Hardin, 1984).

Teaching approaches can be readily applied to a variety of child and adolescent situations. Using a group modality, Knight, Wigder, Fortsch, and Polcari (1990) developed a protocol for teaching children and adolescents on a psychiatric inpatient unit about psychotropic medications. The techniques used were dependent on the developmental functioning of the youngsters and included the use of puppets, art projects, and verbal discussion. After this medication education, the youngsters had an increased understanding of the medications; measures of this knowledge base were not specified, however.

Denehy (1990) noted that the anticipatory guidance provided by nurses has been described as the "giving of information or counseling to a client prior to an anticipated event" (p. 53). The goals of anticipatory guidance include promoting the development and the health of the youngster (Denehy, 1990). The subject matter of the guidance may include child-rearing techniques, problem-solving skills, or assertiveness training.

Puskar, Lamb, and Martsolf (1990) used psychiatric nursing teaching and anticipatory guidance in their program on adolescent coping skills for high-school teen-agers. Using an educational approach, a clinical nurse specialist provided 10 group sessions with didactic presentations on topics such as trust, self-image, stress, and coping. Other group activities included the use of relaxation tapes, role playing, problem-solving exercises, and art projects.

Somatic Therapies

As stated in the ANA standards, "the nurse uses knowledge of somatic therapies with the child or adolescent and family to enhance therapeutic interventions" (1985, p. 17). Somatic therapies are nursing activities focused on stabilizing a youngster's physiological responses; they may include such activities as pain management, dietary interventions, or sleep promotion.

Noting that separation from parents, variations from regular routines, and fears often precipitate sleep disturbances, Schibler and Fay (1990) suggested that meeting the hospitalized child's need for security be made a priority. Specific techniques to make a child feel more secure and promote sleep include rocking, use of a security blanket, tape-recorded stories, and telephone contacts with parents. Attention should also be paid to the management of environmental stimulation and individual sleep rituals. Behavioral management strategies and relaxation techniques may also be used to facilitate productive sleep patterns (Schibler & Fay, 1990).

Documentation of Nursing Interventions

An essential aspect of the implementation process, the documentation of nursing interventions includes notation of the specific nursing interventions implemented and the responses of the child and family to the actions. Communication about nursing care is especially important, given the nature of multidisciplinary settings, such as hospitals and residential treatment centers, where youngsters are often treated. In addition, charting is a legal requirement in all health care systems, and nursing documentation becomes part of the client's permanent health care record (Alfaro, 1990).

Anderson (1983) argued for specific labeling of nursing interventions for four main reasons. First, general labeling of interventions may contribute to trial-and-error approaches by nurses. Second, the use of vague, broad terms confounds nurses' attempts to clarify their role. Third, the specific delineation of nursing interventions increases nurses' accountability for their practice. Fourth, such an explication of nursing actions supports research efforts.

The formats of documentation vary widely. There has been a recent shift from problem-oriented charting (Weed, 1970) to styles more applicable to nursing perspectives. Focus charting, as described by Lampe (1985), better addresses the client's concerns and the use of the nursing process. The "focus" is on nursing diagnoses; the focus is "a statement of what is happening to the patient, sometimes as a result of the medical treatment" (Lampe, 1985, p. 43). Nurses' charting is organized by three categories: data (behaviors, observations, status), actions (plan and nursing interventions), and response (client's responses). Focus charting is more applicable to nurses' concern with human response patterns.

TOOLS OF IMPLEMENTATION

The psychiatric nurse has a variety of tools available to implement interventions with youngsters and their families. Proficiency with these tools is an invaluable aid to the effective implementation of therapeutic interventions and can be developed through clinical practice, self-evaluation, peer review, and supervision.

Types of Skills Needed

Yura and Walsh (1988) described three types of skills essential to the successful implementation of nursing care: intellectual, interpersonal, and technical. Intellectual skills are necessary for the problem solving and decision making required to implement a nursing care plan with a child and family. Perception and judgment are also needed to modify the nursing approach throughout treatment.

Interpersonal skills are also vitally important, because nursing takes place in the context of the nurse-client relationship. These skills include the nurse's ability to convey interest, use verbal and nonverbal cues to facilitate the interaction, and communicate effectively. In psychiatric nursing, interventions are predominantly interpersonal in nature. Therefore, the nurse's therapeutic use of self is an invaluable tool to the nurse.

Technical skills usually refer to the nurse's ability to implement highly technical aspects of care, such as inserting an intravenous line, taking vital signs, and physiological monitoring. Psychiatric nursing does not generally emphasize the technical skills; when used, they are viewed as intricately intertwined with the intellectual and interpersonal skills.

Therapeutic Use of Self

In 1955, the Committee on Psychiatric Nursing of the Group for Advancement of Psychiatry noted the reciprocal nature of the nurse-patient relationship. They stated, "We assume that the behavior of the patient has meaning; that his behavior affects the behavior of those who care for him; and that the behavior of those who care for him affects the patient" (Committee on Psychiatric Nursing, 1955, p. 1). Therefore, a nurse's therapeutic use of self is the most significant tool available in caring for children and adolescents. It can be defined as the use of one's being purposefully to interact and facilitate the achievement of stated goals that have a beneficial effect on another person. This tool can be used in all treatment settings, with all clinical populations, and in conjunction with all nursing interventions. The nurse's therapeutic use of self facilitates effective nursing interventions within the interpersonal context of all client contact.

Travelbee (1971) described the therapeutic use of self as a synthesis of nursing art and science, characteristic of professional nurses. The foundation of nurses' therapeutic use of self is their personal awareness of their own strengths, limitations, and preferences. This awareness originates in an open-minded view of self and continuously evolves through personal reflection, clinical experiences, peer review, and supervision. Watkins (1978) described the underlying dynamics of this technique as a process of resonance. During this process, the person intervening (nurse) co-feels and understands (resonates) the experience of a client. This includes replicating the experience from the child's (client's) perspective as closely as possible—a type of temporary identification.

A nurse's therapeutic use of self can be observed in a responsiveness to the child (Miller & Berg, 1984; Berg, 1987). This responsiveness, which is the extent and way in which the nurse and child react to one another in the context of their relationship, has three key dimensions (Miller & Berg, 1984): style, content, and timing. A nurse's style is a reflection of his or her personality (e.g., warmth, eye contact, energy level), culturally learned behaviors, and the nature of the situation (context of a therapy relationship). A nurse's style of responsiveness may also be related to the cognitive and culturally learned behaviors and patterns of the child and family. Style is evident in a nurse's appearance, verbal and nonverbal communication, and behavior. For example, the distance at which a nurse stands from another person may reflect a style of interaction. The content of the nurse's reaction to the youngster and family reflects decision making and judgment of the child's needs and goals of treatment. The way in which the nurse uses his or her knowledge, experience, and intuition influences the content of responses to a youngster. The timing of the nurse's response is also important. Quick responses may be indicated in situations of providing support; hesitancy in response may prompt a youngster toward emotional expression or exercise of developing skills. Berg (1987) stressed the interactive nature of these dimensions. For example, a nurse may excessively delay a verbal response to a child, but, upon responding, may provide a thoughtful comment that compensates for the perceived delay.

Through the therapeutic use of self, the psychiatric nurse integrates knowledge, skill, and kindness (Travelbee, 1971). This technique is the essence of one individual making an educated, conscious effort to care for another.

RESEARCH

Research on the implementation of psychiatric nursing interventions is sparse, although some investigations have addressed concerns with specific populations of youngsters (e.g., Clatworthy, 1981) and the effectiveness of specific nursing interventions (e.g., Hinds, 1980; Saucier, 1989). Some information about psychiatric nursing interventions has been obtained through survey methods. Spunt, Durham, and Hardin (1984) surveyed 77 nurse psychotherapists with master's degrees to determine the theoretical models and interventions that they use. The most frequently used intervention was education. Other frequently noted interventions included use of self, support or empathy, confrontation, interpretation, and definition of goals. The participants also indicated which techniques they wished to add to their repertoire of skills. Those noted included hypnosis, paradoxial injunction, relaxation techniques, biofeedback, and Gestalt techniques.

Further research in the area of psychiatric nursing interventions is needed. Pillar, Jacox, and Redman (1990) recently called for a classification of nursing technologies, which they broadly defined as physical interventions (e.g., involving medications, computers, and devices), and social instruments (e.g., involving procedures, information systems, and work patterns). Pillar and colleagues argued that nursing's technologies must be specified to delineate nursing as a unique profession and to clarify its services in the overlapping roles of health care providers.

Research is needed to investigate nursing technologies in the areas of safety, efficacy, cost:benefit ratios, and social impact (Pillar et al., 1990). Such research is clearly needed for nursing interventions by psychiatric nurses who work with children and adolescents. The safety and efficacy of nursing interventions, including psychotherapy, is unclear. In addition, the limited research on psychiatric nursing interventions has significantly hampered recognition of nursing's contribution to mental health services with children and adolescents.

REFERENCES

Alfaro, R. (1990). *Applying nursing diagnosis and nursing process: A step-by-step guide* (2nd ed.). Philadelphia: J.B. Lippincott.

American Nurses' Association. (1980). *Nursing: A social policy statement.* Kansas City, MO: Author.

American Nurses' Association. (1985). *Standards of child and adolescent psychiatric and mental health nursing practice.* Kansas City, MO: Author.

Anderson, M.L. (1983). Nursing interventions: What did you do that helped? *Perspectives in Psychiatric Care, 21*(1), 4–8.

Arnold, E., & Boggs, K. (1989). *Interpersonal relationships: Professional communication skills for nurses.* Philadelphia: W.B. Saunders.

Barlow, D.J. (1989). Therapeutic holding: Effective intervention with the aggressive child. *Journal of Psychosocial Nursing and Mental Health Services, 27*(1), 10–14.

Berg, J.H. (1987). Responsiveness and self-disclosure. In V.J. Derlega & J.H. Berg (Eds.), *Self-disclosure: Theory, research and therapy* (pp. 101–130). New York: Plenum Press.

Bowlby, J. (1979). Attachment theory and its therapeutic implications. *Adolescent Psychiatry, 6,* 5–33.

Carkhuff, R. (1969). *Helping and human relations* (Vols. 1–2). New York: Holt, Rinehart & Winston.

Clatworthy, S. (1981). Therapeutic play: Effects on hospitalized children. *Children's Health Care: Journal of the Association for the Care of Children, 9,* 108–113.

Cohen, L.J. (1987). Bibliotherapy: Using literature to help children deal with difficult problems. *Journal of Psychosocial Nursing and Mental Health Services, 22*(10), 20–24.

Committee on Psychiatric Nursing of the Group for Advancement of Psychiatry. (1955). *Therapeutic use of self: A concept for teaching patient care* (Rep. No. 33). Kansas City, MO: Group for Advancement of Psychiatry.

Denehy, J.A. (1990). Anticipatory guidance. In M.J. Craft & J.A. Denehy (Eds.), *Nursing interventions for infants and children* (pp. 53–73). Philadelphia: W.B. Saunders.

Dougherty, J. (1982). Control measures. In J.L. Shuman & M. Irwin (Eds.), *Psychiatric hospitalization of children* (pp. 135–150). Springfield, IL: Charles C. Thomas.

Gardner, R.A. (1971). *Therapeutic communication with children: The mutual story-telling technique.* New York: Jason Aronson.

Gardner, R.A. (1986). The talking, feeling and doing game. In C.E. Schaefer & S.E. Reid (Eds.), *Game play: Therapeutic use of childhood games* (pp. 41–72). New York: John Wiley.

Helmer, L.S., & Laliberte, M. (1987). Assessment groups for pre-school children: A prevention program. *Archives of Psychiatric Nursing, 1*(5), 334–340.

Hinds, P.S. (1980). Music: A milieu factor with implications for the nurse-therapist. *Journal of Psychosocial Nursing and Mental Health Services, 18*(6), 28–33.

Irwin, E.C. (1983). The diagnostic and therapeutic use of pretend play. In C.E. Schaefer & K.J. O'Connor (Eds.), *The handbook of play therapy* (pp. 148–173). New York: John Wiley.

Jones, M. (1968). *The therapeutic community.* New York: Basic Books.

Knight, M.M., Wigder, K.S., Fortsch, M.M., & Polcari, A. (1990). Medication education for children: Is it worthwhile? *Journal of Child and Adolescent Psychiatric and Mental Health Nursing, 3*(1), 25–28.

Lampe, S.S. (1985). Focus charting: Streamlining documentation. *Nursing Management, 16*(7), 43–46.

Leininger, M.M. (1985). *Leininger's identification of cultural care/caring concepts and priority ratings.* Unpublished manuscript.

McGinnis, M. (1989). Gardening as therapy for children with behavioral disorders. *Journal of Child and Adolescent Psychiatric and Mental Health Nursing, 2*(3), 87–91.

Miller, L.C., & Berg, J.H. (1984). Selectivity and urgency in interpersonal exchange. In V.J. Derlega (Ed.), *Communication, intimacy and close relationships* (pp. 161–205). Orlando, FL: Academic Press.

Moscato, B. (1988). The one-to-one relationship. In H.S. Wilson & C.R. Kneisl (Eds.), *Psychiatric nursing* (3rd ed., pp. 720–760). Menlo Park, CA: Addison-Wesley.

Nickerson, E.T., & O'Laughlin, K.S. (1983). The therapeutic use of games. In C.E. Schaefer & K.J. O'Connor (Eds.), *Handbook of play therapy* (pp. 174–187). New York: John Wiley.

O'Connor, K.J. (1983). The color-your-life technique. In C.E. Schaefer & K.J. O'Connor (Eds.), *Handbook of play therapy* (pp. 251–258). New York: John Wiley.

Orem, D.E. (1991). *Nursing: Concepts of practice* (4th ed.). New York: McGraw-Hill.

Pillar, B., Jacox, A.K., & Redman, B.K. (1990). Technology, its assessment and nursing. *Nursing Outlook, 38*(1), 16–19.

Puskar, K.R., Lamb, J., & Martsolf, D.S. (1990). The role of the psychiatric mental health clinical nurse specialist in an adolescent coping skills group. *Journal of Child and Adolescent Psychiatric and Mental Health Nursing, 3*(2), 47–51.

Raynor, C.M., & Manderino, M.A. (1989). "Color your life:" An assessment and treatment strategy for children. *Journal of Child and Adolescent Psychiatric and Mental Health Nursing, 2*(2), 48–51.

Redl, F. (1959). Strategy and techniques of the life-space interview. *American Journal of Orthopsychiatry, 29,* 1–18.

Rowe, J. (1988). Attachment theory and the milieu treatment of children. *Journal of Child and Adolescent Psychiatric and Mental Health Nursing, 1*(2), 66–71.

Saucier, B.L. (1989). The effects of play therapy on developmental achievement levels of abused children. *Pediatric Nursing, 15*(1), 27–30.

Schaefer, C.E., & Millman, H.L. (1977). *Therapies for children: A handbook of effective treatments for problem behaviors.* San Francisco: Jossey-Bass.

Schaefer, C.E., & O'Connor, K.J. (1983). *Handbook of play therapy.* New York: John Wiley.

Schibler, K.D., & Fay, S.A. (1990). Sleep promotion. In M.J. Craft & J.A. Denehy (Eds.), *Nursing interventions with infants and children* (pp. 285–303). Philadelphia: W.B. Saunders.

Schulman, J.L., & Irwin, M. (Eds.). (1982). *Psychiatric hospitalization of children.* Springfield, IL: Charles C. Thomas.

Spunt, J.P., Durham, J.D., & Hardin, S.B. (1984). Theoretical models and interventions used by nurse psychotherapists. *Issues in Mental Health Nursing, 6,* 35–51.

Sundeen, S.J., Stuart, G.W., Rankin, E.A.D., & Cohen, S.A. (1989). *Nurse-client interaction: Implementing the nursing process* (4th ed.). St. Louis: C.V. Mosby.

Travelbee, J. (1971). *Interpersonal aspects of nursing.* (2nd ed.). Philadelphia: F.A. Davis.

Watkins, J.G. (1978). *The therapeutic self.* New York: Human Sciences Press.

Weed, L. (1970). *Medical records, medical education, and patient care.* Cleveland: Case Western Reserve University.

Winnicott, D.W. (1965). *The family and individual development.* London: Tavistock.

Young, J.C. (1988). Rationale for clinician's self-disclosure and research agenda. *Image: Journal of Nursing Scholarship, 20*(4), 196–199.

Yura, H., & Walsh, M.B. (1988). *The nursing process: Assessing, planning, implementing, evaluating* (5th ed.). Norwalk, CT: Appleton & Lange.

11

Preventive Psychiatric Mental Health Nursing with Infants and Young Children

Judith Fry McComish

After reading this chapter, the reader will be able to:

1. identify the focus of promotion and prevention programs for infants and very young children
2. integrate nursing theory with infant mental health theory to develop strategies for preventive nursing interventions for infants at risk
3. describe the nursing assessment process used with high-risk infants and young children
4. examine three treatment approaches that can be used to design nursing interventions with this client population

Infant mental health intervention is a relatively new area of psychiatric and mental health care. It focuses on the provision of prevention services to infants and toddlers up to the age of 3 who are at risk for abuse or neglect, attachment disorders, psychiatric problems, or developmental delay. In June 1989, U.S. Public Law 99-457 was extended to mandate that two groups of infants and toddlers receive services: those with diagnosed developmental delays and those with diagnosed physical or mental conditions that may lead to developmental delays (Benn, 1990). According to the law, individual states can decide whether to provide services also for infants "at risk" for future developmental problems. In view of the fact that approximately 375,000 drug-exposed infants are born annually (Weston, Ivins, Zuckerman, Jones, & Lopez, 1989), 7% of all live births are premature (Benn, 1990), and 26.1% of U.S. children lived in poverty in 1986 (Benn, 1990), the number of infants and toddlers who could benefit from infant mental health services is enormous.

An important domain for psychiatric and mental health nursing is the promotion of the health and well-being of infants, young children, and their families. Psychiatric/mental health nurses are prepared to promote the development of positive attachment relationships, to enhance parent-infant interaction, and to provide therapy to assist parents in resolving common problem areas such as issues related to grief or their own childhood. In addition, psychiatric/mental health nurses can identify and intervene with physiological problems that may impede the formation of the secure attachment relationships and the positive parent-infant interactions necessary for healthy infant development.

CONCEPTUAL FRAMEWORK

Attachment and Infant Mental Health Theory

The attachment theory developed by Bowlby (1982) is the theoretical framework for infant mental health programs. Bowlby became concerned with the response of children who had been separated from their parents, especially from their mothers, through events such as hospitalization or vacation. These children behaved in ways that could be described as depressed; they became quiet, apathetic, lethargic, and increasingly detached. When reunited with their parents, they often appeared disinterested, polite but distanced, or expressed anger. Bowlby postulated that infants have an evolutionary propensity to seek physical proximity to one or a group of adult care-givers, labeled attachment figures and that the purpose of this tendency is to obtain protection and security.

Ainsworth, Blehar, Waters, and Wall (1978) advanced attachment theory by developing a system for classifying attachment. They established one category of secure attachment and three categories of insecure attachment (i.e., avoidant, ambivalent, and disorganized/disoriented), based on the infant's reunion behavior with the parent after a separation. Upon reunion, securely attached infants respond to the parent by showing pleasure, approaching or making contact, and then calmly continuing the interaction with the parent or returning to play. Insecure-avoidant infants continue to play, attending excessively to the environment and actively or subtly showing disinterest in the parent. In contrast, insecure-ambivalent infants focus excessively on the parent to the exclusion of the environment; these children may display approach-avoidance behavior (e.g., run to the parent, but when picked up want to be put down again), may show angry affect, and may resist efforts at consolation (Ainsworth, et al., 1978). Insecure-disorganized/disoriented infants tend to look confused during reunion episodes, sometimes running around in circles or crouching near, but not touching, the parent (Main, Kaplan, & Cassidy, 1985).

Mothers of infants who develop secure attachment relationships tend to be responsive and sensitive to the infants' cues. Mothers of insecure-avoidant infants tend to be rejecting; mothers of insecure-ambivalent infants may be inconsistent; and mothers of insecure-disorganized/disoriented infants are likely to have had very traumatic childhoods, and some of their infants are abused (Cassidy & Kobak, 1988).

Through the attachment relationship, infants form internal representations of the attachment figure, labeled internal working models (Bowlby, 1982). Much attention has recently been given to the way in which these models develop and the function that they serve in the development and maintenance of intimate relationships. Like Bretherton (1985), Main, Kaplan, and Cassidy (1985) believe that infants develop internal working models within the first year as they internalize their parents' responses to their cues. Simultaneously, infants develop a perception of the self that is consistent with the perception of the parent.

Infants develop different internal working models in response to different attachment figures. For example, the internal working model formed in response to the mother is quite different from that formed in response to the father (Main et al., 1985). Once developed, these internal working models are used to anticipate and evaluate responses from other people. As they come into contact with new people and new relationships, infants use the internal working models as prototypes from which to judge both how new people will react and how to respond.

Because internal working models function largely outside conscious awareness, they become immutable to change. As each generation of parents respond to their children in the same way as did the earlier generation, they transmit patterns of attachment from generation to generation. Because they are working models, however, these internal models can be changed through new life experiences and new relationships (Bretherton, 1985). This is what makes the concept of internal working models so positive in terms of nursing interventions in parent-infant relationships.

Rogers' Nursing Theory

Rogers (1970, 1980, 1986) stated that the domain of nursing science and practice is humans and their interactions with the environment. She developed an open systems model in which both humans and the environment are conceived as holistic energy fields that cannot be reduced to parts. Both human and environmental energy fields manifest patterns that are their distinguishing characteristics. These patterns are largely outside conscious awareness in everyday interaction, but they can come into awareness. Individual behaviors are manifestations of the underlying pattern of the person's human field. For example, patterns of sleep and the sensation of time passing vary from person to person. All such patterns, as well as the person's physical body, can be considered manifestations of the underlying pattern of the human field (Malinski, 1986).

Through continuous interaction, human and environmental fields influence one another, and the patterns change, always in the direction of increased complexity and diversity. Rogers labeled the continuous human-environment interaction as the *principle of integrality* and the continuous evolution toward increasing complexity and diversity in patterning as the *principle of helicy*. In addition, Rogers postulated that patterns in human and environmental fields continuously change from lower to higher frequency wave patterns, and she called this the *principle of resonancy* (Rogers, 1986).

The principle of helicy is seen in the concept of nonrepeating rhythmicities. As people interact with their environment, they experience stressful and challenging life events. During these times, they may behave in ways that are similar to earlier patterns of behavior or that appear to be repetitions of family behavioral patterns in past generations. Within Rogers' paradigm, these behavioral patterns are considered nonrepeating rhythmicities; although they are similar to previous behavioral patterns, they are not identical. The person has evolved to a more complex level of functioning since the earlier episode and is in a position to experience the "repeated" pattern differently and learn from the new experience.

Nurses working within Rogers' model have as their primary focus the interaction of human and environmental energy fields. The goal of nursing is to help clients repattern their lives to increase their health and well-being. Because humans are in continuous interaction with, and are continuously influenced by, the environment, nursing interventions are designed to influence the client's environmental energy field. For infant mental health programs, the client is the infant, and the parents, as significant components of the environmental energy field, are an especially relevant focus for intervention.

Attachment, then, can be conceptualized as a developmental pattern that reflects the infant's engagement in continuous, mutual interaction with the environment. The interactional process establishes the child's basic pattern of attachment and internal working models. As the child engages in a wider range of experiences and relationships with other people, the child's patterns of attachment and internal working models are gradually transformed. A new pattern may resemble an earlier pattern, but it is more complex and diverse. Each time the scope and number of attachment relationships increase or are altered in some way by human-environment interaction, the transformation process recurs and completes a new spiral of the life cycle. The transformed pattern reflects the continuity that characterizes the evolutionary process, rather than repetition of an earlier rhythm.

Nurses who use concepts from Rogers' model focus infant mental health interventions on promoting the optimal development of the infant. They accomplish this by assisting the parents in: (1) becoming aware of their interactional patterns with their infant; (2) identifying similarities between current and past interactional patterns, including the influence of internal working models; and (3) developing and selecting alternative patterns of relating that ultimately lead to the development of new internal working models for parent-infant relationships.

NURSING CARE

Joanie London called a parent-infant program requesting help in managing her 17-month-old son, Ronnie, whom she described as hyperactive and unmanageable. He also refused to speak. Joanie, aged 19, and her husband, Reg, aged 25, were also the parents of a 7-month-old daughter, Denise. Joanie described Denise as "perfect."

Joanie had been abandoned by her mother when she was 6 months old, and Reg was from a family with a history of alcoholism and wife abuse, but no reported child abuse. They had marital difficulties, which frequently involved arguing and fighting, and sometimes culminated in Reg's striking Joanie. The children were sometimes present during the fights, and Joanie said that the children cried and tried to protect her at times. Family life was calmer when Reg was employed; the arguments and physical abuse decreased as well. Ronnie's "hyperactive" behavior also decreased when family life was calmer.

Ten months after services were begun, Charles was born. He was the product of an unwanted pregnancy. During his first weeks, the mother and the baby showed evidence of positive attachment (e.g., mutual gaze, modeling). Within the first month, however, Charles developed colic, displayed signs of attachment difficulties (e.g., back arching, gaze aversion), and frequently looked very frightened.

Assessment

Consistent with both the Rogers model and the infant mental health model, in which the family is considered the environment of the infant or very young child, assessment for these clients is process oriented and conducted in the home over a 4- to 7-week period (Fraiberg, 1980; Johnston, 1986). During this time, the nurse begins to establish a trusting relationship with both the infant and the parents. Using a Rogerian approach, the nurse assesses the family as a whole, the individual needs of family members as they relate to the family as a whole, and patterns of family-environment interaction (Johnston, 1986). Because the focus of intervention is the infant, special attention is given to the effect of family patterns on the infant.

Family environment and family support systems are assessed for the provision of safety and nurturance. With the London family, for example, it was important to assess Charles' environment for physical safety and the provision of quiet time so that he could acquire the state regulation needed for sleeping and being quietly alert, for age-appropriate toys, for patterning of family schedules, for intrusions by the older children, and for the affective tone of the family.

The nurse also assesses the developmental level of the infant formally or informally during home visits by observing the infant's interaction with parents or an examiner and coding the child on age-appropriate items from the Bayley Scales, the Denver Developmental Screening Test, the Greenspan Clinical Landmarks Scale, or the Washington Guide to Promoting Development in the Very Young Child (Powell, 1981; Weatherston & Tableman, 1989). The degree of stability within the family and the parents' level of acceptance determine whether the developmental assessment is formal or informal. An additional tool for assessment, which can also be used as an intervention, is a videotape recording of family inter-actions. While viewing the videotape with the parents, the nurse can help them to appreciate the infant's abilities and the ways in which the family interactional patterns facilitate or hinder the infant's development. The infant characteristics assessed include, but are not limited to, temperament, physical or medical prob-lems, appearance, and tone of cry.

Attachment and individuation are assessed through observation of parent-infant interactions. Massie and Campbell (1980) developed a scale for such an assess-ment, focusing on the presence, frequency, and intensity of the following behav-iors during separation and reunion: gaze, vocalization, touch, holding, affect, and proximity. Infant reunion and separation responses can also be used to assess pat-terns of attachment (Ainsworth et al., 1978; Main et al., 1985) and patterns of individuation (Mahler, Pine, & Bergman, 1975).

Carefully observing and listening for possible messages conveyed to the infant through verbal or behavioral interactions reveal internal working models. For ex-ample, on one occasion, Joanie told Ronnie to look for a book in his bedroom, although she knew it was locked in a closet. When he reported that he could not find the book, she smiled and said, "I knew you wouldn't find it." From this inter-action, Ronnie might develop several internal working models that delineate various aspects of parent-child relationships, such as: (1) parents trick children, (2) children are powerless, and (3) children should not show initiative.

Reciprocity and the parent's responsiveness to the infant's cues are also as-sessed through observation of parent-infant interaction. Areas assessed include the clarity of both parental and infant cues; parents' ability to discern and respond to the infant's signals regarding comfort, hunger, socialization, and the need for separation; and the parents' capacity for reciprocal interaction with the infant.

Nursing Diagnoses

Interventions in infant mental health care focus on promoting the optimal de-velopment of infants, whereas diagnoses frequently focus on problems. The iden-tification of potential or existing problems are part of promotion and prevention, but it is also essential to identify healthy aspects of the infant and family in de-fining the focus of intervention. To deal with this issue, Greenspan and Lieberman (1988) have proposed a classification scheme that integrates a clinical perspective with a developmental approach.

Diagnoses applicable to high-risk infants may include: Disorganized Motor Behavior, Hyperactivity, Anxiety, Altered Communication Patterns Not Other-wise Specified, Failure to Attain Language, Potential for Trauma, and Unclear Values (O'Toole & Loomis, 1989). Diagnoses for infants at risk that should be added to the nursing diagnosis classifications are Attachment Disorders, Failure to Thrive, Potential for Child Abuse, and Failure to Attain Developmental Markers.

Nursing Interventions

Nurses who use the Rogerian framework focus on the empowerment of clients in their interventions. Rogers viewed nursing as sharing knowledge and skills, rather than as doing something to or for someone. She described the science of unitary man as "a positive developmental approach" (cited in Johnston, 1986, p. 12). The principles of integrality, helicy, and resonancy guide the practice of these nurses.

This philosophy is consistent with, and complements, the infant mental health model, in which concepts from psychoanalytic theory, attachment theory, and developmental psychology provide the conceptual base for intervention. Typically, treatment takes place in the home, with the therapist making visits at least weekly. Three treatment modalities—support, education, and interpretation—are used throughout treatment (Fraiberg, 1980). Intervention can be provided through dyadic, family, or group modalities.

Support can take two forms: concrete services and emotional support. Although education can take several forms, it is most often provided as developmental guidance informally presented when developmental issues arise in the course of home visits. Intervention focuses on the "baby as client" (Fraiberg, 1980, p. 49). Although unable to speak, infants can eloquently communicate what is happening in their relationships with their parents and other care-givers through nonverbal or verbal behaviors and developmental markers.

Psychotherapeutic interpretation is aimed at helping the parent establish connections between current difficulties in the parent-child relationship and past difficulties in the parent's own life or other psychological blocks that impede the parent's ability to make a positive investment in the infant. This often entails helping the parent identify and alter internal working models of parent-infant relationships.

The London family did not need concrete services as much as they needed emotional support. Although the London family had financial problems, they also had a strong support network for the provision of food, clothing, and transportation. Emotional support was not as evident in the family's support network. The nurse provided such support by acknowledging the difficulty of being parents to three very small and needy infants, encouraging improved interactional and affection patterns between the parents and with the children, and monitoring the protection and safety of the children associated with family violence.

Developmental guidance was an ongoing process throughout the nurse's home visits. Although Joanie was adept at the physical care of her children, she found it difficult to play with them. Both Joanie and Reg would tell a child to "go get a toy" rather than selecting a toy for them or creating and maintaining a play activity. They responded to nondirective suggestions and modeling about ways to structure activities for the children in an age-appropriate way, however, so that both the children and parents began to enjoy play activities more.

Psychotherapeutic interpretation was very important with this family. Both Joanie and Reg were from families who used withdrawal as a method of dealing with conflictual issues, and both were using withdrawal at the initiation of intervention. Joanie's reason for calling the clinic for assistance was a strong urge to abandon her children and husband. Reg was escaping through sports activities, Army Reserves, and work. The parents would spend much weekend time separately with friends or relatives, often each taking a child. By exploring interactions with their children and similarities between past and present life experiences, Joanie and Reg were able to make decisions to stay together; to improve their relationship with each other and their children; and to make conscious, concerted efforts not to abuse or neglect their children. Through this process, the parents were helped to identify and alter their internal working models of marital and parent-infant relationships.

Within the concept of helicy (Rogers, 1970), the parents' interpersonal changes can be viewed as an evolution of the family pattern from one of withdrawal to a desire for intimacy. This represents a movement to a higher, more complex level of interpersonal relating.

Evaluation

Psychiatric nursing interventions with infants and very young children are evaluated for both outcome and process. Outcome measures include the developmental achievements of the infant and the ability of the parent to invest in the infant to promote optimal development. Questions to be asked in this type of evaluation are, With intervention, was the infant's attainment of developmental markers more consistent with the infant's chronological age? Were the parents able to interact with the infant in a way that facilitated development?

Process measures assess the nurse's ability to help the family help themselves. With intervention, was the family able to develop criteria for evaluating change? Did the nurse empower the family to develop their own solutions for change rather than imposing solutions (Johnston, 1986)? With Ronnie, for example, the nurse would evaluate his skills to determine whether they had become more age-appropriate. What family or parent-infant interactions were related to his unwillingness to talk? Was he more able to express his feelings in words rather than in disorganized, hyperactive, or aggressive behavior? Are the parents more able to assess Ronnie's behavior in light of family stress and interactional patterns? Are the parents being assisted to form their own solutions?

NURSING RESEARCH

There is a large body of nursing research on issues directly related to infant mental health intervention, such as mother-infant interaction; development of mother-, father-, or sibling-infant attachment; nursing intervention to prevent developmental delay; parental responses to infant characteristics (e.g., temperament, gender); and instrument development (e.g., infant tenderness needs).

Attachment

Rubin (1977) first described the development of maternal attachment in relation to "binding in," which she believed to occur over the last trimester of pregnancy and the first 12 to 15 months following birth. Through the work of Cranley (1981) and others (Mercer, Ferketich, May, DeJoseph, & Sollid, 1988; Weaver & Cranley, 1983), it has been established that both parents develop an attachment to the fetus in the third trimester. Maternal-fetal attachment is positively related to social support in both young adults and adolescents (Gaffney, 1986). Variables such as anxiety, self-esteem, and parity have produced mixed results over several studies (Gaffney, 1988; Mercer et al., 1988). Situational variables, such as high-risk status of mother and infant (Mercer et al., 1988), use of ultrasound or amniocentesis (Heidrich & Cranley, 1989), and vaginal or cesarean birth (Fortier, 1988) have not been found to be related to parental-fetal attachment.

Carter-Jessop (1981) found that intervention with women in the third trimester of pregnancy enhanced mother-infant attachment after delivery. Carson and Virden (cited in Gaffney, 1988) replicated Carter-Jessop's study with a larger, multiethnic sample of two experimental groups, one of which received the Carter-Jessop intervention while the other received instruction in relaxation during labor. Carson and Virden found no differences in mother-infant attachment between these two groups. These findings may reflect differences in study design and need to be replicated before definite conclusions can be drawn about practice implications.

Holaday (1981) and Capuzzi (1989) examined relationships between mother-infant attachment and chronic illness or handicapping conditions in infants. Holaday compared mothers' responses to the cry of chronically ill infants and healthy infants. Chronically ill infants cried more often than did well infants; among seriously ill infants, the cry waxed and waned more often, making the clarity of the signal more difficult to interpret. Mothers of chronically ill infants showed different patterns of response rather than a single response, such as picking up the infant (Holaday, 1981). Capuzzi (1989) also found differences in the attachment behaviors of mothers of handicapped infants and those of well infants. The mothers of handicapped infants exhibited fewer attachment behaviors at 1 month postpartum, but there were no differences at 6 or 12 months. When maternal prenatal-social support was partialled out, there were no differences in maternal attachment behaviors, suggesting that social support alters the effects of having a handicapped infant.

In a nursing study of child-mother attachment, Fry (1985) compared child-mother attachment in 3-year-old children who were healthy and in children who had congenital heart disease. Reciprocity in mother-child interaction, curiosity, conceptual perspective taking, and delay of gratification were considered measures of attachment. The children with congenital heart disease were more passive and less willing to initiate activities with their mothers. They also did not engage in simultaneous manipulation of objects as often as did the healthy children. Thus, the healthy children demonstrated a higher level of development (individuation) and a more sophisticated form of curiosity than did the children with congenital heart disease.

Nursing Intervention

Since 1971, Barnard and colleagues (1985, 1988) have been studying early risk factors that increase the probability of poor developmental outcomes in high-risk infants. They also developed and tested nursing interventions designed to prevent developmental delay among these infants. Through this program of research, Barnard and colleagues have developed a child health interaction model (Capuzzi, 1989); they postulated that, for effective mother-child interaction to develop, (1) the infant and the mother must both give clear cues, (2) the mother must attend to the infant's cues, (3) the infant must respond to the mother's care-giving, and (4) the environment must facilitate mother-infant interaction.

From an earlier study (Barnard et al., 1985), in which the effectiveness of three nursing intervention models were compared, Barnard and colleagues concluded that, in families with both complicated pregnancies and social problems, the mothers most resistant to intervention were those who had both situational problems and poor support systems. From this conclusion, they developed two intervention models that were tested in a recent study (Barnard et al., 1988). The first model was labeled the mental health model, and the primary focus was to help the mother develop affiliative ties with family and friends through a therapeutic relationship. The second model was labeled the information/resource model, was based on the traditional public health nursing model, and focused on the provision of physical and developmental guidance along with referrals to social agencies.

In a study which tested the two models (Barnard et al., 1985), there were no differences in the Bayley scores of the infants, with means for both groups slightly above 100 at 2 years of age. The study findings indicate that less competent mothers are more likely to stay in treatment through a therapeutic relationship, while higher functioning mothers have better outcomes with the provision of information. This finding was also reflected in the attachment classifications of the children.

Future Research

More research is needed to determine whether interventions derived from the infant mental health model are effective for specific populations. The questions that must be asked include, What therapeutic elements of the infant mental health model are effective? For whom? At what points in time? Would elements of the infant mental health model, in combination with elements of Barnard's mental health or information/resources models, be more effective than either model used alone? With a history of home visiting and the ability to deal with a wide variety of health and social issues, nurses are in an ideal position to conduct this type of research.

REFERENCES

Ainsworth, M.S., Blehar, M.C., Waters, E., & Wall, S. (1978). *Patterns of attachment.* Hillsdale, NJ: Lawrence Erlbaum Associates.

Barnard, K.E., Hammond, M., Mitchell, S.K., Booth, C.L., Spietz, A., Snyder, C., Elsas, T. (1985). Caring for high-risk infants and their families. In M. Green (Ed.), *The psychosocial aspects of the family* (pp. 245–266). Lexington, MA: D.C. Heath.

Barnard, K.E., Magyary, D., Sumner, G., Booth, C.L., Mitchell, S.K., & Spieker, S. (1988). Prevention of parenting alterations for women with low social support. *Psychiatry, 51,* 248–253.

Benn, R. (1990). *Defining eligibility criteria for a state-wide definition under P.L. 99-457: Part H: A research report.* Detroit: Wayne State University, Merrill-Palmer Institute.

Bowlby, J. (1982). *Attachment and loss: Vol. 1. Attachment* (2nd ed.). New York: Basic Books.

Bretherton, I. (1985). Attachment theory: Retrospect and prospect. In I. Bretherton & E. Waters (Eds.), *Growing points in attachment.* Monographs of the Society for Research in Child Development; 50(1–2, Serial No. 209):3–35.

Capuzzi, C. (1989). Maternal attachment to handicapped infants and the relationship to social support. *Research in Nursing and Health, 12,* 161–167.

Carter-Jessop, L. (1981). Promoting maternal attachment through prenatal intervention. *Journal of Maternal Child Nursing, 6,* 107–112.

Cassidy, J., & Kobak, R.R. (1988). Avoidance and its relation to other defensive processes. In J. Belsky & T. Nezworski (Eds.), *Clinical implications of attachment* (pp. 300–323). Hillsdale, NJ: Lawrence Erlbaum Associates.

Cranley, M.S. (1981). Development of a tool for the measurement of maternal attachment during pregnancy. *Nursing Research, 30,* 281–284.

Fortier, J.C. (1988). The relationship of vaginal and cesarean births to father-infant attachment. *Journal of Obstetric and Gynecological Nursing, 17,* 128–134.

Fraiberg, S. (Ed.). (1980). *Clinical studies in infant mental health.* New York: Basic Books.

Fry, J.E. (1985). Reciprocity in mother-child interaction, correlates of attachment, and family environment in three-year-old children with congenital heart disease (Doctoral dissertation, Wayne State University College of Nursing). *Dissertation Abstracts International,* (46; 113).

Gaffney, K.F. (1986). Maternal-fetal attachment in relation to self-concept and anxiety. *Journal of Maternal Child Nursing, 15,* 91–101.

Gaffney, K.F. (1988). Prenatal maternal attachment. *IMAGE, 20,* 106–109.

Greenspan, S.I., & Lieberman, A.F. (1988). A clinical approach to attachment. In J. Belsky & T. Nezworki (Eds.), *Clinical implications of attachment* (pp. 387–424). Hillsdale, NJ: Lawrence Erlbaum Associates.

Heidrich, S.M., & Cranley, M.S. (1989). Effect of fetal movement, ultrasound scans, and amniocentesis on maternal-fetal attachment. *Nursing Research, 38,* 81–84.

Holaday, B. (1981). Maternal response to their chronically ill infants' attachment behavior of crying. *Nursing Research, 30,* 343–348.

Johnston, R.L. (1986). Approaching family intervention through Rogers' conceptual model. In A.L. Whall (Ed.), *Family therapy theory for nursing: Four approaches.* Norwalk, CT: Appleton-Century-Crofts.

Mahler, M., Pine, F., & Bergman, A. (1975). *The psychological birth of the human infant: Symbiosis and individuation.* New York: Basic Books.

Main, M., Kaplan, N., & Cassidy, J. (1985). Security in infancy, childhood, and adulthood: A move to the level of representation. In I. Bretherton & E. Waters (Eds.), Growing points in attachment. *Monographs of the Society for Research in Child Development, 50*(1–2, Serial No. 209), 66–106.

Malinski, V.M. (Ed.). (1986). *Explorations on Martha Rogers' science of unitary human beings.* Norwalk, CT: Appleton-Century-Crofts.

Massie, H., & Campbell, K. (1980). *Manual of the Massie-Campbell Scale of mother-infant attachment indicators during stress.* Unpublished manuscript.

Mercer, R., Ferketich, S., May, K., DeJoseph, J., & Sollid, D. (1988). Further exploration of maternal and paternal fetal attachment. *Research in Nursing and Health, 11,* 83–95.

O'Toole, A.W., & Loomis, M.E. (1989). Revision of the phenomena of concern for psychiatric mental health nursing. *Archives of Psychiatric Nursing, 3,* 288–299.

Powell, M.L. (1981). *Assessment and management of developmental changes and problems in children* (2nd. ed.). St. Louis: C.V. Mosby.

Rogers, M.E. (1970). *An introduction to the theoretical basis of nursing.* Philadelphia: F.A. Davis.

Rogers, M.E. (1980). Nursing: A science of unitary man. In J.P. Riehl & C. Roy (Eds.), *Conceptual models for nursing practice* (2nd ed.). New York: Appleton-Century-Crofts.

Rogers, M.E. (1986). Science of unitary human beings. In V.M. Malinski (Ed.), *Exploration on Martha Rogers' science of unitary human beings.* Norwalk, CT: Appleton-Century-Crofts.

Rubin, R. (1977). Binding-in in the postpartum period. *Journal of Maternal Child Nursing, 6,* 67–75.

Weatherston, D., & Tableman, B. (1989). *IMH services: Supporting competencies/reducing risks.* Lansing: Michigan Department of Mental Health.

Weaver, R.H., & Cranley, M.S. (1983). An exploration of paternal-fetal attachment behavior. *Nursing Research, 32,* 68–72.

Weston, D.R., Ivins, B., Zuckerman, B., Jones, C., & Lopez, R. (1989, June). Drug exposed babies: Research and clinical issues. *Zero to Three, 11*(5), 1–7.

12

Nursing Interventions with Children Experiencing Attention and Motor Difficulties

Edilma Yearwood

After reading this chapter, the reader will be able to:

1. identify behaviors that are characteristic of children with attention and excess motor activity difficulties
2. analyze individual, family, peer, and school dynamics associated with a child who has attention and excess motor activity difficulties
3. identify nursing diagnoses that are applicable to these children
4. develop a comprehensive plan of nursing care for a child experiencing attention and excess motor activity difficulties

The child with attention difficulties and increased motor activity presents a dilemma to parents, teachers, peers, and health care providers. The dilemma often centers around: (1) coping with the demands and needs of this at times difficult-to-manage child, (2) agreeing on the best treatment approach(es) for the child, and (3) accepting the diagnoses when the child exhibits different behaviors with different people. The setting and the demands placed on the child can also affect the severity of the behaviors seen.

The literature points to the incidence of attention and motor activity difficulties as anywhere from 3% to 5% of the child population in the United States. The difficulty occurs mostly in males (a 6:1 ratio) and the existence of a family history of Altered Attention Processes and Excess Motor Activity (AAPEMA) increases a child's potential for developing the disorder.

At some point, the child and/or family usually experiences some type of stress as a result of the child's inability to get along with others, perform well in school, or behave as expected at home. Psychiatric and mental health nurses, because of their education, are particularly well equipped to work with these children and families in order to help them adapt as effectively as possible to their individual situation. Nurses may be involved in one or more of the following:

- the assessment process with the child, the family, and the school
- individual, family, and/or group treatment modalities

- the administration and monitoring of the effects of various medications on the child
- the teaching of appropriate parenting and coping skills to the parents/caregivers
- the teaching of appropriate social and peer interactional skills to children with this disorder
- a variety of research projects aimed at collecting data on assessment criteria and evaluating treatment approaches

ETIOLOGY

There are numerous theories about what causes attention and excess motor activity difficulties. Among these are:

- genetic disturbance (Cantwell, 1975)
- neurological insult (Rutter & Hersou, 1985)
- diet high in sugar and/or additives (Feingold, 1975)
- family dynamics (Cantwell, 1975)
- environmental toxins (Rutter & Hersou, 1985)

Research continues on most of the aforementioned theories in an effort to arrive at a more definitive cause of the disorder. The numerous theories can be confusing to parents who want a definitive cause and a "cure" for this disorder.

APPLICATION OF THE ROY ADAPTATION MODEL

In the Roy adaptation model of nursing (1984), the "person" (individual, family, or group) is viewed as an adaptive system that is made up of internal and external stimuli (input); control processes, which are biological and psychological coping mechanisms; effectors, which include the individual's physiological functioning, self-concept, role function, and interdependence; and output, which can be either an adaptive or ineffective behavioral response (Figure 12-1). There are numerous and frequent stressors on the individual and the family, who are in continuous interaction with the environment. According to Roy, the role of nursing is to promote holistic adaptation or effective coping by using the nursing process of assessment, diagnosis, planning, intervention, and evaluation.

During the assessment, the nurse observes human behaviors and calls upon theoretical knowledge to identify factors that contribute to these behaviors. After reaching an understanding of the individual's and/or the family's response to stressors, the nurse can select areas as the focus for nursing diagnosis. From the diagnosis, interventions to promote system integrity can then be developed.

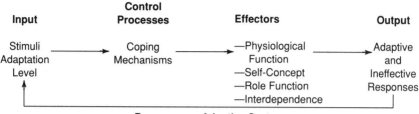

Figure 12-1 The Roy adaptive system. *Source:* From *Introduction to Nursing: An Adaptation Model,* 2nd ed., (p. 30) by C. Roy, 1984, Norwalk CT: Appleton and Lange. Copyright 1984 by Appleton and Lange. Reprinted by permission.

Assessment Process

Diagnosing attention and excess motor activity difficulty requires a complete and thorough examination of the child's biopsychosocial history. The assessment should begin with a comprehensive physical examination, including the child's neurological and neurochemical status, although the results of these tests are usually well within normal limits. Visual and hearing tests, as well as an assessment of the child's behavior at home, in school, and with peers, are crucial. Standardized behavioral rating scales such as the Achenbach checklist (1988a) and the Conners scaler (Goyette, Connors, & Ulrich, 1978) usually yield invaluable data. Cognitive and learning assessments of the child should also be completed (Hunt, 1988).

Child and family interviews are conducted to assess the child's "fit" within the family and to identify existing stressors on the family system. The family interview can be an opportunity to highlight similarities and discrepancies between the interviewer's perceptions of the child and the parent's perceptions, as well as to assess the ways in which the family members are interacting with this child. In order to arrive at a sound holistic nursing diagnosis, a nurse may ask about:

- the course of the mother's pregnancy with this child, including any family history of drug or alcohol abuse; trauma(s) during the pregnancy; type of birth, including duration of labor, use of medication, any occurrence of fetal distress, length of stay in the hospital; any birth complications and treatment; any family history of attention and excess motor activity difficulties
- the characteristics of the child as an infant and preschooler, such as temperament, significant injuries or illnesses, any history of lead poisoning, hospitalizations, use of medications, relationships with siblings and peers, and time frame for achieving developmental milestones
- the child's reaction to limit setting, adherence to rules, activity level, ability to attend to what's being said or asked, and any changes in behavior associ-

ated with a change in physical setting or number of stimuli available in the environment

- the child's behavior in school, including any conflicting reports from the school about the child's behavior, the child's complaints of boredom, the child's ability to get along with friends, argumentativeness, distractibility, excessive number of accidents, quality of the child's schoolwork, need for frequent reminders to resume tasks
- the child's sleep, eating, and self-care history

Six items from the Conner's Parent Questionnaire (Goyette et al., 1978) are included in Exhibit 12-1 to familiarize the nurse with the tool. Specific items on the Scale look at: activity level, inattentiveness, and conduct problems. The points from each of these items are totalled and then divided by the number of items in that category to arrive at the score which indicates whether or not a particular behavior is significant.

Samples from the Child Behavior Checklist Teacher form by Achenbach (1988b) have been included in Exhibit 12-2. The entire scale is comprised of a profile of the child, the I.Q., Achievement test scores and 113 Behavioral items.

There is some controversy in the literature as to the significance of discrepancy between the teacher rating and that of the parent(s) on either the Conners or Achenbach Scales. Barkley proposes that *both* the teacher and the parent need to report symptoms and the symptoms must be across at least 50% of the settings on home and school situation questionnaires (1988).

Exhibit 12-1 Sample Items from Conners' Parent Rating Scale

Name of Child _____ Date _____

Please answer all questions. Beside each item below, indicate the degree of the problem by a check mark (✔)

	Not at all	Just a little	Pretty much	Very much
3. Problems with making or keeping friends.				
11. Restless in the "squirmy" sense.				
25. Fails to finish things.				
31. Distractibility or attention span a problem.				
37. Easily frustrated in efforts.				
38. Disturbs other children.				

Source: Reprinted with permission of Multi Health Systems, Inc., 908 Niagara Falls Blvd., North Tonawanda, NY 14120-2060.

Exhibit 12-2 Teacher Scale

These behaviors should describe the child now and within the past 2 months. 2 = Very true, 1 = Sometimes true, and 0 = Not true. Circle the appropriate number.

0	1	2	2	Hums or makes other odd noises in class
0	1	2	4	Fails to finish things he/she starts
0	1	2	8	Can't concentrate, can't pay attention for long
0	1	2	10	Can't sit still, restless, hyperactive
0	1	2	15	Fidgets
0	1	2	19	Demands a lot of attention
0	1	2	36	Gets hurt a lot, accident-prone
0	1	2	38	Gets teased a lot
0	1	2	45	Nervous, high-strung, or tense
0	1	2	49	Has difficulty learning
0	1	2	53	Talks out of turn
0	1	2	61	Poor school work
0	1	2	72	Messy work
0	1	2	77	Demands must be met immediately, easily frustrated
0	1	2	93	Talks too much
0	1	2	104	Unusually loud

Source: From *Child behavior checklist: Teacher's report form* by T.M. Achenbach. Copyright 1988 by Thomas M. Achenbach. Reprinted by permission.

From these instruments, the nurse has more supporting data about the severity of the disorder and the arena in which the behavior is more problematic. This can guide the nursing diagnosis and interventions.

Attention difficulties can be diagnosed as early as age 3 if the symptomatology is severe enough. These symptoms include gross motor overactivity, such as excessive climbing and jumping, inattentiveness, and the inability to "listen." By the time the child reaches adolescence, the motor activity level may decrease because of hormonal changes, but the fidgetiness, impulsivity, and risk-taking behaviors (e.g., mixed substance abuse) may increase as the youngster tries to cope with the anxiety and motor restlessness experienced (Barkley, 1981).

Using the data collected in the assessment process, nurses should consider the following diagnoses when working with this client population:

1. Alteration in Attention Processes: Etiology Unknown
2. Alteration in Motor Activity: Etiology Unknown
3. Potential for Injury Related to Impulsivity
4. Potential for Noncompliance in the Child Related to Difficulty Attending

5. Potential for Alteration in Nutrition: Less than Body Requirements Related to Excessive Motor Activity and Possible Side Effects of Medication
6. Potential for Sleep Pattern Disturbance Related to Possible Side-effects of Medication
7. Impaired Social Interaction Related to Poor Social Skills
8. Disturbance in Self-esteem (low), Possibly Related to Rejection by Peers, Family, and Adults
9. Potential Alteration in Parenting Related to Knowledge Deficit
10. Potential for Alteration in Sensory Perceptual Processes, Possibly Related to Prenatal Insult (Townsend, 1988).

Clinical Picture

Josie is 7 years old and in the second grade. He is in a class with 22 other children. His teacher is increasingly frustrated because, although he is a bright boy, he does not complete his schoolwork; talks out of turn in class; and distracts the other children by making noises, moving his chair, or fidgeting in his seat. He frequently does not appear to be paying attention and impulsively volunteers for tasks that he does not complete.

During recess, he does not get along with his peers because he is unable to comply with the rules of games, becomes angry and aggressive, and wants to switch from activity to activity. His peers identify him as the least liked child in the classroom.

Using the perspective of Roy's adaptive system (Roy, 1984), the nurse may develop a total profile for Josie's family (Exhibit 12-3). The nurse examines the four major components of the adaptation model in order to identify the areas where coping is adequate and areas where coping is inadequate. The following are guideline questions:

I. Input
   A. Internal Stimuli
      1. What is the cause of Josie's impulsivity, distractibility, and motor activity?
      2. Are his behaviors controlled by the level of stimulant medication present in his blood system at a given time?
   B. External Stimuli
      1. What types of demands are placed on Josie?
      2. How does the family view Josie? Work with him? Reinforce negative or positive behaviors?
      3. Is there a behavioral management plan in place? Is it effective? If not, why not?

4. What type of environment is Josie in? Overstimulating, moderately stimulating or low in stimuli? Describe behaviors in each.

II. Control Processes (Coping Mechanisms)
  A. In class, Josie is described as:
    1. Unable to pay attention
    2. Impulsive
    3. Loud
    4. Active
    5. Unable to follow through
    6. Sloppy with schoolwork
  B. With peers, Josie is described as:
    1. Unable to follow rules
    2. Aggressive
    3. Motorically active
    4. Unable to remain on task

In order to display appropriate coping mechanisms, Josie must be aware of and adhere to a behavioral plan, participate in other treatment recommendations (e.g., medication, therapy), be motivated to get along with peers and "fit" in better, and have the psychological support of the significant adults in his environment.

III. Effectors
  A. Physiological Functioning
    1. What is Josie's nutritional status (weight, height, eating pattern)?
    2. Are there any problems with bowel or bladder elimination?
    3. What time does Josie go to sleep? Wake up? Does he get up in the middle of the night? If so, how long does he remain up?
    4. What are the results of neurological work done on Josie? Was an electroencephalogram done? What are the results?
    5. Does Josie display any difficulty with hearing, seeing, smelling, or tasting? Are tactile senses intact?
    6. What are the results of blood work done on Josie? Is thyroid functioning within normal range?
  B. Self-Concept
    1. How does Josie describe himself? What does he see as his strengths? Weaknesses? Does he like himself? How does he draw himself?
    2. What does Josie want to be when he grows up?
    3. How does Josie think others see him?

Exhibit 12-3 Profile for Josie's Family According to Roy's Adaptation Model

Input	Control Processes	Effectors	Output
Father Age 30 Poor job history Currently unemployed Chronically abused as a child Smokes; poor health; poor appetite Short-tempered Stays away from home frequently Substance abuser Mother Age 30 Bank teller Depressed Has difficulty setting limits on Josie (age 7) Married 8 years Few friends Complicated pregnancy	Father Multiple substance abuser Mother Avoids all situations involving conflict with husband and with Josie	*Physiological* Father Poor nutritional status and poor skin integrity secondary to substance abuse Questionable neurological status secondary to physical abuse, outbursts, and drug abuse Mother Poor nutritional status related to loss of appetite secondary to depression Josie Poor nutritional habits secondary to increased activity level Sensory-perceptual alteration related to prenatal insult *Self-Concept* Father Poor self-concept/self-esteem secondary to chronic child abuse Mother Poor self-concept/self-esteem secondary to marital stress and ineffective parenting skills Josie Poor self-concept/self-esteem secondary to poor school performance, absence of age-appropriate peer relationships and lack of involvement in home/school activities	*Ineffective Parenting* Parents Neither parent is available or effective in setting limits, helping or structuring the environment for Josie. They have missed several appointments with Josie's teacher.

Josie
Age 7
2nd grade
Bright, but performs
  poorly in school
Aggressive/angry
Impulsive
Poor peer interaction
  skills

Josie
Poor attention span
Excess motor
  activity

Role Function
Father
  Ineffective parent, husband, and worker
Mother
  Ineffective parent and wife
Josie
  Ineffective student, peer, and son

Interdependence
Father: nonexistent, minimal
Mother: fair
Josie: poor in school and at home

Josie
Attention
  difficulties,
  excess motor
  activity

C. Role Function

    1. How does Josie describe his position or "fit" within the family? Does he see himself as contributing to the family? To his class? To his peers? If yes, what is the contribution?

    2. How does Josie see himself in relation to his mother? His father? How does he perceive their relationship? How does Josie describe the "ideal" family?

    3. How does Josie describe his school performance? Does he feel he can do better? If so, how?

    4. How does Josie describe his relationship with peers?

D. Interdependence

    1. Who does Josie feel closest to? Who can he trust? Talk to?

    2. Who does Josie feel cares about him?

    3. Who spends quality time with him?

IV. Output (Possible Nursing Diagnoses)

A. Alteration in Attention Process: Etiology Unknown

B. Alteration in Motor Activity: Hyperactivity

C. Impaired Social Interactions Related to Poor Social Skills and Excess Activity Level

D. Alteration in Self-concept Related to Poor School and Peer Interaction Skills

E. Altered Family Processes Related to Family Members' Ineffective Individual Coping

NURSING INTERVENTIONS

When working with the child who has attention and motor activity difficulties, nursing interventions should be comprehensive; the nurse may find it necessary to work with the child, family, siblings, peers, and the teacher/school in order to affect adaptation. The focus should be on improving the child's self-esteem, school performance, peer interaction skills, and achievement of developmental milestones. The specific goals of therapy should include:

- helping the child develop trust in one person, namely, the therapist, which can later be transferred to others. This can be achieved by adhering to the therapy schedule; maintaining a warm, safe, and growth-promoting environment; encouraging exploration of feelings; respecting and accepting the child; and empowering the child whenever possible.

- helping the child learn to get along with peers. This may be achieved by working with the child around particular social skills, such as taking turns, sharing, listening to another, learning and adhering to game rules. Once a positive working relationship has been established with the therapist, work may continue in a dyad group with another child while the therapist monitors and models appropriate behavior.

- fostering ego strengths in the child by dealing with reality, fostering age-appropriate behaviors and pursuits, assisting with improving interactions with peers, dealing appropriately with aggressive impulses, and helping the child to develop a sense of social usefulness.
- setting and helping the child adhere to limits. Expectations should be clear and concise, and consequences should be specified precisely. The child can be helped to adhere to limits by use of explanations, timeouts, and earning/not earning special privileges/things.
- helping the child improve self-esteem by providing tasks/activities at which the child can succeed.
- providing consistent, positive feedback to the child when he or she exhibits appropriate behaviors.
- helping the child understand aspects of the disorder via patient education.

In conjunction with individual therapy, Josie was referred for group therapy twice weekly. The group approach provided opportunities for Josie to interact with same-aged peers in a structured, predictable, and goal-oriented situation. The group was comprised of five 7- and 8-year-old boys, all of whom had difficulty making friends and getting along with peers. There were two group leaders, one man and one woman. Group rules and behavioral expectations were clearly stated at the outset of the group sessions, and they were reviewed periodically to foster positive social interactions. Behaviors such as getting along, listening, and helping others were praised. Stickers were given to reinforce and acknowledge cooperation with these expectations at the end of each session. Josie and his peers were aware that they would not receive stickers for inappropriate group behaviors.

The group activities, which included board games; building projects, such as model airplanes, bird houses and napkin holders; simple cooking activities; and holiday crafts, were aimed at teaching a particular skill and helping the children succeed. Not only did these activities make it possible to avoid relying solely on a talking approach, which may have been ineffective because of the children's age, but also they promoted sharing and helping.

The immediate goal of family therapy for children with attention and excess motor activity difficulties and their families is to engage and set up a working relationship with them. If some family members are resistant to attending sessions, the nurse should continue to try to effect a change in the family by meeting with those who will attend. Work should focus on communication patterns within the family and individual family members' strengths. The parental role is examined in light of the child's developmental needs for consistency, structure, limits, and parent involvement in the child's school and social life. If a behavioral plan is developed (Barkley, 1987), it should be reviewed and revised as necessary and the parents praised for participating in the plan.

Josie and his family participated in weekly family therapy sessions. During these sessions, the family and therapist developed behavioral plans to help the parents work on shaping some of Josie's behaviors at home. For example, the plan to help Josie attend to and complete tasks was as follows:

1. Josie will do homework between 5:00 and 5:30 P.M. on school nights in his room with no television or radio distractions.
2. Homework will be checked nightly, and Josie will receive a star on a graph for completing assignments.
3. Josie and his parents will spend 15 minutes each evening playing a game. During this time, Josie should be praised for attending to stated rules, and for remaining on task for the 15 minutes.
4. Josie should be verbally praised every time he adheres to, rather than ignores, the limits set by his parents.

Josie's parents demonstrated long-term problems regarding abuse, depression, and dependence. Thus, the nurse recommended that they enter marital therapy or their own individual therapy at some point in time.

The entire family needs education about the disorder and about medication, if used. Medication education should include the fact that the drug of choice is usually a stimulant such as methylphenidate (Ritalin), dextroamphetamine (Dexedrine), or pemoline (Cylert). The family should be aware that, if one does not work, another may be tried. These drugs act fairly quickly and remain in the system for approximately 4 hours. Parents should also be aware that baseline height and weight patterns are obtained and monitored periodically throughout the use of the medication to ensure that the child is growing appropriately, because stimulants may inhibit growth and interfere with the child's desire to eat. Smaller, more frequent meals that are high in calories can be offered if this occurs, and finger foods can be provided for this child who is frequently "on the go." This medication also lowers a child's seizure threshold. Finally, the medication should not be administered near bedtime because it may interfere with sleep. Periodically, children are taken off medication to determine whether their changes in behavior result from the medication or from other treatment interventions. As the situation improves at home, parents may opt not to medicate in the evenings or on the weekends.

In working with teachers, the nurse's goals should include:

- ensuring that there is time during the day when this child will have an outlet for his or her excessive motor activity level via involvement in a sport or gym activity
- providing for some quiet time and decreased stimuli in the environment for this child
- setting up and adhering to a behavioral system wherein the child will receive frequent rewards for acceptable behaviors while in class
- evaluating the possibility of special education placement where the child would be in smaller classes with teachers who may be specially trained to work with this more complex individual
- helping the teacher and family work together and follow through by adhering to the same rules/plan at home and in school

RESEARCH

There are myriads of needed research projects that involve children with altered attention processes and excess motor activity. Among them are:

- longitudinal studies of children with attention and motor activity difficulties
- studies of family characteristics/dynamics that foster an increase in self-esteem and social relatedness among children with this disorder
- studies on the effectiveness of male versus female therapists in treating children with this disorder
- studies on the effect of group therapy on children with the disorder
- assessments of the difference in the child's behavior and progress when raised in foster or residential care versus family-of-origin care

REFERENCES

Achenbach, T.M. (1988a). *Child behavior checklist for ages 4–16—Parent form.* Burlington: University of Vermont.

Achenbach, T.M. (1988b). *Child behavior checklist—Teacher's report form.* Burlington: University of Vermont.

Barkley, R. (1981). *Hyperactive children: A handbook for diagnosis and treatment.* New York: Guilford Press.

Barkley, R. (1987). *Defiant children: Parent and teacher assignments.* New York: Guilford Press.

Barkley, R. (1988). *Attention deficit hyperactivity disorders: Diagnosis, assessment and treatment.* Lecture. New York: Saratoga Springs.

Cantwell, D.P. (Ed.). (1975). *The hyperactive child.* New York: Spectrum Publications.

Feingold, F. (1975). *Why your child is hyperactive.* New York: Random House.

Goyette, C.H., Conners, C.K., and Ulrich, R.F. (1978). Normative data on revised Conners parent and teacher rating scales. *Journal of Abnormal Child Psychiatry, 6,* 221–236.

Hunt, R. (1988). Attention deficit disorder and hyperactivity. In Kestenbaum, C.J. and Williams, D.T. (Eds.). *Handbook of Clinical Assessment of Children and Adolescents. Vol. II.* New York: New York University Press.

Roy, C. (1984). *Introduction to nursing: An adaptation model* (2nd ed.). Englewood Cliffs, NJ: Prentice-Hall.

Rutter, M., & Hersou, L. (Eds.). (1985). *Child and adolescent psychiatry* (2nd ed.). Oxford: Blackwell Scientific Publications.

Townsend, M. (1988). *Nursing diagnoses in psychiatric nursing.* Philadelphia: F.A. Davis.

13

Nursing Interventions with Children Experiencing Elimination Difficulties

Louise C. Waszak

After reading this chapter, the reader will be able to:

1. identify the essential features of enuresis and encopresis
2. identify specific treatment goals and interventions for children with enuresis and encopresis
3. examine therapeutic nursing interventions
4. describe methods for evaluating the effectiveness of the interventions and treatment outcome

Difficulties with elimination, such as enuresis and encopresis, are common and persistent childhood problems. Generally, 25% of the children who are encopretic are also enuretic (Barker, 1983). When clinical symptoms of wetting and soiling occur in the absence of medical disease (e.g., infection) or structural abnormality (e.g., neurogenic bladder or aganglionic megacolon), the disturbances are referred to as functional enuresis and functional encopresis. Either disorder can be considered a primary disorder if the child has never been continent for a period of 6 months or longer. If the child begins to wet or soil after achieving continence, however, the disorder is considered secondary enuresis or secondary encopresis, respectively.

The majority of children are successfully toilet-trained by the ages of 3 or 4 years. Should bowel or bladder incontinence persist past the age of 5 years, treatment should be sought for both the child and the parents—not only to assist in the resolution of the disorder, but also to address their feelings of shame, guilt, and blame.

Toilet training is a major developmental task of childhood, and a child's failure to achieve bladder or bowel control produces stress not only for the child, but also for family members. While the incontinent child must contend with the painful awareness of "not measuring up" to family expectations, the parents voice their frustration and embarrassment over the child's soiled clothes and bed linens. In families where functional incontinence has precipitated dysfunctional patterns of behavior, the psychiatric nurse is in an excellent position to implement strategies that will promote adaptive behavior.

ENURESIS

Definition and Prevalence

Enuresis is defined as the involuntary excretion of urine after the age at which the child should have attained bladder control. Nocturnal enuresis or bedwetting occurs more frequently than does diurnal or daytime wetting; nearly one of five children at the age of 5 continues to wet the bed. In most cases, nocturnal enuresis is reported twice as often in boys than in girls. Typically, 30% of the nocturnally enuretic children also have episodes of diurnal enuresis. Even without treatment, 50% of the enuretic children are able to achieve dryness by the age of 10 years (May, 1986).

Contributing and Predictive Factors

In the search for definitive contributing factors, enuresis has been associated with four areas: developmental immaturity, emotional or psychological disturbance, structural or medical problems, and sleep disturbances. Both cognitive and physical maturation are factors in a child's developmental readiness for bladder training. Because learning plays a major role in bladder training, the child must be not only physiologically ready, but also mentally able to understand what is expected and to recognize biological cues, such as the sensation of bladder fullness. Although the child may be beyond the chronological age at which immaturity should be a factor, a disruption in the process of learning bladder control at an earlier age can result in the child's failure to achieve continence.

There are some factors that are predictive of treatment outcome (Butler, Brewin, & Forsythe, 1988). Although the child's age, gender, birth order, family size, and socioeconomic status are not related to the child's response to treatment, unsatisfactory housing conditions, family dysfunction, maternal anxiety, and social inadequacy and withdrawal are predictive of poor treatment outcome.

Assessment and Data Collection

A comprehensive nursing assessment that includes a clinical interview, a history of medical evaluations, and baseline behavioral records is essential to understanding a child's enuresis and determining the appropriate interventions. During the interview, the psychiatric nurse should obtain information about the child's history and pattern of enuresis, prior treatment and its effectiveness, presence of emotional problems, and medical history. The nurse should also inquire about the family's home environment, parental attitudes about the child's enuresis, and the family's medical history. It is important to note any major changes that have occurred in the family and the effects of any such changes on family functioning, especially when the child has secondary enuresis.

A general medical screening is conducted to rule out physiological abnormalities and diseases. Routine laboratory tests, such as a urinalysis, urine culture, and blood analysis, are helpful to determine the presence of an infection or diabetes and to evaluate renal function. More invasive procedures, such as the voiding cystourethrogram and intravenous pyelogram, are not used in the assessment of enuresis unless there is a clear medical indication for them.

A good clinical picture of the child's toileting habits and frequency of enuresis can be obtained through baseline behavioral records of the frequency and approximate times of: (1) both daytime and nighttime wetting episodes and (2) the child's trips to the toilet. It is also important to determine the amount of urine that the child voids when toileting and the size of the wet spot when enuretic. The frequency of voiding, either in the toilet or as a wetting episode, and the amount of urine voided can be used to determine the child's bladder capacity and retention ability. In addition, the effectiveness of the intervention during the initial stages of treatment may be seen as a decrease in the frequency of enuretic episodes and in the size of the wet spots.

The recording of the child's toileting patterns and enuretic episodes should begin at the time of admission and should continue for 1 to 2 weeks in order to obtain accurate baseline information. A form such as that shown in Figure 13-1 can be used to collect data for both diurnal and nocturnal enuretic children.

Graphing the data obtained by means of this form makes patterns in the frequency of both toileting and wetting readily apparent. The child's involvement in activities at the time of the enuretic episodes and the child's report of toileting difficulties should also be noted. Once treatment has begun, data are collected to determine the effectiveness of the intervention (Figure 13-2).

Case Example

Andrew was a 12.5-year-old boy who lived with his biological mother (Mrs. K.), his stepfather (Mr. K.), and a 5.3-year-old stepsister. His mother brought him to the hospital for evaluation of the symptoms of depression and enuresis. According to his mother, Andrew had developed difficulties approximately 2 years earlier after his mother's divorce from his biological father. That year, Andrew became socially withdrawn, did poorly in school, and failed to progress to the next grade. At this time, he also began to have infrequent "accidents at night" (bedwetting). Mrs. K. reported that Andrew had been much less energetic and more irritable in the mornings over the past several months. She noticed that his condition seemed to worsen after she and Mr. K. married 6 months ago. His symp-

Patient: _____ Primary Nurse: _____

GENERAL TOILETING

Date:		Accidents		Independent Toileting		Amount (cc or S, M, or L)	Initial
Time	7 A.M.– 9 A.M.	Y	N	Y	N		
	9 A.M.–11 A.M.	Y	N	Y	N		
	11 A.M.– 1 P.M.	Y	N	Y	N		
	1 P.M.– 3 P.M.	Y	N	Y	N		
	3 P.M.– 5 P.M.	Y	N	Y	N		
	5 P.M.– 7 P.M.	Y	N	Y	N		
	7 P.M.– 9 P.M.	Y	N	Y	N		
	9 P.M.–11 P.M.	Y	N	Y	N		
	11 P.M.– 3 A.M.	Y	N	Y	N		
	3 A.M.– 7 A.M.	Y	N	Y	N		

Figure 13-1 Enuresis and toileting monitoring form to establish a behavioral baseline.

toms included episodes of a depressed mood, decreased self-esteem, increased feelings of guilt and hopelessness, decreased interest in friends and favorite activities, and an increase in the "bedwetting accidents."

In a separate interview, Andrew validated his mother's report. Andrew said that his school performance decreased because he found school boring. He was no longer interested in playing with the other children and was less interested in his favorite sport, football. Andrew had played on the school team the previous year, but was not involved this year because "my stepfather wouldn't give me the money to play because I wet my bed." Andrew also reported that, over the past 6 months, he had much less energy than before and often came home from school feeling very sleepy. He reported difficulty in falling asleep and in awakening, often sleeping 10 to 12 hours on the weekends. Although he admitted to periods of sadness lasting for several days, he denied tearfulness or suicidal thoughts. In ad-

Patient: _____ Primary Nurse: _____

Reinforcer for cooperation: _____

	Fluid Restriction	Prompted Toileting Trips		Strip Bed	Initial
	Cooperative	Cooperative	Productive	Cooperative	
Date					
Time 8 P.M.	Y N	Y N	Y N	Y N	
Bedtime	Y N	Y N	Y N	Y N	
12 A.M.	Y N	Y N	Y N	Y N	

Figure 13-2 Enuresis and toileting monitoring form for intervention phase.

dition, he felt angry when he and his mother moved into her new husband's house and was greatly opposed to their marriage.

Medical History and Physical Examination. Andrew was the healthy, 7-pound, 4-ounce product of an uneventful pregnancy. His medical history was unremarkable, although he had undergone a tonsillectomy and adenoidectomy at the age of 6 years. Prior to Andrew's admission, his pediatrician gave him a complete physical examination and found him to be in good health. The physician's report and laboratory findings indicated that Andrew's enuresis did not have a medical cause.

Family and Social History. Mrs. K. reported that her father had been intermittently hospitalized for alcoholism. Andrew's biological father also drank excessively and had difficulty maintaining full-time employment. While Mrs. K. was married to Andrew's father, the family had lived in a housing project. Mrs. K. was concerned about Andrew's enuresis, but she believed that the problem would resolve itself once he adjusted to their new home. She also felt, however, that Mr. K. was frustrated by the bedwetting episodes and that this was affecting Andrew's relationship with his stepfather.

Developmental History. Mrs. K. described Andrew as a "good baby" who had progressed through the developmental milestones without difficulty. He began to walk at 11 months, and he was toilet-trained for bladder by 2.5 years and for bowel by 3 years. He entered kindergarten at age 5.5 years and progressed through grades 1 through 3 without difficulty.

Data Collection. During Andrew's hospitalization, the staff observed his affect, interpersonal relationships, participation in activities, and sleep patterns. These observations indicated that Andrew was generally bright in the morning and compliant with the activities of daily living. There were times when he appeared depressed, however, and had multiple somatic complaints. As the day progressed, he would either remain isolated in his room for hours or wander about the unit, staying on the fringe of activities, interacting with other children only during very structured periods (e.g., group therapy). He was especially irritable at bedtime and had difficulty falling asleep, although, once asleep, he slept well through the night. Shortly after admission, he became very attached to one particular nurse and would frequently seek her attention. When limits were set on his "clingy" behavior, he became sullen and claimed that he was being rejected.

ENCOPRESIS

Definition and Prevalence

Functional encopresis is the recurrent soiling of the underpants or passage of stool at inappropriate times and places. In addition to its classification as either primary or secondary, encopresis can be subtyped as retentive or nonretentive. Retentive encopresis is characterized by a large accumulation of stool in the lower bowel and rectum. Persistent retention of stool leads to constipation with leakage of liquid stool from the anus. When the bowel is not distended because of the accumulation of a large amount of stool, the encopresis is nonretentive.

The prevalence of encopresis is less than that of enuresis, with an estimated rate of 1% to 5% in young, school-aged children (Barker, 1983). Like enuresis, it occurs more frequently in boys than in girls at a 3–6:1 ratio. If left untreated, this elimination pattern generally resolves by middle adolescence.

Contributing and Predictive Factors

For the most part, children with encopresis do not have severe emotional or behavioral disturbances (Friman, Mathews, Finney, Christophersen, & Leibowitz, 1988; Loening-Baucke, Cruikshank, & Savage, 1987). The two major causes of encopresis are problematic toilet training and chronic or recurrent constipation. Other factors that may cause encopresis are psychogenic in nature, such as anxiety, anger, or stress. Primary encopresis is generally the result of inadequate toilet training or disruptions in the training process while the child is a toddler. Secondary encopresis is usually a response to either emotional stress or organic problems, such as constipation or diarrhea that causes painful defecation.

Retentive encopresis may have either an organic or psychogenic cause. Some medical conditions are associated with painful bowel movements, and the child with such a condition may not pass stool because of the pain. Once the medical condition is resolved, the child may not be able to resume normal bowel habits because of a decrease in muscle and sphincter tone. When there is no organic cause, retentive encopresis can be the result of difficulties in the parent-child relationship. Usually, the toilet-training experience for these children was overly harsh or punitive. Therefore, these children resist having a bowel movement and eventually develop constipation.

Assessment and Data Collection

The assessment process for a child with encopresis consists of a detailed interview with the parents, the child's self-report, a physical examination, and a mental status examination. Information elicited from the parent interview should include: (1) the child's developmental and toilet-training history; (2) parental attitudes; (3) the child's current toileting habits; (4) frequency of encopresis; and (5) eating patterns, including types of foods.

A routine physical examination that includes an abdominal palpation and rectal examination is usually sufficient to determine if there are any major organic causes for encopresis. Children with constipation have a nontender mass in the lower quadrant of the abdomen. Additional screening may include abdominal roentgenograms, a barium enema examination, thyroid function tests, and lead screening.

In children with encopresis, it is also important to note any behavior changes related to the soiling episodes. Somatization is frequently seen in these children; they may complain of intermittent abdominal pain, constipation, nausea, and vomiting. Children who are encopretic generally have a lower self-esteem than do normal peers (Owens-Stively, 1987). While encopretic boys tend to be immature, passive, and feel overwhelmed by their environment, encopretic girls exhibit social withdrawal, hyperactivity, and delinquency.

Case Example

Tony and Rob were 7.3-year-old identical twins who lived with their biological mother (Mrs. C.), 4-year-old half-sister, maternal grandmother, and maternal uncle. Mrs. C. had decided to seek inpatient hospitalization for her sons because of primary encopresis and discipline problems after an unsuccessful period of outpatient treatment. Ever since the boys were 2 years of age, they had been exposed to multiple care-givers and inconsistent toilet training. Mrs. C. had at first used praise for successful toileting, but soon resorted to "trying to force them" through physical punishment. By the time the boys were 4 years old, a negative cycle had developed with intermittent and inconsistent use of praise, spanking, or "simply cleaning up after them." When Mrs. C. tried to get them to wash their soiled underpants, they began to hide them. The only time that they did not soil was while they were at school.

The boys were interviewed separately. Both of them appeared bright, imaginative, clever, and intellectually age-appropriate, although both behaved somewhat immaturely for their age. Socially, Tony was more competent than Rob. During the interview, they both needed frequent limit setting and redirection, to which they readily responded.

Medical History and Physical Examination. Tony had always been the larger of the twins, weighing 6 pounds, 3 ounces at birth compared to Rob's 5 pounds, 10 ounces. At the time of treatment, they weighed 57 and 50 pounds, respectively, and were both 48 inches tall. Neither boy had any childhood illnesses or major medical problems. A comprehensive medical evaluation prior to admission revealed that there was no organic cause for bowel incontinence. Although abdominal roentgenograms showed no fecal impaction, both boys suffered from chronic constipation with leakage. They both stained their underwear daily and every few days had a large, painful bowel movement.

Family and Social History. It had been necessary for Mrs. C. to work since the boys were 2 years of age. Up until that time, Mr. C. (their biological father) had lived with them, but Mrs. C. stated that he was unreliable and had only "begrudgingly" helped with child care. After he had left the household, Mrs. C.'s mother and brother moved in with her to help with expenses and child care. Because of this arrangement, the boys had been exposed to multiple care-givers, including relatives and babysitters. Both sides of the family had a history of alcohol abuse and emotional outbursts.

Developmental History. The boys were the product of a normal pregnancy, and their mother described them as active and noisy as young infants. Their growth and development had been normal, and toilet training had begun at 16 months of age. They had both achieved bladder continence by 2 years of age, but were unsuccessful with bowel training. At the age of 4 years, they had been enrolled in a preschool program, and they were now in the second grade.

Data Collection. During the initial phase of hospitalization, both boys were observed separately for independent toileting, involvement in activities, hygiene skills, and diet. The monitoring of toileting patterns included recording the times of day or night, the frequency, and the number and type of accidents (Figure 13-3).

TREATMENT PLANNING

Nursing diagnoses that are relevant to children with enuresis and encopresis are

- Alterations in Toileting Related to
  1. the Inability to Adapt to Physiological Needs

Patient: _____   Primary Nurse: _____

GENERAL TOILETING

Date:		Accidents		No. and Type (BM, Smear, or Stain)	Independent Toileting		Initial
Date:							
Time	7 A.M.– 9 A.M.	Y	N		Y	N	
	9 A.M.–11 A.M.	Y	N		Y	N	
	11 A.M.– 1 P.M.	Y	N		Y	N	
	1 P.M.– 3 P.M.	Y	N		Y	N	
	3 P.M.– 5 P.M.	Y	N		Y	N	
	5 P.M.– 7 P.M.	Y	N		Y	N	
	7 P.M.– 9 P.M.	Y	N		Y	N	
	9 P.M.–11 P.M.	Y	N		Y	N	
	11 P.M.– 3 A.M.	Y	N		Y	N	
	3 A.M.– 7 A.M.	Y	N		Y	N	

Figure 13-3 Encopresis and toileting monitoring form.

- 2. the Inability to Adapt to Changes in Interdependence
- 3. Knowledge/Learning Deficits during Toilet Training
- Alterations in Feeling Patterns of Guilt and Shame Related to
  1. Personal Failure to Achieve Continence
  2. Failure in Meeting Perceived Expectations of Others
- Alterations in Family Process Related to
  1. Inappropriate or Poor Communication of Expectations of Toileting
  2. Difficulty in Expressing and Listening to Thoughts and Feelings
- Alterations in Social Interactions Related to
  1. Social Withdrawal of the Child Due to Feelings of Shame
  2. Decrease in Community Involvement by Family Members

Once the nursing diagnoses have been established, the treatment goals and plan of action can be formulated. The long-term goals for a child with enuresis or encopresis are as follows:

1. The child recognizes and responds to physiological cues to void/defecate.
2. The child is able to remain dry/unsoiled during daylight hours.
3. The child is able to remain dry at night (enuresis only).
4. The child's feelings of guilt and shame are decreased.
5. The child develops appropriate methods of seeking help, attention, and affection.
6. The patterns of communication among family members are appropriate.

The short-term goals are as follows:

1. The patient will verbalize the function of the bladder/bowel, the importance of regular toileting trips, and good skin hygiene.
2. The patient will bathe and change clothes after each enuretic/encopretic episode.
3. The patient will change bed linen with staff assistance for nocturnal enuresis.
4. The patient will participate in the enuresis/encopresis treatment program.
5. The patient will deal constructively with feelings.
6. The family will identify problems that need to be resolved.

NURSING INTERVENTIONS

Currently, the most effective therapeutic interventions for enuresis and encopresis involve behavioral approaches, such as reinforcement programs and contracting. Other forms of intervention include patient education, supportive counseling, psychotherapy, and pharmacological management. Used alone, none of these other forms of treatment is as effective as the behavioral approaches, but they are essential adjunctive modalities when dysfunctional family issues and treatment resistance are encountered.

Behavioral Programs

Because enuresis and encopresis are often the result of skills deficits, a retraining program in conjunction with reinforcement produces the best outcome. The bell-and-pad system is the most frequently used method for treating nocturnal enuresis, while a urine alarm can be used for diurnal enuresis (Shapiro, 1985). A sensor pad placed in the child's bed or a sensing device placed in the child's underpants alarms or buzzes when the child begins to wet. The alarm alerts the child to go to the bathroom to finish voiding. When coupled with positive reinforcement for successful toileting, this program is 75% to 90% effective, and relapse rates are low. Enuresis generally ceases completely in approximately 5 to 12 weeks. After achieving dryness, the child remains on the program for an additional 3 weeks to ensure treatment effectiveness.

Dry bed training is another behavioral program for enuresis, but it requires a greater degree of staff involvement and time (Doleys & Dolce, 1982). The program includes retention control training, nighttime awakening, and cleanliness training, coupled with positive and negative reinforcement. The child first goes through a practice session, rehearsing participation with all the program's expectations. On the first night, the child is awakened hourly for toileting. Each consecutive night, the child is awakened only once. When the child has had one full dry week, a routine program is put into place to reinforce dry nights or implement the practice sessions for wet nights. Because of the program's complexity, there is a decrease in patient participation, making it less effective than the bell-and-pad system.

> The baseline data collected for Andrew indicated that his bedwetting episodes occurred approximately three to four times a week after 4:00 A.M. Because of Andrew's age, a modified training program was designed to decrease his bedwetting.
>
> 1. At the start of the program, Mr. Williams, Andrew's primary nurse, will meet with Andrew to discuss the way in which the bladder works, factors that contribute to bedwetting, and the program.
>
> 2. Each morning, Mr. Williams will meet with Andrew to determine his progress on the program and complete the monitoring form.
>
> 3. If Andrew independently (a) observes the fluid restriction after 8:30 P.M. and (b) uses the toilet before going to bed, he will earn 2 tokens for each behavior. An evening shift nurse will provide only one reminder for each behavior if Andrew does not perform them independently. If Andrew is responsive to the reminders, he will earn 1 token for each behavior.
>
> 4. Before going to bed, Andrew will set his alarm for 2:00 A.M. to awaken himself to toilet. He will earn 2 tokens for independently awakening and toileting himself, and 1 token if the night nurse must remind him. If his bed is wet at this time, he is to change his sheets and nightclothes and will launder the bed linens in the morning.
>
> 5. If Andrew's bed and nightclothes are dry when he awakens in the morning, he will earn 2 tokens. If his bed is wet, he is to strip his bedding and launder the linens.

6. Andrew's enuresis record and token earnings will be reviewed each morning. Each token equals 1 minute of video game time. He must earn at least 15 tokens before exchanging them.

7. If he has five consecutive dry nights, he will earn an additional 15 tokens.

The most commonly used program for encopresis combines the use of medication, diet, and retraining (Euler-Horner, 1982; Hennessy, 1988; Younger & Hughes, 1983). Depending on the degree of the child's constipation, a combination of laxatives, suppositories, or enemas is used initially to stimulate the rectum and minimize painful defecation. As bowel movements become regular, the amount of medication can be tapered and eventually discontinued. Whole grain cereals, fruits, and vegetables, as well as plenty of fluids, should be regularly incorporated into the child's diet to maintain proper stool consistency.

In the implementation of the retraining program, it is important to establish regular toileting patterns. The child should be toileted three times a day, preferably after meals, with a mechanism for positive reinforcement for stools in the toilet. This type of bowel management program has a 78% treatment effectiveness rate, although relapses and accidents can occur (Younger & Hughes, 1983).

Because the twins, Tony and Rob, had similar patterns of encopresis, one program was developed for both.

PROGRAM OUTLINE

1. At the start of the program, Ms. Davis, the boys' primary nurse, will meet with Tony and Rob to discuss the way in which the bowel works, factors that contribute to soiling and the program.

2. After each meal, Tony (Rob) will go to the bathroom and sit on the toilet for 5 minutes. If responsive, he will earn 2 tokens each trip. If a reminder to go to the bathroom is needed, he will earn 1 token.

3. Each time he defecates in the toilet, he will receive 3 tokens. If the toileting trip is unproductive, the nurse will praise his effort.

4. For each soiling episode, the nurse will

   a. take him to the bathroom to sit on the toilet for 1 minute or to finish the bowel movement

   b. have him remove his soiled clothing and place it in the laundry

   c. assist him in cleaning himself

   d. inform him that he loses 4 tokens for each accident

5. At the end of each day, the nurse will review each boy's monitoring form, earnings, and losses. Ten tokens equals one matchbox car.

A contingency contract is a method of behavioral programming that combines the principles of reinforcement with the components of a contract (Exhibit 13-1;

Exhibit 13-1 Sample Contract

Effective dates: June 17 to July 28

We, the K. Family, agree to perform the following behaviors over the next 6-week period.

For each day that Andrew's bed remains dry, Mr. and Mrs. K. will give him 1 dollar toward the purchase of a new football.

Bonus: For each week that Andrew's bed remains dry, he will earn the privilege of going to one school football game.

Penalty: If Andrew wets the bed three nights in a row, he will lose his weekend late night privileges for the next first full weekend.

Andrew will keep a daily record that will be reviewed with his parents on Friday evenings.

_____
(Andrew)

_____
(Mr. K.)

_____
(Mrs. K.)

_____
(Nurse)

This contract will be reviewed 1 week from the date of agreement.

Leavitt, 1982; Snyder, 1985). Contracting allows the child and parents to become more actively involved in the development of the program. Each family member enters into the agreement with clearly defined responsibilities and expectations. Additional components of a contract include: (1) a penalty clause if either party fails to comply with his or her part of the agreement, (2) additional rewards or bonuses for fulfilling the contract, and (3) a means for monitoring progress and providing feedback. The psychiatric nurse's role in developing a contract is to help the family specify the desired behavior change and establish reasonable expectations. This approach allows the child to gain mastery over the elimination problem while the parents improve their communication skills.

Patient Education

Education of the child and parents is an important phase in the treatment of enuresis and encopresis. Discussions with the family at the onset of treatment should cover the anatomy and physiology of the bladder or lower bowel, toilet training as a developmental process, and the ways in which interventions work. A knowledge of body functions helps the parents toward a better understanding and acceptance of the child's problem. For example, knowing that recurrent constipation makes it difficult for the child to control stool seepage may help to relieve some of the frustration and guilt experienced by both the child and family.

Patient education not only should impart knowledge about the disorder and its management, but also should improve the client's health. Teaching models that use psychoeducational strategies have the highest degree of patient adherence and therapeutic effectiveness (Mazzuca, 1982). In a study of 40 enuretic children, Houts, Whelan, and Peterson (1987) found significant improvement in those who attended training sessions as compared to those who watched a film presentation of the same information. They attributed the difference to the interpersonal interactions that occur in live presentations.

Psychoeducation also involves techniques such as role modeling, reinforcement, communication, and decision making to help the family members implement the information that they have learned. This type of program is often effective as a small group discussion involving families with the same concerns. Many parents feel relief when they find that other families with an incontinent child face similar issues and concerns.

Psychotherapeutic Approaches

Supportive counseling and psychotherapy are useful when psychosocial factors influence the success of the bladder or bowel management program. Supportive counseling for enuresis and encopresis focuses on improving adaptation. Generally, the psychosocial factors that are interfering with the elimination management program are quite conventional. Complaints such as the child "doesn't listen" or adhere to parental expectations, problems with peers, and poor communication between parents are commonplace. In supportive counseling, the psychiatric nurse promotes the use of adaptive responses and interactions while limiting the family's use of maladaptive behaviors. The goals of this approach are to help the child develop a positive sense of self and to promote positive parenting behaviors.

In certain cases, enuresis or encopresis may appear as a symptom of psychopathology, such as depression or problems of separation-individuation. The main goal of psychotherapy in these cases is to treat the major illness; the elimination problem can be expected to resolve through the course of therapy.

Pharmacological Treatment

Of the psychopharmacological agents that have been used for treating enuresis, imipramine hydrochloride has proved to be most effective (Houts, Peterson, & Liebert, 1984). Generally used for the treatment of depression, the mechanism of its effectiveness for enuresis is unclear. Low doses of imipramine, 25 mg for children more than 5 years of age and 50 mg for those more than 12 years of age, are sufficient to be therapeutic. Although imipramine is effective, it is not recommended as the first or only treatment approach because of its side-effects. It is best reserved for treatment-resistant cases.

RESEARCH

There is little nursing research on enuresis and encopresis in children. The majority of the studies in this area have been conducted in the fields of medicine and psychology (e.g., Butler et al., 1988; Houts & Peterson, 1986). For the most part, this body of research demonstrates the effectiveness of medical and behavioral management strategies in treating enuresis and encopresis. The question arises, however, are these programs alone sufficient to treat and correct the problems of elimination?

The nursing literature on bowel management stresses the impact of parental attitudes and the family's understanding of the behavior on the goals of treatment (Euler-Horner, 1982; Hennessy, 1988; Younger & Hughes, 1983). Because enuresis-encopresis are common child health concerns, nurses should become more involved in the overall management of these cases. Many questions about the types of patient education programs and counseling strategies that are the most beneficial to both the child and the family remain to be answered.

REFERENCES

Barker, P. (1983). Enuresis, encopresis and the hyperkinetic syndrome. In *Basic child psychiatry* (4th ed., pp. 121–138). Baltimore: University Park Press.

Butler, R., Brewin, C., & Forsythe, W. (1988). A comparison of two approaches to the treatment of nocturnal enuresis and the prediction of effectiveness using pre-treatment variables. *Journal of Child Psychology and Psychiatry, 29*(4), 501–509.

Doleys, D., & Dolce, J. (1982). Toilet training and enuresis. *Pediatric Clinics of North America, 29*(2), 297–313.

Euler-Horner, M. (1982). The challenge of toilet training–bowel management for the child with psychogenic encopresis or neurogenic deficit. *Pediatric Basics, 32,* 4–10.

Friman, P., Mathews, J., Finney, J., Christophersen, E., & Leibowitz, J. (1988). Do encopretic children have clinically significant behavior problems? *Pediatrics, 82*(3), 407–409.

Hennessy, M. (1988). Pediatric encopresis. *Children's Nurse, 6*(1), 1–4.

Houts, A., & Peterson, J. (1986). Treatment of a retentive encopretic child using contingency management and diet modification with stimulus control. *Journal of Pediatric Psychology, 11*(3), 375–383.

Houts, A., Peterson, J., & Liebert, R. (1984). The effect of prior imipramine treatment on the results of conditioning therapy in children with enuresis. *Journal of Pediatric Psychology, 9*(4), 505–509.

Houts, A., Whelan, J., & Peterson, J. (1987). Filmed versus live delivery of full-spectrum home training for primary enuresis: Presenting the information is not enough. *Journal of Consulting and Clinical Psychology, 55*(6), 902–906.

Leavitt, M. (1982). *Families at risk: Primary prevention in nursing practice.* Boston: Little, Brown.

Loening-Baucke, V., Cruikshank, B., & Savage, C. (1987). Defecation dynamics and behavior profiles in encopretic children. *Pediatrics, 80*(5), 672–679.

May, H. (1986). Functional enuresis: How to help the bed-wetting child. *Pediatric Basics, 44,* 4–7.

Mazzuca, S. (1982). Does patient education in chronic disease have therapeutic value? *Journal of Chronic Disease, 35,* 521–529.

Owens-Stively, J. (1987). Self-esteem and compliance in encopretic children. *Child Psychiatry and Human Development, 18*(1), 13–21.

Shapiro, S. (1985). Enuresis: Treatment and overtreatment. *Pediatric Nursing, 11*(3), 203–207.

Snyder, M. (1985). *Independent nursing interventions.* New York: John Wiley & Sons.

Younger, J., & Hughes, L. (1983). No-fault management of encopresis. *Pediatric Nursing, 9*(3), 185–187.

14

Nursing Interventions with Children and Adolescents Experiencing Communication Difficulties

Sarah Stanley

After reading this chapter, the reader will be able to:

1. describe communication development in children and adolescents
2. examine the basic communicative assessment considerations for stuttering and autism
3. describe nursing interventions for the communicative deficits of autism and stuttering
4. identify an area of nursing research in child or adolescent communicative disorders

Communication is a dynamic, complex, changing process in which human beings send and receive verbal and nonverbal messages in order to understand and be understood by others. The ability to communicate develops systematically, beginning with the birth cry, and the home is the single most important environmental factor in the child's acquisition of speech and language (Weiss & Lillywhite, 1981). If there is no interference, by the age of 3 years, the child will have a comprehension of 3,600 words and will have mastered the expression of 900 words in three- and four-word sentences with minor variations. The child normally communicates clearly by first grade. Children and adolescents with communication disorders experience definite penalties, such as anxiety, embarrassment, confusion, overprotection, name calling, and labeling.

COMMUNICATION PROCESSES

Distorted speech or language is a challenge for most child and adolescent psychiatric nurses, who must assess and organize care specific to the individual youngster's needs (Shanks, 1983; Shanley & Gogliardi, 1988). When considering psychiatric nursing assessments of children and adolescents who are experiencing communication disorders, these nurses should keep in mind that various assessment techniques may also function as therapeutic interventions.

There are several nursing diagnoses related to speech or language deficits: (1) Impaired Communication (verbal and/or written), (2) Anxiety secondary to the communication deficit, (3) Knowledge Deficit related to the condition and ways to provide therapeutic management, (4) Alteration in Self-concept (due to communication deficit), and (5) Social Isolation (secondary to impaired communication). The nursing diagnosis of Impaired Verbal Communication (North American Nursing Diagnosis Association [NANDA], 1987; McFarland & Wasli, 1986) is helpful in formulating the framework of nursing activity for communication disorders in children and adolescents.

The first questions to be answered in the assessment of a child's communication impairment are, Is there something wrong with the child's communication? Are the parents overly concerned? Why is the child's speech/language level lower than that of children who are the same age? For each communicatively impaired client, the nursing assessment should include: (1) careful attention to the youngster's communication abilities and limitations during the interview, (2) determination of the youngster's perception of his or her ability to communicate, (3) observation for impaired and/or dysfunctional communication responses, (4) observation for characteristics that indicate a communication disorder when applied to the developmental stage of the child or adolescent, (5) information about the youngster's network of significant others (e.g., parents, teachers, peers), and (6) determination of others' perceptions of the youngster's ability to communicate.

In the basic assessment, the nurse can evaluate a receptive language disorder by simplifying language spoken to the child; increasing loudness; slowing the rate of speaking; and asking simple questions about events, objects, and persons that are important to the child. The nurse can observe the child and note: (1) his or her coordination of lips and tongue when words are slurred; (2) any eating, chewing, or swallowing problems; (3) choking or tongue thrust; (4) imitation of sticking out the tongue, lip purse, blowing, and sucking through a straw; (5) absence or position of teeth; (6) the raising and lowering of the jaw; and (7) any restricted tongue movement and thumb sucking. Finally, the nurse considers the youngster's ability to: "1) focus on appropriate input, 2) transmit concise, clear and understandable messages, 3) utilize congruent verbal and non-verbal communication, 4) give and accept feedback and 5) experience satisfaction with communication" (McFarland & Wasli, p. 58).

Because many speech or language deficits have multiple, complex causes, the primary psychiatric nursing objective is to facilitate care that will create the greatest gains for the development of the individual child (Goldberg, 1984; Luterman, 1984; MacDonald, 1983; McClowry, Guilford, & Richardson, 1981). Communication specialists are now looking at a child's total communication system and observing developmental levels (which occur before speech) to gain greater insight for planning treatment or programs. In light of this, MacDonald (1983) has identified common problems in the communication methods that adults use with children. For example, the adult may miss the chance to develop the nonverbal communication system that the child needs prior to speech and language by "ignoring new communications" of any level. If the adult responds to the child's body language or sounds, the child will take the "easy way out" and will not be motivated to use words. When the adult communicates far above the child's level, "mismatch" occurs; the child with a few words cannot handle long complex sentences. Also, if the adult drills a child who is not yet developmentally ready on "correct sounds," the child develops "neuroses" and actually makes sounds less frequently. The adult-child communication process is like a tennis game; the players (adult and child) must hit the ball (message) within each other's range to receive a return (response).

For the communicatively disordered child, "longer is harder." Therefore, if adults use utterances that are *just beyond* the child's linguistic level, the child's communication skills will increase. For the nonverbal child, the adult begins with single words. The use of extra emphasis and exaggerated intonation, context and nonverbal cues, facial expressions, gestures, and other hints aid the child's comprehension. Parents, siblings, and significant others can be taught to focus on objects, events, and people in the child's immediate environment to reinforce the child's communication skills.

The psychiatric nurse who works with a communicatively disordered child can adopt techniques from other adult-child communication interactions. McFarlane, Fukiki, and Briton (1984) reviewed modeling, expansion, recasting, and expatiation as helpful techniques. Modeling provides the child with examples of well-formed sentences or phrases; as a young child's toys are placed in a toy box, for example, the nurse states, "ball in, truck in," etc. In the expansion technique, the nurse fills the syntactic gaps in the child's incomplete utterance; for instance "Cookie all gone" is expanded to "Your cookie is all gone." The nurse may also recast the child's statement, reformulating it while maintaining the semantic referent; the child's "I love Uncle Joey" may be recast to "You do love Uncle Joey, don't you?" Recasting is a positive reinforcer of language acquisition, because the child receives enriched input without a loss of content or context. Expatiation involves maintaining the child's lead and topic, but providing additional information. For example, "Kitty cries" becomes "This Kitty cries every night when she is hungry."

The emphasis is not on teaching language, but on fostering interaction and growing communication skills for the child. By de-emphasizing the child's problem(s) and fostering interaction with parents, peers, and significant others, the nurse indicates that sending or receiving a message is the most important aspect of language. Because the purpose of these techniques is to facilitate communication, they must be applied at every opportunity. Inconsistent use or use for only short periods each day will not improve communication. The more real life spontaneous situations that require spontaneous response from the child, the better opportunity for therapeutic intervention.

Children process what is immediately sensed, so parental exchanges must be in the context of here and now. If the communicatively disordered child does not initiate conversation, it is still possible to direct parental utterances to the events or objects to which the child appears to be attending at the time. A valid strategy for assisting the child's communication is to pay special attention to the first and last words of an utterance. The last word of an utterance tends to be held in memory longest and, many times, appears earlier in the response of a young child. Parents are advised of the importance of placing key words in the initial and final position, such as "See the ball" or "Daddy is working."

ARTICULATION DISORDERS: STUTTERING

The most frequent speech problem found in individuals between the ages of 5 and 21 is one of articulation (Sommers, 1983; Van Riper, 1982). The causes of articulation disorders range from nonorganic events, such as lisping, to craniofacial malformations, such as cleft palate/lip. Neurological impairments associated with Down syndrome, cerebral palsy, and other childhood ailments can also compromise articulation.

Social and emotional adjustment problems are found more frequently in children who have articulation communication disorders than in children who speak clearly and fluently. The coping responses of children with articulation difficulties vary greatly. Children with a greater number of misarticulations frequently show weakness in language, reading, and some perceptual functions. Those with a mild degree of articulation disorder may move from grade to grade in school without notice or may simply be labeled underachievers. However, articulation disorders are considered significant dysfunctions by the child, the parents, the educators, and some clinicians.

Van Riper (1982) began a discussion of stuttering by saying that in the beginning was the word—the broken word. Stuttering is described as a disorder of timing, evident as a disruption in the flow of speech or fluency. When a person stutters on a word, there is a temporal disruption of the simultaneous programming of the muscular movements required to produce one of the word's integrated sounds. This mistiming may be attributed to an organic cause or to emotional stress resulting from a struggle and avoidance reaction to mistimed words, as stuttering itself produces fear, shame, and other negative emotional states. When this negative emotion is conditioned to verbal or situational cues, the stuttering child's own perceptions of approaching the difficulty contribute to his or her fracturing words.

There are five levels of possible fluency breakdown: (1) sound, (2) syllable, (3) word, (4) phrase, or (5) sentence. These levels are based on a hierarchy of stability (Van Riper, 1982, p. 418). Sounds have the greatest stability; sentences, the least. The goal for stutterers is to increase their speaking rate from below 100 words per minute in childhood to approximately 125 words per minute by adulthood.

Although fluency disorders compose the smallest percentage of a speech pathologist's caseload, these children are the most noticed, and their condition is the most complex to treat. Stuttering develops before the age of 5 years in 85% of reported cases and is diagnosed in most of the remaining 15% before age 7. The earliest onset was found between 1 1/2 and 2 years of age, and the highest occurrence was at age 3 to 4 years (Wall & Myers, 1984, p. 49). "There is substantial evidence that over 40% of the 5 year old diagnosed group will no longer be stuttering by age 8 years. There is evidence also that recovery from stuttering occurs after 8 years" (Wingate, 1978, p. 13). Peterson and Marquarat (1981) found 3% of the children followed from birth to 16 years (whose stuttering lasted 6 months or more) had begun to stutter before 5 years of age, and no stutterers were found to have begun stuttering after 11 years of age. There were three times as many boys as girls in the stuttering group, and this ratio increased with age (Peterson & Marquarat, 1981).

Assessment of Stuttering

Because there are no tests for stuttering, the adult's evaluation may be a matter of observation and judgment. It is helpful for the nurse to observe the child's speaking (1) to an unresponsive listener; (2) in competition with others; (3) when there is a conflict in the situation; (4) in circumstances that are exciting, fatiguing, bewildering, or confusing; (5) and in situations when the parent-child relationship is unstable. These observations are important data for nurses to incorporate into strategies to help the stuttering child.

Objective data as to the number of repetitions, the number of broken words, and the speech rate are helpful in the assessment. Evaluation must include background information in five major areas: (1) case history; (2) description of speaking behaviors; (3) variability of stuttering; (4) reactions to stuttering; and (5) personality factors, including the child's attitude toward the problem. There are

> seven stuttering danger signs: 1) use of multiple repetitions; 2) the "Schwa" as a filler or starter; 3) the use of prolongations; 4) use of tremors, pitch and loudness; 5) struggle and tension; 6) moment of fear; and 7) avoidance. The first three distort speech patterns, the next four occur as the child reacts to interruptions of his speech. (Peterson & Marquarat, 1981, p. 221)

Nursing assessment should include information from speech clinicians as to the degree of stuttering and what treatment is indicated. Ratings and perceptual scales such as the Iowa Scale of Attitude toward Stuttering (Ammons & Johnson, 1944) and the Stuttering Severity Instrument (Riley, 1972) are given to stutterers, as well as to family members. Receptive language tests measure the child's comprehension skills, and expressive language tests analyze a child's ability to encode language. The expressive tests also demonstrate the child's ability to process and understand language. The pattern of language development must be compared to language observed to be "normal" in other children at a similar level rather than to language observed in adults.

Regardless of the type of assessment used, the nursing assessment must include information about the child's knowledge of stuttering and the child's perception of the possibility of correcting it. The nurse should determine what, if any, prior treatment was planned; whether it was carried out; how long the treatment lasted; and why it ended. If the child and/or parents view the previous treatment as unsuccessful, it is helpful to explore other methods or directions.

Interventions for Stuttering

Because most clinicians agree that stuttering is acquired and maintained by interpersonal dynamics between the child and his or her family, the nurse therapist begins intervention by direct observations of the child's interaction with parents and others outside the family, such as those at school, day care personnel, and babysitters. It is important to determine the child's fluency patterns, the parents' speech, and the interaction. The child whose stuttering pattern is consistent, regardless of the listener or situation, is more difficult to treat. The child who stutters severely, but only in a limited number of situations or with specific individuals, responds more easily to intervention. Behaviors that suggest the more stable stuttering pattern include hand movements, distracting sounds, facial grimaces, body movements, and loss of eye contact associated with stuttering.

The focus of nursing intervention must include psychosocial factors, specifically those involving the adults and peers who are important to the child. Since research has not verified that children who stutter are any more or any less neurotic than the general population, concentration on stuttering in terms of neurosis or psychodynamic conflict has not been helpful in the past. However, the nurse will probably see fragments of neurotic behaviors associated with the emotional anticipation of stuttering.

Therapy approaches for stuttering children can be organized into two categories based on age: indirect and direct therapy. For the preschool child, 3 to 5 years of age, many clinicians choose the indirect approach. They work with the parents rather than the child because they believe that direct attention to speech may exacerbate the stuttering. If they work with the child, they use play therapy and pay no attention to speech production.

Indirect therapies are used primarily to educate the parents about normal speech development and the wide range of fluency possible in all ages. The goal is to teach parents to recognize and observe situational cues to stuttering, such as their talking to the child at a too advanced level. In indirect or filial therapy, the parents are trained to interact with the child in nondirective play sessions. Family therapy is often necessary to address parental guilt and/or anxiety. Many clinicians give families a series of checklists to increase their involvement at home. It is important to work with parents to eliminate criticism, perfectionism, or negative interventions with the child's speech. Situations that foster fluency, such as choral speaking, rhyme speaking, and reciting nursery rhymes are encouraged. Some parents learn to use operant conditioning by selectively attending to their child's speech. Parents keep daily logs of their work with the child, and they review these logs and weekly audiotapes with the clinician. With these techniques, many young children experience a remission of stuttering.

In contrast, the school-aged stutterer is capable of responding to direct techniques of speech management. Although the focus of such techniques remains on the child, parents participate in the treatment by learning to identify, count, and tally stutterings; many learn to adopt a slower rate of speech themselves.

Even with children who appear to be unaware of their stuttering, success in achieving the motor pattern of a word depends on practice. Auditory feedback is very important, because children must vary their pattern to match the model heard. Auditory feedback may be distorted, but children are sensitive to parent or adult response that they have pronounced the word acceptably. A child may sometimes whisper or mouth a word in a pantomime to assist the motoric patterning of the word. Shadowing is a successful technique used with some children who stutter (Van Riper, 1982, p. 424).

The psychiatric nurse becomes one of the significant listeners for the child. As such, the nurse must be aware of the interaction between the speaker and the listener. As stuttering is a disorder of communication (sender-message-receiver), as well as of speech fluency, the nurse therapist (receiver) can have a great impact on the child (sender). A casual curiosity about the stuttering is recommended. Treatment techniques described by Egolf, Shames, Johnson, and Kasprisian-Burrelli (1972; Table 14-1) assist the nurse with interaction response.

In order to help the child or adolescent with an articulation disorder transmit clear, concise, understandable messages, the psychiatric nurse

1. assists the child in increasing communication skills
2. assists the child in mastering speech and language tasks for age and developmental level
3. assists the child with anxieties secondary to communication disorder since bonding, separation, object constancy, body image, self-esteem, and powerlessness can be areas of needed intervention
4. provides parental support for coping with emphasis on language and speech
5. maintains interdisciplinary medical, dental, speech therapy, and educational collaboration
6. refers the child for speech-language evaluation and assistance

Table 14-1 Clinician's Manner of Interaction with the Children

"Reward" refers to the clinician's expressing interest in what the child says. This was most often done by asking a question that required the child to give more information on a topic he initiated.

Child	Manner	Examples
1	Do not accept stuttering. Have child discover new way of talking.	Clinician had child experiment with various ways of talking, to find what was easy for the child to produce fluently.
2	Use puppets to teach child social interaction and to have him experience fluent speech in dialogue.	Clinician began by having dialogues while he and the child were fantasy characters. Gradually, fantasy characters were changed to real characters and puppets were removed.
3	Reward spontaneous verbal output.	Talked about scouting. Discussed badges, projects, stars, camping trips, and bivouacs.
4	Reward verbal output. Give opportunity for success (in verbal and nonverbal tasks) and praise it.	Talked about football. Went over highlights of previous Sunday's game. Set up various offenses and defenses on the blackboard.
5	Do not interrupt child. Reward verbal output.	Went into great detail about music as child played trumpet and drums. Child "taught" clinician about beats, measures, whole notes, scales, and keys.
6	Reward nonaggressive verbal output.	Child brought in his collection of Hot Wheels cars. Discussed various track layouts. Child wrote a play which was presented in his school assembly. Casting, rehearsals, and production were discussed.
7	Give acceptance for ideas and thoughts, and reward verbal output.	Child brought his guitar to therapy. He explained strings, chords, frets, keys, and tuning. Child played and sang a few songs which evoked a lengthy discussion about the differences between speaking and singing.
8	Give praise for coming to therapy and reward verbal output.	Clinician greeted child each week with "I'm glad to see you" or "I was looking forward to today." Talked about school and camping.
9	Listen to child. Be accepting of whatever topic she introduces. Discuss word and situation fears.	Talked about latest trends in the length of skirts and in pop music. Talked about certain words and situations the girl feared. Child talked about her parents' attitudes and contrasted them with her own.

Source: Reprinted from D.B. Egolf, G.H. Shames, P.R. Johnson, and A. Kasprisin-Burelli, "The Use of Parent–Child Interaction Patterns in Therapy for Young Stutterers" in *Journal of Speech and Hearing Disorders*, Vol. 37, p. 222–232, with permission of the American Speech-Language-Hearing Association and the authors.

Frustration, anger, grief, are all found in the family of a child with an articulation disorder. The parents are confused about what to try next and, sometimes, angry about what has not worked in the past. They grieve because they do not have a "normal" child. Lack of economic resources, unavailability of qualified professional help, and unsatisfactory progress in communication all contribute to a resistance or withdrawal from treatment once an appropriate communication system plan has been selected. Parents need support for monitoring the quantity/quality of communication and opportunities for supervised practice with the speech therapist's instructions. Support services to help parents sustain home management and positive attitudes can often be found in the community.

LANGUAGE DISORDERS: AUTISM

A language disorder is the impairment or deviant development of comprehension and/or use of a spoken, written, and/or other symbol system. The disorder may involve the form of language (i.e., the phonologic, morphologic, and syntactic systems), the content of language (i.e., the semantic system), the function of language in communication (i.e., the pragmatic system), or any combination of these. Associated with language disorders is autism, a pervasive developmental disorder that may have an aspect of mild to severe communication dysfunction.

According to Rutter and Schopler (1987), autism was first described as a behaviorally defined syndrome by Kanner in 1943. The condition was formally introduced into the Federal Developmental Disabilities Act in 1976 (Rutter, 1978). The autistic child has a pervasive lack of responsiveness to other people and gross deficits in language development. It may appear during the first months of life, but it is often not noted until basic milestones are missed. The essential features of autism are typically manifested before the child is 30 months of age; they include significant disturbances of: (1) developmental rates and/or sequences; (2) responses to sensory stimuli; (3) speech, language, and cognitive capabilities; and (4) capacities to relate to people, events, and objects.

Autistic children can be found in all parts of the world. There are approximately 4 to 5 such children per 10,000 births, and the condition occurs four times more commonly in males. Sixty percent of autistic children have an IQ below 50; 20% have an IQ between 50 and 70; and only 20% have scores greater than 70 (Kozloff, 1973). The differential diagnosis includes mental retardation, childhood schizophrenia, sensory deficits of deafness or blindness, degenerative brain syndrome, aphasias, and other congenital or acquired developmental disorders related to the central processing of language (Rutter, 1978; Rutter & Schopler, 1987). The autistic person may have a normal life span, and some symptoms disappear with age. The prognosis is generally poor for those with severe forms of the syndrome, however (Gilliam, 1981; Rutter & Schopler, 1987). There are no known predisposing genetic or family factors, and recent studies have found no correlation between autism and parental psychopathology.

Autistic children may have major delays in some areas and relatively minor or no delays in other developmental areas. For example, an autistic child with no language may have relatively strong fine motor skills. Usually, the autistic child has a basic inability to form relationships, along with inadequate understanding of or response to socioemotional cues. The autistic child's failure to recognize when another is happy, angry, or sad is clear from the child's failure to respond with appropriate eye-to-eye gaze, facial expression, body posture, and gestures. The autistic child rarely seeks others for comfort or affection and seldom initiates interactive play with others. This child will not greet others and has no peer friendships. The severe autistic syndromes may include the most extreme forms of self-injurious, repetitive, highly unusual, and aggressive behaviors that are often highly resistant to change and require unique treatment and teaching strategies.

There are reports of comparative studies of autistic and dysphasic children (Rutter, 1978, p. 92). It appears that the overlap of autism with severe developmental disorders of receptive language is unsettled and requires further study. It is certain, however, that nearly all autistic children have severe communication defects, and approximately 50% never develop any useful speech.

Assessment of Language Abilities in Autistic Children

Assessment of the autistic child's speech is difficult because of the child's basic inability to use language for social communication. The child may have immature rhythms of speech, may have only a limited understanding of ideas, and may use words without attaching the usual meaning to them. Autistic language is assessed in terms of: (1) a delay in or total lack of the development of spoken language that is not compensated for by the use of gesture, mime, or prelinguistic babbling; (2) a failure to respond to the communication of others (e.g., no response when someone calls the child's name); (3) stereotypic and repetitive use of language; (4) the use of you when I is meant; (5) idiosyncratic use of wording; and (6) abnormalities in pitch, stress, rate, rhythm, and intonation of speech.

Kozloff (1973) reported that significant diagnostic items for the autistic child less than 2 years of age are: (1) the time of the first word, (2) the child's silence after speaking, (3) the quality of pronunciation of the first words, (4) the child's ability to understand what he or she is saying, and (5) the child's willingness to imitate and repeat the word yes. For the child 2 to 5 years of age, significant speech items are: (1) the child's naming items or using vocabulary out of proportion to his or her ability to communicate, (2) repeating or parroting of words or phrases, (3) ability to answer a simple question, (4) ability to follow oral instructions, and (5) the ability to say "no" or refuse something. An autistic child who is not speaking by age 7 is unlikely to develop useful speech. The combination of no speech by age 5 and a low IQ are associated with a poor communication prognosis.

Although the autistic child appears to lack intentionality, awareness, or competence to use language as a tool to convey a message, communicative abilities should be viewed on a continuum. The autistic child may begin speech efforts by echoing or repeating words spoken by other people, especially the last word or the last few words of a sentence. The child may copy the exact accent of the speaker, as well as the voice pitch. The words seem to have little meaning for the child, however, and are merely echoed. Some children repeat words or phrases heard in the past. This delayed echolalia may occasionally produce an appropriate response.

Echolalia or parroting of words may represent the autistic child's intention to initiate or maintain social interaction in the face of a failure to comprehend the message. Echolalia has been described as a request, a protest, an affirmation, a declaration, a calling, a rehearsal, and/or an effort at self-regulation. The autistic child may be attempting to participate in social interaction, despite a very limited ability to do so.

Interventions for Language Difficulties of Autistic Children

There are several recommended communication treatment packages for autistic children, including behavior modification (Lovaas, 1977), activities therapy and sensory integration therapy (Nelson, 1984), and structured exchange system therapy (Kozloff, 1973). There is no evidence that psychotherapy or psychoanalysis is helpful in treating autism or diminishing the symptoms of the autistic patient. Experiments on the treatment of autistic speech found that teaching an appropriate escape response, such as "Help me," greatly reduced the autistic child's psychotic speech (Durand & Crimmins, 1987).

The behavioral model of treatment fixes the focus of the autistic child's problem as external, involving the child's behavior, not his or her emotional disturbance. Those who advocate this approach believe that the disordered behavior is a direct consequence of external stimulus events. For example, they feel that an autistic child's tantrums, uncooperativeness, or bizarre gestures are often consistently reinforced by the attention given to them, whereas "normal" behaviors or approximations of appropriate behaviors are not reinforced. The operant conditioning programs have been successful in rehabilitating some autistic children and training parents.

Current practice has expanded to include interactional and social exchange techniques, in which the focus is on the behavior of each party in the exchange. The structure exchange system combines interactional social training with operant conditioning. Kozloff (1973) described a training program for an autistic 6-year-old that was designed to strengthen his imitative and functional speech at home by bringing his speech under the stimulus control, to decrease his disruptive speech behavior, and to teach him to occupy his time constructively with play activities.

For the autistic child, the goals of nursing interventions are to help the child attend to appropriate stimuli and transmit clear, concise, and understandable messages. For the parents, the goal is to help them provide care and communication to the autistic child. In order to accomplish these goals, the psychiatric nurse:

1. interprets the treatment plan for parents and child
2. facilitates and supports the use of appropriate behavioral model techniques
3. assists the family with grief work related to the diagnosis
4. includes the parents as co-therapists for the implementation of the care plan
5. coordinates support systems for parents, siblings, and family members
6. maintains interdisciplinary collaboration

Psychiatric nursing interventions for autism depend on the point at which the family and child with the autistic syndrome seek help. With the very young infant to the preschool child, the nurse may be involved in the initial diagnostic process or shortly thereafter. In this event, much nursing effort is directed toward interpreting and implementing the treatment plan for the child. The parents also require a great deal of assistance. They need support as they seek diagnosis and treatment, despite the reaction of other family members; they need assistance with grief work related to the diagnosis and individualized reinforcement of the final treatment plan. The psychiatric nurse can assist in training the parents to be effective teachers and co-therapists.

The child in the middle childhood period of autism, kindergarten through elementary school age, functions best in an education system with behavior modification programs based on the principles of exchange theory. Methods must be established to handle lack of speech; noncooperativeness; inattentiveness; inability to engage in constructive activities; and demanding, destructive, and bizarre behaviors. The behavioral model has become the most important modality in the treatment of the autistic child. The nurse reinforces the behavior patterns necessary for the child to meet his or her potential for participation in the natural community. The nurse also teaches the parents: (1) which *responses* to require of their child and which to regard as unacceptable; (2) how to *initiate* exchange with the child so that new, positive structured exchanges will develop; (3) how to *teach* the child to perform new kinds of behavior (e.g., speech, play, cooperation); (4) how to *reward* appropriate behavior and how to handle inappropriate behavior; and (5) how to *maintain* positive exchanges so that they remain rewarding to parents and child.

When the autistic client is an adolescent, the nurse is challenged to maintain the outlined behavioral program with a physically larger patient. If the adolescent has no speech, communication is a continuation of the patterns that were established in middle childhood. Physical safety issues can be built into the behavioral program. It is very difficult for parents to accept the fact that their child has reached the final level of education and communication possible by the adolescent period, especially when this may be far below their original expectations and hopes. Even though there is no evidence that the parents of an autistic child are responsible for the disorder, many parents need help at this time to deal with lingering guilt issues.

Many parents of autistic children who have struggled to understand and accept their child's disorder have also expressed their feelings about the value of professional help. Forty-eight percent of the parents reported "professional's defective communication with the parents" about their autistic child, and 27% reported "no direct help for the child" (DeMyer, 1979, p. 179). Other areas of concern to parents were "child in need of more treatment than receiving, professional's failure to take parental observations seriously, lengthy wait for appointments and professional's active avoidance of seeing parents" (DeMyer, 1979, p. 178).

Generally, professionals from more than one health care discipline participate in the care of an autistic child or adolescent. The psychiatric nurse can serve as liaison or coordinator for the parents. Once parents have accepted the diagnosis of autism, they may focus primarily on the child; they may be so caught up in the care of the autistic child/adolescent that they neglect their personal growth, marital health, and needs of the other children. Family therapy may be necessary to assist parents and other children in attending to their own needs.

Nursing goals for the impaired communication of the autistic child will be achieved through a structured, well-developed, frequently reassessed behavioral program. Therapeutic listening; believing the parents; directive, nonjudgmental problem solving; role modeling with the child; limit setting; and periodic re-assessment of the behavioral program are each a necessary part of nursing care for an autistic child or adolescent. The youngster's ultimate level of attending to appropriate stimuli and transmitting clear, concise, and understandable messages depends on the severity of the autistic syndrome and other accompanying disorders. In order to achieve the goal for parental care, the psychiatric nurse must be comprehensive, persistent, and consistent with support—not rescue—and work with parents to release their energies to meet the task of raising an autistic child.

When parents are not available or not willing to be part of the treatment plan, nurses can incorporate other creative means for communication learning. Members of Head Start programs, community education groups, Big Brothers/Big Sisters, and extended family members can be recruited to meet some of the communication roles of significant others for the child or adolescent with speech or language difficulties.

RESEARCH

Nursing research in the area of communication disorders of children and adolescents is sparse to nonexistent. Therefore, there are numerous opportunities for nurses to examine family issues, nursing care aspects, and treatment modalities for communication difficulties. Because nurses must direct a major portion of their efforts toward those significant in the child's environment, information about parental and sibling interactions and coping abilities is also necessary.

Nursing research about the effect of preventive programs directed toward increasing parental knowledge and experience about prelinguistic (infant) and early childhood speech and language development would be helpful, as would more information about techniques that extinguish undesirable communication behaviors, such as stuttering. An examination of the development of standardized nursing assessment tools for age-appropriate speech and language is needed.

Finally, many children will never achieve verbal expression, so nursing treatment methods and care plans that use augmentative means must be studied. Nursing research efforts may focus on the effectiveness of augmentation methods such as communication boards, mechanical communication devices, nonspeech symbol systems, finger spelling, pantomime and gesture, sign language, and biofeedback for nonverbal children.

Despite their difficulties, children and adolescents with communication problems have much in common with normal children, and psychiatric nurses are challenged to intervene knowledgeably to improve the quality of their daily life.

REFERENCES

Ammons, R., & Johnson, W. (1944). The construction and application of a test of attitudes toward stuttering. *Journal of Speech and Hearing Disorders, 9,* 39–49.

DeMyer, M. (1979). *Parents and children in autism.* New York: John Wiley & Sons.

Durand, M., & Crimmins, D. (1987). Assessment and treatment of psychotic speech in an autistic child. *Journal of Autism and Developmental Disorders, 17*(1), 17–28.

Egolf, D., Shames, G., Johnson, P., & Kasprisian-Burrelli, A. (1972). The use of parent-child interaction patterns in therapy for young stutterers. *Journal of Speech and Hearing Disorders, 37*(2), 222–232.

Gilliam, J. (1981). *Autism.* Springfield, IL: Charles C. Thomas.

Goldberg, R. (1984). Identifying speech and language delays in children. *Pediatric Nursing, 10*(4), 252–259.

Kozloff, M.A. (1973). *Reaching the autistic child: A parent training program.* Champaign, IL: Research Press.

Lovaas, I.O. (1977). *The autistic child.* New York: Irvington.

Luterman, D. (1984). *Counseling the communicatively disordered and their families.* Boston: Little, Brown.

MacDonald, J. (1983). A conversational approach to language-delayed children: Problem solving for nurses. In S. Shanks (Ed.), *Nursing and the management of pediatric communication disorders* (pp. 103–164). San Diego: College–Hill Press.

McClowry, D., Guilford, A., & Richardson, S.O. (1981). *Infant communication: Development, assessment and intervention.* New York: Grune & Stratton.

McFarland, G., & Wasli, E. (1986). *Nursing diagnosis and process in psychiatric mental health nursing.* Philadelphia: J.B. Lippincott.

McFarlane, S., Fukiki, M., & Briton, B. (1984). *Coping with communicative handicaps.* San Diego: College-Hill Press.

Nelson, D. (1984). *Children with autism and other pervasive disorders of development and behavior: Therapy through activities.* NJ: Slack.

North American Nursing Diagnosis Association. (1987). *Classification of nursing diagnoses: Proceedings of the 7th conference.* St. Louis: C.V. Mosby.

Peterson, H., & Marquarat, T. (1981). *Appraisal and diagnosis of speech and language disorders.* Englewood Cliffs, NJ: Prentice-Hall.

Riley, G. (1972). A stuttering severity instrument for children and adults. *Journal of Speech and Hearing Disorders, 37,* 314–322.

Rutter, M. (1978). Language disorders and infantile autism. In M. Rutter & E. Schopler (Eds.), *Autism: A reappraisal of concepts and treatment* (pp. 85–104). New York: Plenum Press.

Rutter, M., & Schopler, E. (1987). Autism and pervasive developmental disorders: Concepts and diagnostic issues. *Journal of Autism and Developmental Disorders, 17,* 159–186.

Shanks, S. (1983). *Nursing and the management of pediatric communication disorders.* San Diego: College-Hill Press.

Shanley, D., & Gogliardi, B. (1988). The nurse's role in identifying children with communication disorders. *Journal of School Health, 58*(2), 75–77.

Sommers, R. (1983). *Articulation disorders.* Englewood Cliffs, NJ: Prentice-Hall.

Van Riper, C. (1982). *The nature of stuttering.* NJ: Preng Association.

Wall, M., & Myers, F. (1984). *Clinical management of childhood stuttering.* Baltimore: University Park Press.

Weiss, C., & Lillywhite, H. (1981). *Communication disorders: Prevention and early intervention.* St. Louis: C.V. Mosby.

Wingate, M. (1978). Disorders of fluency. In P.H. Skinner & P. Shelton (Eds.), *Speech, language and hearing: Normal processes and disorders* (pp. 13–256). Reading, MA: Addison-Wesley.

15

Nursing Interventions with Children and Adolescents Experiencing Conduct Difficulties

Louise C. Waszak

After reading this chapter, the reader will be able to:

1. identify the essential features of conduct difficulties, such as aggressive or violent behaviors toward the environment and toward others, and dysfunctional behaviors
2. develop specific treatment goals and interventions for children and adolescents who are experiencing conduct difficulties
3. examine selected treatment strategies for this client population

When a child loses emotional and physical self-control, the child's educational and developmental progress is disrupted, family conflict ensues, and there is a potential for physical harm. The child's difficulties are often compounded by the presence of a dysfunctional family and social system. If these unwholesome behaviors and situations are allowed to continue, the child is likely to develop persistent interpersonal deficits and become an antisocial adult.

Because children with conduct disturbances often have complex, multisystem problems, an open systems framework, such as that proposed by King (1981), can guide the psychiatric nurse through the nursing process. Eliciting information about the child's actions and interactions with the environment and determining the child's perceptions about self, communication, and decision-making skills are important aspects of the psychiatric nurse's assessment. Treatment goals should be developed in collaboration with the child to address the child's personal, interpersonal, and social systems. Most important, the psychiatric nurse needs to be skillful in management strategies that target not only the child's difficult behavior, but also the child's deficiencies in problem solving, social interactions with family and peers, and social awareness.

RISK FACTORS AND PREVALENCE

Chronic rule breaking and frequent disregard for societal codes are behavioral characteristics of children who are experiencing conduct disturbances. These youngsters exhibit a broad range of antisocial behaviors, such as lying, stealing, disobedience, vandalism, truancy, running away, and aggression. For some children, these habitual, unmanageable, and destructive behaviors are common occurrences at home and in school. These disruptive behaviors may even continue into adulthood. Although the exact cause of behavioral disturbances in children is unknown, certain individual characteristics of the child, as well as certain parent and family factors, are predictive risk factors.

Behavioral Development

Genetic factors do not appear to be a contributing factor in conduct disturbances, but the child's inherent personality style does play a role in behavioral maldevelopment. From birth, the child has a way of behaving that affects the actions of parents and others in the environment. Some children appear to have a difficult temperament, manifested by defiant, hostile, and demanding behavioral characteristics. These children often find it difficult to adapt to routine changes, let alone stressful or challenging events. Even normal growth may frustrate temperamental children. Often, these children perceive the socialization process as a negative experience, and this perception diminishes their ability to relate to others. The inability to make friends and develop lasting relationships is common among children with poor social skills.

Although the lack of social skills does not in itself constitute a disturbance in conduct, it is highly associated with a wide range of other problems, such as substance abuse, acting out or aggressive behaviors, and extreme dependency. The child's inability to develop relationships with peers often leads to antagonistic behavior toward others and social withdrawal. Such a child has few friends and rarely engages in normal childhood activities.

Family Factors

Biological factors and environmental factors, such as family conditions, parental attitudes, and child-rearing practices, influence and shape each child's individual behavioral attributes or personality style. Early parent-child interactions and the home environment play an important role in the development of the child's behavioral expressions.

Conduct disturbances in children can result from a certain combination of parental actions and behaviors in relation to discipline. Socially withdrawn, self-abusive, and quarrelsome children often have parents who are hostile and excessively controlling in their manner of discipline. Antisocial and delinquent behaviors are more frequently seen in children whose parents are indifferent and neglectful or in children whose parents use rejection, angry threats, and verbal and physical abuse as a means of punishment. While hostile and ineffective parental management contributes to conduct disturbances, family conflict, discord, and disorganization also have a pathological influence on child development.

Prevalence

Within the U.S. population the prevalence of childhood disturbances of conduct ranges from 2% to 12% (Kazdin, 1985). Both parents and teachers report a higher occurrence of delinquent behavior, such as stealing, fighting, and truancy, in boys than in girls (Patterson, 1982). Typically, more boys than girls are referred for treatment at a rate of 3–10:1. Of all the children and adolescents referred to mental health services, one-third to one-half exhibit a variety of conduct disturbances.

> Maria, a 14-year-old girl, was referred for admission to an adolescent psychiatric inpatient unit from a residential setting for hitting two staff members and attempting to injure another staff member with a chair. The residential staff reported that, for the past week, Maria had been very moody with frequent aggressive outbursts at staff and other residents. At times, she appeared to be sexually preoccupied and inappropriately grabbed male staff members. There was no report of self-injurious behavior, substance abuse, or psychotic symptoms.

DATA COLLECTION AND NURSING ASSESSMENT

The use of three methods of data collection—interviewing, record review, and observation—allows for a higher degree of validity in the information obtained. The nurse's first task, however, is to establish a therapeutic relationship with the child and family. This may be accomplished by meeting with the child and parents before conducting the interview with the child alone. In addition, this meeting may help to identify family needs other than the child's problems.

Upon the youngster's admission to the hospital, the nurse conducts an initial interview to determine the presenting symptoms, the probable causes, and the environmental or situational factors that have affected the child over time. The youngster's coping abilities, strengths, and support systems should also be assessed. When interviewing children with conduct disturbances, the nurse must remember that youngsters may not perceive themselves as having a problem or needing hospitalization. Adolescents tend to be more difficult to interview because of the negative feelings associated with hospitalization. Although adolescents are better reporters than are younger children, it may be necessary to rephrase some questions to ensure accuracy. It may be best to obtain information about problematic interpersonal relationships by phrasing the parent's, teacher's, or peer's behaviors in context with the youngster's behaviors, such as "What happens when you do something your teacher dislikes?"

In most cases, the hospitalized adolescent has had a problematic past and, therefore, has had previous psychiatric evaluations. If possible, the nurse should review these past records in order to delineate further the child's conduct disturbances and the associated circumstances.

> Because Maria's mother was unwilling to cooperate with the treatment team and her father was incarcerated for theft, background information was obtained from several other sources, including past reports and records from her school, outpatient services, and the residential facility. The reports reflected a complex social history in that Maria had been in several foster homes since the age of 7. Her older brother continued to live at home with the mother, and a younger sister resided with a foster family.
>
> During the previous five years, Maria had been in outpatient counseling. Her school behavior in the fourth grade was the original reason for the referral. School reports indicated that, during this time period, she did not have one perfect day at school; she was constantly getting into trouble, hitting other students, and walking out of the classroom. While in the fifth grade, her negative behavior intensified and resulted in her suspension from school for yelling at the teachers and for frequent truancy. The foster family found that the school problems were being carried into the home setting. Although the foster family had learned home management strategies, these techniques became less effective as Maria became increasingly bold in her misbehavior. After trying to set the furniture on fire in the foster home, Maria was moved to the residential facility.

The child's conduct disturbances may make it impossible to obtain a full nursing history on the child's admission. Therefore, the nurse must quickly and directly assess the child's immediate needs. In determining the factors that increase the child's out-of-control behaviors, the nurse must ascertain the event that precipitated the admission, in the child's words, and the circumstances that surrounded the event. Questions such as "Do you recall doing ____?" "What provoked you to ____?" "How did you feel before? During? Afterward?" permit a quick assessment of the child's speech content, affect, and mood while allowing the child to feel that his or her point of view is important.

> On her admission to the inpatient unit, Maria was noted to be extremely irritable and very guarded. Her irritability rapidly gave way to loud, threatening, and aggressive behavior. Maria's primary nurse noted that she had extreme difficulty in establishing trusting relationships, making friends, and feeling close to people. She experienced a good deal of disappointment in that her mother rarely called or visited. In addition, she

seldom took her prescribed medications and did not follow the unit rules and expectations.

In conjunction with interviewing, the nurse must observe the child's current behaviors. Careful and controlled observations of the conduct disturbances on the inpatient unit validate information obtained from interviews, reports, and prior records. Observations made during the first few days after the child's admission provide "baseline data" that are later used to measure the efficacy of the treatment program.

A variety of methods may be used to observe and record behaviors. First, the target behaviors must be clearly defined. Aggressive behavior is a frequent problem in children with conduct disturbances, for example, and the observer determines the magnitude of the child's aggression by monitoring specific acts, such as physical attacks on people, cruelty to others, explosive outbursts, and physical fighting. One method of observation is a continuous assessment of the behavior, whereby all aggressive acts are recorded throughout the day. Another method of observation is time sampling, whereby the child's behaviors are monitored for predetermined periods at pre-established intervals throughout the day and aggressive acts that occur within these time periods are recorded (Exhibit 15-1). For example, an observer may monitor a child's behavior during the first 15 minutes of an unstructured play period. Whatever method of observation is employed, the defined acts and time period must remain constant throughout the monitoring.

In addition to monitoring the frequency of a behavior, the observer should note the circumstances before (antecedents) and after (consequences) the event, as well as the setting or location and other factors (Exhibit 15-2). Often, the circumstances surrounding a particular behavior stimulate and reinforce the behavior. For example, a child with poor reading skills may use an explosive act in order to be removed from the classroom and, thus, to avoid reading aloud in front of his peers. In this situation, removal from the classroom is a positive reinforcer for the behavior, as the child successfully avoids a task that he finds unpleasant. Removing a child from a play activity for an explosive act may be perceived as punishment or a negative reinforcer, however.

Certain behaviors, such as stealing or the possession of contraband, are not always readily observable. Both of these behaviors may be monitored through periodic room checks (Exhibit 15-3). Prior to the initiation of room checks, a complete inventory of each client's belongings is made, to be updated as needed. All clients should be informed that periodic room checks will be conducted for unauthorized or stolen items.

TREATMENT PLANNING

Because a child's strengths or abilities are the basis for growth, a care plan for a child with conduct disturbances should include goals for both the reduction of

Exhibit 15-1 Aggressive Behavior Rating Form

Child's Name: _____ Setting: _____
Rater: _____ Unit: Day ____ Evening ____
Date: _____ Classroom: _____
Day: S M T W TH F S   Activity: _____

Intervals

Behaviors	1	2	3	4	5	6	7	8	9	10	11	12
Arguments												
Cruelty/meanness												
Defiance												
Destruction of property												
Explosiveness												
Physical fighting												
Attacks on others												
Threats to people												

Exhibit 15-2 Behavioral Analysis Recording Sheet

Child's Name: _____ Date: _____

Location	Activity	Others Present	Antecedent Conditions	Behavior	Consequences

Exhibit 15-3 Room Check

Child's Name: _____

Specific items of concern: _____

This record is used to record any items found in the child's room that do not belong to him/her according to his/her room inventory list.

Date: _____ Room check: Contraband/Stolen items found   Y   N

Time: _____ Observation: Possession   Y   N

Comments/List of items: _____

_____

Date: _____ Room check: Contraband/Stolen items found   Y   N

Time: _____ Observation: Possession   Y   N

Comments/List of items: _____

_____

aggressive behavior and the development of appropriate behavior. Applicable nursing diagnoses include:

- Potential for Violent/Aggressive Behavior Directed at the Environment or Others Related to
  1. Inability to Control Impulsive Actions
  2. Inability to Cope or Adapt to Situational or Maturational Changes Adequately
  3. Inability to Tolerate Stressful Events
- Altered Interpersonal Processes Related to
  1. Inability to Develop Trust in Others
  2. Dysfunctional Parent-Child Relationship
  3. Inability to Participate in Age-Appropriate Activities
- Potential for Dysfunctional Behaviors Related to
  1. Inability to Adhere to Expectations, Rules, and Societal Norms
  2. Inability to Problem Solve

The long-term goals in the treatment of conduct disturbances are to help the client:

1. eliminate violent acts that destroy property
2. eliminate violent or injurious acts against self and others
3. eliminate dysfunctional/inappropriate behaviors
4. develop coping skills as an alternative response to aggression
5. develop positive methods of expressing anger
6. develop a trust relationship with care-giver

The short-term goals are to help the client:

1. decrease aggressive behavior, as evidenced by the Aggressive Behavior Rating Form (see Exhibit 15-1)
2. interact with others without using aggression to solve conflicts
3. identify feelings of anger
4. deal constructively with feelings of anger
5. increase problem-solving skills
6. develop self-control skills

The treatment goals should be measurable, time-oriented, and validated with the child and parents.

> The nursing staff viewed Maria as a management problem because of her multiple conduct disturbances. Her treatment plan included behavioral strategies for her aggressive and uncooperative behaviors, group therapy to increase her ability to develop positive peer relationships and to promote her emotional and physical self-control, and individual therapy with the primary nurse to work on developing a trusting relationship with an adult. In Maria's case, affirmation of the treatment plan was used to develop problem-solving skills and to facilitate cooperation.

NURSING INTERVENTIONS

Therapeutic Milieu

The first and perhaps most important aspect of nursing care is patient safety. Therefore, the therapeutic environment of the inpatient unit should be structured not only to provide a living situation that will help the youngsters to modify their behavior and develop competency skills, but also to ensure that they cannot hurt themselves or others. The therapeutic milieu for youngsters with a high potential for out-of-control behavior must have clearly defined verbal and physical approaches for managing aggression.

Verbal Interventions

The purpose of verbal interventions is to help youngsters recognize their own distress and regain control. At the first sign that a child is becoming agitated and disruptive, the nurse should verbally acknowledge the child's discontent and set expectations for appropriate behavior. For example, "Maria, I know you are angry about not getting a phone call from your mother today. However, if you want to watch TV with the rest of the group, you will have to stop swearing."

In addition to their use for limit setting, verbal techniques may be used to facilitate adaptive ways of dealing with anger. The nurse may want to move the youngster to another setting in order to discuss the child's behavior by means of re-expression, in which the nurse helps the child to identify and appropriately verbalize feelings of anger, or problem solving, in which the nurse helps the child to recognize the alternatives or consequences of behavior in the hope that the child will select the most adaptive option. The goals of verbal intervention are to refocus the child away from disruptive behavior and to help the child deal with reality.

Timeout

The child whose behavior escalates beyond the point of verbal reasoning should be given an exclusionary timeout. This procedure removes the child from a reinforcing environment for a specified period of time. The basic steps of a timeout procedure are as follows:

1. Issue a warning first. Call the child by name, state the inappropriate behavior, and inform the child that a timeout will be given if the behavior continues.

2. Approach the child and state, "Since you did not stop [disruptive behavior] you will take a timeout now in [location]." The location can be a designated area a few feet from the activity, the hallway outside the room, or the child's room.

3. If the child does not walk to the timeout area, guide or lead the child by the hand. State the time interval and the conditions for leaving timeout, such as "You may rejoin the group in 5 minutes when you are quiet." The time period should be adjusted according to the child's age and ability to regain control (e.g., 5, 10, or 15 minutes). Another option with an older child or adolescent is to let the youngster determine when control has been regained.

4. Discuss the behavior only after the timeout period when the youngster has regained control and is able to reason.

5. After the timeout, observe the child for appropriate behavior and praise appropriately.

This procedure can be implemented when the child does not respond to verbal interventions and continues inappropriate behavior or when the behavior has escalated to verbal threats and limit testing.

Physical Interventions

If the child's level of aggression is potentially harmful to self or other individuals, physical controls such as seclusion or therapeutic holding are indicated. Seclusion is a procedure that removes the child from a reinforcing environment to a closed, quiet area devoid of any objects that may be used as a weapon. The steps used to seclude a child are similar to those of a timeout.

1. State the child's name, specify the unacceptable behavior, and indicate that the child must go to the seclusion area.
2. When possible, give the child the opportunity to walk to the seclusion area. If the child is uncontrollable, however, the nursing staff must employ physical restraining techniques to move the child to the seclusion area.
3. Once in the seclusion area, inform the child of the time period for the seclusion and the conditions for leaving.
4. Remove potentially dangerous clothing, explaining the rationale.
5. Limit conversation with the child to essential information, such as the child's remaining time in seclusion.
6. Discuss the child's behavior only after the seclusion period is over.

During the seclusion process, the nurse's primary concern is to ensure the child's safety and control of the situation. To be out of control is a frightening experience for the child. Therefore, all verbalizations should be firm, brief, and direct to let the child know what is happening. After the seclusion period is over, the child may feel guilty, may be angry, or may fear punishment for losing control. In order to reestablish therapeutic rapport, the nurse and the child should discuss the event and the child's feelings.

Therapeutic holding is a form of physical restraint that has proved useful with aggressive children (Barlow, 1989). The technique requires several nurses with a clear understanding of each one's assignment. Once it has been determined that therapeutic holding is the preferred intervention, the nursing staff should follow a basic procedure.

1. Inform the child that holding will occur in order to help him or her regain control.
2. Approach the child cautiously and calmly. Safety is an important concern for both the child and the nursing staff. Therefore, it is important to avoid a confrontational appearance.
3. Preferably, remove the child to a quiet and safe area away from the other children. This can be done by holding the child securely with a nurse to

manage each arm. If the child refuses to walk voluntarily, the team can carry the child to an appropriate area.

4. Place the child in a prone position on a blanket or pad. A nurse straddles the child's buttocks while holding the arms crossed at the small of the back. To prevent the child from kicking the nurse, a pillow may be placed between the nurse and the child, or the nurse may place his or her feet across the child's inner knee. A second nurse can secure the child's head by loosely holding it with a towel or small blanket to minimize the child's attempts to spit or bite. The rest of the team should be nearby if assistance is required.

5. Inform the child that he or she will be released when control is regained. Release the child gradually, giving the child step-by-step instructions, such as "I am going to release one arm. If you can remain calm, I will release your other arm."

6. After the child has been fully released, talk with the child about actual and alternative behaviors.

Both forms of physical intervention should be implemented in a manner that helps the child to regain control without physical or emotional harm. Physical controls are generally the last treatment choice for managing aggression. Prevention and supportive techniques are preferred to physically restrictive measures.

Behavioral Approaches

Behavioral treatment procedures are relatively easy to implement and monitor for effectiveness, because they follow the basic principles of learning and use highly specific goals. Once the goals have been identified, treatment can be implemented through reinforcement, a token economy, or contracting in an individually tailored or group program.

Reinforcement

The use of reinforcement techniques can be a part of either the natural setting or a planned program to increase the frequency of a desired behavior or extinguish unwanted behaviors. The type of reinforcement should be chosen carefully to achieve the desired outcome and support the development of a positive self-concept. Programs based on positive reinforcement are preferred; negative reinforcement programs are used only in select circumstances.

As part of the treatment team, the child's primary nurse provides essential information about the child's conduct disturbance, such as frequency, time of day, setting of occurrence, and suitable reinforcers in the development of a reinforcement program.

One of Maria's problems was the frequent use of profanity, for which her primary nurse recommended the following program:

1. When Maria swears, she is to be given a warning to stop swearing or she will not earn TV time. The nurse will instruct Maria to use appropriate language when angry.
2. If Maria does not stop swearing after the warning, she will receive a mark for that hour on her daily monitoring sheet. For each hour that she does not have a mark, she will earn 5 minutes of TV time for that evening.
3. The nurse will praise Maria if she independently uses appropriate language when angry.
4. Every third day, Maria's primary nurse will review her progress on the program.
5. After 10 days, the treatment team will reevaluate the program.

Token Economy Programs

In a comprehensive token economy program, a child receives tokens for positive behavior or for cooperating with defined expectations. The child can also lose tokens by continuing to demonstrate a conduct disturbance. At a specified time (usually 2 or 3 days to 1 week after the initiation of the program), the child can use the tokens to purchase a special privilege or item. Token economies can be developed as individual programs, structured on a larger scale for a group, or used in all aspects of the milieu. This type of program has distinct advantages in that expectations can be specified for one or several behaviors and activities. Furthermore, a program can be developed for a small group that will ultimately affect the entire milieu.

Maria, Cathy, Brian, and Peter all used abusive language. A token economy was developed to decrease the use of abusive language by this group, to decrease the use of abusive language by all clients in the unit through the positive role model of this group, and to increase positive interaction and cohesiveness in this group. The program was designed as follows:

1. Maria, Cathy, Brian, and Peter will meet as a group with their primary nurses each morning to discuss the major points of the program.
   a. The use of abusive language has increased on the unit because of this group's verbally abusive behavior.
   b. Although this type of language may be common in their age group, the frequent use of such language is not appropriate within the community setting and increases their chances of being involved in aggressive conflicts with others.

    c. The members of this group are to serve as positive role models for their peers by not using verbally abusive language and demonstrating good impulse control.

2. The day is divided into four monitoring time periods: 7 A.M. to 11 A.M., 11 A.M. to 3 P.M., 3 P.M. to 7 P.M., and 7 P.M. to 11 P.M.

3. As a group, these four clients will not be given a warning for the use of abusive language. Should a group member use abusive language, that member will lose two tokens immediately and will be informed of the loss.

4. If no group member has lost more than two tokens per time period, each member will earn five tokens. If any group member has lost more than two tokens, that member will not earn any tokens for that time period, while the group members who have lost two or fewer tokens will earn only three tokens.

5. One of the program nurses will review the token record sheet with the group at the end of each time period and post the earnings and losses for group members.

6. Losses in tokens will be posted immediately by the nursing staff giving the loss.

7. The nursing staff will praise the group members for both appropriate language and group interactions throughout the time periods.

8. Group members have the choice of exchanging 20 tokens for a late bedtime or banking their tokens for a special group outing at the end of the week for 100 tokens.

Contracting

A type of program that combines behavioral principles with concepts of a contract or formal agreement (Snyder, 1985), contracting can be used to target conduct disturbances or difficulties in relationships between peers or between parent and child. The contract specifies in writing the expected behaviors, reinforcement strategy, and time period involved. This program works well with older school-aged children and adolescents, as it is developed in collaboration with the youngster.

Trust Contract

Effective dates: July 10 to July 30

I, Maria, have difficulty in earning and keeping the nursing staff's trust. This weekend I stole a knife from the cafeteria and was restricted to the unit for three consecutive meals. The first time I was allowed to return to the cafeteria, I stole another knife. Because everyone on the unit is concerned with safety, the nursing staff and my peers feel that my actions have placed them in danger. In order to earn back everyone's trust, I must show them that I can be trusted.

Step 1. I will be restricted to the unit for activities and for meals with finger foods. I must follow the unit rules and our "special trust rules." To move to Step 2, I must demonstrate all six trust rules in three of four time periods in that day.

Step 2. I will remain restricted to the unit for activities and for meals with plastic utensils.

Step 3. I will remain restricted to the unit for activities and for meals with silverware.

Step 4. I will remain restricted to the unit except for meals. I can go to the cafeteria for meals with my group and use silverware.

Step 5. I am no longer restricted to the unit and, therefore, may resume all of the regular privileges of my peers on the unit. I have regained everyone's trust.

Special Trust Rules

1. Volunteer to help prepare materials for group activities.
2. Volunteer to help a younger peer clean his or her room with staff supervision.
3. Stay involved in group activities rather than remaining alone in room or whispering to another peer.
4. Stay out of other peers' rooms.
5. If someone is having a problem, try to be helpful.
6. Be safe and trustworthy—DO NOT HIDE DANGEROUS OBJECTS.

Progress through Steps

1. I will be rated by nursing staff during four time periods: 7 A.M. to 11 A.M., 11 A.M. to 3 P.M., 3 P.M. to 7 P.M., and 7 P.M. to 11 P.M.
2. If I follow the special trust rules, I will receive a (+). If I break any rule, I will receive a (0). I must have three of the possible four (+) marks in the same day to move to the next step.
3. If I do not receive three of the four possible (+) marks in the same day, I remain at that step until I do.
4. If I break Rule 6 at any time, I go back to Step 1.

(Maria)   (Nurse)

Group Therapy

Inpatient group therapy is a short-term therapy used as an adjunct to other treatment modalities during a youth's hospitalization (Slavson & Schiffer, 1975). The overall goal of group therapy for youngsters with conduct disturbances is to provide a therapeutic experience that diminishes their conduct disturbances, builds positive interpersonal relationships, and promotes the development of self-esteem by helping each youngster to become a valued member of the group. A variety of methods can be used in group treatment. The ages, levels of function, and personality styles of the client population often determine the method of choice. In general, group therapy sessions are scheduled to meet two to three times per week for approximately 50 to 60 minutes for younger children and 1 to 1½ hours for adolescents.

Play Group Therapy

For children aged 4 to 10 years, play group therapy is most effective (Schaefer, 1976). Groups for this age range should have no more than 6 to 8 children, with two nurse co-leaders. The purpose of a play group is to help children who have difficulty in dealing with parent and peer relationships or in understanding or expressing feelings, specifically anger and negativism. The children explore relationships and the expression of feelings through the use of play materials, fantasy, and conversation. Even though the children are allowed freedom of expression, each therapy session has limitations or boundaries that teach them to express themselves in an acceptable manner. The selection of play materials is very important. For instance, toys such as building blocks, tinkertoys, crayons and drawing paper, clay, and hand puppets can be used in many ways by the children and nurse to test reality and express feelings.

Activity Group Therapy

The school-aged child can develop his or her sense of self and deal with problems associated with peer and sibling relationships, self-esteem, responsibility, and life event changes (e.g., separation and loss) through activity group therapy. These groups use structured activities to facilitate the group process and to improve behavior by planning, applying, and negotiating rules, as well as by developing an internal organization. The structured activities help the child to work through conflicts, frustrations, and hostilities without having to engage in open communication. Therefore, activities that support peer play, such as games or competitive sports, or that resemble those of a club or organization are used to promote social adjustment and better relationships between the youngsters and to develop their sense of cohesiveness and leadership skills.

The composition of an activity group for aggressive children is a key factor in achieving the desired climate. When selecting children for the group, the therapist must consider each child's chronological age, maturation, physical abilities, and personality to provide for a more homogeneous balance. When most children in the group are aggressive with poor impulse control, the number of group members should be limited, with two to three nurse co-leaders for 8 to 10 children.

Social Skills Training

Children who demonstrate uncooperative, aggressive, or acting out behavior typically have problems with social interactions and peer relationships. Because a child's inability to interact appropriately with other children and adults often generates a negative response, the socially maladjusted child feels rejected, frustrated, and angry.

Social skills training is a therapeutic modality used to alter social behaviors through the use of modeling, rehearsal and practice, feedback, and social reinforcement (Michelson, Sugai, Wood, & Kazdin, 1983). The program teaches new social behaviors that will receive positive responses from the other people in the environment, such as the child's teachers, parents, and peers. The training often includes role playing to help the child apply newly learned skills in multiple settings with different persons.

Adolescent Group Therapy

Adolescents generally benefit from a group program that focuses on interpersonal learning, such as control of emotional and impulsive responses, appropriate expression of anger, and communication skills (Feindler, 1987; Lichstein, Wagner, Krisak, & Steinberg, 1987). In addition to a discussion group format, modeling and role playing can be used to develop the youngster's coping skills and understanding of conduct disturbances. A group session can be devoted to relaxation training, decisional control, imagery, or social skills training. The use of therapeutic games helps the youngsters apply the learned skills to other settings.

An adolescent group should include clients who are not in acute distress, possess the potential for interpersonal learning, and have common problems. Because adolescents with conduct disturbances are often difficult to work with, specific techniques must be used to maintain a degree of structure. The nurse co-leaders should begin by establishing group goals or developing a group therapy contract. The group co-leaders play an interactive role in the sessions by serving as role models for appropriate behavior, facilitating interaction and cohesion, and acting as technical experts in skills training.

RESEARCH

To date, there has been very little nursing literature that addresses aggressive or disruptive behavior in children and adolescents. The focus of current nursing research is on verbal and physical interventions for aggression (Barlow, 1989; Pond,

1988). Although research on the management of aggressive behavior should continue, there is a strong need for clinical research that demonstrates the effectiveness of various nursing interventions to promote interpersonal learning and skill building in both the child and family systems. Studies that describe intervention strategies by psychiatric nurses such as contracting, social skills training, group therapy, progressive relaxation, parent training, and decisional control are essential in helping children with conduct disturbances achieve a healthy outcome.

REFERENCES

Barlow, D. (1989). Therapeutic holding: Effective intervention with the aggressive child. *Journal of Psychosocial Nursing, 27*(1), 10–14.

Feindler, E. (1987). Clinical issues and recommendations in adolescent anger-control training. *Journal of Child and Adolescent Psychotherapy, 4*, 267–274.

Kazdin, A. (1985). *Treatment of antisocial behavior in children and adolescents.* Homewood, IL: Dorsey Press.

King, I.M. (1981). *A theory for nursing: Systems, concepts, process.* New York: John Wiley & Sons.

Lichstein, K., Wagner, M., Krisak, J., & Steinberg, F. (1987). Stress management for acting-out, inpatient adolescents. *Journal of Child and Adolescent Psychotherapy, 4*, 19–31.

Michelson, L., Sugai, D., Wood, R., & Kazdin, A. (1983). *Social skills assessment and training with children: An empirically based handbook.* New York: Plenum Press.

Patterson, G. (1982). *Coercive family process: A social learning approach* (Vol. 3). Eugene, OR: Castalia Publishing.

Pond, V. (1988). The angry adolescent: Treatment versus containment practices. *Journal of Psychosocial Nursing, 26*(12), 15–17.

Schaefer, C. (1976). *Therapeutic use of child's play.* New York: Jason Aronson.

Slavson, S., & Schiffer, M. (1975). *Group psychotherapies for children: A handbook.* New York: International Universities Press.

Snyder, M. (1985). *Independent nursing interventions.* New York: John Wiley & Sons.

16

Nursing Interventions with Children Experiencing Difficulty in Expressing Feelings

Billie J. Hayward

After reading this chapter, the reader will be able to:

1. identify the human response pattern of difficulty in expressing feelings
2. differentiate between the factors that influence the development of acceptable expression of feelings and the development of difficulty repressing feelings
3. design clinical goals for nursing interventions with youngsters who have difficulty in expressing their feelings and their families
4. develop therapeutic nursing strategies to help youngsters identify, express, and manage their feelings constructively in age-appropriate ways
5. develop therapeutic strategies to help parents and other care-givers facilitate their children's expression of feelings

> "It just hurts. All over," moaned 10-year-old Courtney as she moved her hand gingerly across her abdomen. "And my head hurts. I'm dizzy and tired. I feel like I'm going to throw up," she continued with a worried expression. "But nobody believes me. Everybody says I'm imagining it—that I'm making myself sick. It really does hurt! I'm not just making it up."

Alteration in comfort is a significant challenge for nurses who work with children and adolescents. When the discomfort arises from somatic responses to anxiety and stress rather than from physical pathology, however, nurses are often puzzled about the best ways to help. Youngsters also face a dilemma when significant adults and health professionals suggest psychological explanations, implying that a youngster's pain is exaggerated or does not have a "real" basis. Parallel with this, these children often suspect that their pain results from something dangerous, mysterious, and perhaps untreatable. Their fear is accompanied by a sense of helplessness because interventions do not "make it go away" rapidly.

Learning to communicate both positive and negative feelings in age-appropriate ways either through words or through other constructive outlets is an important developmental task for children and adolescents. By the time that they reach school age, children who have experienced an enabling environment that fostered a sense of safety and acceptance generally communicate their feelings spontaneously and honestly (sometimes bluntly).

Children who do not master the developmental task of expressing their thoughts and feelings reflect their anger, anxiety, elation, envy, fear, grief, guilt, sadness, and shame through patterns of behavior that indicate difficulty in expressing feelings. Some of these youngsters are inhibited, shy, fearful, mistrustful, and socially isolated. Conversely, some are overexpressive, impulsive, silly, aggressive, and rebellious. Others internalize their uneasiness and communicate their emotions through a pattern of somatic distress, usually reported as pain in the abdomen, head, limbs, or chest.

"Bottled-up" feelings communicated as somatic distress are reportedly present in 10% of school-aged children between ages 6 and 15 years (Schaeffer, Millman, & Levine, 1979). The expression of troubling feelings through altered comfort can be devastating to a youngster's health, social effectiveness, academic achievement, and personal competence. Helping youngsters learn to identify and express emotions constructively while mastering culturally expected self-control is of special importance to nurses who practice in child psychiatric, pediatric, community health, and school settings.

DEVELOPMENTAL FRAMEWORK

According to behavioral and psychoanalytic theories of personality development, the communication of feelings progresses from somatized reactions to undifferentiated emotions in neonates toward verbal responses to differentiated emotions in adolescents. At birth, there is little discrimination between physiological and psychological experience, as infants have only a vague perception of their bodies. Unpleasant feelings of distress and pleasant feelings of delight elicit body sensations automatically. Feelings are expressed as gross physical movements and/or loud vocalizations that capture the attention of adults quickly.

The recognition of emotions begins between 6 and 12 months of age. By 9 months, infants respond to adults' facial and vocal expressions of negative emotions with frowning, crying, or sobering. By 12 months, they follow nonverbal facial cues of frowning or smiling from mothers in avoid-approach situations (Bretherton, Fritz, Zahn-Waxler, & Ridgeway, 1986), demonstrating early differentiation and expression of feelings in ways other than somatization.

As youngsters grow, their perceptual and expressive abilities become increasingly differentiated. Toddlers between the ages of 18 and 36 months make rapid strides in communicating their feelings verbally. Preschool children respond verbally to emotion-related situations with increasing accuracy and clarity (Bretherton et al., 1986). When they are old enough to go to school, youngsters are usually capable of using language to communicate a wide variety of feelings. Concurrently, they learn that the direct expression of some feelings is not acceptable. They may then stifle their feelings to avoid trouble and embarrassment, maintain self-esteem, support relationships, and meet social norms (Saarni, 1977). Deliberately controlled verbal responses take precedence over automatic reactions.

While children master the selective verbal and nonverbal expression of emotions, their attention to body sensations diminishes. Happy or disturbing thoughts and situations continue to arouse emotions that speed up internal body processes, but children begin to be only minimally aware of this increase in activity. Despite this desomatization of emotions, school-aged children are naturally attuned to their changing physical bodies. They notice the transient discomfort often referred to as "growing pains." The increased attention to their bodies, together with the environmental, social, and cultural constraints that inhibit the direct expression of feelings, helps explain why children may begin to communicate their feelings unconsciously through somatic distress during this developmental period.

Sarnoff (1976) identified three factors that influence this phenomenon. First, the direct expression of emotions becomes less acceptable during the latency phase, and children learn to suppress their feelings. Second, language contains few words to represent feelings so "it is customary during latency in America for the affects of early childhood to be consigned to nonverbal organ language and psychosomatic forms of expression" (p. 161). Third, competency in controlling feelings requires selecting behaviors that are "right" from many options. Consequently, children in this age group may learn to "be nice" and curtail direct verbal and motoric expression of their feelings.

While learning not to show negative emotions, children may convince themselves that they are not feeling anger, anxiety, envy, fear, grief, guilt, sadness, or shame. When the normal expression of feelings is blocked, emotions may appear as somatic distress. A problem arises when a youngster develops a pattern of consistently holding in feelings and expressing them through physical discomfort that interferes with the pursuit of age-appropriate activities and interpersonal relationships.

INTERPRETATIONS OF ALTERATION IN COMFORT

Explanations for somatic distress in the absence of any apparent physical cause are varied and predictable. Parents, who are often puzzled by the notion that pain can be associated with difficulty in expressing feelings, generally attribute youngsters' discomfort to physical conditions. For example, headache is usually attributed to "sinuses" or "eye strain." Discomfort is occasionally ascribed to "excitement" or "being worked up about school." Even when pain is attributed to stress, parents tend to believe that the child will "grow out of it."

Health care clinicians generally believe that pain does not exist if the physical source cannot be identified. In fact, many professionals believe that pain symptoms without an apparent physical cause are deliberately produced or exaggerated.

Their explanations for intentionally "bringing on" pain include efforts to win sympathy and attention, escape responsibilities, avoid some distressing activity, control troubling situations, or prolong recuperation after physical illness. Nurses must examine their own beliefs and responses in these situations in order to be more therapeutically effective and to ensure that their inaccurate assumptions will not be unwittingly communicated to suffering, worried children and their families. An accepting, caring, compassionate, growth-promoting atmosphere will enhance youngsters' success in learning to identify, express, and control their feelings.

NURSING PROCESS

Psychiatric nurses who work with youngsters who communicate feelings through somatic distress use individualized approaches. They adjust their interventions to the developmental level of the children, age-appropriate responses to stress, family situations, and environmental factors.

Assessment and Planning

The behavioral responses of youngsters and families have unique characteristics. There are some patterns of discomfort commonly seen in youngsters with difficulty in expressing feelings, however, and a knowledge of these patterns is useful in assessment and planning.

Pattern of Discomfort. Youngsters who communicate feelings through alteration in comfort appear to be healthy. Their pain is varied and erratic, and it seldom awakens them from sleep. Pain may interfere with school attendance and other age-appropriate activities. Recurrent abdominal pain is often accompanied by pallor, dizziness, and headaches. Physical findings are normal except for some abdominal tenderness over parts of the colon on deep palpation (Barbero, 1982).

Psychosocial Variables. Discomfort generally begins after youngsters experience distressing changes or uncontrollable situations in their lives, such as the death of or separation from an important person, physical illness or chronic disability in a sibling or parent, psychiatric illness in a parent, severe marital discord, alcoholism or drug abuse in primary care-givers, parent-child conflict, punitive limit-setting practices, child abuse or domestic violence, and peer problems or learning difficulties at school (Green, 1967).

Interpersonal Skills. Parents describe youngsters who communicate their feelings through body aches as shy; socially insecure with few friends; eager to please others, especially close relationships with their parents; dependent on the parents for support; and worried about the parents' having accidents or illness. Parents often report uncertainty about their youngsters' ability to handle experiences on their own (Stone & Barbero, 1970). Parental sensitivity and closeness can have a negative impact on a youngster's attempts to cope with discomfort.

Assessment Goals. Nursing goals specific to assessing a difficulty in expressing feelings with a youngster and family include:

- establishment of an open, supportive communication
- exploration of the youngster's pain experience and the responses of significant others
- determination of the beliefs of the youngster and family about the reason for the symptoms
- identification of the stressors that elicit the discomfort
- exploration of the meaning of the pain to the youngster
- provision of feedback about findings and recommended interventions

Nursing Diagnosis and Interventions

After a thorough diagnostic work-up by a pediatrician has revealed no identifiable physical causes, pain is suspected to be a symptom of anxiety and other emotions. The nursing diagnosis for youngsters with this pattern of difficulty is Alteration of Comfort related to difficulty in expressing feelings.

Goals of Interventions

Nursing interventions are designed to help youngsters and their families attain the following goals. Youngsters will:

1. identify, label, and connect feelings with their physical, mental, and emotional responses
2. express both positive and negative feelings safely and constructively in age-appropriate ways
3. experience mastery, competence, and self-confidence in managing and dealing directly with external and internal stress in their lives by using the skills learned through selected therapeutic modalities, patient education, and practice in therapeutic settings

Parents and significant others will:

1. facilitate and allow their youngsters' expression of both positive and negative feelings
2. create an empathic, nonjudgmental, and safe environment to foster their youngsters' expression of feelings
3. identify, label, and connect altered comfort with emotions and confirm their understanding of their youngsters' feelings
4. experience mastery, competence, and self-confidence in helping their youngsters deal directly with internal and external stress in their lives

In addition, psychiatric and mental health nurses' main goals for intervening with children who communicate feelings through alteration in comfort are to:

1. accept youngsters' reports of pain, empathize with their suffering, and assist them in learning to express their feelings constructively
2. alleviate specific fears not supported by clinical findings
3. establish and maintain a therapeutic relationship and environment that facilitates the effective expression of positive and negative feelings in age-appropriate ways
4. select nursing interventions congruent with youngsters' developmental, cultural, and therapeutic needs and paced to match their progress
5. educate, coach, guide, and encourage parents in learning, allowing, and supporting their youngsters' expressions of feelings

Types of Interventions

Nurses may use several different approaches when intervening with youngsters whose difficulty in expressing feelings manifests itself as physical health problems. These strategies include individual psychotherapy; expressive therapies using play, puppets, cartoons, drawing, music, books, and storytelling; education about the physiological relationship between feelings and altered comfort; relaxation and imagery; parental guidance, counseling, and modeling; and environmental restructuring to facilitate the age-appropriate expression of feelings.

Individual Psychotherapy. Sarnoff (1976) suggested that the most effective way of dealing psychotherapeutically with children is to discuss their problems with them directly. Mainly supportive, psychotherapy encourages the open expression of feelings, either through words or other activities. During sessions, youngsters often call attention to their difficulty in expressing feelings by reporting somatic symptoms of emotional distress or by massaging the area of their body that hurts. Individual psychotherapy is helpful with youngsters from the ages of 10 or 11 years and older who prefer direct conversations. Some youngsters as young as 6 or 7 years old may also want this approach, however.

Expressive Therapies. Children sometimes need a bridge between communicating their feelings through body upsets and being able to talk about them. Fantasy and play are good techniques to use in therapy with children who have difficulty in verbalizing their feelings (Sarnoff, 1976). Children have active imaginations that are reflected through their play, drawings, and the stories that they tell. These natural, enjoyable modes of expression allow youngsters to express their feelings more openly and freely. Any one of these three creative forms of expression can be used singly or collectively as directed activities to initiate therapeutic relationships, stimulate interaction between nurses and children, and address the specific therapeutic problem of learning to express feeling constructively (Pothier, 1976). In addition, expressive therapies allow children to relieve tension and play out dilemmas from their personal lives. They can learn and practice coping skills that foster a sense of mastery, competence, and self-confidence.

Specific strategies include games, mutual storytelling, and drawing cartoons. A therapeutic board game that is especially helpful in encouraging youngsters to express feelings is the Talking, Feeling, Doing Game (Gardner, 1973). The game can be adapted to meet the specific needs of individual children.

Mutual storytelling helps youngsters put their feelings into words (Deering, 1986). Children tell stories that reflect their fears, worries, and feelings. The nurse tells another version of the same story in which the characters express their feelings openly and demonstrate that it is acceptable to describe negative and positive feelings (Piché, 1978).

Allegorical stories can also be effective avenues for helping youngsters express feelings. The nurse composes or selects stories that relate to the child's experience, including characters with whom the child can identify and a metaphor with the theme of the child's worry (Fossom & deQuan, 1984). Children tend to express their own concerns and feelings after listening to thematic stories.

Lastly, cartoons can help children master fear, pain, or worry and express their feelings (Crowley & Mills, 1989). Youngsters are encouraged to identify a cartoon friend who can help them with their particular difficulty. The nurse then selects a pretend technique and encourages the child to visualize, tell a story, or draw what the worry, fear, or pain is like. The child then describes or draws what the difficulty will be like when it is "all better" (Crowley & Mills, 1989).

CASE EXAMPLE

Mrs. Carter sought therapy for her 10-year-old daughter, Courtney, because she believed that her daughter's stomachaches and headaches were stress-related. A pediatrician had been unable to find a physical cause for Courtney's pain. During the past year, several uncontrollable life changes had occurred in the family. The two most troubling for Courtney were a recurrence of her mother's cancer and her family's move from another state.

Courtney sat stiffly on the sofa close to her mother. She listened attentively as Mrs. Carter described her as "a very good child who tries hard to please and worries too much." Courtney was solemn and massaged her forehead as she responded thoughtfully to questions. As her anxiety increased, she scratched her arms and said, "I always itch when I'm nervous." One fear she reported was that her stomachache might indicate she was getting cancer, too. Courtney's mother was surprised to learn this. When the nurse therapist expressed an understanding of Courtney's worry and reassured her that stomach cancer is uncommon in children, her mother joined in helping alleviate this fear.

Because Courtney was suffering from pain that interfered with her usual activities, the initial assessment focused on her stomachache and headache. Pain assessment tools designed by McCaffery (1982), and McMillan, Williams, Chatfield, and Camp (1988), were used to help Courtney describe the multidimensional aspects of her pain. Courtney chose a red crayon to color the location of her pain on a drawing of a child. Using a visual analogue scale of intensity in which 0 was no pain and 10 was the worst pain imaginable, Courtney rated her headache as 8 and her stomachache as 7. Courtney was most aware of her pain during school and at bedtime when she was thinking about her mother. Lying down near her mother and placing a cool cloth on her forehead made the pain better. Courtney perceived "worry" to be a cause of her discomfort, but she found that being told to "stop worrying" made it worse. She felt guilty about causing extra concern for her mother and father. Courtney had no ideas about what she personally could do to control her pain.

Courtney spoke softly, jiggled her foot, and twisted the handle on her purse as she continued. "I haven't told anybody what I'm really afraid of because I'm afraid, if I say the word, it might make it happen." After explaining to Courtney that nobody ever completely gets over the fear that thinking awful thoughts or saying scary things aloud might make them happen (LeShan, 1972), the nurse reassured her that thinking and talking about things do not make them happen. She moved nearer her mother and said, "I'm afraid Mom is going to die, and I'm not sure I can get through it." Courtney's mother held her close as they wept together.

After a few minutes of silence, the nurse said, "I'm sorry your mother has cancer again. I can understand why you are sad and scared. I've talked with other girls and boys your age whose parents have cancer. They were worried and angry because they didn't think it was fair to go through this a second time. In fact, they often mentioned that they wished it had happened to somebody else's mother instead. I know that these feelings are normal. I'm glad you told us."

Using a children's book about feelings as a guide (LeShan, 1972), the nurse taught about the interaction of thinking, feeling, and body pain. "Feelings are very complicated. They influence everything we do. When we understand our feelings, we can decide what we want to do about them. You are a smart girl. You've already noticed that your head hurts when you worry about your mother. You're unhappy and your body is unhappy because your mind and your body are one. When girls like you are very nice, they sometimes believe they shouldn't let their feelings show. But feelings that hurt and have nowhere to go don't give up. Those feelings come out as headaches and stomachaches because they have to go somewhere.

"Now, let's talk about some things you can do to help yourself hurt less when you get afraid and upset. First, it takes a lot of courage to think about your feelings (LeShan, 1972). It will be a lot easier on your head and stomach if you let yourself feel your sad and angry feelings instead of trying not to have them. Some things are worth feeling sad and angry about. Leaving your friends, going to a new school, and having your mother's cancer come back are important reasons for feeling sad and mad. These feelings are normal in your situation.

"The next thing you can do is find someone you can talk to about your feelings. When boys and girls find out they can think about how they feel and find someone they can talk to about their feelings, they can begin to control what they do about them [LeShan, 1972]. It will be easier on your stomach and your head if you talk about your feelings more openly. Think about who you can talk with."

Courtney identified her father and her Aunt Margaret as two people who would listen and understand, but she had reservations about "hurting them" if they knew her worries. The nurse reassured her that it is the job of grown-ups to listen and to comfort their children. "By trying to protect them," the nurse continued, "you keep them from doing their job." The nurse reminded Courtney that she felt left out when her parents did not keep her informed about happenings and told her that her father had said that he wanted Courtney to speak up about her thoughts and feelings. "Talking with your dad at bedtime about your worries and the good things that happened during the day will help you put your mind at ease and let you fall asleep. You may take this book home with you to read alone and share with your parents."

The final self-care interventions introduced in this first meeting were passive relaxation and creative thinking. Children and adolescents can learn to control mental processes that influence a wide variety of physical processes. Relaxation and imagery are effective strategies for helping them reduce tension and anxiety through conscious control over breathing and naturally active imaginations.

Because it is necessary to relax before using imagery so that motor responses, thoughts, and external stimuli do not compete with the production of images (Acterberg, 1985), Courtney was initially taught to use the four basic components necessary to elicit the relaxation response: a quiet environment, a mental device, a passive attitude, and a comfortable position (Benson, 1975). Once Courtney gained control over her breathing and was able to relax, she received instruction in imagery, which serves as an integrative mechanism between mental and physical processes (Acterberg, 1985), to help control her headache and distract her from fear and worry.

The supportive involvement of Courtney's parents allowed them to learn additional coping skills together as a family. Courtney's mother was already using relaxation and guided imagery to help manage her own anxiety and pain. Courtney was interested in learning these skills also because of her strong identification with her mother. Courtney practiced relaxation every day for 10 minutes after school with her mother and at bedtime with her father. The nurse provided an audio tape that began by encouraging her to be patient with herself when her mind wandered, to remember that mastering relaxation takes as much practice as learning to read, and to have positive expectations for success.

In the second meeting, the nurse spent part of the time teaching Courtney guided imagery to help her relieve headache pain. After an explanation of the procedure, Courtney sat in a chair and used breathing to relax. When she was ready, she listened to selected parts of an audio tape (Ulene & Diamond, 1986). Courtney followed the voice on the tape as it guided her through three images that could help relieve headaches. In the first, she imagined feeling very light as she floated in warm, clear air. She saw her headache take on a bright red color, slowly change to a very dark red, and then become a soothing blue as she concentrated on feeling it become cool. Second, she visualized a bright electric light bulb that slowly became a softer light until it was out, and her headache was gone. Finally, she was guided to imagine putting her headache in a box that gradually became smaller until it disappeared from view, taking her headache with it. Courtney liked the imagery and agreed to practice at the times previously set aside and at times when she had a headache.

In the third meeting, Courtney spent part of the time relaxing and using imagery to reflect on a happy time. When asked to think about a favorite place, she focused her mind's eye on a recent trip to the zoo with her family when her mother was "feeling good." Because imagery is most effective when all senses are used, the nurse encouraged her to report the details aloud as they came to mind. Courtney described the color and warmth of a bright summer day, the sounds and smells of the zoo, and the taste of treats. The nurse concluded by telling Courtney that she could go back to this special place anytime she wanted—especially before falling asleep at night. Getting in touch with happier times helped her balance the sadness, anger, and worry of her present circumstances and maintain hope. Imagery, like pretending, allows youngsters to change an unpleasant situation temporarily to one that is more tolerable and positive. This cognitive distraction gives them a heightened sense of being in control.

Over the course of 6 months, the nurse therapist continued to see Courtney individually or with her parents. Courtney found the following strategies helpful in expressing her feelings constructively and reducing her physical discomfort: writing about her feelings in a journal; compiling a worry list and assigning the nurse responsibility for thinking about her mother while Courtney was at school; reading books selected to match her situation (LeShan, 1986); using positive self-talk (e.g., I can do it; I'm OK); exercising vigorously five times a week (e.g., swimming and bike riding); and permitting herself to have fun, then sharing it with her parents. The outcomes for Courtney were improved mood, verbal expression of a wider range of emotions, increased discussion of feelings within the family, decreased occurrence of somatic distress when emotionally upset, increased tolerance for separation, and improved concentration at school.

RESEARCH

There has been little research on nursing practice with children who reflect their difficulty in expressing feelings through alteration in comfort. Nurses are frequently in positions where they have the authority and responsibility for deciding how and when alteration in comfort will be treated, however, and pain of "unknown cause" is particularly challenging. Therefore, a study of the patterns of nurses' responses toward youngsters who communicate pain through somatic distress is warranted. In addition, an effort could be made to determine if there is a correlation between positive, accepting nurse attitudes and therapeutic nursing interventions.

The effectiveness of nursing interventions with children, such as the effectiveness of relaxation training as an intervention with children, could be explored. The area of prevention could be addressed to determine if children who are taught to view themselves as in control of their lives stay healthier than those who are not taught this view.

REFERENCES

Acterberg, J. (1985). *Imagery in healing*. Boston: Shambhala Publications.

Barbero, G.J. (1982). Recurrent abdominal pain in childhood. *Pediatrics in Review, 4*(1), 29–34.

Benson, H. (1975). *The relaxation response*. New York: William Morrow.

Bretherton, I., Fritz, J., Zahn-Waxler, C., & Ridgeway, D. (1986). Learning to talk about emotions: A functionalist approach. *Child Development, 57,* 529–548.

Crowley, R.J., & Mills, J.C. (1989). *Cartoon magic*. New York: Magination Press.

Deering, C.G. (1986). The inhibited child. *Journal of Psychosocial Nursing, 24*(2), 17–21.

Fossom, A., & deQuan, M. (1984). Reassuring and talking with hospitalized children. *Journal of the Association for the Care of Children's Health, 13*(1), 37–44.

Gardner, R.A. (1973). *The thinking, feeling, and doing game*. Cresskill, NJ: Creative Therapeutics.

Green, M. (1967). Diagnosis and treatment: Psychogenic abdominal pain. *Pediatrics, 40,* 84–89.

LeShan, E. (1972). *What makes me feel this way?* New York: Macmillan.

LeShan, E. (1986). *When a parent is very sick*. Boston: Little, Brown.

McCaffery, M. (1982). Initial pain assessment tool. Unpublished manuscript.

McMillan, S.C., Williams, F.A., Chatfield, R., & Camp, L.D. (1988). A validity and reliability study of two tools for assessing and managing cancer pain. *Oncology Nursing Forum, 15*(6), 735–741.

Piché, J.C. (1978). Tell me a story. *American Journal of Nursing*, 1188–1193.

Pothier, P.C. (1976). *Mental health counseling*. Boston: Little, Brown.

Saarni, C. (1977). Children's understanding of display rules for expressive behavior. *Developmental Psychology, 13,* 3–10.

Sarnoff, C. (1976). *Latency*. New York: Jason Aronson.

Schaeffer, C.E., Millman, H.L., & Levine, G.J. (1979). *Therapies for psychosomatic disorders in children*. San Francisco: Jossey-Bass.

Stone, R.T., & Barbero, G.J. (1970). Recurrent abdominal pain in childhood. *Pediatrics, 45*(5), 732–738.

Ulene, A., & Diamond, S. (1986). *How to relieve a headache*. New York: Feeling Fine Programs and Random House.

17

Nursing Interventions with Children and Adolescents Experiencing Substance Abuse

Linda M. Finke

After reading this chapter, the reader will be able to:

1. discuss the scope of child and adolescent substance abuse
2. describe the psychiatric nursing assessment for substance abuse in a child or adolescent
3. describe the formulation of nursing diagnoses for children or adolescents with a substance abuse problem
4. examine primary, secondary, and tertiary nursing interventions for children or adolescents with a chemical dependency problem
5. identify treatment approaches for children and adolescents with substance abuse problems
6. identify areas for future research concerning substance use and abuse by children and adolescents

Substance abuse among children and adolescents is a major health problem. Although there has been a recent decline in the use of marijuana daily, there has been no change in the prevalence of abuse of alcohol, cocaine, and heroin. Furthermore, younger children are experimenting with drugs and developing problems as a result (Johnston, Backman, & O'Malley, 1985). All drug use is a potential problem for this vulnerable age group and can be detrimental to their physical and psychosocial development.

Client systems (individuals and families) are in constant interaction with environmental stressors (Neuman, 1988). Psychiatric nurses need to be aware of the stressors, both internal and external, that have a potential impact on children and adolescents. Internal stressors may be related to poor self-esteem, while external stressors may be living in a dysfunctional family or associating with peers who abuse alcohol and drugs. These stressors either may lead to substance abuse or may be the result of substance abuse.

Nurses can intervene to assist children and adolescents who are abusing drugs or alcohol by strengthening the lines of defense of these young people and their families through effective prevention programs, complete assessments, and appropriate referral and treatment. Nurses can also intervene to facilitate adaptation or to modify internal and external stressors through effective therapy techniques. Nursing interventions can be made at the primary, secondary, or tertiary level.

SYNTHESIS OF THEORY AND ASSESSMENT DATA

Scope of Child and Adolescent Substance Abuse

The nurse working with children and adolescents who are experiencing a substance abuse problem must synthesize existing theory with individualized assessment data to design interventions appropriate for each client system. Therefore, the nurse must start with an understanding of the scope of the problem.

It has been estimated that as many as 1 in 4 young people become involved in drug and alcohol abuse. Ninety-two percent of all high-school graduates stated that they have used alcohol, and more than half (56%) said that they began to use alcohol in the sixth to ninth grades (Carnegie Council, 1989).

The number of problem drinkers in the school-aged group is alarming. Fifteen percent of students in the 10th to 12th grades are considered heavy drinkers; that is, they drink at least once a week and consume 5 to 12 drinks on a single occasion. Three of four high-school students drink alcoholic beverages, and one of seven drink enough to interfere with their daily functioning. Sixty percent of U.S. high-school seniors have tried marijuana, and one of fourteen uses marijuana daily. One of every five high-school students uses drugs on a weekly basis (Johnston et al., 1985).

Children with a family history of substance abuse are at high risk for developing substance abuse. There are multiple theories concerning the familial linkage of substance abuse, which includes both genetic and socialization factors. Substance abuse may be the maladaptation of a child with a poor self-esteem because of family dysfunction or individual differences. The causes of the abuse are not predictive of the difficulty children will develop nor the progression of the problem.

The use of chemical substances by children and adolescents can become a chronic problem that is progressive and can be fatal. Drugs are toxic to the body, especially to the body of a fast growing youngster, and have drastic effects on the psychological development of a child (Exhibit 17-1). All children experience some difficulty at various stages of their development, but a child who is using drugs may actually stagnate at a developmental phase and be unable to accomplish the tasks necessary to achieve emotional maturity.

As a result of drug use, young people develop wide mood swings, have little control of their behavior, and overreact to stimuli. Reflexes are impaired, and resistance to infection is reduced. Drug use can interfere with the development of effective coping strategies and can cause feelings of failure, loss of control, and

Exhibit 17-1 Drugs of Abuse and Some of Their Effects

Depressants

Examples and Comments: Alcohol, barbiturates, Placidyl, Doriden, Valium, Xanax and many others. Any drug used to calm or sedate could be in this category and may be called downers.

Usual Forms Found: Alcoholic beverages and legitimate looking tablets and capsules.*

Potential for Excessive Use Leading to Physical (Ph) and Psychological (Ps) Dependence: High for both Ph & Ps, varies somewhat among drugs. Ph withdrawal effects can be life threatening.

Common Effects at Peak of Drug Response: Inebriation, impaired speech & judgment, confusion, sleepiness.

Possible in Overdoses: Death from depression of breathing & from dangerous behavior under influence.

Stimulants

Examples and Comments: Amphetamines and most related diet drugs, amphetamine look-alikes (contain caffeine and other legal stimulants), cocaine (crystalline) and processed (freebase, crack) and caffeine.

Usual Forms Found: Legitimate looking tablets and capsules,* crystals, powders (usually white).

Potential for Excessive Use Leading to Physical (Ph) and Psychological (Ps) Dependence: Ph low to moderate, Ps high; severe depression can occur on withdrawal and has led to suicide (except caffeine which can cause moderate depression and headaches upon withdrawal).

Common Effects at Peak of Drug Response: Jitteriness, jolly or high feeling, talkativeness; may become irritable, fearful (paranoid), and aggressive.

Possible in Overdoses: Hallucinations, increased blood pressure, death from heart rhythm defects and/or convulsions.

Narcotics/Opioids

Examples and Comments: Heroin, morphine, Demerol, Dilaudid, codeine, Methadone, opium, Talwin, T's & B's (Talwin & an antihistamine), Stadol; most all drugs prescribed for severe pain.

Usual Forms Found: Legitimate looking tablets and capsules; powders (white, brown, or gray), and injectable liquids.

Potential for Excessive Use Leading to Physical (Ph) and Psychological (Ps) Dependence: High for both Ph & Ps; varies somewhat between drugs. Ph withdrawal effects very uncomfortable but rarely life threatening.

Common Effects at Peak of Drug Response: Initially may vomit, then become very calm (on the nod) and euphoric.

Possible in Overdoses: Death from depression of breathing and severe & unique toxic effects from contaminants (e.g., Parkinsonism from MPTP impurity).

Hallucinogens

Examples and Comments: LSD (acid, window-pane, blotter, microdot, blue stars), mescaline, psylocybin, MDMA, etc. These drugs can alter perceptions of reality.

Usual Forms Found: Tablets, capsules, liquid or impregnated on blotters, stamps, pieces of clear gelatin, or other items.

Potential for Excessive Use Leading to Physical (Ph) and Psychological (Ps) Dependence: No Ph; extent of Ps unknown, probably low.

Common Effects at Peak of Drug Response: Incoordination, hallucinations, changes in space & time perception, may make irrational verbal statements and movements.

Possible in Overdoses: Severe toxic effects unlikely; death can occur from dangerous behavior while under influence (e.g., driving).

Delirients

Examples and Comments: Phencyclidine (PCP, THC, angel dust) and any drug with actions like belladonna (such as Jimson Weed). Produce hallucinations & delirium at doses causing significant toxic effects.

Usual Forms Found: Tablets, capsules, powder, seeds; may be in other drugs.

Potential for Excessive Use Leading to Physical (Ph) and Psychological (Ps) Dependence: Low for Ph (gastro-intestinal & muscle symptoms are reported); moderate to high for Ps.

Common Effects at Peak of Drug Response: Blank stare, confusion, disturbed speech, agitation, hostile behavior, gross incoordination, floating sensation.

Possible in Overdoses: Death from heart & breathing system effects or dangerous behavior, convulsions, increased blood pressure.

Inhalants

Gasoline & Solvents

Examples and Comments: Almost any vaporous liquid or aerosol may be inhaled for a temporary high.

Usual Forms Found: Certain glues, typing correction liquids, spot removers & other solvents.

Potential for Excessive Use Leading to Physical (Ph) and Psychological (Ps) Dependence: Ph & Ps varies greatly with agent patterns of use.

Common Effects at Peak of Drug Response: Inebriation, impairment of judgment & coordination, delirium.

Possible in Overdoses: Sudden sniffing death possible with overdose.

Inhaled Gases

Examples and Comments: Laughing gas, whippets intended for use in charging whipped cream canisters.

Usual Forms Found: Nitrous oxide is usually found in small metal containers.

Potential for Excessive Use Leading to Physical (Ph) and Psychological (Ps) Dependence: Ph unlikely & Ps varies greatly with patterns of use, but has been reported.

Common Effects at Peak of Drug Response: Laughing episodes of euphoria.

Possible in Overdoses: Death from oxygen deprivation.

Inhaled Nitrites

Examples and Comments: Rush, poppers, amyl, etc.

Usual Forms Found: The nitrites are very strong smelling solutions generally in small brown bottles.

Potential for Excessive Use Leading to Physical (Ph) and Psychological (Ps) Dependence: Ps occurs; Ph questionable.

Common Effects at Peak of Drug Response: Sudden lowering, then rising of blood pressure & heart rate, suffocating sensation, flushed prickly heat feeling.

Possible in Overdoses: Less than an ounce has caused death when accidentally or intentionally swallowed. Death from cardiovascular collapse, blood disorders, convulsions.

continues

Exhibit 17-1 Continued

Marihuana

Examples and Comments: Sinsemilla, grass, reefer, pot, Thai sticks; concentrated forms include hashish and hash oil.

Usual Forms Found: Generally as dark green or brown small plant particles; often in plastic bags or as cigarettes, black or brown cakes or concentrated oily liquid.

Potential for Excessive Use Leading to Physical (Ph) and Psychological (Ps) Dependence: Ph low (reported symptoms vary); Ps low for most users, moderate to high for a few. Some cases of significant Ps occur.

Common Effects at Peak of Drug Response: Mild stimulation & giddiness followed by relaxed euphoric feeling, red eyes, interference with thinking, judgment, recent memory.

Possible in Overdoses: Severe immediate toxic effects unlikely; death can occur from dangerous behavior while under influence (e.g., driving).

Cigarettes & Tobacco Products

Examples and Comments: Cigarettes, cigars, & other smoking preparations. Snuff, chewing tobacco.

Usual Forms Found: Brand name & generic cigarettes, dried & chopped leaves & "plugs."

Potential for Excessive Use Leading to Physical (Ph) and Psychological (Ps) Dependence: Ph moderate, Ps high. Withdrawal syndrome: nervousness, confusion, agitation, drug seeking behavior.

Common Effects at Peak of Drug Response: Dizziness, nausea, increased heart rate, peripheral vasoconstriction.

Possible in Overdoses: Not typical with usual use. Accidental ingestion by young children can be medical emergency.

Anabolic Steroids

Examples and Comments: Testosterone, Winstrol, Anavar, Android, Halotestin, Methandrostenolone

Usual Forms Found: Injectable: long acting oil and short acting water base, oral: capsules and tablets.

Potential for Excessive Use Leading to Physical (Ph) and Psychological (Ps) Dependence: Narcotic type withdrawal symptoms have been reported, many case reports of Ps.

Common Effects at Peak of Drug Response: Increased aggression ("'roid rage"), insomnia, violent behavior.

Possible in Overdoses: Single, acute exposure not severe, long term high doses used by athletes lead to many hormonal changes.

---

*Fake "look-alikes" exist for some drugs in this category. No one can be absolutely certain of the content or quality of any street drug without analysis.

Source: Primary support for DPIC services is provided by the Alcohol and Drug Addiction Services Board of Hamilton County, University of Cincinnati Medical Center, Children's Hospital Medical Center, Cincinnati Health Department, Ohio Department of Health, Ohio Department of Alcohol and Drug Addiction Services, Drackett/Bristol Myers Companies, Hoffmann-La Roche Foundation, and 30 Member Hospitals. Additional contributors include The Procter & Gamble Company, Dowbrands Corporation, Kroger Company, Marion Merrell Dow, Inc., Hamilton County Pharmaceutical Association, local pediatricians and individuals.

low self-esteem. Problems with judgment can lead to increased sexual activity, as well as to illegal and violent behavior. All of these problems contribute to a continuing downward spiral. Suicide becomes a significant risk, which is heightened by the frequency of polydrug use and the potential for lethal overdose.

Drug use by children and adolescents often follows a pattern (Schwartz, 1985). The initial experimentation with drugs is usually the result of pressures from peers at a party, and the youngster frequently finds the first experience unpleasant. With continued use, however, the beginner learns to "achieve the high"—the illusion of well-being and power. The youngster actually begins seeking the mood change, takes the initiative in obtaining the drugs, and moves to more frequent use. The youngster becomes very knowledgeable about the drug and takes pride in his or her ability to handle the drug. As the youngster enters the drug culture more deeply, the circle of friends changes to include others who are using drugs, the manner of dress becomes altered, and grades quickly drop. A drug culture is established. The youngster becomes obsessed with obtaining drugs and the euphoric high that is now viewed as the only way to tolerate life.

Blackouts are danger signs; they are short-term memory lapses that affect a youngster while on drugs and are indications of the toxic effects of those drugs. A youngster who has reached this point has probably lost communication with his or her family and has become withdrawn and apathetic.

Assessment for Substance Abuse

Because the prevalence of substance abuse is high, the assessment for alcohol and drug use should be part of every examination of a child or adolescent. A problem of substance abuse can be defined as the repeated use of a chemical substance that causes behavior that interferes with the individual's health, interpersonal and social relationships, or school and community interactions. Many signs of substance abuse are very obvious, and the health care professional should heed easily detected clues, as well as those that require more extensive investigation.

An assessment of substance use in a child or adolescent should include a determination of intrapersonal, interpersonal, and extrapersonal stressors. Such an assessment consists of four parts: (1) history, (2) current use, (3) behaviors and feelings related to substance use, and (4) desire to change. The focus should be on drug and alcohol use without any judgment concerning abuse.

The history should include the age when the drug use began (prescription or otherwise), pattern of use at the time, length of time on drugs, amount, and state of mind while on drugs. The nurse must keep in mind that polydrug use is very common, and youngsters tend to underreport drug use, just as adults do. Determining the behavior and feelings of the youngster while on drugs is very important, because it may reveal the client's willingness to accept treatment. The possible behaviors to consider are blackouts, tremors, hallucinations, sleep disorders, depression, suicidal thoughts, paranoia, anxiety, eating disorders, physical illness, sexual activity, and illegal actions. An exploration of the client's interaction with friends, family, peers, and school personnel may also provide insight.

Children and adolescents who abuse drugs often have several physical signs of the abuse, such as bloodshot eyes, dilated pupils, slurred speech, and loss of weight. These individuals are often either restless or very sleepy, and they may demonstrate signs of clumsiness. They are often very susceptible to illnesses, such as colds and flu. As the chemical dependency progresses, the signs of substance abuse become more obvious. The drug user may also talk freely about drug use, even to the point of bragging. Parents may find bottles, pipes, and other drug apparatus actually lying around the home. The youngster no longer fears being caught.

Less obvious signs, but often good indicators of a drug problem, are changes in behavior. School attendance problems may arise, and grades may drop suddenly. Children or adolescents having a problem with drugs tend to avoid contact with parents, teachers, and other adults. New friends also avoid meeting the youngster's parents. Life becomes increasingly chaotic for those with a problem.

Parents often have noticed behavior changes and are concerned about the youngster's behavior. Questionnaires may be effective to assist some parents in recognizing the problem (Exhibit 17-2).

> Steven was a 14-year-old who was brought in for therapy by his parents. Steven's parents had found a bottle with diazepam (Valium) and codeine in Steven's desk drawer in his room. His parents were distraught and very concerned.
>
> Steven was from an upper middle class family. His father, a chemical engineer, had recently started his own consulting firm. Steven's mother, although not employed outside the home, was a college graduate with a degree in business and was very active in the community as a volunteer. Steven had an older brother who was a freshman in an out-of-state college.
>
> Steven's parents stated that there had been a recent dramatic change in his behavior. His school performance had dropped suddenly and severely, and he had begun to have frequent unexplained absences from school. He also had been involved in several fights at school and had been disrespectful to teachers and school administrators. The parents had also noticed that Steven had stopped bringing friends home with him after school. They were deeply puzzled by his behavior because, prior to this school year, Steven had been an honor roll student, an active member of the student government, and a member of the reserve wrestling team. They had tried to discuss the situation with him, but they were frustrated by his unwillingness to communicate.

Exhibit 17-2 Questions for Parents

You may suspect that your child or teenager is having trouble with alcohol and other drugs, but short of smelling liquor on the breath or discovering pills in pockets, how do you tell? While symptoms vary, there are some common tipoffs. Your answers to the following questions will help you determine if a problem exists.

1. Has your youngster's personality changed dramatically? ____ Does he or she seem giddy, depressed, extremely irritable, hostile without reason? ____ Do his or her moods change suddenly, intensely and without provocation? ____

2. Is your supply of liquor, mood or diet drugs dwindling? ____ (Unless you keep a close inventory, you may not detect diminished amounts for months.)

3. Is your youngster less responsible about doing chores? ____ About getting home on time? ____ About following instructions and household rules? ____

4. Has he or she lost interest in school? ____ In extracurricular activities, especially sports? ____ Are grades dropping? ____ Has the teacher complained that your youngster is sleeping or inattentive in class? ____ Is your youngster skipping school? ____ (Problems at school are frequent warning signs.)

5. Has your youngster changed friends and started hanging out with a drinking and drug-taking group? ____ Are there weekend-long parties? ____ (A youngster having problems with alcohol or other drugs will abandon old friends and seek out those with similar attitudes and behavior.)

6. Are you missing money or objects which are easily convertible into cash? ____ (A young abuser's need for alcohol or other drugs increases and becomes more expensive. Eventually, the need for drugs overcomes any guilt about stealing from family members or others.)

7. Have neighbors, friends or others talked to you about your youngster's behavior or drug-taking? ____ (These reports may have substance.)

8. Has your youngster been arrested for drunkenness? ____ Driving under the influence of alcohol or other drugs? ____ Disorderly conduct? ____ Delinquent acts? ____ (Encounters with the legal system often indicate underlying problems with alcohol and other drugs. There is a strong correlation between alcohol and/or other drug abuse and delinquency.)

9. Does your youngster strongly defend his or her right to use alcohol and other drugs? ____ (People defend that which is most important to them.)

10. Does your youngster "turn off" to talks about alcohol and other drug addictions? ____ (Abusers would rather not hear anything which might interfere with their behavior, while the nonabuser will listen without becoming defensive.)

11. Does your youngster get into fights with other youngsters? ____ With other family members? ____ (More than 70 percent of all beatings, stabbings and assaults have occurred when one or both participants has been drinking or abusing other drugs.)

12. Are there medical or emotional problems? ____ (Check for ulcers, bronchitis, high blood pressure, acute indigestion, liver and kidney ailments, hepatitis, nose bleeds, malnutrition, weight loss, depression, memory lapses, talk of suicide. Alcohol and other drugs take their toll. Youngsters on "uppers" or "downers" usually lose their appetite. The taking of PCP, "Angel Dust," leads to paranoia and hallucinations. Long-term marihuana users often de-

continues

Exhibit 17-2 Continued

velop bronchitis. Heavy drinkers experience problems with digestion, malnutrition and depression.)

13. Do you detect physical signs—alcohol on the breath, change in pupil size in the eyes, hyperactivity, sluggishness, slurred or incoherent speech? ____ (These are all strong clues.)

14. Does your youngster lie to you and others often? ____ (For young abusers, lying becomes automatic. They fib without reason. There is a saying: "Young alcoholics and other drug abusers have two things in common—they have a terminal attack of the 'cool' and are stuck in 'sneak' gear.")

15. Does your youngster volunteer to clean up after adult cocktail parties? ____ (Draining half-empty glasses is a cheap high.)

16. Do you find bottles or drugs in the bedroom, garage, van? ____ (Parents of abusers are amazed to find stashes of alcohol or drugs under mattresses, in stereo speakers, behind insulation in garages.)

17. Is your youngster irresponsible in using the family car—taking it without permission, making excuses for not getting it home on time? ____ (Many teenagers drink in cars and then drive. They frequently cause motor vehicle accidents.)

18. Does your youngster stay alone in his or her bedroom most of the time, bursting forth only occasionally? ____ Does he or she resent questions about activities and destinations? ____ (Some secrecy, aloofness and resentment on the part of teenagers is normal. But when carried to extremes, these may signal problems with alcohol or other drugs.)

19. Have your youngster's relationships with other family members deteriorated? ____ Does he or she avoid family gatherings which were once enjoyed? ____ (An abuser's ability to relate to others suffers. The primary family relationships are affected first.)

20. Has your youngster been caught dealing in drugs or giving them to friends? ____

Alcohol and other drug abuse can create "Mr. Hydes" out of once happy youngsters and isolate them from those who love them. The youngsters become strangers and sources of frustration, irritation and disruption to the family.

Source: Courtesy of CareUnit Hospital of Cincinnati, 3156 Glenmore Avenue, Cincinnati, Ohio 45211. CareUnit® is a registered trademark of Comprehensive Care Corporation.

Steven was pale and thin for his 5 foot, 8 inch frame. During the interview, he was quiet and only responded to questions. He rarely looked at the nurse. He said that no one cared what he did anymore. No matter how hard he tried, his parents did not seem pleased with his performance. He missed his brother and felt that he now had no one to talk with. He did admit that he frequently used diuretics and laxatives, as well as diet pills, to control his weight for wrestling. He said he drank only occasionally at parties. He knew about alcohol and drugs, and about the effects of these substances on the body. The nurse was informed during the interview that Steven's routine blood examination showed a high level of blood alcohol.

NURSING DIAGNOSIS

Following a thorough assessment of the client's status, the psychiatric nurse should analyze the data to determine an individualized nursing diagnosis. Each client has a unique nursing diagnosis, depending on the particular circumstances (American Nurses' Association & National Nurses Society on Addictions, 1988; O'Toole & Loomis, 1989). A client who is under the influence of hallucinogens may have a nursing diagnosis of Sensory-Perceptual Alteration, Sleep Pattern Disturbance, Potential for Injury, Alteration of Thought Process, or Impaired Communication. Another client, whose circumstances are different, may have the nursing diagnosis of Alteration in Self-concept, Social Isolation, Alteration in Nutrition, or Ineffective Individual Coping. There is no one nursing diagnosis that is appropriate for every client who has a substance abuse problem. The nursing diagnosis should be individualized according to the specific situation of each client and family, as viewed by the client, family, and nurse.

Following the interview with Steven and his parents, the nurse formulated the following nursing diagnoses: Alteration in Conduct/Impulse Control, Potential for Violence Toward Self.

INTERVENTION FOR SUBSTANCE ABUSE

Primary Nursing Interventions

Prevention, of course, is the most desirable intervention against substance abuse. Nurses can play a major role in teaching children and their families about substance abuse. Education is the best weapon against substance abuse and cannot begin too early. Indeed, investigations have found that even preschool prevention programs are needed and can be effective (Hahn & Papazian, 1987).

Several prevention programs are available for elementary school children. These programs attack the problem by promoting the psychosocial development of the child. They present activities that increase the child's self-awareness and decision-making ability. They help children to identify qualities of relationships with friends and to examine the values and beliefs of their families, peers, and self in regard to drug use.

Burpo (1988) developed a drug education program for school-aged children that presents basic knowledge of drugs, information about abused drugs, and opportunities for critical thinking by the students. Students make collages, role-play, and debate the topic. This type of program can also be useful in group therapy for children who abuse drugs or alcohol.

> In Steven's case, a primary prevention intervention might have been an education program designed for athletes. It could have emphasized the harmful effects of drugs on the body. Self-esteem exercises might also have been helpful to prevent Steven's use of drugs to alter his feelings.

Secondary Nursing Interventions

Interventions at the secondary level are often the most challenging, because the client and family must come to see the relationship between drug use and the identified problems. The nurse should confront the child or adolescent who is suspected of having a drug problem directly with the identified behavior. The suspicion should be founded on facts, however. It is very difficult for a child or family to admit to a problem, and denial is usually a very strong defense. In order to break through the denial, the nurse must report actual facts—observations that are signs of substance abuse, such as physical complaints, declining school behavior, poor social interaction, and low emotional status.

Motivational therapy is another useful technique to help clients become aware of their substance abuse problem. By discussing the client's behavior, the nurse helps the client to relate undesirable outcomes with drug use. The client is not directly confronted, but is allowed to reach the conclusion that drug use is causing problems (Miller, 1982). The client's behavior is repeatedly fed back to the client in a nonjudgmental, nonconfronting manner.

> *Nurse:* You have frequent arguments with your boyfriend.
>
> *Client:* Yes. We fight a lot.
>
> *Nurse:* What happens before these arguments?
>
> *Client:* We usually have fights after a party.
>
> *Nurse:* What has happened at the party?
>
> *Client:* We usually drink and listen to music with our friends.
>
> *Nurse:* You usually drink?
>
> *Client:* Yes, we usually drink beer—sometimes a lot of beer.
>
> *Nurse:* Do you fight other times?
>
> *Client:* No, usually just after a party. Maybe it's the beer that clouds my thinking.

Sometimes a group confrontation of an individual with a substance abuse problem is effective in breaking through denial. The group may include such people as family members, friends, teachers, school administrators, counselors, or coaches—people who care about the client and have personal experiences to relate. Facilitated by the nurse therapist, each group member individually relates observations that he or she has made about the client's substance use and the effects of that use. This confrontation should be done calmly, without attacking, yelling, or blaming. The group members should be ready to emphasize the need for treatment and the consequences if the behavior does not change. The nurse's role is to prepare and support group members and the client, and to keep the experience within therapeutic boundaries. The nurse should role-play the meeting with the group members before the actual confrontation and should debrief the members following the experience.

Once a youngster has been made aware of a substance abuse problem, treatment should be immediate and tailored to the needs of the client and family. The nurse should provide a structured and supportive environment that will assist the client in recognizing unhealthy interactions and in developing effective coping skills.

There are various treatment programs for substance abuse available, ranging from long-term inpatient therapy to individual and family outpatient counseling. Many inpatient treatment programs for substance abuse are founded on the Alcoholics Anonymous (AA) steps for personal change. They involve detoxification, self-help group meetings, and education programs. Such programs usually involve 4 to 6 weeks of inpatient care with outpatient follow-up. To be helpful to children and adolescents, the AA model must be adapted to meet the cognitive needs, as well as the psychological needs, of the young clients. The abstract concepts of AA must be made concrete. The nurse must break through the egocentric barriers that are often a part of adolescence (Beck, 1988).

Other programs, such as Kids Helping Kids and Get Straight, Inc., are resocialization models and involve intense inpatient therapy, followed by structured outpatient activities. Because resocialization is a total family experience, it requires a strong family commitment. Families become an integral part of the therapy for other children, as well as for their own child, as each child lives with a family other than his or her own during a phase of the treatment. While in treatment, the client is separated from family and friends, and functions within narrow limits. The client "earns the right" to return home and is encouraged to develop a new group of friends.

Individual or family therapy is another important option for some clients. As discussed earlier, the abuse of chemical substances can be a maladaptive coping mechanism. To intervene in the substance abuse problem, the therapist must identify the precipitating problem and tailor the intervention to resolve that problem. The elimination of the substance abuse will probably not be longlasting if the precipitating problem remains.

Secondary interventions for Steven may include: (1) confrontation about suspected substance abuse, (2) inpatient treatment for detoxification and treatment, (3) exploration of the behavior and possible causes for unwanted outcomes, (4) exploration of feelings and present coping with Steven, (5) discussion of acceptable coping alternatives, and (6) family education programs.

Tertiary Nursing Interventions

After the immediate intervention, the client and family need tremendous support and reassurance to sustain changed coping patterns and a self-esteem that promotes social changes. It is very difficult to return to school and social situations following treatment. Support groups are often helpful, and open communication among the school, the parents, and the treatment agency is necessary.

Special attention should also be given to siblings in the family. They may feel guilty, ashamed, or even neglected because of all the attention that their brother or sister has been receiving. Siblings, therefore, also need interventions to promote self-esteem and understanding.

Tertiary interventions for Steven may include: (1) role-play, problem-solving techniques and communication; (2) relaxation techniques; (3) group therapy with peer group; (4) family counseling; and (5) open communication with his school.

RESEARCH

Nursing research in the area of child and adolescent drug use and abuse has been limited. There has been almost no development or adaptation of nursing theory to this problem. Instead, nurses have tended to use theories developed by other disciplines with little testing (Compton, 1989).

Investigations are needed on the causes of childhood and adolescent addiction, effective treatment methods, and long-term success rates. The effectiveness of support groups such as Alcoholics Anonymous and prevention programs for children and adolescents should be measured, and the influence of these programs on the drug use of children and adolescents needs to be determined.

The area of substance use among children and adolescents is a rich area for nursing research. The unique role and holistic perspective of nursing can offer important insights into the substance abuse problems of children and adolescents.

REFERENCES

American Nurses' Association and National Nurses Society on Addictions. (1988). *Standards of addictions nursing practice with selected diagnoses and criteria.* Kansas City, MO: American Nurses' Association.

Beck, S. (1988). Adapting the Alcoholics Anonymous model in adolescent alcohol treatment. *Holistic Nursing Practice*, 28–33.

Burpo, R. (1988). A step beyond "Just Say No." *American Journal of Maternal/Child Nursing, 13*(6), 428–431.

Carnegie Council on Adolescent Development. (1989). *Turning points: Preparing American youth for the 21st century.* Washington, DC: Carnegie Corporation of New York.

Compton, P. (1989). Drug abuse: A self-care deficit. *Journal of Psychosocial Nursing, 27*(3), 22–26.

Hahn, E., & Papazian, K. (1987). Substance abuse prevention with preschool children. *Journal of Community Health Nursing, 4*(3), 165–170.

Johnston, L.D., Backman, J.G., & O'Malley, P.M. (1985). *Use of licit and illicit drugs by America's high school students 1975–1984* (DHHS Publication No. ADM 85-1394). Washington, DC: U.S. Government Printing Office.

Miller, W. (1982). Motivational interviewing with problem drinkers. *Behavioral Psychotherapy,* (11), 147–172.

Neuman, B. (1988). *The Neuman systems model: Application to nursing education and practice.* Norwalk, CT: Appleton-Century-Crofts.

O'Toole, A.W., & Loomis, M.E. (1989). Revision of the phenomena of concern for psychiatric mental health nursing. *Archives of Psychiatric Nursing, 3*(5) 288–299.

Schwartz, R. (1985). Frequent marijuana use in adolescence. *American Family Physician, 31*(1), 201–205.

18

Nursing Interventions with Children and Adolescents Experiencing Altered Sensory-Motor Processes

Patricia C. Pothier

After reading this chapter, the reader will be able to:

1. discuss the concepts of sensory-motor development and altered sensory-motor processes
2. examine strategies for nursing identification and assessment of altered sensory-motor processes
3. develop nursing interventions for altered sensory-motor processes

Michael, a 6-year-old first grader in an inner city urban school, lived with his mother and three younger siblings. His mother had a long history of substance abuse. Michael's teacher had referred him to the school-based child mental health nurse for thorough evaluation because he was having difficulty in adjusting to the school environment. More specifically, he was failing academically, and his aggressive and hyperactive behavior was increasingly difficult to manage in the classroom. A teacher behavior rating scale also indicated that Michael had difficulty with fine motor tasks and was extremely clumsy in his physical education activities.

Increasingly, children like Michael are being referred for psychosocial evaluation because of emotional and behavior problems. Often, referring persons express concern that the child is clumsy, is accident-prone, has difficulty with fine motor tasks, or exhibits other behaviors that may interfere with some aspect of the child's development or academic performance. At other times, there may be a suspicion of some type of neurological involvement, but the impact of neuromuscular problems on development is less clear. For adolescents, some of the early sensory-motor alterations may be resolved with maturation, but secondary emotional responses and poor self-concept may result from earlier sensory-motor alterations.

Sensory-motor alteration has been associated both theoretically and empirically with autism (DeMyer, 1976; Ornitz, 1976; Ornitz & Ritvo, 1976), childhood schizophrenia and childhood psychosis (Bender, 1956; Bender & Helme, 1953; Silver & Gabriel, 1964), hyperactivity (Werry, 1972), adolescent behavior disorders (Ross & Ross, 1976), and other emotional disturbances (Rider, 1973; Silberzahn, 1975). Friedlander, Pothier, Morrison, and Herman (1982) demonstrated a significant presence of neurological signs in groups of children who had been labeled emotionally disturbed.

BASIC CONCEPTS OF SENSORY-MOTOR DEVELOPMENT

The underlying assumption of sensory-motor development is that the integration of sensory-motor stimuli is intimately related to the cognitive and emotional development of the infant and young child. In this schema, it is impossible to separate sensory, motor, and perceptual components because they are so intertwined in the total response of the infant/child. Perception, however, may be distinguished from sensory processes, as it involves the ability to recognize and relate stimuli to previous experience. Cognition, in contrast to perception, is the process by which sensation and perception assume meaning in terms of symbols. Thus, during infancy and early childhood, sensation, perception, and cognition are interrelated with movement and are the base for later cognitive and social-emotional learning (Morrison, Pothier, & Horr, 1978).

According to the developmental psychology of Piaget, children are born with an innate capacity for learning (Flavell, 1963). This capacity reaches its potential through children's interactions with their total environment. In order to maximize children's learning potential, the environment must stimulate them, and they must be able to use the stimulation that their environment offers. Children are in a continual process of adaptation in which their inborn reflex mechanisms become differentiated and integrated with experience. Piaget also stated that intelligence, whether that needed for simple forms of play or that needed for complex logic, is derived originally from motor actions on concrete objects. The growth of intelligence in children is viewed as the progressive transformation of motor patterns into thought patterns. As the reflex structure of children becomes more differentiated through experience, they are able to conceive of objects, space, time, causality, and logical relationships more adequately.

Ayres, an occupational therapist, offered a neurobehavioral theory as a base for understanding the underlying processes of sensory-motor alterations. Drawing on her knowledge of neuroanatomy, neurophysiology, neurodevelopment, and extensive clinical practice, Ayres (1972) devised a series of standardized tests that reveal sensory-motor alterations. She hypothesized that sensory-motor alterations result from a disturbance in the ability to integrate stimuli appropriately. These problems are seen in varying degrees in children of normal intelligence with learning disabilities, in mentally retarded children, and in those with severe emotional and developmental disabilities.

Ayres (1972) agreed with Piaget that perceptual and sensory-motor experience form the base for more abstract learning. As babies are touched, moved, and cuddled, they receive tactile and vestibular input. The babies' attempts to adjust to the movement inhibit certain reflexes, resulting in a change in muscle tone that allows a new automatic movement to occur. When the movement completely inhibits the reflex, it is integrated into a normal movement pattern. Normal automatic movements free children to explore, to make further use of their senses, and to learn at a higher cognitive level. Ayres termed this the process of sensory integration.

Nurses use these theoretical concepts to formulate a holistic, developmental approach to assessment, diagnosis, and treatment of sensory-motor alterations with children. The nursing process takes into account all the factors that impinge on children's development within the framework of their current developmental stage and the concept of developmental progression as a natural phenomenon in children.

Normal Sensory-Motor Processes

Newborns are essentially helpless in that they are totally dependent on others, often not even able to raise their heads. They cannot maintain any position against the pull of gravity and, without support, fall over. Gradually, as the brain matures, they begin to exert control over the force of gravity and gain progressive control over body movement. The changes in infants' neurological systems that facilitate this process are the automatic changes in tension in the muscles of the body that serve to maintain balance and posture. These automatic reactions are beyond infants' usual awareness, are controlled by higher brain processes, and are refined through neurological maturation and environmental interactions. The development of normal movement patterns follows a series of stages in which the specific tasks accomplished in each stage form the base of movement patterns for the next stage. Within each stage, there can be a great deal of variability regarding onset and completion; however, progression from one stage to another is fairly constant.

Perceptual development begins before birth with tactile, vestibular, and proprioceptive information coming to the fetus through random movement. Infants learn that information comes from their own body, and they begin to investigate body parts and what they can do. In the next stage, children develop a mental picture of their body, its parts, and the ways in which they move. Children also learn how much space their body occupies and develop concepts of laterality and directionality in relation to their own body.

In subsequent stages, children learn motor planning (praxis). In order to determine where and how to move, children must have the ability to use sensory input cognitively to plan appropriate motions. This ability develops through the integration of the tactile, proprioceptive, and visual impulses that arise through either purposeful or nonpurposeful, random motor activity.

Through maturation and experience, children also learn to judge the relationship of self to the environment. The specific spatial relationships learned are prepositional concepts (e.g., under, over, beside, in front, behind); directional (e.g., away from, toward, right, left); form (e.g., shape, size, dimension, distance); and Gestalt, or making a whole out of parts.

Altered Sensory-Motor Processes

The child or adolescent who has altered sensory-motor processes has a dysfunction of the motor and/or integration centers of the brain. These centers may be either physically damaged or so immature that the automatic reactions necessary for normal development are not fully available for the child's use in motor learning. In addition, the primitive reflexes that are present in infancy may not disappear as is expected in normal development. If they are not well integrated into more advanced movement patterns, their presence may interfere with the development of normal movement sequences and the fine motor coordination that is necessary for academic achievement.

Sensory-motor alterations occur on a continuum from mild, such as some learning disabilities, to almost complete impairment of perceptual and sensory-motor functioning. The cause of the cerebral dysfunction is often not known, but has been associated with: (1) viral infections and substance use in the mother during the period of myelination of the fetus, (2) damage during the birth process, (3) postnatal infection, (4) accident, (5) deprivation, and (6) abuse.

> Michael's prenatal and postnatal history revealed that he had been exposed to the substance abuse of his mother during her pregnancy.

Most youngsters with altered sensory-motor processes also have associated handicaps, such as sensory deficits, learning disorders, seizure disorder, intellectual deficit, behavior problems, delayed speech, and speech disorders. Some of the characteristics that may be observed in youngsters with altered sensory-motor processes are: (1) clumsy, awkward movement; (2) difficulty in fine motor activities; (3) hyperactivity; (4) distractibility; (5) tactile defensiveness; (6) irritability; (7) inability to cross midline of the body; (8) difficulty with right/left discrimination; (9) difficulty in identifying shapes; (10) unusual or difficult sensory processing; (11) poor body concept; and (12) impaired ability for motor planning.

ASSESSMENT OF ALTERED SENSORY-MOTOR PROCESSES

Sensory-motor assessment must be viewed within the context of a total assessment process that is designed to reveal a picture of the whole child in relation to the developmental norms for the child's age. This type of assessment requires only minimal equipment, because it usually involves observation of the child in different types of body movements. The child's shoes and socks should be removed, along with any clothes that would hamper movement or the observation of movement. The room should be warm and free of extraneous distractions or sounds, and it should have a mat or pad on which the child can lie comfortably.

Because normal movement patterns are usually characterized by smoothness of flow and symmetry, it is important to note the following types of movements: jerky, uncoordinated, exaggerated, involuntary movements in other body parts; tremors; tics; and asymmetry. In addition, the observer should note the accuracy of movement when accuracy is required. Many of these responses can be observed during the overall, holistic assessment.

Assessment of Specific Movement Responses

Muscle tone, which is present at birth, reflects the amount of proprioceptive input that is available to the central nervous system. Throughout the assessment procedure, the examiner has the opportunity to feel and see the child's body tone, both when the muscles are at rest and when the muscles are stimulated. To assess differences in tone in various parts of the body, the examiner moves each extremity through the range of motion. Muscle strength can be tested by asking the child to squeeze the examiner's hands alternately with each hand. Body posture can also be observed throughout the assessment procedure. The major criteria for good posture are straight alignment of body parts, symmetry, and standing with a narrow base.

By 18 months of age, children should be able to cross the midline of their body in order to reach objects on the opposite side. The child should be asked to reach across the middle of his or her body for an object and to demonstrate the ability to bring the hands together at midline by catching a large ball.

The degree to which a child has balance can be observed throughout the assessment procedure. Balance can be assessed by asking the child to stand first on one foot and then the other, with the eyes closed. Balance can also be assessed by pushing the child slightly to the right, then to the left, with both the child's feet on the ground. Normally, the body compensates by increasing tension on the same side as the pushing and extending the extremities on the opposite side.

Motor planning is the child's ability to coordinate motor activities in order to achieve goals. In its simplest form, an infant moves the hand to the mouth in order to suck the fingers. The examiner can observe motor planning in a preschool child by asking him or her to climb in and out of a box. An older child can be asked to lock and unlock the door with a key, tie shoelaces, retract a ballpoint pen, or snap the fingers.

To assess coordination, the examiner may ask the child to touch finger to nose, touch forefinger to thumb, turn hands rapidly, hop on one foot or do tandem walking (one foot in front of the other). The ability of the child to reproduce symbols on request, such as letters of the alphabet or shapes, is dependent on the development of perceptual and motor integration. School-aged children can be asked to copy the alphabet, numbers, or shapes.

Body image, a child's awareness and use of the body, is linked to self-esteem and understanding of self. The examiner should observe how the child uses his or her body in various activities. In addition, the young child can be asked to name body parts as the examiner points to them or touches them. Laterality and directionality are two concepts related to the understanding of body image and the ability to cross the midline. These concepts are particularly significant for successful academic achievement. Children who do not have these concepts clearly integrated are likely to have difficulty with reading and writing. To test for laterality, the examiner should ask the child to place an object to the right of a table, then to the left; for directionality, on top of and under the table.

Although visual acuity can be checked by means of the Snellen E chart, observation provides clues as to the way in which children use their eyes in coordination. The examiner should note the symmetry of the eyes, strabismus, and turning of the head from side to side to focus on the visual field. Auditory acuity may be tested by calling a word quietly from behind, as well as from each side, and asking the child to repeat the word. The sense of smell can be assessed by asking the child to identify, with the eyes closed, odors that are commonly known to most children, such as peanut butter, cinnamon, peppermint, and vanilla.

The sense of touch begins in utero and continues to be refined and developed throughout life. The examiner should note whether the child appears to withdraw from contact with persons or objects, whether the child's toes curl on contact with the floor or mat, and whether the child avoids touching surfaces with the hands by drawing up the fingers so that only the knuckles touch the surface. Other ways to elicit observable responses to touch are to tickle the child with a feather under the chin, administer a light pin prick, and ask the child to identify the point of touch on the body with the eyes closed.

Reflex testing is aimed at detecting remnants of primitive reflexes that should previously have been integrated into normal movement patterns. The asymmetrical tonic neck reflex is best assessed with the child in the quadruped position with the head straight. The stimulus for the reflex is to turn the head from one side to the other. Normally, there is no reaction in the arms or legs. An abnormal response is the extension of the arm and/or leg on the side to which the head is turned and flexion of the arm and/or leg on the opposite side. The stimulus should be repeated five times, because the abnormal response may not occur until more tension is placed on the neuromuscular system.

Postural Reactions

As discussed earlier, some children with altered sensory-motor processes who are engaged in specific movements may have involuntary movements in other parts of their body. For example, when a child lies on the back on a mat and squeezes a soft rubber ball, there is normally no increase in body tone or movement; with dysfunction, however, an arm or leg on the opposite side of the body may move or become more tense. These associated reactions can be observed throughout the procedure.

Body righting reactions emerge at approximately 6 months of age. This righting reaction can be tested by having the child roll across the room to a specific point and then back. Normally, the body turns segmentally, with rotation of the trunk between the shoulders and pelvis. The rolling movement should be coordinated, and the child should be able to roll to a target. The child with sensory-motor alterations may have difficulty in rolling or in rolling to a target, and the body may move as a whole "like a log" rather than segmentally.

Protective extension is an automatic reaction that also develops at approximately 6 months of age. This reaction is necessary for protection in falls. To test this response, a child can be suspended in air at the waist and then stimulated with a sudden movement toward the floor. Normally, there is an immediate extension of the arms and fingers to protect the head. With delays in development, there is a lag in the extension of the arms; in severe cases, the arms may withdraw or flex.

> Michael was in good health, and he had normal muscle tone and straight, aligned posture. He was able to cross the midline easily, and he did not seem to have any abnormal responses to touch. He did have difficulty with balance, however, and was unable to maintain his balance with his eyes closed. Also, he was unable to tie his shoelaces or snap his fingers. He was found to have difficulty in discriminating left/right concepts and in reproducing shapes and words with any degree of accuracy. Testing of his reflexes and righting reactions indicated a mostly normal picture, except for some remnant of the asymmetrical tonic neck reflex when he was tested in the quadruped position. These findings suggested some degree of sensory-motor alteration that may have been contributing to Michael's inability to function well in the classroom. His behavior problems were judged to be secondary to his altered sensory-motor processes; most likely, his behavior was a reaction to his poor school adjustment and academic failure.

NURSING MANAGEMENT OF ALTERED SENSORY-MOTOR PROCESSES

Following assessment, the nurse can organize the assessment data into specific nursing diagnoses, establish priorities for the nursing diagnoses, and develop a treatment plan that addresses the child's major specific altered sensory-motor processes within a developmental framework.

There is considerable documentation for the effectiveness of intervention in normalizing the responses to stimuli by youngsters at risk for, or with, altered sensory-motor processes (Ayres, 1974; Bronfenbrenner, 1968; Chapman, 1984; Eddington & Lee, 1975; Evans, 1981; Godfrey, 1975; Kephart, 1964; Koniak-Griffin & Ludington-Hoe, 1988; Maloney, Ball, & Edgar, 1970; Montgomery & Richter, 1980; Morrison & Pothier, 1972, 1978; Rausch, 1981). Sensory-motor interventions for disabled children have been developed over the past 20 years primarily by occupational and physical therapists, by psychologists and educators, and by nurses for infants at risk for alteration. Sensory-motor intervention programs involve the clients in a series of repeated, prescribed sensory and motor activities that are based on a detailed assessment. This assessment provides the baseline data for an ongoing evaluation of the effectiveness of the intervention.

The major goal of an intervention program is to facilitate the development of more normal or mature sensory-motor functioning and perceptual processes. More specific goals are: (1) to facilitate the integration of primitive reflexes; (2) to develop more normal responses to tactile stimulation; (3) to increase the occurrence and maturity of righting, equilibrium, and automatic reactions; and (4) to increase awareness of body image and motor planning. The assumption underlying the interventions is that, because the neuromuscular system of the client is immature, it is still flexible so that the corrective experiences actually influence both the nervous system and the integration centers of the brain (Chess, 1979).

Nursing Interventions with Infants

Nurses who work with infants often must teach the parents how to provide their infant with sensory-motor stimulation during the usual daily care, interactions, and play. Demonstration, modeling, and anticipatory guidance are important strategies in this endeavor. For the infant younger than 3 months old, the most important interventions relate to touch and positioning. Touching, which comes with the closeness during feeding, holding, and handling, is a part of the natural bonding process between infant and mother. The infant with, or at risk for, abnormal sensory-motor responses needs additional tactile stimulation, such as patting and stroking; rubbing with different textures, pressures, and temperatures; cuddling; and rocking. These activities should be accompanied by verbalizations that reinforce the touching.

In order to foster more normal body alignment, the infant's sleeping posture should be changed often. Side lying with the support of small pillows or blanket rolls is the position of choice, because this position minimizes the influence of gravity and stimulation of abnormal reflex activity. In addition, the environment should supply the infant with interesting stimuli, such as toys that move and make sound. Loud stimuli and quick movements should be avoided, however, to prevent stimulation of the startle reflex.

In infants up to 1 year old, normal movement patterns can be facilitated first by passive flexion and extension of the arms and legs, then by rolling from side to side. Head control can be fostered by placing a towel roll under the shoulder girdle as the infant lies in the prone position. A toy can then be used to entice the infant to raise the head to follow this interesting stimulus. Similarly, as the infant begins to gain more control over his or her body against the force of gravity, the infant can be encouraged to roll over by crossing one leg over the other to help with trunk rotation. Because sitting posture is dependent on head control, trunk control, and balance, all the previous activities prepare the infant to sit, then to creep, crawl, stand, and walk. Any type of vestibular stimulation, such as rocking from side to side, swinging in a blanket or a swing, rolling in a barrel or large ball, and rocking on a horse, helps with learning to balance.

Nursing Interventions with Children

The nurse may have the opportunity to carry out sensory-motor interventions with older children in school, in the home, or in clinical settings. The equipment and space required are similar to those required for the assessment process.

The nurse can facilitate correct rolling (i.e., by means of trunk rotation) by having the child lie in the supine position and manually turning the head in the direction in which the child is expected to roll. When the child is able to roll correctly without manual direction, the nurse can encourage the child to roll across the room to a target, such as a toy.

To facilitate righting reactions, the nurse can help the child to perform somersaults by placing a hand on the back of the child's neck so that its head is flexed during the somersault and by guiding the child's body in straight alignment for completion. Also to develop equilibrium, the child can be guided while walking on a balance beam. This beam should be of variable length and should be made with smoothly finished wood. The board is raised to different heights with different-sized blocks. In the beginning, the beam should be low and wide. The child may need some gentle support either by holding his or her arms or, even better, holding him or her on either side of the head; it is important to provide minimal external support in order to foster the internal balancing system. As the child develops better balance, the beam can be narrowed and raised. Further vestibular stimulation can be provided through jumping on a trampoline, twisting on a twist board, and rolling over a barrel. Optical righting reactions can be facilitated by having the child ride prone on a skateboard with encouragement to raise the head.

Because a remnant tonic neck reflex can interfere with fine motor movements, such as drawing and writing, it is necessary to facilitate the integration of this reflex. An activity that helps with this integration is a passing game in which the child passes an article to another person, first to one side and then the other.

The game of "wheelbarrow" is helpful for children with poor protective extension reactions. The child's legs are raised, and he or she is verbally encouraged to walk forward on his or her hands.

The prescriptive activities that have been described, as well as a number of other facilitating activities, can be built into the client's play structure as appropriate for the client's developmental stage. The young child can be involved in games that require crawling or walking through mazes or tunnels; games of start and stop, such as Simon Says; rhythm instruments; relay passing games; rowing games; and hopscotch. For older children who are clumsy, are accident-prone, and have difficulty in mastering sports, it is appropriate to coach specific skills, such as shooting baskets; throwing and catching balls; and hitting with a bat, paddle, or racquet. As the youngsters master each of these physical skills, they learn that they can have more control over their bodies and experience an associated increase in self-esteem.

As a result of his assessment and diagnosis, it was recommended that Michael be involved in short-term focused individual play therapy to work through some of his emotional responses to his school failure and his home situation. In addition, a program of sensory-motor activity was developed to treat his problems in balance, the reflex remnant, fine motor coordination, laterality, and his general incoordination in physical activity. At his school, Michael was enrolled in an activity group with other children who had similar sensory-motor alterations. The group met for 45 minutes, three times a week, for a 6-month period. The interventions were planned by the school-based child mental health nurse in collaboration with an occupational therapist and were carried out by nonprofessional volunteers who were trained by the occupational therapist and supervised by the child mental health nurse.

Michael received a great deal of vestibular stimulation through a variety of games and group activities. He regularly practiced on the balance beam, performed somersaults, bounced on the trampoline, and twisted on the twist board. To work on his tonic neck reflex, he regularly engaged in relay races in which he and his group passed a beanbag back and forth to each end of the line. In addition, along with the other children, Michael was coached in throwing, catching, and kicking in games of kickball.

At the end of the 6-month treatment program, the nurse repeated the detailed sensory-motor assessment, and the teacher repeated the behavior rating of Michael. He was observed to be much less clumsy in his physical activities and seemed to be more sure of himself generally. His coordination was greatly improved, and the asymmetrical tonic neck reflex was completely integrated. In the classroom, his hyperactive and aggressive behaviors occurred less frequently; however, he was still experiencing difficulty with word recognition and reversals of letters, and he was referred for more defined work on his specific learning disabilities. Clearly, there was more work to be done to foster Michael's development and to remediate some of the damage that had probably occurred prenatally, but the prescribed activities had improved his sensory-motor status, and the short-term play therapy had helped him to resolve some of his emotional responses to his past experience.

Adolescent Issues and Management

Adolescence is generally one of the most stressful stages of development. The degree of difficulty that an individual faces at this stage depends on his or her successful coping with past experience and physical status. Sensory-motor alterations may be resolved or greatly decreased simply through the maturation process. In fact, altered sensory-motor processes are found in adolescents and adults significantly less often than in the pre-adolescent population (Ross & Ross, 1976). For those who have more serious deficits in childhood, however, the signs of altered sensory-motor processes may remain to some degree during adolescence. The major manifestation of previous altered sensory-motor processes in adolescents is their inability to master adolescent developmental tasks.

Common characteristics of adolescents with longstanding sensory-motor alterations are: (1) poor school performance, (2) poor self-image, (3) poor relationships with family and peers, (4) difficult personality, and (5) a tendency toward antisocial and delinquent behaviors (Ross & Ross, 1976). Although these behaviors are usually considered secondary to the physiological problems, there is some evidence that these behaviors may be due primarily to the physiological status of the sensory-motor system (Ross & Ross, 1976). A reasonable assumption is that both sources may be operational at the same time. An adolescent may be somewhat physically awkward and accident-prone because of the remnants of sensory-motor alterations, but may also be extremely depressed because of a long history of academic failure and poor peer relations. Another adolescent may manifest his or her response to the same situation through antisocial behavior.

Because the behaviors of these youngsters are often typical of the behaviors of disturbed adolescents, it is important for the nurse in the assessment process to obtain a detailed developmental history that includes indications of school adjustment problems at an early stage. The nurse must also be particularly alert for any remaining signs of sensory-motor alterations. For adolescents, the major focus of nursing intervention is to help them (1) resolve feelings of being different or of being a failure in a society that highly values academic achievement, (2) accept the disability, and (3) cope with the residue of disability in light of adolescent developmental tasks. The psychiatric nurse who comes into contact with adolescents with previous or current sensory-motor alterations can offer individual, goal-directed psychotherapy. The nurse can also help significant others in the adolescent's life to understand both the reasons for the behavior and the delicate balance between volitional and nonvolitional behaviors.

CONCLUSION

In the United States today, increasing numbers of children are identified as having school adjustment problems or are referred for psychosocial evaluation because of emotional problems. There is growing evidence that, for some of these children, the cause of their behavior may be deficits in sensory-motor status. The goals of early identification, assessment, and intervention of sensory-motor alterations is to prevent a more complex disability in infants and children and to prevent potential emotional disorders in adolescents.

REFERENCES

Ayres, A.J. (1972). *Sensory integration and learning disorders.* Los Angeles: Western Psychological Services.

Ayres, A.J. (1974). *The development of sensory integration theory and practice.* Dubuque, IA: Kendall/Hunt.

Bender, L. (1956). *Psychopathology of children with organic brain disorders.* Springfield, IL: Charles C Thomas.

Bender, L., & Helme, W. (1953). A qualitative test of theory and diagnostic indicators of childhood schizophrenia. *Archives of Neurological Psychiatry, 70,* 413–427.

Bronfenbrenner, U. (1968). When is infant stimulation effective? In D.C. Glass (Ed.), *Environmental influences.* New York: Rockefeller University Press.

Chapman, J.S. (1984). Longitudinal follow-up of prematurely born children: Outcomes of home stimulation program. *Nursing Papers/Perspectives on Nursing, 16*(2), 49–65.

Chess, S. (1979). The plasticity of human development. *Journal of American Academy of Child Psychiatry, 17,* 80–91.

DeMyer, M. (1976). The nature of the neuropsychological disability in autistic children. In E. Schopler & R. Reichler (Eds.), *Psychopathology and child development.* New York: Plenum Press.

Eddington, C., & Lee, T. (1975). A home centered program for parents in sensory motor stimulation. *American Journal of Nursing, 75*(1), 60–61.

Evans, M.A. (1981). High risk infant follow-up program. *California Nurse, 77,* 8–9.

Flavell, J. (1963). *The developmental psychology of Jean Piaget.* New York: Van Nostrand.

Friedlander, S., Pothier, P., Morrison, D., & Herman, L. (1982). The role of neurological-developmental delay in childhood psychopathology. *American Journal of Orthopsychiatry, 52*(1), 102–108.

Godfrey, A.B. (1975). Sensory-motor stimulation for slow to develop children: A specialized program for public health nurses. *American Journal of Nursing, 75*(1), 56–59.

Kephart, N.C. (1964). Perceptual-motor aspects of learning disabilities. *Exceptional Children, 31,* 201–206.

Koniak-Griffin, D., & Ludington-Hoe, S. (1988). Developmental and temperament outcomes of sensory stimulation in healthy infants. *Nursing Research, 37*(2), 70–76.

Maloney, M.P., Ball, T.S., & Edgar, C.L. (1970). An analysis of the generalizability of sensory-motor training. *American Journal of Mental Deficiency, 74,* 458–469.

Montgomery, P., & Richter, E. (1980). *Sensorimotor integration for developmentally disabled children.* Los Angeles: Western Psychological Services.

Morrison, D., & Pothier, P. (1972). Two different remedial motor training programs and the development of mentally retarded pre-schoolers. *American Journal of Mental Deficiency, 77,* 251–258.

Morrison, D., & Pothier, P. (1978). Investigation of the effect of sensorimotor training on the language development of retarded pre-schoolers. *American Journal of Orthopsychiatry, 42*(2), 310–319.

Morrison, D., Pothier, P., Horr, K. (1978). *Sensory-motor dysfunction and therapy in infancy and early childhood.* Springfield, IL: Charles C Thomas.

Ornitz, E. (1976). The modulation of sensory input and motor input in autistic children. In E. Schopler & R. Reichler (Eds.), *Psychopathology and child development.* New York: Plenum Press.

Ornitz, E., & Ritvo, E. (1976). Medical assessment. In E. Ritvo (Ed.), *Autism: Diagnosis, current research and management.* New York: Spectrum Publications.

Rausch, P.B. (1981). Effects of tactile and kinesthetic stimulation on premature infants. *Journal of Obstetric, Gynecologic, and Neo-Natal Nursing, 10,* 34–37.

Rider, B. (1973). Perceptual-motor dysfunction in emotionally disturbed children. *American Journal of Occupational Therapy, 27,* 316–320.

Ross, D.M., & Ross, S.A. (1976). *Research, theory, action.* New York: John Wiley & Sons.

Silberzahn, M. (1975). Sensory integrative function in a child guidance clinic population. *American Journal of Occupational Therapy, 29,* 28–34.

Silver, A., & Gabriel, H. (1964). The association of schizophrenia in childhood with primitive postural responses and decreased muscle tone. *Developmental Medicine and Child Neurology, 6,* 495–497.

Werry, J. (1972). Studies of the hyperactive child: VII. Neurological status compared with neurotic and normal children. *American Journal of Orthopsychiatry, 42,* 441–451.

19

Nursing Interventions with Children and Adolescents Experiencing Role Performance Difficulties

Nancy D. Opie, Kathleen Zink Bradley, and Susan Lea Ziegler

After reading this chapter, the reader will be able to:

1. define role performance
2. describe the three major roles associated with childhood and adolescence
3. identify causes of role performance problems in children and adolescents
4. apply the theoretical frameworks of symbolic interactionism, humanistic philosophy, and Peplau's theory of interpersonal relations in nursing to the psychiatric nursing care of youth with role performance problems
5. apply the nursing process to the mental health care needs of the children and adolescents with role performance problems
6. discuss the use of individual, family, group, and behavior therapy and consultation as nursing interventions for role performance problems
7. identify implications for research

The role performance behaviors of children and adolescents are learned, shaped, and given meaning within the context of interpersonal life experiences. The primary roles for children and adolescents are associated with family, play, and school, and the performance of these roles is based on the meaning and value assigned to them by children, families, teachers, and significant others. The meaning and value of roles for children and adolescents are in a formative stage of development and are subject to change.

Children and adolescents normally learn social roles by practicing the behaviors that are demonstrated by significant others. From infancy through adulthood, individuals learn and acquire a variety of roles necessary to interact with the external environment. "The child learns to act, to feel, and to perceive the world in the manner expected from someone in his position" (McCall & Simmons, 1978, p. 208). Thus, role performance can be defined as a situation-specific set of behavioral and interactional expectations placed on an individual.

In the home environment, role responsibilities for the child include beginning to understand the importance of relationships by making the connections with siblings and significant adults. The family serves as the social unit in which the child learns about intimacy and sharing. Through play, the child practices the behavior associated with the social roles that he or she may be asked or may desire to perform in the future. McCall and Simmons (1978) described play as anticipatory socialization that "leads to the gleaning of notions about all aspects of a role: the performances that seem to portray it, the self expectations and social expectations that it involves, and the self-conceptions and perspectives on social objects germane to it" (p. 209). In the student role, the child is expected to attend school, complete academic work, learn, and develop peer and adult relationships. Role performance in all three areas involves adhering to rules, learning values, assuming responsibilities, and developing the ability to interact with others in a socially acceptable manner.

Role performance problems in children and adolescents may develop when the meanings and values assigned to the roles that youngsters have learned are inadequate, inconsistent, and unhealthy. Role problems directly affect the child's ability to carry out the activities of daily living in a socially acceptable manner. Such problems occur primarily in the home, at play, and in school environments. When the child is consistently unable or unwilling to behave in accordance with societal expectations, given a specific environment, an alteration in role performance develops. The causes of role performance problems are varied, but they are primarily factors that interfere with the development of relationships and social skills. According to Gordon (1987), they include:

- alterations in parenting
- social isolation, rejection, or deprivation
- alterations in relationships related to poor social skills, poor self-concept, self-esteem disturbances
- cultural differences, values and beliefs contrary to socially presented mores
- ineffective coping with change
- situational crisis
- developmental crisis

Gordon also noted individual factors that contribute to role performance problems:

- developmental delays or disorders
- limited intelligence (e.g., mental retardation)
- learning disability
- emotional/behavioral illness (e.g., school avoidance/phobic disorder, conduct disturbance, adjustment disorder)
- physical disability or physical illness

An understanding of role performance enables the nurse to determine if the child or adolescent has a disturbance in any particular area of social interaction (e.g., family, play, or school). A disturbance in role performance is a "change, conflict, or denial of role responsibilities" (Gordon, 1987, p. 234). The psychiatric and mental health nurse helps to alleviate role performance problems by intervening to improve the child's level and quality of functioning. The nurse assists the child, family, teachers, and significant others in learning new meanings, values, and behaviors for the roles that have resulted in performance problems for the child. Nursing's holistic orientation to health care reinforces the importance of looking at the total person, including environmental and cultural influences.

THEORETICAL FRAMEWORK

Nurses who care for children and adolescents with role performance problems need a working knowledge of a variety of theories, such as symbolic interactionism, the humanistic approach, and the theory of interpersonal relations in nursing. The use of adjunct theories (e.g., developmental, psychodynamic, behavioral) enables the nurse to design goals and care plans to meet the unique needs of each individual.

Symbolic Interactionism

First labeled by Blumer (1969), symbolic interactionism developed from the work of George Herbert Mead and Charles Cooley. The theory emphasizes that self-concept is very much dependent on interactions with others, that individuals learn who they are and how to behave through an interactive process. In the process of acquiring information about self from others, the individual gradually develops the concept of self as separate and distinct from others, yet having characteristics similar to those of others.

Individuals become aware also of their own ability to affect the interactive process, to give it and the objects involved (such as self) labels and meaning. Roles and associated behaviors are objects that are shaped and also given meaning in the interactive process. Meaning includes cognitive conception, values, attitudes, and associated feelings. Meanings that are attached to the self include self-concept (cognitive conception) and self-esteem (value and attitudes). Meanings that are associated with self and the roles acquired or taken on provide the basis for action (Stryker, 1980).

Social interaction is a lifelong phenomenon, and most individuals engage in new relationships throughout their lifetimes. Each new relationship and interactive process provides a new opportunity to experience different dimensions of the self and to adjust attitudes toward self and others. New roles may be taken on and old ones modified in meaning and enactment. Symbolic interactionism is based on three major assumptions: (1) human beings act toward things on the basis of the meaning that the things have for them; (2) the meaning of things in a person's life is derived from the social interactions that one has with others; and (3) people handle and modify the meanings of the things that they encounter through an interpretive process (Stryker, 1980).

Humanistic Philosophy

The humanistic framework presupposes that individuals have within them the capacity for self-healing. The psychiatric and mental health nurse establishes a sensitive, caring, and supportive relationship with the client. The nurse takes into account the social and cultural milieu, as well as the developmental and individualistic needs of the client. Nurse therapists use themselves to facilitate their clients' exploration of the meaning of their experiences. They help their clients arrive at new meanings and develop more productive and satisfying ways of relating to self and others. A nurse's effective use of self in the relationship is the primary factor in bringing about a successful outcome.

Interpersonal Model of Nursing

The nursing model developed by Peplau (1952) is consistent with symbolic interactionism and humanistic philosophy. Peplau asserted that behavior is meaningful and should be understood in the context of the situation and needs experienced by the client. Nurses, according to Peplau (1969) "utilize established knowledge for beneficial purposes" (p. 33) and assist "patients to gain intellectual and interpersonal competencies beyond that which they have" (p. 37). Peplau (1952) believed that nurses must help clients to master current tasks and problems so that more mature and complex needs could emerge. Thus, the nurse functions to promote the normal developmental process.

Within the context of the interpersonal relationship, the nurse plays various roles (e.g., teacher, collaborator, leader, resource, counselor) to help the client reduce tension by finding satisfactory and socially acceptable ways to fulfill needs. Through this process, the nurse assists the client in becoming aware of the conditions required for health and in identifying situations that produce undue tension and threaten the well-being of the individual. The nurse and client work together in the evolving interpersonal relationship to facilitate learning (i.e., modify the meaning of self, roles, and conflictual objects) and goal achievement (i.e., enactment of roles in more socially acceptable and rewarding ways). Peplau's theory also directs the nurse to use expert communication skills, especially those of clarifying, listening, accepting, interpreting, collaborating, and setting goals together.

NURSING INTERVENTIONS

The child psychiatric and mental health nurse selects interventions for role performance problems according to the individual needs of the child or adolescent.

When role performance problems involve the school, the nurse uses intervention strategies that promote change rapidly and efficiently. Because school failure will only compound the child's self-esteem problems and sense of overall failure, the most efficient and effective use of therapeutic time is mandated. Interventions take into account the severity of the problem, the environmental and cultural constraints, and the individual nature of the child (e.g., developmental level, cognitive capacity, and physical limitations). More than one technique is often required. Individual, group, family, and behavior therapy, as well as consultation, are all appropriate interventions.

Individual Therapy

Within individual strategies, play therapy is most commonly used in working with children. As children and adolescents learn to communicate more openly and directly, play activities are used less frequently; verbal communication strategies more frequently (Sarnoff, 1987).

Play therapy, which is based on a natural activity of children, makes it possible for children to express and explore their conflicts, fears, fantasies, and feelings. Through the use of play activities and play productions, the nurse therapist helps the child to gain cognitive clarity of rules and expectations for behavior. The nurse therapist provides an accepting and respectful environment in which the child can explore alternative and more appropriate behaviors. The expression of feelings; the clear understanding of values, rules, and expectations; and the opportunity to explore and try out new behaviors reduce anxiety and lead to improvements in role performance. In working with children with role performance problems, the building of a trusting relationship is essential. The use of an active and directive approach is preferable—once the relationship has been established (Gumaer, 1984).

Group Therapy

Commonly used for youngsters, group therapy is often the most effective strategy for intervention in adolescent role performance problems. Individuals are born into, live, and work in groups throughout life. Formulating identities and learning behaviors associated with various roles are dynamic, interactive processes that occur most often in groups. Group therapy takes advantage of the group interactive process to explore interpersonal fears, fantasies, conflicts, and feelings. In group therapy, the therapist attempts to establish and maintain a permissive, accepting, and democratic environment. Individuals use the group process to improve their interactive skills, gain acceptance and peer support, and give and receive corrective feedback. The group experience enhances the individual's identity and improves the capacity to perform in expected and selected roles (Gumaer, 1984).

Group therapy with children involves the natural and structured play activities of children, guided by a permissive, accepting adult who maintains the physical safety of the group members. The therapist uses the normal conflicts that arise in the group to help the group members give and receive corrective feedback. Members are able to use the feedback to promote their personal growth and to increase effective interpersonal functioning. Group activities are useful at all developmental levels for improving role performance.

Family Therapy

Treatment of the family is often indicated for a child or adolescent who has a role performance problem, particularly when the problem has developed within the family system. Since the 1950s, several models of family theory have been established (e.g., family systems, structure, and communication). Although theoretical foundations differ, issues common to family therapy remain. Family therapy may be used alone or in conjunction with other therapies. The nurse therapist must decide which family members will participate in therapy. Maurin and Clements (1985) suggested that all members of the nuclear family be involved in family therapy if a child is presented as the problem or the identified client. The primary objective of family therapy is to enable family members to identify and to develop new ways of relating to self and others.

Behavior Therapy

According to the behaviorist, symptoms associated with behavioral or emotional problems are learned in an interpersonal context and persist because they are gratifying or rewarding to the individual and reinforced by significant others (Patterson & Fleischman, 1979; Wilson, 1988a). If learned behaviors are socially unacceptable, role performance problems may develop.

The primary goal of behavior therapy is to change behavior, thus enabling the individual to fulfill role responsibilities. Behavior therapy includes the use of reinforcers or contingencies to: (1) encourage and reward desirable behavior or (2) extinguish undesirable behaviors by withholding rewards or attention. In consultative work with the school system, behavior therapy provides a mechanism whereby the child psychiatric nurse, student, parents, and teachers work together to establish a mutually agreed upon treatment contract intended to improve the child's school performance. The nurse facilitates changes in the child's performance by teaching behavior techniques to parents and teachers (Wilson, 1988b).

The teacher-student relationship is an important factor to consider in determining if behavior therapy is likely to improve student role performance. If the student views the relationship with the teacher as positive and desirable, the teacher's praise and other positive regard statements will increase the student's motivation to please the teacher. Parents may also be included in a behavior therapy plan by learning to reinforce their child's successful home study habits or other desired behaviors.

Consultation

Psychiatric nursing consultation is an essential technique and skill in assisting children and adolescents with role performance problems (Opie & Slater, 1988). Because children's behavior is developed in a dynamic interactive process within environments largely shaped and controlled by adults, behavior therapy is effective in the consultation process (O'Leary, 1984). Parents, teachers, siblings, and peers all affect the behavior of children and adolescents. Often, parents and teachers unknowingly or inadvertently reinforce or evoke nonproductive behavioral responses.

Several models of consultation are available to the child psychiatric nurse. One effective model for intervening with problems related to individual children is that of client-centered case consultation, a collaborative process in which the nurse meets with significant others (e.g., parents, teachers) who seek assistance in facilitating appropriate role performance in the child. The nurse helps to improve the child's level of functioning by helping the responsible adults understand the dynamics of the child's problem, including the adult-child relationship. The nurse consultant provides the adults with information or skills, such as classroom management or the development of family rules (Gumaer, 1984; Lange, 1987). Improvement of the child's behavior is facilitated when the teachers and parents work with the nurse to implement the goals and plan of care for the child (Opie & Slater, 1988).

CASE EXAMPLE

Gary, an 11-year-old sixth grader, had poor school attendance; he frequently missed 1 or 2 days in a week. When he was in school, he was disruptive. He argued with the teacher, rarely did his homework, and was failing in mathematics and science. He was referred for treatment following a conference of Gary's primary teacher, the school psychologist, Gary's mother, the school psychiatric nurse, and the guidance counselor.

Assessment

Gary was quiet and exhibited little energy at the initial session. He had a worried expression and smiled only infrequently. He responded appropriately to questions, but did not initiate conversation or topics. Thought content was age-appropriate, and he talked softly, with no obvious dysfunction. His eye contact was fair. He was able to attend and stay on topic. Gary defined his problems as: (1) the teacher's not liking him and picking on him and (2) not having enough time to get his work done. Gary said that he stayed home often because he had to take care of his little sister or because he did not feel well. His mother defined Gary's problems as irresponsibility and laziness. Gary's mother said that Gary stayed home because he complained of headaches or stomach upset.

Gary's history suggested that the precipitants for this crisis included the recent hospitalization of his mother, a new school setting (from elementary to middle school), and the death of his maternal grandmother. Gary was coping by not completing homework assignments, clowning in the classroom, having verbal arguments with his mathematics and science teachers, complaining of physical problems, and relying on the school counselor. He had also been resistant and argumentative at home, especially about performing household tasks and caring for his younger sister. Gary did not know the reason for his mother's hospitalization, nor did he demonstrate cognitive clarity of his grandmother's death.

Since Gary's entry into middle school, his grades had dropped steadily, and his classroom behavior had become increasingly problematic, especially in science and mathematics classes. His school attendance had decreased dramatically. Gary had been an average student, earning C and B grades. He was generally described as a "good," but quiet student in previous school records. Now, however, Gary sat in the rear of the classroom and attempted to engage other students in playful, but disruptive activities (e.g., making paper airplanes, joking, and making fun of other students). He had become increasingly disruptive and unresponsive to discipline by the teacher.

Gary's family consisted of his mother, his father, and two younger siblings—Danny, 8 years, and Jessica, 2 1/2 years. His father worked as a truck driver, but was home most evenings and weekends. The family had regular mealtimes, and Gary was expected to help in the preparation of meals and the cleanup afterward. He was asked to fold laundry and to entertain his sister. Gary's mother stated that her recent hospitalization was the result of weakness and fatigue, but would not discuss her problem beyond that. Gary's mother added that, while they were sad that Gary's grandmother had died and missed her help, they had resigned themselves to the loss and had not talked about her since the funeral (8 1/2 months earlier).

Gary and his family lived in a semirural area. The family had lived in the same house since Gary was 7 months old. They belonged to the Unitarian church, but rarely went to services. Gary had not been allowed to have friends visit (in the house) for the past year "because his mother needed her rest."

A recent school physical examination revealed that Gary's health was good. He had weighed 7 pounds at birth and had no health problems other than occasional colds, sore throats, and one episode of pneumonia at 4 years of age. He was short in stature, thin, and pale. Developmental milestones were within normal limits. Gary was reported to have an average IQ (school records), but was underachieving because of poor work and study habits, poor self-esteem, and low motivation. Gary questioned the value of learning and following rules. Although Gary stated that sometimes he wished he had never been born, he did not have a history of suicide gestures or threats of self-harm.

Nursing Diagnoses, Goals, and Interventions

The nursing diagnoses established for Gary were Altered Student Role, Altered Family Role, Altered Play Role, and Altered Self-esteem (Table 19-1). The goals for the nurse-client relationship were established in discussion with Gary, his mother, his teacher, and the psychiatric nurse. The diagnoses, corresponding goals, interventions, and evaluation criteria are presented in Table 19-2.

Table 19-1 Nursing Diagnoses for Gary

Nursing Diagnosis	Etiology	Defining Characteristics
Altered Student Role	Anxiety Knowledge deficit of mother's current health status and grandmother's death	Poor school attendance Disruptive classroom behavior Refusal to do academic work Verbally expressed hostility toward teacher Underachievement in two subjects
Altered Family Role	Unrealistic parental expectations for Gary's family role performance	Parent expression of unrealistic expectations for child's work and play roles Inadequate communications and expression of feelings related to significant family events Child's complaints of having insufficient time to accomplish homework Child's expression of need to stay home due to family responsibilities Child's argumentativeness about roles and responsibilities in family Lack of cognitive clarity of mother's illness and grandmother's death
Altered Play Role	Unrealistic parental expectations for Gary's play role performance	Undervaluing of play role, restriction of friends visiting in home Insufficient time allowed for play No established family leisure activities
Altered Self-esteem	Unrealistic parental expectations for Gary's family role Performance anxiety regarding self and life's problems and events Unproductive negative relationships with significant adults	Negative self-statements Lack of initiative and low motivation Expressed feelings of inadequacy Worried expression Somatic complaints without physical evidence

Table 19-2 Goals, Interventions, and Evaluation Criteria for Gary

Nursing Diagnosis	Goals	Interventions	Evaluation
Altered Student Role	Gary will improve school attendance, relationships with teachers and peers, and performance of academic work at home and school.	In family meetings, facilitate clarification of expectations and values assigned to student role.	Parents will describe expectations for Gary in student role, based on own values and beliefs.
		Reinforce parental expectations and support efforts to have child attend school and complete homework.	Nurse will monitor own responses to family.
		Provide positive feedback to child and family for efforts to resolve problems.	Reinforcing statements and verbal recognition by parent of child's efforts will increase.
		Recognize feelings and demonstrate ways to express feelings more directly.	
		Keep record of school attendance.	Nurse will monitor school attendance, looking for increase in daily attendance with absence only for valid illness.
		Have adults verbalize expectations that Gary attend school and participate in academic work.	
		Assist Gary's family in establishing time and place for Gary to complete homework.	Parents and child will report where and when Gary completes homework.
		Ask teachers to provide feedback to parents and Gary regarding homework completion.	Teacher will monitor completion of homework assignments and provide feedback to parents and Gary.
		Assist family in identifying and establishing rewards for improvements in student role.	Family will clearly identify ways to reward cooperation and report use of rewards.

Altered Family and Play Roles	Parents will establish appropriate expectations for child's family role and play role.	Collaborate with teachers; provide information about behavior management principles and techniques. Develop a plan to reinforce positive classroom behaviors.	Teacher will report an increase in Gary's cooperation in the classroom. Teachers will initiate behavioral program with emphasis on positive reinforcement for acceptable classroom behavior.
		Provide adolescent growth and development information to parents. Facilitate family discussion and problem solving related to work and play behavior expectations, and value of and benefit from play (leisure activities) and peer relationships.	Parents will verbalize realistic expectations for child's family and play role.
		Explore values and establish realistic guidelines for peer activities and play/leisure activities within family. Provide family with positive feedback based on ongoing evaluation of progress.	Nurse will monitor progress in establishment and reinforcement of rules, schedules for work and play. Nurse therapist will monitor own communications for positive reinforcing statements.
		Explore with family opportunities to increase peer and play activities.	Family members will verbalize options available to them to increase peer and play activities.
		Assist family in identifying opportunities for group experiences for Gary (e.g., school, church, community) and provide information as needed.	Family will identify at least one group experience for Gary, and encourage and support his involvement.

continues

Table 19-2 Continued

Nursing Diagnosis	Goals	Interventions	Evaluation
	Gary will gain cognitive clarity of grandmother's death and mother's illness and health status.	In family meetings, facilitate and support family discussion and expression of feelings related to loss of grandmother and mother's illness/health status.	Nurse will monitor parent's expression of feelings and information about grandmother's death and mother's health.
		Provide information about reactions of children and adolescents to loss and need for knowledge.	Parents will verbalize understanding and acceptance of Gary's expression of loss.
		In individual sessions with Gary, encourage and support expression of feelings of loss. Explore feelings, fears, and conflicts regarding meaning of illness and death.	Nurse will monitor Gary's clarity related to grandmother's death and mother's illness, increased investment in other relationships, increased ability to identify and label own feelings, expression of feelings with appropriate affect.
		Assist Gary to identify, develop, and use appropriate coping strategies, such as relaxation techniques, talking with friends and supportive adults, physical activity, and keeping a journal about his feelings and events.	
	Gary will demonstrate cooperative behavior in family and play roles.	Provide encouragement and positive feedback to Gary when he reports on family leisure and play roles.	Nurse will monitor Gary's verbalization and expression of feelings about play, peer relationships, and family leisure activities.
			Nurse will monitor own positive feedback to family and Gary.

| Altered Self-esteem | Gary's concept of self as worthy and capable will improve. | Include Gary in contracting and planning for his care.
Establish relationship with Gary; meet at regularly scheduled time each week for one class period.
Use discussion and activities (e.g., clay, drawing, games) to encourage ventilation of feelings, express concerns, and problem solving. | Nurse will observe for increase in smiling, initiative, ability to decide on activities, suggestions for content of discussions, expression of own feelings, ability to problem solve, positive self-statements. |

Phases of Therapy

Orientation. During the orientation phase, the nurse worked to establish a trusting relationship with Gary, his family, and his teachers. A contract was formulated; it included a plan for weekly meetings with Gary during an independent study time and four 2-hour meetings with Gary's family. The contract specified the content of the family meetings (e.g., discussion of family/play roles, behavioral expectations and role performance, family losses, relationships, and mother's illness). The contract also included a meeting with Gary's teacher to discuss behavioral interventions and communication strategies for working with Gary. A second meeting with Gary and his teacher was used to establish specific goals, to clarify the rewards for appropriate behavior, and to outline the consequences for failure to work on the goals.

During their weekly meetings at the school, the nurse played interactive games with Gary. The nurse used this time to assess Gary's defenses and coping strategies. The nurse helped Gary to learn the rules associated with the games he selected and ways to negotiate variations in the rules. As Gary began to trust the nurse and looked forward to the time spent with her, they began to negotiate the content and process of the therapy (e.g., the content of family meetings and activities to be included in the sessions with the psychiatric nurse). Trust was facilitated as Gary negotiated his own role in the three arenas of therapy. Self-esteem and self-worth were promoted as Gary was recognized as an important person and was included in the decision-making process.

Identification. The identification phase of the therapeutic relationship is the beginning of the "working" phase. In this stage of the relationship, the therapist and the client become better known to one another and become more aware of the client's feelings, dissatisfactions, and functioning in interpersonal relationships. In this phase, the psychiatric nurse therapist maintains an attitude of acceptance and helps the client to understand problem(s) more clearly.

Gary's nurse therapist began more intensively to explore with Gary his feelings and dissatisfactions about his three major roles: family, school, and play. Initially, Gary was most comfortable discussing his school role. In the early sessions of the identification phase, Gary projected the cause of his feelings and his problem behaviors onto other people. The nurse therapist helped him to clarify situations and his feelings, and supported Gary in looking at his own behavior. As she remained accepting and open to his experiences, Gary was able to accept more responsibility for negative outcomes in his interpersonal experiences.

During this phase, Gary, the nurse, Gary's teachers, and his family negotiated more specific goals and objectives. Consultation was used to assist the teachers in negotiating a behavior management plan to help Gary behave more appropriately in the classroom. Plans were also established with the family for modifications in

Gary's schedule and activities at home (e.g., care of his younger sister, time spent on chores, play activities, and schoolwork).

Exploitation. In the exploitation phase, emphasis is placed on resolution of the identified problems. The nurse therapist works to maintain the safety of the therapeutic relationship and provides support and encouragement so that the client can use available resources to meet his or her needs. The school psychiatric nurse continued to meet individually with Gary to allow him time to explore and clarify his feelings and concerns related to each of his roles, the death of his grandmother, and his mother's illness.

Gary struggled with dependence/independence issues with the nurse therapist, gradually displaying an increasing reliance on himself as his problem-solving skills improved. As the nurse therapist recognized Gary's reluctance to trust an adult, she encouraged Gary to role-play new behaviors with her. Homework assignments were also used to help Gary develop trust in others and confidence in his ability to manage his own life events. For example, Gary was first engaged in role playing with the nurse to request a change in the number of household duties that he was expected to perform at home and then given a homework assignment to renegotiate his household task responsibilities. In the subsequent session, the nurse provided positive reinforcement for Gary's attempts to undertake, complete, or succeed at the assignment.

The nurse therapist provided support and assistance to Gary in engaging in treatment and performing homework assignments. As a result, Gary was able to use the treatment to express feelings, and to recognize and discuss family, social, and academic problems and their potential solutions. Gary identified select individuals with whom he could talk about his feelings (e.g., therapist, teacher, and friends). He also spoke about his own classroom behaviors and began to associate socially acceptable behaviors with positive attention from others.

Family meetings centered around Gary's accomplishments and remaining problems. The nurse supported the parents in their reinforcement of rules and in their initiation of recreational activities with the children. She also supported and facilitated the family discussion and expression of feelings related to the loss of the grandmother and the mother's illness. Gary and the younger children were encouraged to use nonverbal techniques (e.g., drawings) to help them express their feelings and concerns. Dramatic play has also been found to assist children in reducing anxiety toward conflictual objects or events (Milos & Reiss, 1982).

Resolution. The resolution phase of the relationship centers on the termination of the nurse-client relationship and the facilitation of liaisons with supportive others in the client's natural environment. The therapist's role in termination is to continue to act in a supportive, clarifying, and encouraging role as the client becomes increasingly independent in meeting his or her own needs. Through a discussion of feelings, an exploration of potential relationships, and the encouragement of the therapist to initiate interaction, Gary formed a relationship with a small group of peers with similar interests. The mathematics teacher whom Gary had seemed to dislike so much at the beginning of the school year was taking a mutually satisfying interest in Gary and was helping Gary to expand his interest in and knowledge of sports cars. Gary was consistently completing his homework in mathematics and science, and his grades were gradually improving.

During the resolution phase, an outcome evaluation was conducted with Gary and his family. Although Gary had been given permission to have friends come to his home, he had not yet invited anyone. He continued to carry out the same work roles in the family, but his complaints had diminished. At this time, he told the nurse that he was worried about his mother and wanted to help her as much as possible. He expressed a desire to be a doctor when he grew up. Prior to termination of the nurse-client relationship, Gary and his father began to play checkers regularly one evening a week.

With Gary's consent, the nurse recommended Gary for a peer group experience in the school setting. Facilitated by a school guidance counselor, the group focused on peer support, self-concept, and communication skills.

RESEARCH

Little research has been conducted regarding the provision of psychiatric nursing services within school settings. Research on client outcomes, impact on the school system, cost of services, and needs and problems encountered by psychiatric mental health nurses in the provision of such services would be extremely useful. There is also a need for research specific to role performance. By studying children's behaviors in various roles and identifying potential causes of role performance problems, the psychiatric mental health nurse can work more effectively with children, their families, and the school.

REFERENCES

Blumer, H. (1969). *Symbolic interaction: Perspective and method.* Englewood Cliffs, NJ: Prentice-Hall.

Gordon, M. (1987). *Nursing diagnosis: Process and application* (2nd ed.). New York: McGraw-Hill.

Gumaer, J. (1984). *Counseling and therapy for children.* New York: Free Press.

Lange, F. (1987). *The nurse as an individual, group or community consultant.* Norwalk, CT: Appleton-Century-Crofts.

Maurin, J.T., & Clements, I.W. (1985). Family approaches. In D.L. Critchley & J.T. Maurin (Eds.), *The clinical specialist in psychiatric mental health nursing: Theory, research, and practice* (pp. 258–274). New York: John Wiley & Sons.

McCall, G.J., & Simmons, J.L. (1978). *Identities and interactions: An examination of human associations in everyday life* (rev. ed.). New York: Free Press.

Milos, M., & Reiss, S. (1982). Effects of three play conditions on separation anxiety in young children. *Journal of Consulting and Clinical Psychology, 50*(3), 389–395.

O'Leary, K. (1984). The image of behavior therapy: It is time to take a stand. *Behavior Therapy, 15*, 219–233.

Opie, N., & Slater, P. (1988). Mental health needs of children in school: Role of the child psychiatric nurse. *Journal of Child and Adolescent Psychiatric and Mental Health Nursing, 1*(1), 31–35.

Patterson, G., & Fleischman, M. (1979). Maintenance of treatment effects: Some considerations concerning family systems and follow-up data. *Behavior Therapy, 10*, 168–185.

Peplau, H. (1952). *Interpersonal relations in nursing.* New York: G.P. Putnam's Sons.

Peplau, H. (1969). Theory: The professional dimension. In M. Norris, (Ed.), *Proceedings of the first nursing theory conference.* University of Kansas Medical Center, Department of Nursing Education, Kansas City, KS.

Sarnoff, C. (1987). *Psychotherapeutic strategies in late latency through early adolescence.* Northvale, NJ: Jason Aronson.

Stryker, S. (1980). *Symbolic interactionism: A social structural version.* Menlo Park, CA: Benjamin/Cummings.

Wilson, H. (1988a). Conceptual frameworks for interdisciplinary psychiatric care. In H.S. Wilson & C.R. Kneisl (Eds.), *Psychiatric nursing* (3rd ed., pp. 70–89). Menlo Park, CA: Addison-Wesley.

Wilson, H. (1988b). Philosophical perspectives. In H.S. Wilson & C.R. Kneisl (Eds.), *Psychiatric nursing* (3rd ed., pp. 3–9). Menlo Park, CA: Addison-Wesley.

20

Nursing Interventions Focused on Enhancing the Self-Concept in Children and Adolescents

Hertha L. Gast

After reading this chapter, the reader will be able to:

1. describe various components of the self-concept
2. demonstrate the use of Orem's model of nursing to provide direction for nursing care as it relates to the self-concept
3. identify principles for guiding clinical assessment of the self-concept in children
4. examine strategies for enhancing children's self-conceptions as they pertain to their experiences of self as subject
5. develop strategies for helping children meet their developmental requisites related to self-concept

For the child psychiatric nurse, concern about a client's self-concept is a necessity. Virtually all children who have mental health problems and many children who have serious physical health problems have self-concept–related difficulties. Moreover, mental health promotion and mental illness prevention invariably include efforts to foster the development of a healthy self-concept in children. Thus, it is incumbent on the child psychiatric nurse to have: (1) a clear conceptualization of the self-concept, (2) a perspective within which to view nursing care as it pertains to the self-concept, (3) sensitive clinical assessment strategies, and (4) a repertoire of nursing interventions that support healthy self-concept development.

CONCEPTUALIZATIONS OF THE SELF-CONCEPT

Simply stated, the self-concept is the way in which children experience and describe themselves. In the constructionist view advanced by Hartner (1983), the self-concept is considered a cognitive structure, actively constructed and reconstructed by children in their interactions with the environment. Factors in these interactions are the maturational levels of children, particularly as they determine their cognitive capacities, and the information that they take in about how they are affecting their environments and how they are being perceived by others.

The self-concept has two different, but intertwined aspects: (1) the experience of self as subject, as observer, as "I" and (2) the experience of self as object, as the observed, as "me." Much of the literature on the self-concept is about the experience of self as object, and several instruments have focused on the normative contents of the self-concepts of school-aged children in terms of this experience (Fitts, 1965; Petersen, Schulenberg, Abromowitz, Offer, & Jarcho, 1984; Piers, 1984). The Piers-Harris Children's Self-Concept Scale (Piers, 1984), for example, classifies the content of the self-concept by means of the following dimensions: behavioral self, intellectual self, physical self, anxiety, popularity, and happiness. Contents of the self-concept in children have also been described from a developmental perspective; self-concept is generally thought to progress from a focus on concrete, observable characteristics in preschool children, to a focus on traits in school-aged children, to the notion of personality in adolescence (Selman, 1980). Children's experiences of self as subject have received less attention in the literature, although the experience of self as subject is thought to be captured somewhat in notions such as perceived competence (Hartner, 1982), personal agency (Dickstein, 1977) internal locus of control (Rotter, 1966, 1975), self-efficacy (Bandura, 1977, 1981), and existential self (Lewis & Brooks-Gunn, 1979).

According to Hartner (1983), the self-concept, self-esteem, and self-control make up the self-system. The self-concept refers to the child's self-description; self-esteem refers to the child's evaluation of the contents of this self-description; and self-control is the extent to which the child directs the course of his or her own behavior.

THE SELF-CONCEPT IN NURSING CONCEPTUALIZATIONS

Even a cursory review of the nursing literature from 1983 to 1990 reveals more than 150 citations about the self-concept of clients. Moreover, all the existing taxonomies of nursing diagnoses have self-concept–related diagnoses. Indeed, among the various broad conceptualizations of nursing, the well-known and widely used adaptation model proposed by Roy and Andrews (1991) places the self-concept in a central position, depicting it as one of only four broad types of adaptive outcomes of unique concern to nurses.

Although the self-care model of nursing developed by Orem (1991) does not give explicit attention to the self-concept, it provides a framework that differentiates various aspects of the self-concept surprisingly well. In this model, persons to whom nursing care is directed have self-care agency, and perform self-care to meet their self-care demands. Self-care agency refers to the abilities of persons that enable their self-care. These abilities are of three types: (1) foundational dispositions and traits; (2) general abilities, such as a knowledge of self-care or motivations for self-care; and (3) specific abilities used when a self-care action is undertaken. In this formulation, the self-concept can be viewed as a foundational disposition that underlies general and specific abilities for self-care. For example, an overweight adolescent who sees herself as unattractive may lack the motivation to go on a weight reduction diet.

Broadly speaking, self-care agency also encompasses the notion that individuals have some degree of control over their health and well-being, that is, they experience themselves as actors on behalf of their own health, not just as persons acted upon. This notion parallels the self as subject–self as object distinction in conceptualizations of the self-concept. Children with a well-developed sense of self as subject (i.e., personal agency) experience themselves as able to effect outcomes of interest to themselves.

Self-care refers to persons' actions on behalf of their own health and well-being. When related to the self-concept, the notion of self-care is in some respects analogous to Hartner's contention that children actively construct and reconstruct their self-conceptions. Epstein (1973) argued that the self-concept is more a theory than a concept and that the process used to develop this theory is akin to that used to develop scientific theories. In this process, hypotheses are derived from an existing theory, and the results of various empirical tests of these hypotheses are used to develop the theory further. In childhood, new hypotheses regarding the self are constantly being generated and tested. An adolescent, for example, may revise his negative self-theory by incorporating the consistent positive feedback that he receives from his peers in a psychotherapy group.

Self-care demand refers to persons' actions that are required for their health and well-being—actions that meet universal, developmental, or health care needs. Universal self-care needs occur regardless of age, culture, or health status. In the case of the self-concept, for example, it is necessary to manage the dissonance experienced when feedback from others is markedly different from the individual's self-conception, either by modifying the self-conception or by rejecting part or all of the incongruent feedback. Developmental self-care needs relate to healthy growth and development, including the development of the self-concept (Damon & Hart, 1982; Livesley & Bromley, 1973; Montemayer & Eisen, 1977; Rosenberg, 1979; Selman, 1980). Self-care needs may also arise because of health problems, such as structural defects or illnesses that make it necessary to protect or reorder the self-concept. For example, the adolescent with diabetes must incorporate that fact into her self-concept. The outcome to which self-care is directed is health and well-being. In conceptualizations of mental health, the notion of a positive, well-defined, and age-appropriate view of self is central (Offer & Shabshin, 1974).

Social and environmental factors may impinge on self-care through basic conditioning factors, dependent care agency, and dependent care. Basic conditioning factors are factors known to influence various aspects of self-care, such as culture, socioeconomic class, family system factors, and conditions of living. These factors have a marked influence on the self-concept as well (Bishop & Ingersoll, 1989). Dependent care agency refers to the abilities of care-givers to engage in actions that foster the health and well-being of persons who are unable to manage their own care, and dependent care refers to actions of care-givers directed toward the health and well-being of others. With regard to the self-concept, children are clearly dependent on parents and significant others for input that will allow them to construct healthy self-concepts (Killeen, 1988a, 1988b).

NURSING INTERVENTIONS

The foregoing conceptualization, which aligns distinctions made in the self-concept literature with concepts in the self-care model (Figure 20-1), suggests that interventions should be directed at: (1) clarifying connections between the self-conceptions of children and their behaviors; (2) enhancing children's self-conceptions as they pertain to the experience of self as subject; (3) engaging children in processes that foster the construction of healthy self-concept; (4) helping children meet universal, developmental, and illness-related requirements for a healthy self-concept; and (5) facilitating interactions between children and their social environments that have a positive impact on their self-concepts.

Clinical Assessment of the Self-Concept

Issues that arise in the clinical assessment of the self-concept in children and adolescents are decidedly complex. First, evaluation scales such as the Piers-Harris Children's Self-Concept Scale (Piers, 1984) and the Tennessee Self-Concept Scale (Fitts, 1965) are generally made up of fixed sets of self-statements and are used to make normative assessments of children in a given age group. Because clinicians are also interested in idiosyncratic self-revelations and unique self-descriptions, the usefulness of such scales in clinical assessment is limited. Assessment techniques are needed that make it possible for children to demonstrate both normative and idiosyncratic aspects of their self-descriptions.

Second, adults are able to share their self-conceptions directly in that they can represent their experiences of self abstractly, differentiate various aspects of the self, and take a reflective position vis-à-vis the self. Children do not have all these abilities. For example, preschool children may use words to describe themselves, but the meanings of these words are highly personal, arising from their experiences rather than from a shared understanding of the critical attributes of concepts. Moreover, preschoolers characteristically describe themselves solely in terms of physical qualities and are, for the most part, incapable of self-reflection. Assessment techniques should accommodate such cognitive limitations.

Third, because they are profoundly and inescapably dependent, children typically respond to adults in ways that court their favor and are cautious about mak-

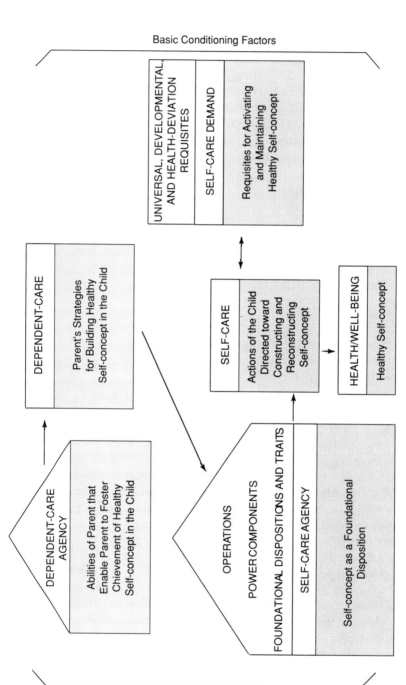

Figure 20-1 Orem's model applied to the self-concept in children.

ing potentially unacceptable self-revelations. Therefore, assessment techniques that have face-saving mechanisms are needed.

Fourth, more often than not, self-concept assessment is done from the perspective of a child's view of self as if the child were looking in a mirror—an actual mirror or a social mirror. In this view, the child is an object that can be seen by others. An assessment with this perspective does not capture the child's experience of self as subject, however, as the one who is looking into the mirror, the one who is actively constructing a view of self. Assessment techniques are needed that include data about this aspect of the self.

There are some assessment techniques that meet these criteria. For preschool children, for example, spontaneous play, puppet play, or drawings may reveal how they experience themselves. For school-aged children, spontaneous stories, artwork, and games (e.g., the Talking, Feeling, Doing Game [Gardner, 1986]) may serve this purpose. For adolescents, personal journals or psychodramas may facilitate self-revelations. Such strategies generally use metaphors to capture a child's sense of self. Metaphors have been shown to be rich in meaning when interpreted in the context of other data about the child by the experienced clinician (Mills & Crowley, 1986). They have the advantages of involving relatively concrete symbols and of having an inherently face-saving quality because they are understood by the child to be "just pretend" or "only a story." Moreover, they often communicate what the child considers important about the self and can reveal the child's experience both of self as subject and of self as object.

> Maria, an 11-year-old girl from a large Mexican-American family, was brought into treatment because she had threatened suicide. Maria's mother reported that Maria was the most difficult of her children and that, in the past, she and the family had coped with Maria's stormy behavior by sending her to Mexico to spend a few months with her natural father. In the inpatient milieu, Maria was alternately withdrawn and contentious with her peers. She neglected her personal hygiene and appearance, attending to them only when the staff insisted that she do so, and she was sullen and shared only superficial information about herself in individual psychotherapy sessions.
>
> In an effort to get her to reveal more about herself, the therapist asked her to draw a picture of her family, which she did, drawing each family member with considerable detail. The picture she drew had a major impact on her course of therapy. Unlike the other family members in this picture, Maria was depicted as a cavewoman dressed in an animal skin. Two horns protruded through her bushy head of hair, forming an interesting contrast to the benign expression on her face. The therapist hypothesized that Maria's depiction of herself in this drawing represented her sense of self in the context of her family; that is, she perceived her-

self as different, incorrigible, wild, perhaps even dangerous, but at the same time, pleasant and well-meaning.

Although surprised at her self-revelation, Maria confirmed this hypothesis and became more open about her longstanding sense of marginalization and the way in which she viewed herself as a "black sheep" in her family. When Maria showed her drawing to her family during family therapy, it evoked surprise, concern, and considerable empathy from her mother and some of her siblings. At the same time, it stimulated several productive confrontations from her siblings about some of her behaviors that they experienced as difficult. Eventually, changes in Maria's sense of herself, especially in the context of her family, resulted in improvements in her behavior. Her quarreling with peers in the milieu and her siblings became less intense. She became more interested in her appearance. Her sense of hopelessness about being acceptable to her family lessened.

Enhancement of the Experience of Self as Subject

In order to promote a positive self-concept in children, the nurse should foster a general sense of competence in them and should help them acquire a broad repertoire of abilities so that they experience themselves as able to affect their environments.

A Competency-Based Approach to the Care of Children

The nurse who uses a competency-based approach endeavors to help children become more able to manage their lives. Thus, the nurse focuses primarily on supporting competencies that the children already have and helping them acquire an increasingly more diversified competency repertoire. In some settings, it may not be easy to maintain such a focus; however, the nurse is likely to do so successfully by adopting a philosophy of care and a conceptual model of nursing that supports the notion of competency.

The nurse who wears a "competency lens" when working with children notices strengths where others see weaknesses. Zinker (1977) argued that even problematic behaviors can be considered to be strengths; they are problematic for the most part not because there is something inherently wrong with them, but because they are overused or used to the exclusion of other behaviors. For example, the silence of the child who has learned to say little rather than risk criticism is typically considered problematic, but it can be viewed as an understandable form of self-protection—even as a behavior that, in some circumstances, is highly prized. Zinker's approach is to appreciate the usefulness and value of behaviors characteristically viewed as problematic and to help people change by adding new behaviors rather than by controlling or eliminating so-called problematic behaviors. With the silent child, the nurse may begin by noticing and admiring the child's capacity for silence—acknowledging it as an inordinately well-developed competency. The nurse may then invite the child to develop other competencies, among them those related to verbal expression. Important in this approach is the accent on competencies, existing ones and ones that can still be developed.

Interactive Styles That Foster Self-Reliance

Certain interactive styles foster a healthy sense of self as subject in children. Baumrind (1989) summarized findings from an extensive longitudinal study of the influence of parental styles on the rearing of competent children. Two broad types of social competence were delineated: agency and communion. Agency is the drive for independence and self-aggrandizement, status in social relationships, and a sense of justice in resolving social conflicts. In contrast, communion is the need to be of service and engaged with others, solidarity in social relationships, and a sense of compassion in resolving social conflicts. Optimal social competence was defined as high levels of both agency and communion. Baumrind found that an authoritative parental style that is high in demandingness (i.e., structure and control) and high in responsiveness (i.e., warmth and respect for individuality), results in competent, confident children. Of importance is the balance between demandingness and responsiveness in parenting and the development of a reciprocal pattern between the parent and the child. It is necessary to have a balance in which the child is required to be responsive to parental demands and the parent accepts the responsibility to be as responsive as possible to the reasonable demands of the child and to show interest in the child's point of view.

With the assumptions that how children think affects what they do and that improved interpersonal *cognitive* competence results in improved interpersonal *behavioral* competence, Shure and Spivak (1978) advocated a type of dialogue to foster a sense of competence in children. Using everyday interpersonal conflicts and frustrations, adults guide children in: (1) identifying interpersonal problems, (2) considering how they and others involved might feel in a specific problematic situation, (3) anticipating what might happen next, (4) recognizing that there is more than one way to solve a problem by generating alternatives, and (5) deciding on and experimenting with one or more alternatives. The emphasis in these exchanges is on the process used to resolve interpersonal difficulties rather than on the content. Shure and Spivak's extensive studies provide ample evidence that children who learn this process through formal structured lessons or in naturalistic dialogues generalize what they learn from one interpersonal situation to another and come to experience themselves as efficacious in a global sense. The following two exchanges, adapted from dialogues described by Shure (1981, 1989), demonstrate the differences between an interactive style between adults and children that is all too typical and a style designed to enhance social competence.

Adult: John, why did you grab that toy from Larry?

John: He never shares.

Adult: You can't grab toys. Larry doesn't like that. You should ask.

John: It's not fair. He won't give it to me.

Adult: If you grab like that, he won't play with you anymore.

John: I don't care.

Adult: John, I told you to ask him for it.

Adult: John, what happened when you grabbed that toy from Larry?

John: He hit me and grabbed it back.

Adult: How did that make you feel?

John: Mad.

Adult: How do you think Larry feels?

John: Mad.

Adult: You're mad and Larry's mad. Can you think of a *different* way to get Larry to let you have that toy?

John: Ask him.

Adult: That's one way. Go ahead and ask him.

John: Can I play with that toy?

Larry: No!

John: See—he won't give it to me!

Adult: I know you're feeling frustrated, but I bet if you think real hard, you'll find another idea. You could ask or . . . ?

John: (after several seconds) I'll give it back when I'm finished.

Larry: (reluctantly) OK.

Adult: Very good, John. You thought of another way to get Larry to let you play with that toy. How do you feel now?

John: (smiles) Happy.

Adult: I'm glad, and you thought of that all by yourself.

In the second dialogue, the adult provides the child with opportunities to learn to connect means to ends, to consider the effects that his behaviors have on others, and to generate alternative strategies for solving a problem. Shure and Spivak argued that a general sense of competence rests on learning these skills.

A Typology of Psychosocial Competencies in Children

In order to adopt a competency-based approach, the nurse must know what psychosocial abilities children must develop if they are to have a healthy sense of self as subject. Strayhorn (1983) argued persuasively that, at their core, all psychotherapies foster the development of psychosocial competence; to that end, he developed a taxonomy of psychosocial skills that gives a comprehensive description of the critical psychosocial competencies of adults. A similar taxonomy for children and adolescents would clearly be useful. In the nursing literature, the "tools and tasks" analysis proposed by Fagin (1972) could be said to presage such a taxonomy.

Gast (1986) recently developed a tentative typology of the psychosocial competencies of children. This typology has the advantage of being derived from a series of interviews with experienced child psychiatric clinical nurse specialists. These nurses considered 14 types of mental health–related competencies to be underdeveloped in most children in psychiatric treatment. To test the validity of this typology, a self-report instrument made up of 70 items describing these 14 types of competencies was constructed and tested with both children in treatment and children not in treatment. Children in psychiatric treatment were found to have significantly poorer scores for 13 of the 14 types of competencies. Furthermore, as the severity of psychiatric problems increased, the level of competence decreased (Edford, 1990; Stumpf, 1990). Although these findings are preliminary, they are at least a first step in outlining a competency-based approach to the psychiatric nursing care of children. Following are the 13 types of competencies found to be underdeveloped in children who were undergoing psychiatric treatment:

1. the ability to maintain a sense of self-esteem. Included were positive self-talk, realistic self-expectations, acceptance of positive feedback, and openness to learning from mistakes.
2. the ability to identify and express feelings. Included were skills in identifying, modulating, and expressing feelings, as well as a vocabulary for talking about feelings.
3. personal hygiene and physical health care skills. These included good grooming skills and good health habits, such as good eating patterns, adequate exercise, and responsible substance use.
4. peer relationship skills. Included were skills in establishing new friendships, sharing with friends, resolving disagreements, maintaining a degree of autonomy vis-à-vis friends, and valuing friends.
5. general social skills. These included the capacity to trust persons who are trustworthy, comfort in giving and receiving affection, and good manners.
6. self-control. Included were respect for reasonable rules and for persons with authority, as well as the capacity to monitor impulses in the absence of adult supervision.
7. age-appropriateness. These pertained to awareness of and comfort with age-appropriate roles and responsibilities.

8. assertiveness skills. Included were comfort in seeking help and skill in asking for things clearly and directly.

9. insight and responsibility. These included self-awareness, a willingness to accept responsibility for one's actions, and a willingness to be accountable when given a job to do.

10. problem-solving skills. Included were skills in means-end thinking, the generation of alternatives, and decision making.

11. recreation, play, and study skills. These included a capacity for humor and fun, the ability to use free time, and a repertoire of interests.

12. flexibility and openness to change. Included were a positive attitude toward change, a willingness to try new things, and comfort with difference.

13. skill in relating to the wider world of family and community. Included were skills in finding positive resources in the community and in relating to various family members.

Developmental Requisites for a Healthy Self-Concept

As stated previously, the conception of self as "me" is thought to be constructed largely from the reflected appraisals of significant others—from looking into the "social mirror." At the same time it is the product of maturational and developmental factors that govern social cognition.

Preschool Children

Selman (1980) characterized preschool children as "radical behaviorists" in that they are outer-directed and describe themselves in terms of observable characteristics. Beginning with the toddler, self-descriptions pertain to the body self (e.g., nose, eyes, ears, toes) and physical actions (e.g., jumping, wiggling, running), progress to the more categorical descriptions of the young preschooler (e.g., "I am a boy," "I am a child," "I am a human being not an animal"), and then turn to distinctions made by the older preschooler about observable skills (e.g., "I'm a good runner—I can run the fastest of any kids in my school"). Hartner (1983) depicted the self-concept–related task of preschool children as featural recognition and labeling. Children in this age group proliferate labels for physical aspects of themselves, but, because they emerge from personal experiences, these labels are somewhat idiosyncratic and lack stability. In the course of social experience, preschoolers learn the critical attributes of concepts and thus achieve a level of consensus and a degree of constancy in the labels that they use in self and person descriptions. Preschoolers must also crystallize a sense of self, that is, they must differentiate invariances and variances with regard to the self—to establish, for example, that "I will always be Janie, and I will always be a girl, even though I will get bigger and go to school like my older brothers and sisters."

Finally, according to Selman (1980), preschoolers have little sense of the ways in which they are seen by others or of the differences between their perceptions and those of others. Moreover, because they do not differentiate feelings or intentions from actions, they are confused about psychological causality. For example, they may juxtapose cause and effect, as in the statement "My mommy gave me a treat, so I am a good girl." Thus, children at this age must begin to distinguish, in themselves and others, the psychological from the physical; the subjective from the objective; thoughts, feelings, and intentions from behaviors.

The self-concept–related tasks of children, when viewed in the context of the self-care model of nursing, can be considered developmental requisites. Nursing interventions that help children meet these requisites, which are limited only by the resources and creativity of the nurse, are shaped to a degree by the treatment modalities selected. The following principles can be used in designing self-concept–enhancing interventions for preschool children:

1. To be comprehensible, feedback to children at this age must be about observable characteristics rather than psychological features. A statement such as "I like the way you are sitting quietly while I talk to your mother" is preferable to "You are such a polite little girl."

2. Preschool children need help recognizing attributes in themselves and others, and in developing a repertoire of labels for describing persons. Preschoolers love to be observed and delight in the "running commentary" that adult observers provide. This commentary, especially as it challenges them to make new distinctions and learn new labels, helps them develop a vocabulary for talking about themselves. Pointing out attributes of persons in books and pictures can also serve this purpose.

3. Preschool children need help developing a stable sense of self. Feedback from adults can help them recognize aspects of themselves that will not vary, such as humanness (I will always be a human being and cannot turn into a rabbit), personhood (I will always be me and cannot become my older sister), gender (I will always be a boy), name (I will always be Sally), and birth order (I will always be my mother's second child).

4. Children at this age have a necessary egocentrism. They cannot take the perspective of another and are not governed by a sense of what others are thinking. The perspectives of others need to be pointed out to them in simple ways. For example, "You and Jerry both want to go down the slide, so let's figure out a way for each of you to have a turn."

5. Preschoolers need help in beginning to construct a subjective self—the self of thoughts, feelings, and intentions—and they need help in understanding how this self is causally related to their behaviors. Older preschoolers, especially, can profit from inquiries about the relationship of their feelings and intentions to their behaviors.

School-aged Children

If preschool children are "radical behaviorists," school-aged children are "trait psychologists." According to Selman (1980), school-aged children's self-descriptions progress from a focus on observable skills, to a focus on habitual ways of acting that incorporate both attitudes and actions, to a focus on clusters of enduring traits. Among the self-concept–related tasks that children must accomplish during this period is the development of a classification system for concepts about personal attributes; concepts in this system have demonstrable referents. For example, the trait smart may be used to classify a person who gets good grades, is in the top reading group, or wins the spelling bee. Theoretical terms such as personality, ego, and unconscious motivation are not understood at this age.

School-aged children must also develop the capacity to differentiate a subjective self, a self of feelings, intentions, and thoughts. With regard to subjectivity, children at this age begin to realize that they can have more than one feeling. At first, they understand subjectivity as a progression of feelings ("First I feel sad and then I am happy") and eventually as mixed feelings ("I feel a little sad and a little happy at the same time"). This suggests that another self-concept–related task during this period is to clarify the subjective self of feelings, thoughts, and intentions and the objective self of observable behavior and then to connect these two.

Self-awareness and the "looking glass" self emerge during this period. Although young school-aged children come to realize that the thoughts of others may differ from their own and become concerned about the impact of their actions on the feelings of another, it is not until middle-school age that they take a second-person perspective vis-à-vis themselves. Moreover, the capacity to take a third-person perspective, an observing ego that monitors the self in relation to others, does not develop until late school age or early adolescence. Thus, an additional self-concept–related task for the school-aged child is to construct an objective sense of self based on how the child believes that he or she is seen by others and to modify such beliefs in the course of social interaction. Principles that guide interventions with children in this age group include the following:

1. Feedback to school-aged children can be about their unique habits and traits, that is, about relatively stable aspects of themselves. For younger school-aged children, particularly, it is helpful to point out that generalizations about them arise from specific observations, for example, "You are such a kind person—you always remember your grandmother's birthday, you look out for the new kids in school, and I've never heard you say mean things about others, even when you don't like them."

2. The necessary egocentrism of children at this age is a function of the fact that they tend to view the conclusions that they draw from experience as certainties. For example, a school-aged child, having concluded on the basis of several successes at bowling that he is a good bowler, views this

conclusion as immutable, not as a tentative hypothesis to be validated or invalidated in the course of subsequent experience. This egocentrism needs to be respected.

3. Interactions with school-aged children should attend to their feelings, thoughts, and intentions—not just their behaviors. Among the numerous strategies for expanding children's subjective selves are games or activities designed to increase the range of feelings that they can identify, the use of "life-space" interviews in which their problematic behaviors are reviewed and their intentions and outcomes are clarified, and consistent interest in and inquiries about their feelings, intentions, and thoughts.

4. Children first become self-conscious at this age; they begin to worry about what others think about them. Moreover, they begin to incorporate second-person perspectives vis-à-vis themselves into their self-conceptions, making these conceptions somewhat less open to inspection and external influence. A child at this age may, for example, view herself as "a nerd" if she believes that her peers view her as such. To change this view, she may need to share it with someone who can help her understand whether and how this view is connected either to her behavior (e.g., perhaps infantile) or to the social context in which it evolved (e.g., perhaps a peer group of "tough" youngsters intimidated by her pleasantness). With this understanding, she may change her view of self by learning new behaviors or by taking in new feedback that challenges the feedback she used to construct a distorted view of self.

Adolescents

It is not until adolescence that children (1) represent their self experiences using abstract symbols; (2) view themselves from a third-person perspective; (3) describe themselves as unique, complex personalities with a past history and evolving future; and (4) understand themselves using abstract theoretical notions, such as unconscious motivation and defenses, organizing personality structures, a guiding philosophy or system of values, and culture as a determinant of behavior. Self-concept–related tasks in this age group are myriad and complex. First, because of their emerging capacity for abstract thinking, adolescents begin to view themselves in the context of the hypothetical, the possible, the ideal; thus, they must incorporate these dimensions into their self-theories.

Second, adolescents take on a third-person perspective from which to view self in relation to others. Elkind (1976) noted that the third-person perspectives of adolescents typically involve over- or underattributions. When adolescents overattribute thoughts to others, they tend to experience themselves as scrutinized by a critical imaginary audience; similarly, when they underattribute thoughts to others, they tend to construct a personal fable about the uniqueness of their experiences, a uniqueness that others cannot understand. Thus, adolescents must discover how they are actually being seen by significant others, especially peers.

Third, adolescents begin to understand personality as a product of childhood experiences and as a complex dynamic system with unconscious forces that are not readily understood or accessed. Their approach to change with regard to the self system not only is less naive than is that of the school-aged child, but also is less direct and optimistic. Finally, adolescents have the task of forming a sense of self separate from, albeit shaped by, an interpersonal, social, and cultural context; this means clarifying and claiming at least a set of values, a career, a life style, and a social network. These developments suggest the following principles for guiding self-concept–related nursing interventions:

1. The enchantment of adolescents with the hypothetical, the ideal, and the possible is thought by some to contribute importantly to the circumspect world of adults. With regard to the self-concept development of adolescents, this idealism should be supported, not prematurely foreshortened. At the same time, adolescents may need help in striking a balance between the hypothetical and the actual, the ideal and the real, the possible and the probable.

2. The over- and underattributions that adolescents make when taking on a third-person perspective vis-à-vis themselves usually become more veridical as they share their thoughts and concerns with others. Peer interactions are particularly important in correcting these misattributions.

3. Adolescents sometimes overwhelm themselves with such ideas as unconscious forces; personality structures; developmental, historical, and cultural determinism; and psychopathology. One of the things that they need from adults is useful, accessible understandings of personality dynamics and a sense of optimism about their ongoing development.

4. In preparation for adulthood, adolescents are faced with challenging identity tasks, such as clarifying their values, establishing social networks, considering career choices, and experimenting with life styles. They need access to adult models, pertinent life experiences, thoughtful and respectful discussions with adults that help them clarify their values, and responsibilities commensurate with their abilities.

Child psychiatric nurses can have considerable impact on the self-concept of children. They can help children expand their competence repertoires and thus achieve a more healthy sense of self as subject. Additionally, they can use their knowledge of growth and development to help children accomplish the developmental tasks that shape their emerging self-conceptions.

REFERENCES

Bandura, A. (1977). Self-efficacy: Toward a unifying theory of behavioral change. *Psychological Review, 84,* 191–215.

Bandura, A. (1981). Self-referent thought: The development of self-efficacy. In J.H. Flavell & L. Ross (Eds.), *Social cognitive development: Frontiers and possible futures* (pp. 200–239). New York: Cambridge University Press.

Baumrind, D. (1989). Rearing competent children. In W. Damon (Ed.), *Child development today and tomorrow* (pp. 349–378). San Francisco: Jossey-Bass.

Bishop, S.M., & Ingersoll, G.M. (1989). Effects of marital conflict and family structure on the self-concepts of pre- and early adolescents. *Journal of Youth and Adolescence, 18,* 25–38.

Damon, W., & Hart, D. (1982). The development of self-understanding from infancy through adolescence. *Child Development, 53,* 841–864.

Dickstein, E. (1977). Self and self-esteem: Theoretical foundations and their implications for research. *Human Development, 20,* 129–140.

Edford, D. (1990). *The Self-esteem Subscale of the Child Mental Health Self-care Inventory: A validity study.* Unpublished master's thesis, Wayne State University, Detroit.

Elkind, D. (1976). Cognitive development and psychopathology: Observations on egocentrism and ego defense. In E. Schopler & R.J. Reichler (Eds.), *Psychopathology and child development* (pp. 167–183). New York: Plenum Press.

Epstein, S. (1973). The self-concept revisited or a theory of a theory. *American Psychologist, 28,* 405–416.

Fagin, C.M. (1972). Tools and tasks. In C.M. Fagin (Ed.), *Nursing in child psychiatry* (pp. 13–27). St. Louis: C.V. Mosby.

Fitts, W.H. (1965). *Tennessee Self Concept Scale.* Nashville, TN: Counselor Recordings and Tests.

Gardner, R.A. (1986). *The psychotherapeutic techniques of Richard A. Gardner.* Cresskill, NJ: Creative Therapeutics.

Gast, H.L. (1986). *Developing an inventory to measure mental health self-care in children.* Paper presented at the Annual Research Conference of the Council of Directors of Graduate Programs in Psychiatric Mental Health Nursing, Washington, DC.

Hartner, S. (1982). The Perceived Competence Scale for Children. *Child Development, 53,* 87–97.

Hartner, S. (1983). Developmental perspectives on the self system. In E.M. Hetherington (Ed.), *Handbook of child psychology: Vol. 4. Socialization, personality and social development* (pp. 275–385). New York: John Wiley & Sons.

Killeen, M.R. (1988a). Self-concept of children of alcoholics: Part I. Family influences. *Journal of Child and Adolescent Psychiatric and Mental Health Nursing, 1,* 25–30.

Killeen, M.R. (1988b). Self-concept of children of alcoholics: Part II. Developmental considerations. *Journal of Child and Adolescent Psychiatric and Mental Health Nursing, 1,* 77–81.

Lewis, M., & Brooks-Gunn, J. (1979). *Social cognition and the acquisition of self.* New York: Plenum Press.

Livesley, W.J., & Bromley, D.B. (1973). *Person perception in childhood and adolescence.* London: John Wiley & Sons.

Mills, J., & Crowley, R. (1986). *Therapeutic metaphors for children and the child within.* New York: Brunner/Mazel.

Montemayer, R., & Eisen, M. (1977). The development of self-conceptions from childhood to adolescence. *Developmental Psychology, 13,* 314–319.

Offer, D., & Shabshin, M. (1974). *Normality: Theoretical and clinical concepts of mental health.* New York: Basic Books.

Orem, D. (1991). *Nursing: Concepts of practice* (4th ed.). New York: McGraw-Hill.

Petersen, A.C., Schulenberg, J.E., Abromowitz, R.H., Offer, D., & Jarcho, H.D. (1984). A Self-image Questionnaire for Young Adolescents (SIQYA): Reliability and validity studies. *Journal of Youth and Adolescence, 13,* 93–111.

Piers, E.V. (1984). *Piers-Harris Children's Self Concept Scale.* Los Angeles: Western Psychological Services.

Rosenberg, M. (1979). *Conceiving the self.* New York: Basic Books.

Rotter, J.B. (1966). Generalized expectancies for internal versus external control of reinforcement. *Psychological Monographs, 80*(1, Whole No. 609).

Rotter, J.B. (1975). Some problems and misconceptions related to the construct of internal versus external control of reinforcement. *Journal of Consulting and Clinical Psychology, 43,* 56–67.

Roy, C., & Andrews, H.A. (1991). *The Roy adaptation model: The definitive statement.* Norwalk, CT: Appleton & Lange.

Selman, R. (1980). *The growth of interpersonal understanding: Developmental and clinical analyses.* New York: Academic Press.

Shure, M.B. (1981). Social competence as a problem-solving skill. In J.P. Wine & M.D. Syme (Eds.), *Social competence* (pp. 158–185). New York: Guilford Press.

Shure, M.B. (1989). Interpersonal competence training. In W. Damon (Ed.), *Child development today and tomorrow* (pp. 393–408). San Francisco: Jossey-Bass.

Shure, M.B., & Spivak, G. (1978). *Problem-solving techniques in childrearing.* San Francisco: Jossey-Bass.

Strayhorn, J.M. (1983). A diagnostic axis relevant to psychotherapy and preventive mental health. *American Journal of Orthopsychiatry, 53,* 677–696.

Stumpf, Y. (1990). *The Problem Solving Subscale of the Child Mental Health Self-care Inventory: A validity study.* Unpublished master's thesis, Wayne State University, Detroit.

Zinker, J. (1977). *Creative process in Gestalt therapy.* New York: Brunner/Mazel.

21

Nursing Interventions with Children and Adolescents Experiencing Difficulties with Socialization

Beth Bonham and Sandra J. Wood

After reading this chapter, the reader will be able to:

1. identify the impact of developmental issues on the socialization of children and adolescents
2. examine the relationship of inhibition and oppositionality to the socialization of children and adolescents
3. develop nursing interventions for children and adolescents experiencing difficulties with socialization

Nurses who work with children professionally in physicians' offices, schools, clinics, and hospitals sometimes must cope with the disruptive behavior of acting-out (antisocial) children. These children demonstrate antisocial behavior in play groups, preschool, Sunday school, or any setting in which other children are present. Because these problems begin early, disrupt various activities, and lead to censure for affected children, it is important to intervene early. This helps change behavior before a cycle of acting out, punishment, and rejection makes the children isolated and unhappy and the adults who relate to them frustrated and despairing.

Nurses also encounter quiet, anxious children who avoid interaction. These asocial children also prompt concern. Skill in behavioral observation, together with a strong grounding in normal growth and development, helps nurses recognize that quiet children are also at risk for future dysfunction. Interacting with most children individually or in small groups, the nurse attends to reticent children more easily.

Because nurses deal with individuals holistically, they examine all aspects of functioning—physical, social, cognitive, and emotional. Being health-based, nurses are less likely to label clients or to use a purely medical/illness-oriented treatment approach. Nurses can also recognize positive aspects of behavior, despite the socialization difficulties of a child or adolescent.

BEHAVIORS BASED IN INHIBITION

The phenomenon of inhibition and its associated behavior is complex and multifaceted. Anthony (1976b), however, gave a succinct and simple definition: "Inhibition . . . is characterized by an absence of reaction and can almost be regarded in negative terms as a mode of nonbehavior" (p. 103). Anthony further commented that inhibition does not reflect opposition or lack of desire to cooperate, but reflects the youngster's difficulty in understanding cooperation or lack of drive toward cooperation.

According to Deering (1986), the inhibited child has deficiencies in several areas of expression and behavior, including initiative, achievement, assertion, motor activity, and expression of feelings. Although these children and adolescents lack the open, carefree attitude associated with childhood, they do not wish to be alone. They crave closeness, but are afraid to initiate contact and/or reveal their feelings. They guard against the expression of strong emotions, particularly sexual and aggressive drives. This concern about their own reactions makes them fearful, constricted, and nonexpressive. The longer this behavior pattern continues, the more ingrained it becomes (Anthony, 1976b; Deering, 1986).

Overstimulation vs. Understimulation

In exploring the genesis of inhibition, Anthony (1976b) noted Freud's suggestion that individuals possess a stimulus barrier to assist them in coping with external stimuli. During the third month, the infant's neurological development progresses to the point that the stimulus barrier regulating stimulus input and output is active. Thereafter, the barrier should function to protect the child from being overstimulated and, thus, overwhelmed.

When overstimulated, the child can avert gaze, rock, coo, or suck fingers or thumb to diminish anxiety. When the parents and significant others recognize the child's cues of being overwhelmed, they should decrease the stimuli in order to calm the child. If the parents are not physically or emotionally available or if the child is constantly faced with a noisy, tension-filled environment, however, the child may retreat and begin to shun contact with others. No longer does the child seek the parents' stimulation or respond to care-givers. The child avoids the anxiety and discomfort caused by too much contact with others. Although such a reaction may be fairly adaptive in the short run, critical deficits in age-appropriate social skills and motivation toward academic and vocational achievement develop over time (Anthony, 1976b).

The child who is understimulated (i.e., is rarely handled or exposed to external stimuli during the first few months of life) is likely to remain passive and asocial because of the lack of contact with others who can teach social skills and serve as role models of appropriate behavior. Neglect by parents and care-givers has a cumulative effect on a child's growth and development. First, there is little bonding with parents, which limits the child's ability to trust others. Second, the child often lacks the external limit setting that paves the way for internal self-control. Finally, lack of parental involvement limits the inculcation of values that permit the development of morality (Anthony, 1976b).

Risk for Dysfunction

Both the overstimulated child and the understimulated child are at risk for dysfunction in childhood and adolescence. The short-term consequences of inhibition include diminished academic performance and lack of normal friendships because of poor social skills. In school, children are expected to be assertive and inquisitive. Although the passive, quiet child may achieve satisfactory grades, the teacher rarely perceives that child as outstanding and so does not praise and challenge that child as much as the bright, active student. The same child is often ostracized by peers because the child lacks the social skills that encourage others to seek friendship with him or her (Rubin, 1980). Deering (1986) pointed out that inhibited children have trouble connecting emotions with events or objects, making it difficult for them to express their feelings.

Children who do not master the tasks of competition, compromise, and cooperation with same sex peers in latency and preadolescence are poorly equipped to manage socialization with the opposite sex in adolescence. Adolescents who are significantly inhibited fear and repress their sexual impulses and drive. They avoid all but superficial contact with the opposite sex, having few social skills with which to initiate and maintain either friendship or love. These cumulative deficiencies may leave them unprepared for a deep commitment to the opposite sex in young adulthood. As a result, the inhibited adolescent who marries in late adolescence or early adulthood is likely to divorce quickly due to the inability to maintain a lasting relationship. Furthermore, the inhibited late adolescents or young adults who were neglected as children often lack parenting skills and are likely to neglect their own children, thus perpetuating this destructive social pattern (Bornstein, Bellack, & Hersen, 1977).

The neglected adolescent who is inhibited may use alcohol or drugs to be sociable and gain peer acceptance. Unfortunately, unhappiness with self and environment, together with a lack of social skills, can lead the inhibited adolescent to abuse substances rather than merely to experiment with them. The inhibited teenager's concerns about social acceptance and perceived inability to learn to relate successfully to others puts that youth at risk for suicide, depression, and/or an anxiety disorder. Unless the youngster receives treatment to learn skills and achieve an appropriate social adjustment, the problematic behavior seen in the childhood or adolescence of an inhibited youngster may lead to Schizoid Personality Disorder, Depression, or Addiction in Adulthood (American Psychiatric Association, 1987).

It behooves all nurses and other health care professionals who work with infants and young children to be cognizant of the devastating effects of overstimulation and understimulation. Nurses can assist parents and other care-givers in monitoring and controlling external stimuli. Nurses can also teach neglectful parents positive ways to interact that are enjoyable for both child and parent.

BEHAVIORS BASED IN OPPOSITIONALITY

Oppositional behavior is a normal part of child and adolescent development. Anthony (1976a) described the pioneering work of David Levy, who defined normal opposition as a logical outcome of socializing children to conform to their particular environment. Oppositionality can be viewed along a behavioral continuum, with the normal developmental crisis of opposition at one end and a "psychotic negativism" at the other (Anthony, 1976a). Behavior can range from simply refusing to eat to a generalized oppositional character disorder. The 2-year-old may display temper tantrums in a quest for autonomy; the adolescent may break established rules in searching for independence and identity. An oppositional disorder may be observed in children as young as 3 or 4 years of age and is obvious by early adolescence. In differentiating normal oppositional behavior from problematic oppositional behavior, the nurse considers duration, frequency and intensity of response, the area of involved function, and the people most involved.

As a child becomes increasingly mobile, the child frequently hears the word *no* when exploring the environment and acquiring self-control. In controlling self, the child entertains a delicate balance between what Anthony (1976a) called yes and no decisions. These decisions represent the difference between pleasure and reality, independence and conformity, and omnipotence and impotence. The healthy outcome is a child who blossoms into a self-confident, self-reliant, and self-controlled person. This process may not be obvious in the easygoing latency-aged child who outwardly accepts the information about the self and the world given by adults. With the advent of preadolescence and adolescence, however, that earlier negativism resurfaces to force a new way of interacting for some families and become a battleground for others. Played out in treatment, the clinician may see the adolescent whose rebellion or delinquency is no longer tolerated by the family. Thus, negativism becomes a presenting complaint for treatment.

It takes at least two people to produce oppositional behavior. The controlling, authoritarian parent who uses overly harsh, coercive methods to force behavioral compliance may unwittingly increase a youngster's acting-out behavior. The controlling adult may perceive the 2-year-old or the adolescent who is being developmentally oppositional as a threat, and the ensuing interactions can establish an intractable negative pattern. The oppositional parent may be refighting his or her own childhood battles while the youngster is struggling for identity (Anthony,

1976a). The parent who is depressed or emotionally unavailable can foster a benign neglect and fail to set appropriate limits. In trying to force the parent to respond and receive needed limits, the youngster may become more oppositional. Neglect and lack of limit setting cause the child to have great difficulty in defining and internalizing values (Anthony, 1976a).

There are secondary oppositional reactions. As children become independent and autonomous, both the children and their parents have many feelings. Some parents feel that their child no longer loves them. Some children want to retaliate for rules that they perceive as too strict. Parents and children are often unaware of the feelings that dictate their reactions. Unacknowledged feelings of guilt, shame, and embarrassment (arising from earlier events for the adult) are reactivated in the parent-child interaction. The adult, unaware of this, reacts to the behavior of the child and perpetuates the cycle of reaction without knowing the reasons (Anthony, 1976a).

The oppositional child frequently loses his or her temper, argues with significant adults, blames others for mistakes, is resentful and vindictive, and has difficulty in all areas of life. In response, adults become more resentful and more controlling. Peers do not play with the oppositional child, and the child becomes a loner. The child may become the class clown and, subsequently, be excluded from the classroom for this behavior. Academic performance decreases until interest in school is lost. In adolescence, when the peer group takes on special importance, the adolescent loner cannot socialize according to group rules and perpetuates the cycle of antisocial behavior. These adolescents are at risk for destructive behaviors, such as substance abuse, eating disorders, and delinquency (Anthony, 1976a). If left untreated, early antisocial behaviors may become increasingly severe in adulthood. The oppositional adult may: (1) become addicted, (2) become involved with the legal system, or (3) have difficulty in staying employed.

Adults who commit offenses such as assault, rape and burglary previously displayed severe antisocial responses to others. These offenses have roots in earlier oppositional behaviors (Gottman, Gonso, and Rasmussen, 1975).

It is important for nurses and other professionals to determine the reason for the oppositional behavior of children and adolescents. Nurses can assist parents and professionals by educating them about the normal growth and development of children and adolescents. Parents can be taught appropriate parenting skills and ways to redirect the behavior of oppositional children.

PSYCHIATRIC NURSING DIAGNOSES

In categorizing socialization problems, nursing diagnoses are helpful. The broad categories of inhibition and opposition in the Revision of the Phenomena of Concern for Psychiatric Mental Health Nursing Practice provide a framework to classify child and adolescent socialization problems (O'Toole & Loomis, 1989; see Appendix B for specific nursing diagnoses that apply to inhibited and acting out youngsters).

NURSING INTERVENTIONS

Children and adolescents who are experiencing difficulty with socialization can benefit from a variety of treatment interventions. Some modalities, such as play therapy, are most productive with children; others, such as peer counseling and psychodrama, are better suited to preadolescent and adolescent populations. Certain treatment modalities, such as art therapy, are appropriate for both children and adolescents.

Play therapy can offer the anxious, inhibited child the emotional outlet needed for improved social skills and can assist the acting-out child in exploring nonaggressive means of relating to others (Axline, 1969). Art therapy can be employed as a means to assess self-concept (through self-portrait drawing) and as a therapeutic treatment. For the repressed youngster who resists treatment because of anxiety and for the angry youngster who resists treatment because of a need to control others, art therapy provides a nonverbal outlet for feelings. Art therapy can pave the way for better relations with others and more direct expressions of feelings (Oster & Gould, 1987). Journal writing is also a less direct means to express and gain control of feelings, as well as to solve problems in relationships with others. Bibliotherapy offers children and adolescents the opportunity to learn about socialization by reading about the experiences of others (Gardner, 1975). Adolescents who take part in peer counseling learn from others directly through the modeling of appropriate behavior and the provision of immediate feedback regarding interactions with others (Strain, 1981).

Three innovative interventions are particularly well suited to the unique abilities and talents of nurses. These three interventions are developmental games, social skills training, and group therapy.

Developmental Games

A new intervention for youngsters who are experiencing socialization problems is the developmental game technique designed by Shapiro (1984). He has applied the technique primarily with children and adolescents who have learning disabilities, Attention Deficit Disorder, and antisocial behavior (e.g., Conduct Disorder). It was designed for children who do not respond to traditional play therapy because their perceptual and learning problems make it difficult for them to reveal their feelings and learn through a verbal mode. Shapiro (1984) suggested that some benefits of this type of therapy are "assistance with the transfer of learning from one situation to another, allowing as much repetition as needed without diminishing enjoyment of the process, guaranteeing success for the child and providing a concrete, realistic, manageable situation in which the child can learn" (p. 106).

In developmental game therapy, the therapist designs and builds a game that deals with a particular problem that keeps the child focused. If a child is confronting multiple issues, a different game can be created for each problem. The youngster's interest and active participation are integral parts of the development and construction of the game. Once constructed, the game can be played with any adult (not just the therapist), which extends the value of treatment.

In some cases, the developmental game is competitive, so the youngster learns how to lose. For an aggressive child or an adolescent who needs to learn cooperation, a game with no individual winners may be more appropriate. Rewards for success with the game may be points, tokens, prizes, or social interaction. The ultimate goal of a developmental game is helping the youngster give up longstanding negative behavior patterns and build appropriate socialization skills (Shapiro, 1984).

Social Skills Training

Children acquire social skills in a variety of ways: through their culture; through their social group; and through modeling of appropriate behavior by parents, relatives, teachers, and peers. A child's interaction depends on situation, personality, past interaction experiences, observations of other people, and the impression formed of them (Wilkinson & Canter, 1982). Communication, both verbal and nonverbal, is an important part of social skills acquisition.

If their social skills acquisition is impaired because of inadequate modeling, decreased opportunities for learning, impaired intellectual functioning, physical illness, emotional difficulties, or any other reason, a social skill development program can be modeled on work initiated by Dr. Emory Cowen at the University of Rochester, (Cowen, Pederson, Babigan, Izzo, & Trost, 1973). The assessment of social skills in children is accomplished by teacher and parent surveys and questionnaires. The Behavioral Assertiveness Test (Bornstein et al., 1977) or the Matson Evaluation of Social Skills with Youngsters (MESSY; Matson, Rotatori, & Helsel, 1983) may also be helpful for assessment. Behavioral goals may include enhancement of positive self-image, improvement of ability to help others and understand self, and better understanding and expression of feelings (Cowen et al., 1973).

One such social skills program was developed for 60 children in an elementary school's summer enrichment program. The children had completed kindergarten or first grade and were 6 and 7 years old. The program focused on one theme per week for 4 weeks. Age-appropriate activities and training techniques of coaching, feedback, behavior rehearsal, modeling, and teacher praise accompanied each theme.

Week I's theme was self-concept. At the core of a child's mastery of skills and environment is the way that the child feels about self. If the child acts capable, competent, and confident, the chance of a positive response from others is increased. The child's negative self-perception impairs the attainment of self-confidence, however. The first step in the program was to list the day's agenda while modeling desired social behavior. A sharing circle was established. Everyone sat in a large circle facing each other, which facilitated eye contact and participation. Each day began with the circle, so the children became comfortable with it and knew what to expect. The gradual acquisition of participation skills (e.g., talking, listening, and asking questions) was encouraged. *Liking Myself* (Palmer, 1977a), a book developed for assertiveness training, was used to introduce concepts of "I'm valuable" and "I can identify positive things about myself." Activities used to follow up discussion included drawing favorite things to do and self-portraits.

Week II's theme was feelings. Because of their developmental and cognitive levels, children are not yet familiar with the words used to describe their feelings. Six cardboard faces depicting emotions, such as sad, happy, and surprised, were used to introduce feeling words and nonverbal facial expression. The chapter on feelings of *Liking Myself* (Palmer, 1977a), as well as the chapter on "Warm Fuzzies" from *T.A. for Tots and Other Prinzes* (Freed, 1974), were read to the children. Individual and group activities helped the children become aware of their own feelings and encouraged modeling, rehearsing, and affirming feelings. In one individual activity entitled "Many Faces We Make," children were asked to draw facial expressions to illustrate such sentences as "Are you friendly to new people?" and "Do you speak kindly of your friends?" Another activity was drawing a booklet of feelings associated with sentences such as "This is happy me" and "When I feel good inside, I . . . ." A group activity focused on feelings was the pride line. Each student was asked to describe a specific area of personal behavior in a sentence beginning with "I'm proud that I . . . ." Another group activity involved one person's describing what he or she liked, knew, or appreciated about another person in the group. The discussion centered on how people feel when they hear someone say pleasant things about them.

Relationships was the theme for Week III. To relate to other people, children need to know how they feel and how their body feels in a particular situation. The chapter on "Body Talk" from *Liking Myself* (Palmer, 1977a) was used to introduce those concepts. Children were asked to describe their body feelings when they experienced sadness, anger, or fear. To accomplish the objective of learning to relate to other people, activities were done in groups. In one activity, groups of four children planned and painted group pictures of themselves, their families, and their houses as if they lived side by side. Another activity involved selecting and pasting magazine pictures of people who were showing each other respect.

Assertiveness, which incorporated all previously taught concepts, was the theme of Week IV. Previous concepts were reviewed, and the book *The Mouse,*

The Monster and Me (Palmer, 1977b) was used to introduce the concepts of strength and power. Coaching was used first to help students identify personality characteristics and then to empower them to verbalize situations in which they are in charge. One activity was drawing a self-portrait that matched a child's description of self; the portrait was then made into a button for the child to wear. In another activity, the children described a scary situation that involved a monster; then one child role-played the monster and another role-played an empowered child. The children then reversed the roles. As a result of such programs, children can gain confidence, self-awareness, and assertiveness.

Group Therapy

Children and adolescents with socialization difficulties often benefit from group therapy. The content or "the reason for the group" can be as varied as its members—sexual abuse, substance abuse, low self-esteem, normal growth and development, or a significant loss. Groups can be led by one therapist or by cotherapists, who may or may not be of one gender. Membership can be open or closed. Group sessions can be structured or unstructured. Because the peer group takes on enormous importance for the preadolescent and the adolescent, group work becomes a natural way to "do therapy" for that age group.

The intent of this chapter is to describe socialization issues as they occur in each stage of group development. Regardless of the reason for the group, socialization occurs during the process. Planning is the first step of preparing for a group, and recruitment is one aspect of planning. In the following example, planning was accomplished in discussions with the teacher and recruitment was easy because of the "captive audience."

> A teacher of gifted and talented third- and four-grade students was concerned about the way that the children talked to and treated each other. The teacher observed disrespectful peer interactions, clique formations, and intense competition. A group was formed, first with the girls and then with the boys, that met weekly to discuss behaviors, feelings, and normal developmental issues. As the process continued, it was obvious that positive socialization was occurring, as each participant interrupted less and disclosed more. The teacher commented that the children were interacting more respectfully in the classroom.

A second stage of the group process is exploration or "the honeymoon." This period is important for group trust and ownership to occur (Siepker & Kandaras, 1985). One author led a group with ten junior high girls.

> Each group meeting was preceded with comments such as "I love this group" and "My other friends ask if they can come, too." As the group progressed, the girls began to tell their stories, which were respectfully

listened to and gently confronted. Clarifying statements were heard ("you mean that . . . ."), as well as questions seeking information ("what did you do when your mom . . . ?") An example of responding to nonverbal cues occurred when one group member became tearful, and another silently offered her a tissue. These examples of communication demonstrated that the socialization skills of listening, clarifying, and observing both verbal and nonverbal cues, modeled by the therapist, were learned.

The third stage or working phase of the group process is filled with anxiety (Siepker & Kandaras, 1985). There is much movement, both internal and external.

Two therapeutic play groups were formed for 14 kindergartners because of their undersocialized and/or aggressive classroom behaviors. As the two groups met, the working phase was fraught with movement. One boy was banging away on toy soldiers, two girls were feverishly drawing picture after picture, and two boys were being physically aggressive with the large plastic "stress reducer." Because these children were acting out their aggressions in a safe place and in a safe manner, it was important to allow that behavior. The therapist commented to the group that what they were doing and the objects that they had chosen were appropriate for anger displacement. The commentary was instructive and clarifying, two components of modeling desired social behaviors.

The goal of the working phase of group therapy is to move the child or adolescent into an awareness of the group process through internalization of the group (Siepker & Kandaras, 1985).

The fourth stage or cohesive phase brings a sigh of relief, both to the members and to the therapist (Siepker & Kandaras, 1985). A sense of anticipation ensues, and the talking/working really begins. Group members rely less on the therapist for direction and begin to direct their own play (children) or to verbalize their stories and feelings (adolescents).

In a group of fifth-grade boys and girls meeting because their parents had divorced, one girl said that she felt abandoned by her mother. This was particularly significant because, in 2 years of individual therapy, this young lady had steadfastly refused to discuss her mother.

In the final stage of termination, the anxiety-filled moments of the working phase return. Regressive behaviors resurface. (One fifth-grade boy in the divorce group conveniently had himself removed from the group at the termination meeting.) Members may ask to continue the group, and they commonly express anger, denial, and sadness. Young children can be asked to draw a picture of how it feels to say goodbye. For adolescents, a goodbye party can assist in resolving termination issues. These behaviors help children to manage future terminations successfully. Because group work with children and adolescents can be very intense, it is also helpful for the therapist and/or co-leaders to have a debriefing with a colleague.

TREATMENT DIRECTIONS

Nurses, whether they are inpatient staff, clinical specialists, or presidents of their local parent-teacher associations, have knowledge that should be articulated and disseminated to the community. The health promotion model of nursing emphasizes preventing illness. In a proactive stance, nurses can demonstrate wellness by actively educating the public through community groups, churches, and schools.

The identification of populations that need care and the accessibility of care are also important treatment considerations. Who will identify the youngster who needs care—parents, teachers, nurses, police, or others in the community? Once a client has been identified, who will provide care? The proliferation of adolescent psychiatric units and hospitals is well-known, but many of the adolescents who are receiving care in these facilities are white and middle class. Lower income adolescents also need and deserve treatment, but may be excluded from care by their financial status. Because of their community health backgrounds, nurses are well prepared to treat these excluded groups. Affordable health care, including mental health care, is an issue that requires scrutiny and support at the local, state, and national levels.

Staff nurses can be educated to use socialization interventions; however, more child and adolescent psychiatric clinical nurse specialists are needed. This requires a concerted effort by the community at large, including agencies such as the National Institute of Mental Health, that can provide increased funding for graduate nurse education.

RESEARCH DIRECTIONS

In the area of research on youth socialization, there are two immediate problems—the lack of recent research by all disciplines and the limited nursing research in the area. Although psychologists and social workers generated research in the 1970s and early 1980s, there is very little current work. Nurses can develop and investigate research questions in the area of childhood socialization. For example, what treatment modality is best for specific clients? Which treatment is most effective for a particular cultural group? How effective is health promotive and primary preventive treatment for normal and at risk populations?

REFERENCES

American Psychiatric Association. (1987). *Diagnostic and statistical manual of psychiatric disorders* (3rd ed., rev.). Washington, DC: Author.

Anthony, E.J. (1976a). The genesis of oppositional behavior. In E.J. Anthony & D.C. Gilpin (Eds.), *Three clinical faces of childhood* (pp. 1–8). New York: Spectrum Publications.

Anthony, E.J. (1976b). The genesis of inhibition. In E.J. Anthony & D.C. Gilpin (Eds.), *Three clinical faces of childhood.* (pp. 103–110). New York: Spectrum Publications.

Axline, V.M. (1969). *Play therapy.* New York: Ballantine Books.

Bornstein, M.R., Bellack, A.S., & Hersen, M. (1977). Social skills training for unassertive children: A multiple baseline analysis. *Journal of Applied Behavior Analysis, 10*(2), 183–195.

Cowen, E.L., Pederson, A., Babigan, H., Izzo, L.D., & Trost, M.A. (1973). Long-term follow up of early detected vulnerable children. *Journal of Consulting and Clinical Psychology, 41,* 438–446.

Deering, C.G. (1986). The inhibited child. *Journal of Psychosocial Nursing, 24*(2), 16–21.

Freed, A.M. (1974). *T.A. for tots (and other prinzes).* Sacramento, CA: Jalmar Press.

Gardner, R. (1975). *Psychotherapeutic approaches to the resistant child.* New York: Jason Aronson.

Gottman, J., Gonso, J., & Rasmussen, B. (1975). Social interaction, social competence, and friendship in children. *Child Development, 46,* 709–718.

Matson, J.L., Rotatori, A.F., & Helsel, W.J. (1983). Development of a rating scale to measure social skills in children: The Matson Evaluation of Social Skills with Youngsters (MESSY). *Behavior Research and Therapy, 2*(1), 335–340.

Oster, G.D., & Gould, P. (1987). *Using drawings in assessment and therapy: A guide for mental health professionals.* New York: Brunner/Mazel.

O'Toole, A.W., & Loomis, M.E. (1989). Revision of the phenomena of concern for psychiatric-mental health nursing. *Archives of Psychiatric Nursing, 3*(5), 288–309.

Palmer, P. (1977a). *Liking myself.* San Luis Obispo, CA: Impact Publishers.

Palmer, P. (1977b). *The mouse, the monster and me.* San Luis Obispo, CA: Impact Publishers.

Rubin, Z. (1980). *Children's friendships.* Cambridge, MA: Harvard University Press.

Shapiro, L.E. (1984). *The new short-term therapies for children: A guide for the helping professions and parents.* Englewood Cliffs, NJ: Prentice-Hall.

Siepker, B.B., & Kandaras, C.S. (Eds.). (1985). *Group therapy with children and adolescents: A treatment manual.* New York: Human Science Press.

Strain, P.S. (Ed.). (1981). *The utilization of classroom peers as behavior change agents.* New York: Plenum Press.

Wilkinson, J., & Canter, S. (1982). *Social skills training manual: Assessment, programme design and management of training.* Chichester, England: John Wiley & Sons.

22

Nursing Interventions with Children and Adolescents Experiencing Self-Destructive Tendencies

Sharon M. Valente

After reading this chapter, the reader will be able to:

1. examine the risk factors and warning signs of child or adolescent suicide
2. evaluate the suicide risk of a child or adolescent
3. describe the characteristics of the suicidal child or adolescent
4. develop nursing strategies to assess the suicide risk of children and adolescents
5. examine psychiatric nursing interventions that reduce depression and suicide risk in children and adolescents

The haunting question is, Why do children commit suicide? Why do they no longer want to live after seemingly temporary, ordinary setbacks, such as failing grades? There is no single dynamic that explains youth suicide. Because most children and adolescents give warnings before they attempt suicide, however, many suicides can be prevented. Psychiatric and mental health nurses who evaluate clues to suicide may reduce tragic loss of life, as they can detect suicide warnings and help a youth explore alternatives to self-destruction.

> His parents were stunned when Teddy, their sweet-faced 14-year-old, left a suicide note saying, "I'll love you forever, but I've decided to end it. I'm sorry. Love, Teddy." Before Teddy's suicide, no one had guessed that the sandy-haired youngster with large eyes was planning suicide. He enjoyed his friends, delivered papers for pocket money, hated school, and could not wait to grow up. After a failing report card, he crawled out his bedroom window and hung himself. Teddy's parents had believed his mood swings, rebelliousness, depression, and argumentative nature to be teen-age growing pains. Teddy had believed that no one cared about him. After Teddy's suicide, his parents, teachers, and friends worried that they had missed the warning signs of suicide.

MAGNITUDE OF THE SUICIDE PROBLEM

Suicide constitutes a major social, medical, and economic problem. A child or adolescent who does not want to live shocks family, confuses friends, and challenges nursing staff. Many children and adolescents who attempt suicide feel hopelessly unhappy, unloved, alienated, and worthless. They perceive themselves as unlovable failures. Often, they cannot identify any one significant event that triggered their suicide attempt, but they feel overwhelmed by daily events that symbolize their feelings of rejection, alienation, and hopelessness. They cannot put their distress into words. At highest risk are youngsters who have frequent suicidal thoughts that they cannot control and a specific plan and method.

Suicide ranks as the third leading cause of death among youth aged 15 to 19. The increase in adolescent suicide is both real and substantial; according to the Centers for Disease Control (CDC; 1985), the incidence of adolescent suicide has increased 257% in the past 30 years. Suicides before age 10 are not tallied. Although the number is small, suicide rates among children below age 12 have also doubled. Males die by suicide four times more often than do females; this ratio is reversed for suicide attempts (CDC, 1985). There is no explanation for these gender differences, however.

Statistics reflect an underestimation of the frequency of suicidal behaviors. For youth, there may be 7 to 200 attempts for every completed suicide (McIntosh & Jewell, 1986). Accurate statistics are unavailable because: (1) some suicides are reported as accidents, (2) statistics clump age groups of under 14 and 15 to 19 together, (3) families and medical examiners are hesitant to label a death suicide without evidence, and (4) youths rarely leave suicide notes.

Since 1980, both males and females have preferred guns as a suicide method (CDC, 1985). Recent suicide rates for 1988 show that those aged 15–24 with 13.2 suicides per 100,000 have higher risk than those age 5–14 with 0.7 suicides per 100,000 (National Center for Health Statistics, USDHHS, November 26, 1990). High suicide rates also occur among Black and hispanic adolescents and some American Indian tribes. Although Navajos have a suicide rate close to the national average (11.8–12/100,000), Southwest Apaches have had suicide rates ranging from 20.8 in 1950 to 43.3/100,000 in 1978. Indian communities with high suicide risk also have high rates of alcoholism and drug and solvent abuse and early loss of caretakers among adolescents. High suicide rates occur among Indians adopted by non-Indian families and those who attend American Indian boarding schools (Berlin, 1987).

THEORETICAL PERSPECTIVE

Theories derived from adult suicide research identify key biological, psychological, and sociological variables and dynamics, but they lack clear guidelines for the evaluation of the developmental theories regarding suicide or for interventions with children or adolescents. Psychoanalytic theory (Freud, 1916/1949) suggests that suicide may occur when loss evokes mourning, melancholia, and death wishes, and when death wishes toward another are internalized. This theory highlights the importance of evaluating loss, whether perceived or actual, and intervening to help children and adolescents work through the experiences of loss. Psychodynamic theory emphasizes the evaluation and treatment of depression, poor self-esteem, and hopelessness.

Family theory emphasizes current family and peer interactions and the way in which youngsters cope with developmental tasks. It is not known how the turbulence or stress of development increases vulnerability to suicide; it is known, however, that childhood trauma, alienation, degree of support, and the adequacy of parenting alter this vulnerability. In the past decade, child and adolescent suicide has been defined as a family problem, for the family is in a position to prevent suicide. Families that teach children to cope with problems through secrecy and self-destructive behaviors may inadvertently teach youngsters to manage problems by suicide (Valente, 1987a). Some youngsters also mimic family role models who talk about or attempt suicide (Valente, 1987b).

Developmental theorists emphasize important developmental tasks and the vulnerability of children who lack abstract thinking capacities and mature self-concepts. Youth suicide is embedded in a family context. The pressures of mastering developmental tasks (e.g., developing an identity, forming stable values, establishing responsible sexuality, selecting student or work roles, creating independence from parents, and developing relationships) can precipitate suicide attempts (Gilead & Mulaik, 1983; Valente & Saunders, 1987).

Children younger than age 8 use concrete thought processes and do not see much difference between ideas and actions (e.g., thinking about suicide is the same as doing it). Because of immature cognitive processes, some children may not realize that death is permanent and irreversible until they reach age 12. Children who grow up amid violence understand the permanence of death earlier. Despite limited concepts of death, children as young as age 2½ have wished for death and impulsively swallowed poison or darted in front of cars. Although some psychoanalysts still argue that children cannot be suicidal unless they know that death is permanent (Valente, 1987b), the nurse must respond to all self-destructive behavior.

The theoretical perspective of self-care developed by Orem (1985) provides guidance for nursing assessment and interventions with youngsters at risk for self-destructive behaviors. The model emphasizes assessment of the youth's self-care agency, or the capability to engage in self-care actions. A deficit exists if the self-care agency is unable to meet the client's needs for safety and self-care (Taylor, 1989). This may occur when a suicidal patient lacks the knowledge, motivation, skill, or reasoning needed to avoid self-destructive behavior. When a patient possesses—but fails to activate—strengths, knowledge or skill for self-care, the nurse helps the patient initiate self-care. Collaboratively, the nurse and youth plan interventions that enhance self-care capacities.

Because the self-care perspective emphasizes the importance of empowering clients, it is a relevant nursing theory for youth who feel helpless and/or hopeless, or have low self-esteem. Instead of doing "for" the client, the nurse helps the child or teen-ager develop self-care capabilities. The nurse evaluates the youth's ability to cope and helps him or her learn to improve social skills (Orem, 1985). Using this theory, the nurse does not expect the child or adolescent to meet all his or her needs, but rather to be dependent during suicidal crises (Kerr, 1985). This dependence is an important aspect of the therapeutic alliance during a suicidal crisis. Later, the nurse supports increased independence as self-care capacity improves and suicide risk declines.

A strength of nursing is its orientation toward patient strengths—not just pathology. Because nurses have the skill and insight to identify and highlight a patient's strengths, as well as a patient's deficits, nurses can encourage and develop an adolescent's self-esteem and self-concept.

ASSESSMENT

To evaluate suicide risk in a child or adolescent, the nurse considers risk factors; warning signs; and the lethality of the suicide plan, method, means, and intent. For the younger or less verbal child, play, art, and psychodrama may elicit suicidal themes better than words (Pfeffer, 1986). For verbal youngsters, questionnaires and interviews facilitate data gathering (Pfeffer, 1989). Approximately 60% of normal high school students report suicide ideas (Smith & Crawford, 1986).

Risk Factors

A past or present history of incest, child abuse, chemical dependence, family suicide, schizophrenia, early death of a parent, or depression places a child or adolescent in a group that has a high suicide rate (Valente & Sellers, 1989). Other high-risk groups are runaways and those individuals who have been in jail for less than 48 hours. Among these groups, black male teenagers have high suicide rates, while gay and lesbian adolescents have high suicide attempt rates.

Suicide can be a youngster's attempt to get help for a problem or to reduce family tension. The nurse should determine whether any recent events may increase suicide risk. When Gould and Shaffer (1986) studied the role of imitative behavior in suicidal teen-agers during 1984 and 1985, they found a significant increase in both completed and attempted suicides 2 weeks after broadcasts of TV movies about suicide. Their results highlight the importance of assessing the risk of suicide by imitation.

Family theory highlights the impact of constructive and disturbed interactions between the child or adolescent and family. Knowing that suicidal ideas in one individual may represent or trigger similar ideas in another family member, nurses should routinely assess the suicide potential of each family member (Richman, 1986). The assessment of a youngster's support network is also important, for a suicidal friend may increase a child's risk of suicide. When a youth has run away from home, the nurse must determine how the youth has internalized and interpreted family messages about self-esteem, deliberate self-harm, and coping with suicidal thoughts.

Danger Signals

Suicide warnings may be overt (e.g., "I don't want to be alive, and I'm going to kill myself") or covert, self-destructive behavior that may appear accidental (e.g., ingesting poison or running in front of a car). For instance, one 7-year-old ran in front of a car because he wanted to be with Grammy, the only one who loved him, and she had gone to heaven. Statements about not wanting to live should be explored. Nurses must seriously assess jokes about suicide or suicidal thoughts that are subsequently denied.

Suicide warnings include behaviors such as withdrawal, self-mutilation, depression, running away, or aggressive acting out. Other signals may involve changed eating, sleeping, or social behavior. Recurrent moods of helplessness, hopelessness, and ambivalence are important, despite occasional happy days. If no one responds to these warnings, the youngster may decide that no one cares or has time to listen until "I seriously attempt suicide."

Other suicide clues include giving away prized possessions; disclosing thoughts of suicide; or warning of suicide in diaries, essays, play, or art. In figure drawings, a slash mark piercing the wrist, neck, chest, or other body parts may forewarn the observer of a suicide plan and method. In other drawings, loops or nooses that are part of the sky, decoration, or background may imply a suicide message. The nurse should ask the child or adolescent to explain such drawings. One 12-year-old hospitalized patient illustrated his choice of suicide method by draping the hospital "call bell" cord around his neck and jokingly asking staff what it would be like to be dead. His message was serious, as was his subsequent attempt to hang himself.

Lethality

When the danger signals of suicide appear, the nurse should explore the youngster's feelings; consider the family interaction around suicide; and examine any suicide plan for its specificity, method, means, and intent. The risk increases if the youth desires death rather than rescue or relief, the family resources are exhausted, support is unavailable, or family messages encourage suicide (Richman,

1986). For example, some adolescents believe that their death would solve the family's problems.

A youth who can explore the possibility that life may be worth living and can create an action plan with realistic goals has a lower suicide risk than does one who is hopeless about the future. When a youth has a precise, immediate, lethal suicide plan and means, safety is the first priority. If an outpatient attempts suicide, the nurse should consult colleagues; an attempted suicide may signal the need for hospitalization.

Possible Assessment Aids

Although Lester (1974) reports that no instrument evaluates suicide risk as accurately as an interview, reliable and easily administered measurement instruments for suicidal behavior of children and adolescents exist. These include: Spectrum of Suicidal Behavior Scale (Pfeffer, 1989), Schedule for Affective Disorders and Schizophrenia for School Age Children (K-SADS), Diagnostic Interview Schedule for Children (DISC), Schedule for Affective Disorders and Schizophrenia (SADS), Children's Depression Inventory (CDI), Scale for Suicide Ideation, and the Suicide Intent Scale. The severity of suicidal behavior should be defined and measured (Pfeffer, 1989). Depression inventories help the nurse monitor depression in those youngsters whose suicide risk is linked with depression (Pfeffer, 1989).

The Minnesota Multiphasic Personality Inventory (MMPI; Pope & Scott, 1967) is a paper-and-pencil test with a subscale that has been used to measure suicide potential in adults and adolescents. Critics of this instrument have been concerned about the frequency of false-positive results. Newer versions of the inventory may remedy these faults.

Suicidologists agree that clinical evaluation and observation are the most effective ways of determining suicide risk, because assessment scales have a degree of unreliability and inaccuracy (Lester, 1974).

One effective assessment interview format is a conference in which the family, the client, and significant others list the client's strengths, discuss concerns, and plan strategies. The problem is defined as "how can we all work together to help Jerry feel better about himself, use safe coping strategies, and improve the quality of life." The action plan can boost hope and reduce feelings of helplessness and alienation.

The family conference also allows the nurse to evaluate perceived or actual family messages about the importance of the suicidal youth. Messages may encourage suicide by implying that the child is a burden, that the family would be better off without the child, and that love or approval is contingent on the child's disappearance (Kerfoot, 1984). When families are involved in treatment rather than blamed, suicide risk can be reduced.

NURSING DIAGNOSES AND PLANNING

A nursing diagnosis serves to organize observations and direct interventions. For self-destructive youths, the nursing diagnoses may include Alteration in Feeling State, Alteration in Self-esteem, and Alteration in Social Interactions. Two nursing diagnoses deserving particular consideration for children at risk for suicide are Potential for Injury and Inadequate Individual or Family Coping (Valente & Sellers, 1989). Although other diagnoses may also be considered, the diagnosis of Potential for Injury or Self-harm alerts the nurse to the importance of evaluating the patient's mood, comments, and behavior and to the need for precautions to prevent self-harm. An adolescent's goal (e.g., "I want to feel better about myself") may translate into a diagnosis of Inadequate Individual Coping Related to Low Self-esteem.

In the planning phase of the nursing process, the nurse, youngster, and family establish the outcomes or desired health state to be achieved. Safety of the adolescent is always the key priority. The child and the nurse then discuss how therapy can help achieve these outcomes. Orem (1985) emphasized mutual collaboration on goals and interventions. The task is to match the child's capacity for creative or verbal expression with the type of therapy. For example, the nurse may strongly recommend art or play therapy to children who feel intimidated by talking, adding family therapy when the child feels able to interact in a group setting.

INTERVENTIONS

Based on Orem's (1985) theory of nursing systems, nursing interventions can be divided into wholly compensatory, partly compensatory, or supportive-educational interventions. Many interventions that ensure safety are used for all clients, however, regardless of their self-care agency and nursing system.

Wholly Compensatory

Safety Issues. Evaluations of the youngster's need for safety determine the level of protection required; the client's need for safety must be balanced with the client's need for therapy. As most parents and nurses know, some risks are inherent in the process of allowing growth during adolescence. For instance, the total restriction of an adolescent would reduce the risk of suicide, but would also preclude growth. The goal of therapy is to provide a therapeutic environment with a balance between opportunities for growth and provisions for safety.

An initial focus of nursing interventions for the acutely suicidal child or adolescent is the provision of a safe environment. The therapeutic plan includes hospitalization with suicide precautions; a no-suicide contract; and a team conference with the client, family, and school representative. An effective no-suicide contract is embedded in a therapeutic nurse-client relationship. The nurse asks the youth to promise not to cause self-harm until a specified date and time. The youth can specify limitations to the contract; the nurse renegotiates the contract before it expires. The use of the no-suicide contract allows the nurse to assess the youth's willingness to make a life-saving commitment and to accept the support of a caring relationship. Impulsive adolescents who have poor object constancy or who lack control over suicidal thoughts require close supervision, however, because their anxieties may invalidate their no-suicide commitment.

During a suicidal crisis in which a youngster has highly lethal plans that indicate the potential for violence, the nurse actively provides supervision and takes suicide precautions to ensure the youngster's safety. Based on an assessment of the youth's impulsivity and ability to avoid responding to suicidal thoughts, the nurse determines the level of supervision required. Some youngsters may be closely observed at irregular intervals; others may be placed on suicide precautions so that the nurse is always within arm's length. Often, the multidisciplinary team discusses the level of precautions or observation required and the behaviors that the youth must demonstrate to attain more freedom. The themes being explored in therapy and behavior may serve as an index of suicide risk, but it is difficult in suicide assessment to determine the clients' internal feelings and impulse states based on their thoughts, behaviors, and actions.

Milieu Management. Suicidal youths are placed on psychiatric units where nurses help them to understand and manage problematic behaviors. A therapeutic milieu reinforces the idea that each person (1) has value, can manage problems safely, and can upgrade his or her level of self-care; (2) can be happy and learn to contribute to the community; and (3) can express feelings without harming people or objects. Other messages may be that certain behaviors are unacceptable, each person can be someone who counts, and failure is not the end of the world. Failure is, in fact, a learning experience.

Within this milieu, nurses assist clients in developing a community where they learn self-responsibility and self-management. Psychiatric clients also learn to use self-care strategies, such as building self-esteem, forming relationships, and monitoring symptoms. Underwood (1980), recognizing that a psychiatric client's deficits in perceptions, thoughts, and motivation influenced the ability to meet basic physical and psychological needs, formally integrated self-care concepts into inpatient psychiatric care. Underwood believed that self-care "provides the nurse with a way of assessing and planning that supports the client's own control over daily living" (p. 16).

Because some suicidal youths give partial suicide messages to different people, suicide risk should be discussed in staff conferences before privileges or passes are awarded. Suicidal youths often test limits, project negative attitudes, and complain that there is little meaning in life. This behavior can frustrate and test everyone.

Unit policies should prescribe restrictions and the safe control of sharp items, dangerous objects, and medications. Because most hospital suicides involve hanging or jumping, Farberow (1981) advised installing break-away bathroom fixtures to prevent hanging and assigning patients to ground floor, well-supervised rooms. Nurses should investigate unsafe conditions and supervise or safeguard tools, equipment, or bags brought by visitors, housekeepers, maintenance staff, or other people who enter the unit. The use of safety scissors, cutlery, and occupational therapy tools should be supervised. Each unit needs a suicide precautions and surveillance policy that sets standards for suicide observation, documentation, and staff-client ratios.

Partly Compensatory

As the youth's control over suicidal impulses improves, the nurse should encourage independence and strategies that improve self-esteem; reduce depression; develop social skills; and increase hope, help seeking, and constructive use of power. In order to demonstrate improved impulse control, the youth usually needs to respect rules, attend meetings and school, and meet homework and behavior objectives. Contracts that specify the target behaviors and appropriate rewards for cooperation are often useful for youth when staff set limits without being angry or punitive. Before a youth's privileges are increased, staff may need to see that the youth initiates discussion of suicidal ideas, improves self-esteem, and has some goals or plan for living. In addition, the youth can demonstrate safer coping strategies (e.g., exercise) when stress occurs.

Staff and family members continue to monitor suicide ideas and to evaluate all suicidal behavior—even joking. If the youth is depressed, staff remain particularly alert for suicide potential as the depression lifts, for suicide risk may increase at this time. When the youth goes home for a visit, the staff meet with family to discuss the monitoring of warning signs and precautions for safety (e.g., keeping medication in a locked container and having an adult dispense it, avoiding alcohol).

Art and Play Therapy. As the child or adolescent demonstrates less self-destructive behavior, the nursing interventions become more focused on improving the patient's agency. Art and play therapy help youths express suicidal ideas and master self-destructive impulses. Nurses can explore themes that emerge during play as clues to diagnosis, suicide methods, and treatment. They can comment on themes linked with suicide potential, such as separation, loss, repeated dangerous or reckless behavior, misuse or destruction of toys, and omnipotent fantasies. For instance, when a child makes a puppet act dangerously or destroy toys, the nurse may comment empathically on how sad, angry, or unhappy the puppet feels and the good reasons for those feelings. The nurse may wonder aloud, "what might happen if things got worse," "maybe the puppet feels no one loves him," or "maybe the puppet feels so bad he wishes he were gone." Such an exploration of themes unfolds slowly as the nurse empathizes with the child's viewpoint and feelings, and suggests that parents and staff who love a child do not want that child to be hurt. The nurse may also explain that the child who is developing a "self" and self-regard needs to learn not to allow any harm to the self.

Family Interventions. In family therapy, the nurse helps families lower suicide risk by improving communication, sharing feelings, reducing blaming, and enhancing self-esteem and constructive coping (Richman, 1986). Richman emphasized that a youngster's symptoms may indicate a family problem. Intervention with the family may mobilize resources and reduce distress. When nurses ignore the family dynamics that underlie potential suicide, the interventions with an individual child or adolescent may be ineffective or even counterproductive.

After a suicide attempt, families and clients typically deny or discount it. It is critically important to involve the family and youth in a meeting to: (1) understand the youth's feelings, (2) examine the messages of the attempt, (3) clarify the dynamics surrounding the suicide attempt, and (4) explore suicide risk among family members. Families who deny the serious nature of a suicide attempt can be encouraged to participate in a meeting; the nurse may say, for example, "Well, maybe you are right, and you know your child. However, the risk of ignoring any potential suicide is too high. Let's have a meeting to discuss what happened and find some safer solutions." The meeting can then focus on family communication, listening, and feelings.

Before the family meeting, the nurse may meet briefly with each family member to invite collaboration and to ask: (1) what that person thinks led up to this suicide attempt, (2) how this problem can be resolved, and (3) what are the family strengths and limitations? Richman (1986) recommended that each family member complete a drawing of a person and that these drawings be evaluated for suicide clues. Activities such as family sculpting, in which each member builds a people sculpture of family interaction according to his or her personal view, is a nonverbal technique useful with children or teen-agers. The nurse assesses family communication, rules, suicide risk, support systems, family interactions or norms, and evaluates the need for therapy to improve communication or interactions and to reduce suicide risk.

If the family refuses therapy and the youth is not an immediate suicide risk, the nurse should encourage the family to return by stressing the importance of monitoring suicide clues or warning signs and by asking each family member to make a no-suicide contract. The child or teen-ager can also be encouraged to return or to call teen hotlines or mental health services if distress or suicidal impulses recur. If the youth does not demonstrate these help-seeking abilities, the family should be alerted to the possibly increased suicide risk.

Individual Therapy. With the child experiencing suicidal ideation, the nurse should build a therapeutic alliance and focus on exploring feelings, improving self-esteem and social skills, developing safe coping strategies, examining development and conflict, and monitoring suicide risk.

As the nurse and Joy, aged 12, explored the meaning of Joy's suicide attempt and death wishes, they talked about other safety issues and potential hazards (e.g., use of seat belts, safe sex, safe dieting, and alcohol/drug use). To enhance self-esteem and coping, the nurse commented that Joy's overdose might have been her way of coping with painful feelings. After Joy talked about those feelings, the nurse asked what other, safer strategies might reduce the problems that trigger suicidal ideas.

Based on evidence that Joy had the capacity for many self-care activities, such as personal hygiene, nutrition, grooming, and socialization, the nurse planned a partly compensatory nursing system. Joy had self-care deficits in self-esteem, self-protection, and plans for living. Joy was motivated to improve her self-esteem, but was not sure how. Joy and the nurse identified the actions that each would take to reduce these deficits and decided to evaluate the actions and deficits weekly.

The nurse gave Joy an assignment to strengthen her self-esteem. Joy's task was to ask each teacher to praise one positive behavior and to ask each staff nurse what he or she liked about Joy. The nurse also asked Joy to identify three of her attributes that she herself liked. When Joy said, "nothing," the nurse noted that this is often a difficult task and requires practice. The nurse first held up a mirror and asked, "Do you like your hair, nose, or eyebrows?" Then, the nurse suggested positive attributes, such as "a really friendly smile."

The nurse also encouraged art therapy to help Joy express her feelings and develop self-esteem. At each session, the nurse explored any increase or change in suicidal feelings, depression, or self-esteem. Joy needed reminders that the nurse would implement safety precautions if Joy's suicidal feelings increased. Joy and the nurse agreed to monitor her feelings and coping strategies together.

Unless the client is having a suicidal crisis, suicide should not be the entire focus of therapy. This emphasizes a problem and neglects strengths and efforts to improve. Suicide risk requires careful monitoring, however.

Another task that Joy worked on with the nurse was creating a plan for living that included pleasurable activities to make life worthwhile. Joy enjoyed earning "off the ward" privileges and looked forward to going out for ice cream or a movie with the nurse.

According to Orem (1985), it is important to assess the ways in which youngsters at risk for suicide use their time to balance their needs for solitude and social interaction. For suicidal youths, long periods of time in solitary activities, such as watching TV or listening to music alone, are discouraged, and time with others in constructive, noncompetitive activities is encouraged.

When Joy reported feeling less suicidal, she started testing the staff. She said that, if "things didn't go well," she might become more suicidal. The nurse wanted to examine the dynamics behind these feelings; typically, youngsters feel anxious and frightened—and suicide risk may rise—as they improve. Although Joy's threats appeared to be manipulative, the nurse suspected that Joy was frightened; she feared that no one would care about her if she got well. The nurse needed to shore up Joy's self-esteem and asked care-givers to provide more attention and monitoring.

The nursing staff felt resentful that Joy was "threatening" to relapse into suicidal behavior; they recognized their countertransference feelings—fear that Joy might get worse; anger at apparent manipulation; and desire to overprotect and, perhaps, punish Joy with restrictions. When the therapist, multidisciplinary staff, and Joy discussed these interactions, Joy shared her fear of getting well and being abandoned. The group discussed Joy's keeping her family "focused" on her suicide threats and considered other ways to get attention and concern. Joy learned that the nursing staff would take threats seriously and would observe her carefully until her fear and suicide risk diminished. The staff also met with a consultant to discuss their countertransference.

Supportive-Educational Interventions

High-school suicide prevention programs help students, staff, faculty, administrators, and parents recognize danger signals and prevent suicide. Fearing that these programs may do more harm than good, critics have noted: (1) the lack of data to show that prevention programs reduce suicide rates, (2) the absence of program evaluation components, (3) the inadequate evidence of program cost-effectiveness, and (4) the concern that increasing suicide awareness may trigger suicides (Valente & Saunders, 1987). Nurses who understand adolescent development and suicide prevention can be instrumental in planning effective high-school prevention programs.

These programs offer diverse interventions. Some programs are linked to community mental health services that provide support groups or drop-in counselors. Some schools train students to become peer counselors who assess and refer students with depression or suicide risk. Teen-agers often share their suicidal ideas with peers, but the pressures on these peer counselors are unknown. Professional support and supervision should be available for peer counselors who grieve when their interventions have not prevented a suicide.

Most programs have no provision to reduce the impact of grief on the other students when one high-school student commits suicide, although bereavement may increase suicide risk. The most effective prevention programs are collaborations of school, community, and professional resources with select competent suicide prevention trainers. Nurses with valuable skills in assessing normal growth and development, as well as in preventing suicide, are important resources.

RESEARCH

Because nursing interventions with suicidal children and adolescents have been neglected by researchers, this is a fertile field for nursing research. There have been few comparative studies of youngsters who feel important, valued, capable, and loved, and who typically do not attempt suicide, and youngsters who do attempt suicide to identify the differences between these two groups.

Parker (1988) examined the relationship of life change events to adolescent suicidal behavior and found that adolescents who had attempted suicide had experienced more life change events than had other teen-agers. The psychometrics of the study have not yet been verified, however, so the basis for extending the results to other groups has not been established. Research data on risk factors, ethnicity, and primary methods of suicide are important as they help clinicians identify and evaluate teens at risk. Multiple variables are associated with suicidal behavior among hospitalized adolescents. Variables include:

- prior suicidal behaviors;
- depressive, personality and substance abuse disorders;
- hopelessness;
- preoccupation with death; problems with family, health, and friends.

Repeated suicidal behavior is associated with not being in the parental home, severity of initial suicidal behavior, age, gender, and ethnicity, and stress and loss (Pfeffer, 1989).

Nursing research should focus on several areas of suicide as it affects children and teen-agers: (1) identification of risk factors for children and adolescents, (2) effectiveness of high-school suicide prevention classes, (3) impact of bereavement on teen-age suicide, (4) effectiveness of selected nursing interventions on decreasing suicide attempts, (5) peer grief after an accidental death, and (6) at risk youth who do not attempt suicide.

REFERENCES

Berlin, I. (1987). Suicide among American Indian adolescents. *Suicide & Life Threatening Behavior,* *17*(3), 218–232.

Centers for Disease Control. (1985). *Suicide surveillance, 1970–1980.* Atlanta: U.S. Department of Health and Human Services.

Farberow, N. (1981). Suicide prevention in the hospital. *Hospital and Community Psychiatry, 32,* 99–104.

Freud, S. (1949). *Mourning and melancholia: Vol. 4. Selected Papers.* London: Hogarth Press. (Original work published 1916).

Gilead, M.P., & Mulaik, J.S. (1983). Adolescent suicide: A response to a developmental crisis. *Perspectives in Psychiatric Care, 21*(3), 94–101.

Gould, M.S., & Shaffer, D. (1986). The impact of suicide in television movies. *New England Journal of Medicine, 315,* 690–694.

Kerfoot, M. (1984). Assessment of the young adolescent. In C.L. Hatton & S.M. Valente (Eds.), *Suicide: Assessment and intervention* (2nd ed., pp. 195–208). Norwalk, CT: Appleton & Lange.

Kerr, J.A.C. (1985). A case of adolescent turmoil: Use of the self-care model. In J. Riehl-Sisca (Ed.), *The science and art of self-care* (pp. 105–112). Norwalk, CT: Appleton-Century-Crofts.

Lester, D. (1974). Demographic versus clinical predictors of suicidal behaviors. In A.T. Beck, H.L.P. Resnick, & D.J. Lettieri (Eds.), *The prediction of suicide* (pp. 71–84). MD: Charles Press.

McIntosh, J., & Jewell, B. (1986). Sex difference trends. *Suicide and Life Threatening Behavior, 16,* 16–27.

Orem, D.E. (1985). *Nursing: Concepts of practice* (3rd ed.). New York: McGraw-Hill.

Parker, S.D. (1988). Accident or suicide? Do life change events lead to adolescent suicide? *Journal of Psychosocial Nursing and Mental Health Services, 26*(6), 15–19.

Pfeffer, C. (1986). *The suicidal child.* New York: Guilford Press.

Pfeffer, C. (1989). Suicidal preadolescents and adolescent inpatients. *Suicide & Life Threatening Behavior, 19*(1), 58–77.

Pope, B., & Scott, W.H. (1967). *Psychological diagnosis.* London: Oxford University Press.

Richman, J. (1986). *Family therapy for suicidal people.* New York: Springer.

Smith, K., & Crawford (1986). Suicidal behavior among "normal" high school students. *Suicide & Life Threatening Behavior, 16*(3), 313–325.

Taylor, S.G. (1989). Nursing theory and nursing process: Orem's theory in practice. *Nursing Science Quarterly, 3,* 111–114.

Underwood, P. (1980). Facilitating self care. In P. Pothier (Ed.), *Psychiatric nursing* (pp. 18–30). Boston: Little, Brown.

Valente, S.M. (1987a). Assessing families with a suicidal teenager. In M. Leahey & L. Wright (Eds.), *Families and psychosocial problems* (pp. 78–94). Springhouse, PA: Springhouse.

Valente, S.M. (1987b). Preventing childhood suicide. *Journal of Pediatric Health Care, 1,* 1–5.

Valente, S.M., & Saunders, J.M. (1987). High school suicide prevention programs. *Pediatric Nursing, 13,* 108–112, 137, 139.

Valente, S.M., & Sellers, J.R. (1989). Effective coping. In D. Corr & C. Corr (Eds.), *Nursing care in an aging society.* New York: Springer.

23

Nursing Interventions with Children and Adolescents Experiencing Thought Disorders

Geraldine S. Pearson

After reading this chapter, the reader will be able to:

1. define the etiology of disorders in thinking and differentiate the various ways in which they may be manifested
2. elaborate on behavior implications of a thought disorder in children and adolescents
3. describe the nursing implications of the psychotropic medications used in the treatment of the thought-disordered child or adolescent
4. delineate the planning and coordination of nursing care of the thought-disordered child or adolescent within various treatment settings and with various treatment modalities
5. develop nursing intervention strategies with youngsters experiencing alterations in thought processes
6. discuss the nursing research implications of the clinical management of the thought-disordered child or adolescent

Thought disorders in children and adolescents are relatively rare phenomena, yet nurses who work in a variety of psychiatric and nonpsychiatric settings are likely to encounter children and adolescents with such disorders. The nursing care required by these individuals presents particularly difficult challenges. The manifestation of the disorder, its severity, and the age of onset all influence the nursing process. Often, these individuals have disturbed peer and family relationships that also require nursing interventions.

A thought disorder is considered one part of the diagnostic matrix encompassing psychosis. Diagnosing a thought disorder in a preverbal or mute child is difficult, because verbal cues most often help nurses identify the content and nature of the disturbance. Nurses are frequently the first professional health care contact (e.g., in school or in a health clinic), however, and they may be first to note any oddity in speech or behavior suggestive of a thought disorder. With adolescents,

329

the assessment of a disturbance in thinking is usually easier because verbal norms are more easily assessed and identifiably violated.

Psychotic disorders in youngsters are characterized by altered contact with reality. The psychotic individual is attempting to adapt to a subjectively distorted concept of the world. The onset of such a disorder generally falls into one of two time frames. Those disorders that occur in the first year or two of development are characterized as pervasive developmental disorders; they seriously distort development and result in long-term residual deficits. Barker (1983) pointed out that it is almost impossible to determine the level of cognitive functioning that a psychotic child might have achieved had the child not become psychotic. Hence, it can be difficult to differentiate a psychosis from a mental handicap. Currently, children with early onset psychosis who may appear autistic are categorized as developmentally impaired.

In later childhood, more particularly in adolescence, psychoses are more likely to resemble the process of adult schizophrenia (Rutter, 1976; Vrono, 1974). These individuals have had a more developmentally normal history, and the psychosis or thought disorder occurs after verbal and cognitive abilities are more fully developed.

Obviously, for psychiatric nurses, an understanding of thought disorders, their etiology, and their manifestations is imperative to providing nursing care. Wilson's (1988) concept of "humanistic interactionism" moves the psychiatric nurse away from a medical/biological explanation of the disorder and instead encourages a view of the dysfunction within a holistic framework that encompasses the individual's mind, body, and the associated environmental interactions.

DEVELOPMENT OF THOUGHT DISORDERS

Schizophrenia is extremely rare during the school-age years; 15 to 20 years is a common age for its initial onset. The causes of schizophrenic psychosis in childhood and adolescence are unknown. Although genetic predisposition probably plays a part, metabolic or biochemical abnormalities, environmental stresses, or family behavior have not been proved to be causes of psychosis.

As Burgess (1985) noted, there are several types of thought disorders:

- blocking: an abrupt stop in the middle of a sentence or thought with no explanation for the ending.
- circumstantiality: verbalization of unnecessary, extraneous detail before articulation of the central idea of thought.
- delusions: unusual or bizarre beliefs unexplained by logic or experience. Types include persecutory, somatic, grandeur, guilt, and influence.
- echolalia: repetition of words used by another person or an echoing of another's statements.

- flight of ideas: thoughts that lack logical connections.
- hallucinations: disorders in perception. Types include visual, auditory, olfactory, tactile, gustatory, or visceral.
- loose associations: lack of logical order in the content of the thought.
- perseveration: same response to different questions or situations.
- retardation: a slowing of thoughts with labored speech and difficulty formulating an idea.
- word salad: a nonsensical mixture of words.

Clinically, children with thought disorders appear odd or shy. They are often withdrawn from peers and family; they may have experienced language delays. "At the outset there is a change of personality and alteration of the contact the child makes, on an emotional level, with the environment" (Barker, 1983, p. 112). Emotional reactions to people or events may not fit the reality of the situation. Thought disorders may be identifiable, although it may be difficult to differentiate delusions from fantasy. Auditory hallucinations may occur. Behavioral cues include a drop in school performance, self-isolation, or bizarre movements or postures.

In addition to the behaviors that have been described, adolescents can exhibit signs of a Paranoid Schizophrenia. This disorder rarely develops in childhood, but is common in the teen-age years. The adolescent with this type of thought disorder falsely believes that he or she is being persecuted. Signs of Paranoid Schizophrenia can include impulsivity, aggressiveness, and hallucinations.

Systemic infections, intracranial infections, acute brain injury, and chemical intoxications can trigger transient thought disorders in children and adolescents. The thought disorders caused by these conditions usually resolve when the cause is removed.

ASSESSMENT OF THOUGHT DISORDERS

The presence of a thought disorder is best assessed by listening to the content of an individual's speech. Any unusual flow or rhythm, or any other peculiarities, may indicate a need for further assessment. It is important to determine whether the individual communicates thoughts in a clear, coherent manner, although the evaluator must take into account the fact that articulation disorders, developmental delays, and age-appropriate behaviors can influence responses. The circumstances of the assessment must also be considered. Anxiety about a strange setting and unfamiliar people might contribute to poor communication patterns, for example. The younger the child, the more age-appropriate such disorientation. Although an adolescent also normally experiences some initial discomfort in a new situation, the adolescent is likely to have more social ease. Disorientation to the point of stress should not be taken alone as sign of a thought disorder. Careful assessment over several interactions is necessary for definitive assessment. It is helpful to adopt a systems approach to assessment with children and adolescents who have a thought disorder.

Personal System: Assessment of Mental Status

As defined by King (1981), the personal system is composed of perception, self, growth and development, body image, time, and space. These concepts, as well as a knowledge of normal growth and development, help nurses understand individuals as dynamic open systems. An assessment of mental status is one way to begin understanding individual children and adolescents.

Two levels of data are obtained in a mental status assessment (Greenspan, 1981). The first is the descriptive level (i.e., observed behavior), while the second is the age-appropriate level (i.e., developmental stage functioning). Nurses must assess both levels when assessing a thought disorder. For example, a 3-year-old with an imaginary friend is expressing age-appropriate fantasies, but such thoughts in a 12-year-old are deviant from age-appropriate norms.

The assessment of mental status in children differs radically from the formal mental status examinations done with adults. Assessment of the child is more subjective, less structured, and related to a broad range of developmental norms. Formal adult mental status examinations can be used with older adolescents, however. Exhibit 23-1, adapted from the *Mental Status Examination of Children*, developed by Goodman and Sours (1967), is useful for both children and adolescents.

Interpersonal System: Assessment of Relationships with Others

The concept of interpersonal systems involves the interaction and communication between individuals and groups (King, 1981). When assessing the relationships of the child or adolescent with others, first consideration must be given to the nuclear family. Beyond that, the interpersonal system widens to include relationships with extended family, neighborhood peers, and other adults.

Assessment involves identifying the child's role in the nuclear family and the child's relationship with parents, siblings, and others who live in the home. Typically, the youngster who has a thought disorder causes stress in the family system. Wynne (1970) noted that family members are often preoccupied with establishing a "sense of relatedness" with the youngster at the expense of self-differentiation, goal directedness, and language usage generally accepted by others. In other words, family members often try to deal with the child or adolescent who has a thought disorder by denying their own needs. Such a youngster requires many levels of intervention, often at the expense of family members.

It is also necessary to examine family members' individual feelings about the youngster. Is blaming or guilt part of the reaction? Do the parents search exhaus-

Exhibit 23-1 Assessment of Mental Status in Children and Adolescents

While the assessment of mental status involves a number of other areas of function, including level of activity, coordination, and intellectual capacity, the following areas are addressed as they pertain most clearly to thought disorders in both children and adolescents. Each category is divided into areas for observation and corresponding questions that can be asked by the nurse.

General Appearance

- Observations
  1. How does the child look?
  2. What is the child's level of activity? Does he/she appear nervous, bite fingernails, suck his/her thumb or fingers, or walk on tiptoe?
  3. What is the child's level of alertness?
  4. How are the child's skills in grooming and self-care? Are they age-appropriate to normative?
  5. Does the child lick, smell, or habitually touch objects in the environment?
- Questions
  1. What is your favorite aspect of your body?
  2. What don't you like about your body?
  3. Draw me a picture of a person or of yourself.

Speech

- Observations
  1. Are there any articulation defects?
  2. What are receptive capacities versus expressive capacities?
  3. Does the level of meaningful conversation correspond with age-appropriate norms?
  4. Are the rhythm, rate, organization, and syntax of speech normal?
  5. How is anxiety represented in speech patterns?
  6. Is the child echolalic?
  7. Does the child use correct gender pronouns?
- Question
  1. Direct a complex question to the child; for example, what kinds of snacks do you and your friends eat when you come home from school?

Modes of Thinking and Perception

- Observations
  1. Does the preschooler express thought through motoric action? Does the school-aged child rely on speech to express thought?
  2. What is the child's self-concept?
  3. Is the child mistrustful of unfamiliar adults or overly friendly?
- Question
  1. Tell a story about something happy/painful/sad that happened at school. (Note organization of thinking and the ability to express organized thoughts.)

continues

Exhibit 23-1 Continued

Emotional Reactions

- Observations
  1. When does the child show emotion and how is it expressed?
  2. What is the child's general mood, and how does it vary?
  3. What range of emotions are expressed?
- Question
  1. Describe situations that make you sad, mad, happy, or scared.

Manner of Relating

- Observations
  1. What is the child's level of independence relative to his/her age?
  2. Does the child make eye contact?
  3. Is the child curious?
  4. Is the child negativistic or oppositional?
- Question
  1. Do you want to ask me any questions about myself?

Fantasies and Dreams

- Observations
  1. Is the child's concept of a dream as a "real" occurrence an appropriate belief relative to age?
  2. Are fantasies vivid, structured, repetitive, and pleasurable or frightening, scary, and accompanied by pressured speech and lack of behavioral control?
  3. What themes are evident in fantasy stories or dreams?
  4. Do fantasies engulf the child's thoughts, making reality orientation difficult?
  5. Does the child have an ability to distinguish which fantasy thoughts are real and which are not?
- Questions
  1. Do you think your dream really happened?
  2. If you could have three wishes, what would they be? Explain.
  3. What is your most favorite and least favorite animal? Why?

Character of Play

- Observations
  1. Is play persistent, repetitive, age-appropriate, or orderly?
  2. What is the level and type of emotional intensity?
  3. Can the child initiate play when provided with play materials such as paper, crayons, dolls, puppets, or a dollhouse?
  4. Is play goal directed or fragmented?
  5. What is the child's attention span?

tively for reasons why their child is not "normal"? Do nuclear family members have to defend the affected child to extended family members who have a poor tolerance or understanding of behavioral aberrations? Does the family try to hide or deny the child's thought disorder?

Recent and past changes in the youngster's relationships with others outside the family may indicate the changing degrees of disordered thought presented to others. Parents can indicate the level of tolerance in the community. In some small, close-knit neighborhoods, tolerance can be quite high; in others, there is more scapegoating. The broader interpersonal relationships with neighborhood peers and adults are likely to involve more rejection of these children, less understanding of their problems, and decreased tolerance for odd speech or behavior.

In general, the nurse should assess the youngster's level of relatedness to others, the status of peer relationships, and the precipitating events around the request for psychiatric care. The nurse must also carefully assess the youngster's verbal and nonverbal communication patterns and the ways that these patterns affect relationships.

Social System: Assessment of Functioning in the Community

According to King (1981), social systems represent the dynamics of society in which the change process alters the environment. "A social system is defined as an organized boundary system of social roles, behaviors, and practices developed to maintain values and the mechanisms to regulate the practices and rules" (King, 1981, p. 115). Social systems include family systems, religious or belief systems, or educational and work systems.

As individuals mature, they become part of more and more social systems beyond the initial system of the family. Thus, young children are likely to be involved with fewer social systems than are their adolescent counterparts. For both populations, the nurse must examine the impact of the system's rules and boundaries on the individual's behavior, as well as the individual's impact on the system's functioning.

It is important to determine whether the individual's level of socialization is age-appropriate. To what degree does the youngster's functioning deviate or conform to the norms of the social systems within which he or she functions? The nurse must also determine whether the youngster's behavior fits within the cultural expectations of the community. Defining the ways in which a youngster with a thought disorder has violated normative values, behavior patterns, and prescribed roles is crucial to planning interventions that help the youngster begin to function within the culture of the community. Most often, the greater the disorder of perception and communication patterns, the greater the deviation from social system norms.

NURSING INTERVENTIONS

The systems framework of nursing, when used in planning care, is especially useful for children and adolescents with a thought disorder. Because of their youth and their obvious involvement with home, school, and community, interventions ideally involve multiple arenas of their lives. King (1981) noted that patients and nurses "communicate information, mutually set goals, and take action to attain goals" (p. 157).

Personal System Interventions

Nursing interventions in the personal system are focused on helping youngsters with a thought disorder process information from the environment and "give meaning and stability to their world" (King, 1981, p. 19). Children and adolescents may be hospitalized in a psychiatric milieu if their disturbed thought compromises their functioning in home or community. Many milieu interventions are applicable to individual or family treatment.

King (1981) stated that "perception is each human's representation of reality" (p. 20). For thought-disordered youngsters, this reality is distorted. In their minds, some people may assume unreal or macabre identities, the walls in their room may move or crawl with snakes, and it may seem that people are staring or laughing. Nursing interventions focus on understanding the perceptions of self, others, and the environment and on continually clarifying these perceptions.

Nursing diagnoses can assist in this clarification. Diagnoses that apply to the thought-disordered child or adolescent include Altered Knowledge Processes, as development is often compromised when mental deficiencies result in a knowledge deficit; Altered Memory, in which memories may be distorted and delusional; Abuse Response Pattern, which may be characterized by flashbacks in which the youngster relives the trauma of abuse and may, therefore, appear thought-disordered; and Altered Communication Processes, which may be manifested as difficulty in expressing thoughts and odd, nonverbal ways of expression (e.g., grimaces or hand gestures).

Poor peer relationships and social isolation suggest the nursing diagnosis of Altered Social Interaction. Other nursing diagnoses that could apply to the thought-disordered individual include Altered Self Concept and Altered Sensory Perception. The nursing care plan can be developed after identification of the most pertinent nursing diagnoses.

Orientation to the Milieu

Separation from family can be difficult as the child or adolescent comes onto the psychiatric unit. The nurse must take a firm and supportive stance, clarifying, with both the family and the client, the boundaries around visits and telephone calls. Helping youngsters show family members their room can ease the transition away from family.

When orienting a youngster who has a thought disorder to the rules of the unit, it is imperative that the nurse speak clearly, slowly, and in simple terms, gearing communication to the youngster's ability to understand at that moment. It may be necessary to repeat directives several times before the youngster comprehends them, and the youngster may forget ward rules at times of stress when thought is most disordered. The youngster may need frequent reminders about staff and patient names, orientation to time and place, and specific rules.

Behavioral cues that the youngster may feel sensory overload include covering the ears or eyes with the hands, walking away during a conversation, making repetitive movements (e.g., rocking), and talking in incoherent word salads. The goal of care at this time is to decrease stimulation and restore stability, gearing the orientation to the youngster's level of tolerance for new information.

The unit program for thought-disordered youngsters should be predictable and clear, as these youngsters easily distort time and other factors of reality. They feel safest when nursing staff and unit routines are most consistent.

Self in Relation to the Environment

The youngster who has a thought disorder may need protection from peers on the unit during the early stages of the hospitalization, when the setting is unfamiliar and the youngster has not learned the cultural rules of the milieu. These youngsters need constant reminders of time and space boundaries, such as mealtimes and the location of their rooms. Visual aids, such as charts or written schedules, assist in this process. For youngsters with poor reading skills, pictorial charts are useful.

Nurses must constantly monitor the peer issues that can emerge with these youngsters on an inpatient psychiatric unit. It is imperative to assist other children and adolescents on the unit in understanding the behavior that can sometimes be presented by a psychotic youngster. Peers can be directed to assist in orientation to the unit rules and can be coached to ignore behaviors that may seem attention seeking, but are in reality the result of the disordered thinking.

Attainment of Age-Appropriate Skills

The initial assessment of a youngster's ability to perform the activities of daily living (ADL) may be inaccurate if the youngster was acutely disordered and in crisis at the time. Frequent assessment of ADL skills is essential. Teaching is planned according to what the client can tolerate interpersonally. Certainly, the youngster who is actively hallucinating is less likely to understand teaching around ADL skills, and his or her condition must be stabilized, usually with psychotropic medication, before teaching can take place. The nurse's role with the most actively psychotic individual is to support strengths without creating unnecessary dependency while normalizing age-appropriate ADL skills. Simplifying the intervention to coincide with the youngster's level of distortion in perceptions, avoiding the infantilization of the youngster, and maximizing functioning are all nursing care goals.

Safety

The use of seclusion allows nurses to maintain a youngster's safety. It gives the child or adolescent a chance to regain equilibrium. Nurses maintain a youngster's safety in a number of ways. Seclusion should be used judiciously, however, especially if the client is actively hallucinating or is likely to become frightened by the confines of a seclusion room. Nursing interventions include frequent checks on the client and short timeouts in seclusion, whether in a quiet room or in a bedroom. The goal is to help youngsters avoid isolation while keeping them safe. Reintegration into the milieu as quickly as possible is essential.

Use of Psychotropic Medications

Although the use of medication is known to be effective for adult patients with a psychotic disorder, there has been no systematic review of the use of antipsychotics for treatment of a thought disorder in children and adolescents (Campbell & Spencer, 1988). It has been hypothesized that the reason for this is the rarity of a schizophrenic diagnosis prior to the onset of puberty (Kydd & Werry, 1982). Even though psychosis becomes more evident during puberty, only a few studies have been published pertaining to the use of antipsychotic medication in this age group (Pool, Bloom, Mielke, Roniger, & Gallant, 1976; Realmuto, Erickson, Yellin, Hopwood, & Greenberg, 1984).

Campbell and Spencer (1988) noted that, according to limited clinical experience, antipsychotics are indicated in prepubertal schizophrenic children, but they are much less effective in these children than in adults. They postulated that the early onset of a psychotic disturbance has a more pervasive effect on developing functions in a child than in an adult. They also recommended that the drugs of choice may be high-potency antipsychotics, such as haloperidol and thiothixene, because of their lesser sedative effect at therapeutic dosages. It is imperative that baseline and interval blood studies be conducted to monitor blood cell count and liver function. Four weeks is recommended as an appropriate trial period.

The goal of medication use is to allow the youngster to maximize functioning and to continue moving along a continuum of age-appropriate growth and development that would be compromised if the thought disorder were left untreated. As with all medications, nurses must be alert to the acceptable pediatric dosages and side-effects of psychotropic medications. Side-effects can include extrapyramidal symptoms, such as muscle spasms, motor restlessness, and tardive dyskinesia. Anticholinergic side-effects can include blurred vision, dry mouth, nasal congestion, constipation, and urinary hesitancy or retention (Harris, 1988).

Children and adolescents are entitled to an explanation of the purpose of their medication, its benefits, and its possible side-effects. The treatment team, including the nurse, usually decides the complexity of the explanation possible, based on the severity of disorder and the developmental stage of the client. Yet, it is the nurse who teaches children and families about psychotropics and deals with ongoing questions and day-to-day management.

Nurses must be aware of the provisions of state statutes regarding the right of a child or adolescent to refuse a medication and the right of parents to deny permission for the administration of medication to their child. Nurses can assess potential resistance prior to the actual refusal and can begin immediate assessment and intervention. Family cooperation is imperative for the success of drug therapy.

Interpersonal System Interventions

Nursing interventions in the interpersonal system of the child or adolescent who is experiencing a thought disorder initially focus on helping the youngster begin to understand the verbal and nonverbal cues in the environment in order to maximize functioning. Identifying the exact nature of the thought disorder and the ways in which it is manifested clarify the child's ability to understand such cues. The nurse must continually reassess the ability of these children to interact with their environment.

Play therapy with these children should include structured games and activities geared toward reality orientation. For adolescents, talking therapy may improve socialization skills. For both groups, the goal is to avoid fantasy activities that perpetuate the delusional system.

Group treatment is sometimes beneficial for the individual with a thought disorder, usually after a period of stabilization. The nurse must assess the other group members' level of functioning relative to the individual, however. Children who have a thought disorder often do well in groups of children with various levels of functioning, but careful monitoring is necessary to ensure that they are not scapegoated. The group can also, at times, use the individual's bizarre behavior to avoid dealing with their own issues. This is more likely to occur in a milieu psychotherapy group than in a community meeting where individual issues may be diluted. Because psychotic youngsters are unable to tolerate affective stimulation, it may be wise to include them in group psychotherapy for only short periods. Introduction to community meetings in the milieu, which facilitate reality testing and orientation, is a positive way of integrating the thought-disordered individual. These youngsters are frequently unable to tolerate the intensity of group psychotherapy to deal with past issues and feelings.

Interpersonal system interventions include the family. Many nurses have found a psychoeducational model useful in working with the families of children with thought disorders. In this model, parents and siblings are helped to understand the disorder, the use of medication in treatment, and treatment strategies that can be applied at home. Management issues are often major concerns, and families need support to provide structured discipline and reality orientation. Nurses can help families foster age-appropriate independence, as overprotectiveness is a common response to the child or adolescent who seems unable to care for self.

Parents need to grieve for the loss of what they may previously have perceived as a "normal" child. Olshansky (1965-1966) cited the presence of "chronic sorrow" in parents who have a child with a disability, especially if the child's disability compromises his or her future level of adult independence as a psychiatric disorder does. This grief process is not readily resolved and usually lasts the lifetime of the child, becoming particularly intense during each acute episode of psychosis. Family members are key players in helping the youngster maintain a functional level of adjustment, however. The care that they provide can often help avoid hospitalization and can help the youngster maximize potential.

Finally, nurses and other staff who work with thought-disordered children or adolescents must be aware of their own feelings for the youngsters and their sometimes bizarre behaviors and verbal communications. While adolescents tend to be verbal with their delusions and hallucinations, young children act out. These children tax the creativity of a milieu staff, and feelings of countertransference require close monitoring.

Social System Interventions

Nurses intervene most effectively in social systems by assessing attitudes held about the thought-disordered youngster within these systems. It is essential to clarify perceptions and associated feelings generated by past or present dysfunctional behaviors. A well-documented baseline of behaviors makes it possible to predict the points at which more intense intervention is needed. The nurse can educate those in schools and community settings about the child's predictable reaction to their environment, for example.

Nurses work with community agencies, often arranging needed services, decreasing hesitancy around providing services, and educating personnel about psychiatric disorders. Correcting misperceptions about individuals with a thought disorder is one of the most important tasks of psychiatric nurses. Sometimes, the simple explanation that the child with a thought disorder is not dangerous may secure an opportunity for the child to receive needed services in the community. Children with a thought disorder are frequently in special school programs where teachers and administrators are able to meet their needs. The availability of needed psychiatric services to stabilize behavior at a point of crisis facilitates the community system's willingness to resume providing care.

RESEARCH

Although there is a paucity of nursing research on the outcomes of effective nursing care with youngsters who are experiencing thought disorders, there is some literature on management of these clients from a nursing perspective (Grossman & Herrmann, 1985; Wilkinson, 1983). Other disciplines have focused their current research on the use of psychotropic medication with thought disorders; outcome measures around the efficacy of community services; and the etiology of the disorder, especially in children (Arboleda & Holzman, 1985; Caplan, Guthrie, Fish, Tanguay, & David-Lando, 1989; Kolvin, 1971; Tanquay & Cantor, 1986). They have found that psychotropic medication assists in management of thought disorder and that community services help patients avoid psychiatric hospitalization. The etiology of thought disorder in children has been less clearly delineated by research.

Future nursing research focused on King's (1981) personal, interpersonal, and social system perspectives could be very helpful. In the personal system, for example, research might reveal the types of nursing interventions that are most effective in milieu treatment and the behavioral cues that indicate the progress of these children in the system. Research from an interpersonal system perspective could focus on the nuances of communication or environmental factors that assist the individual in regaining ADL skills or improved reality testing. Nurses could investigate educational models for effectively teaching ADL, the use of peer interaction to facilitate change, and the use of group therapy.

Within the social system, youngsters with a thought disorder are frequently grouped with children who are deemed chronically mentally ill (Looney, 1989). This population of children receives poor and uncoordinated service, especially if the children are from an economically deprived background. Nursing research could focus on methods for the early detection of thought disorders and the most effective ways to ensure that treatment begins early and continues in a coordinated way throughout the child's life.

REFERENCES

Arboleda, C., & Holzman, P.S. (1985). Thought disorder in children at risk for psychosis. *Archives of General Psychiatry, 42,* 1004–1013.

Barker, P.B. (1983). *Basic child psychiatry* (4th ed.). Baltimore: University Park Press.

Burgess, A.W. (1985). *Psychiatric nursing in the hospital and the community* (4th ed.). Englewood Cliffs, NJ: Prentice-Hall.

Campbell, M., & Spencer, E.K. (1988). Psychopharmacology in child and adolescent psychiatry: A review of the past five years. *Journal of the American Academy of Child and Adolescent Psychiatry, 27,* 269–279.

Caplan, R., Guthrie, D., Fish, B., Tanguay, P.E., & David-Lando, G. (1989). The Kiddie Formal Thought Disorder Rating Scale: Clinical assessment, reliability, and validity. *Journal of the American Academy of Child and Adolescent Psychiatry, 28,* 408–416.

Goodman, J.D., & Sours, J.A. (1967). *The child mental status examination.* New York: Basic Books.

Greenspan, S.I. (1981). *The clinical interview of the child.* New York: McGraw-Hill.

Grossman, J., & Herrmann, C. (1985). Nursing care of the child with a psychiatric or social disorder. In S. Mott, N. Fazelcas, & J. James (Eds.), *Nursing care of children and families* (pp. 811–842). Menlo Park, CA: Addison-Wesley.

Harris, E. (1988). The antipsychotics. *American Journal of Nursing, 88,* 1508–1511.

King, I.M. (1981). *Theory for nursing: Systems, concepts, process.* New York: John Wiley & Sons.

Kolvin, I. (1971). Studies in childhood psychoses. *British Journal of Psychiatry, 118,* 381–384.

Kydd, R.R., & Werry, J.S. (1982). Schizophrenia in children under sixteen years. *Journal of Autism and Developmental Disorders, 12,* 343–357.

Looney, J.G. (Ed.). (1989). *Chronic mental illness in children and adolescents.* Washington, DC: American Psychiatric Press.

Olshansky, S. (1965-1966). Parent responses to a mentally defective child. *Mental Retardation, 3-4,* 21–23.

Pool, D., Bloom, W., Mielke, D.H., Roniger, J.J., & Gallant, D.M. (1976). A controlled evaluation of loxitane in seventy-five adolescent schizophrenic patients. *Current Therapeutic Research: Clinical and Experimental, 19,* 99–104.

Realmuto, G.M., Erickson, W.D., Yellin, A.M., Hopwood, J.H., & Greenberg, L.M. (1984). Clinical comparison of thiothixene and thioridazine in schizophrenic adolescents. *American Journal of Psychiatry, 141,* 440–442.

Rutter, M. (1976). Infantile autism and other child psychoses. In M. Rutter & L. Herson (Eds.), *Child psychiatry: Modern approaches* (pp. 717–747). Oxford: Blackwell.

Tanquay, P., & Cantor, S. (1986). Schizophrenia in children: Introduction. *Journal of the American Academy of Child Psychiatry, 25,* 591–594.

Vrono, M. (1974). Schizophrenia in childhood and adolescence. *International Journal of Mental Health, 2,* 1–116.

Wilkinson, T. (1983). *Child and adolescent psychiatric nursing.* Boston: Blackwell Scientific.

Wilson, H.S. (1988). Philosophical perspectives. In H.S. Wilson & C.P. Kneisl (Eds.), *Psychiatric nursing* (3rd ed., pp. 2–9). Menlo Park, CA: Addison-Wesley.

Wynne, L.C. (1970). Communication disorders and the quest for relatedness in families of schizophrenics. *American Journal of Psychoanalysis, 30,* 100–114.

24

Nursing Interventions with Children and Adolescents Experiencing Eating Difficulties

Catherine Gray Deering

After reading this chapter, the reader will be able to:

1. identify the major characteristics and dynamics of eating problems
2. describe the specific considerations for nursing assessment of adolescents who have eating disorders
3. discuss nursing interventions that can be implemented through milieu, group, individual, and family therapy

Eating problems, particularly anorexia and bulimia, have become increasingly prevalent over the past 50 years (Russell, 1985). Most clinicians and theorists believe that this is due to current societal emphasis on slimness and perfect body shapes, especially for women. The common eating problems of childhood and adolescence include obesity, pica, anorexia, and bulemia. Obesity is not usually conceptualized as a mental health problem, but its effects on a child's development, self-esteem, social interactions, and physical health are obvious. Because of this, many innovative approaches have been developed to prevent and treat childhood obesity. Pica, the persistent ingestion of nonnutritive substances (e.g., paint or plaster), is a much less common eating problem that usually accompanies other significant mental health problems. In essence, both obesity and pica are symptoms of more generalized individual or family problems that often become the major focus of child psychiatric nursing interventions. Rarely is a child admitted for psychiatric treatment for obesity or pica alone. In contrast, anorexia and bulimia are pervasive mental health problems that are frequently the focus of child psychiatric treatment.

Anorexia and bulimia are basically problems of female adolescence. Some 90% to 95% of anorexics and bulimics are female (Garfinkel & Garner, 1982). These disorders are estimated to affect 5% to 18% of young women (Halmi, Falk, & Schwartz, 1981; Pope, Hudson, & Yurgelun-Todd, 1984a, 1984b). Whereas the usual onset of anorexia is around the time of puberty, bulimia most often begins in middle to late adolescence. Although bulimia is known to be much more common than anorexia, it is easier to conceal and often goes undiagnosed.

There is considerable overlap between anorexic and bulimic behavior. The problems may shift back and forth, but one pattern usually predominates. The hallmark of anorexia is severe weight loss. The major nursing diagnoses associated with the anorexic pattern include Alteration in Nutrition (less than body requirements), Alteration in Body Image, Altered Thought Content (obsession with food and weight), and Altered Hormone Regulation (loss of at least three consecutive menstrual periods).

The main characteristic of bulimia is the binge-purge cycle, which consists of the rapid eating of large amounts of food followed by the implementation of a weight control method, such as induced vomiting, laxative or diuretic abuse, starvation, or compulsive exercise. The main nursing diagnoses associated with bulimia include Altered Eating (compulsive binge episodes); Altered Self-concept (low self-esteem, poor body image); and Potential for Fluid Deficit or Electrolyte Imbalance due to Vomiting, Laxative Abuse, or Diuretic Abuse. Bulimia goes beyond the normal periodic eating binges associated with adolescence and involves at least two major binges per week. These binges are highly distressing to the adolescent and lead to a frightening sense of a lack of control. Bulimic adolescents also have more than the usual concerns about their body shape and weight, even though they are usually within optimal weight ranges.

ASSESSMENT

The nursing care of clients who have eating problems can easily be viewed from the perspective of systems theory, because the symptoms affect all levels of the biopsychosocial system. In addition to a thorough general assessment process, some specific aspects of each subsystem should be explored in the nursing history.

Biological Subsystem

A thorough physical examination is very important in view of the serious physical problems that can result from anorexia and bulimia. The symptoms of anorexia develop in reaction to severe weight loss. They may include hypothermia, bradycardia, hypotension, cardiac arrhythmia, amenorrhea, constipation, dizziness, edema, lanugo, stunted growth, hair loss, osteoporosis, and death from starvation. Signs of bulimia may include muscle weakness, menstrual irregularities, esophagitis, pharyngitis, gastritis, bloody diarrhea from laxative abuse, swollen parotid glands, hemorrhages in the conjunctiva, erosion of dental enamel, abrasions on the knuckles caused by inducing vomiting, and, in rare cases, death by cardiac arrest. A review of laboratory findings may reveal other evidence of starvation or vomiting, including potassium depletion, electrocardiogram changes, elevated blood urea nitrogen (BUN) levels, a low white blood cell count, decreased concentrations of triiodothyronine (T_3) and thyroxine (T_4), decreased levels of luteinizing hormone (LH) and follicle-stimulating hormone (FSH) (Bennett, Pleak, & Silverman, 1988). Because clients often deny the seriousness of eating problems, an emphasis on these concrete physical findings may help to underscore the need for intervention. As treatment progresses, the ongoing nursing assessment should include daily weighing and careful monitoring of changes in any of these physical symptoms.

For taking the initial history, the nurse should have a checklist of supplementary questions that track fluctuations in weight and focus on the methods of weight control used, including starvation, excessive exercise, bingeing, vomiting, laxative or diuretic use, diet pill use, and ipecac-induced vomiting. The use of ipecac is particularly dangerous, because it may cause fatal cardiac arrhythmias (Adler, Walinsky, Krall, & Cho, 1980). Most clients conceal their eating habits out of shame, fear, or denial. Direct questions about specific weight control methods are necessary to elicit accurate information, and they convey the nurse's willingness to discuss this sensitive area. Without direct questioning, significant behaviors are likely to remain secret.

Psychological/Emotional Subsystem

Adolescents with eating problems have a fairly uniform pattern of typical concerns. The most striking is the constant preoccupation with food and weight, and the fear of loss of control over eating. Some adolescents develop obsessive-compulsive behavior (e.g., constantly checking the scales, exercising compulsively, following rigid diet patterns), as well as anxiety attacks that seem to originate in their fear of losing control. Their harsh, negative, distorted views of their bodies cause them to focus constantly on the need for weight control. For anorexic adolescents, the body image distortion may be of delusional proportions, as they view themselves as fat even when their weight drops below 100 pounds. This overconcern with physical appearance often masks a generalized low self-esteem and a tendency toward self-deprecating thoughts in all areas of their lives. Other typical patterns include problems with separation-individuation, sexual identity and/or sexuality, perfectionism, self-control, assertiveness, and intimacy.

There is a subgroup of clients with eating problems who have more extensive psychopathology, such as borderline or mixed personality disorders characterized by chronic instability of mood, interpersonal relationships, and self-image (Halmi & Falk, 1982; Masterson, 1977). Many bulimic patients abuse drugs or alcohol (Johnson, Stuckey, Lewis, & Schwartz, 1982; Pyle, Mitchell, & Eckert, 1981), and many are clinically depressed (Herzog, 1984). The apparent link between depression and bulimia has led to the use of antidepressants for some patients (Herzog & Brotman, 1987). It is unclear whether antidepressants work by relieving the depressive component of the bulimia or by otherwise reducing bulimic symptoms.

Social Subsystem

Assessment should include an exploration of family dynamics, peer relationships, and the effects of the eating problem on the adolescent's life style. For example, some patients avoid social gatherings because they are afraid that they will overeat. Some develop strange rituals, such as bingeing through a sequence of restaurants or vomiting into paper bags. The exhaustion and compulsion of binge-purge cycles may leave no time for normal activities. In addition, many patients with eating problems have food-related jobs (e.g., waitress, grocery store clerk) or hobbies that perpetuate this narrow emphasis and exacerbate their symptoms.

INTERVENTION

Milieu Therapy

Although eating problems can often be treated with outpatient therapy, some adolescents with such problems require hospitalization. Indications for hospitalization include severe weight loss, frequent bingeing and purging, suicidal ideation, crisis, or lack of improvement with outpatient therapy. Hospitalization provides an opportunity to observe the adolescent and family more closely and may uncover key problems that have been blocking previous treatment efforts.

The first task of milieu treatment is to establish a therapeutic alliance with the adolescent (Deering, 1987). Anorexics usually resist hospitalization because they fear weight gain and tend to deny the seriousness of the problem. If the nurse can establish a dialogue with the anorexic adolescent on topics other than food, however, a relationship may form that allows the adolescent to discuss feelings such as loneliness, anger, and fear of failure. This will happen only if the nurse can reach out to the adolescent through repeated contacts and can actively direct the discussion away from the obsession with weight.

It is easier to form a therapeutic alliance with bulimic adolescents, because they usually feel that they have lost control of their bingeing and may be desperate for help. The nurse may seem like an almost magical source of external support and a guardian to prevent bingeing. Because of this, the nurse must emphasize the adolescents' role in their own recovery while helping them to build self-control and self-confidence.

The nurse-client relationship is the supporting structure for milieu therapy. Behavioral, cognitive, and group interventions are specific modalities often used in conjunction with milieu therapy.

Behavioral Interventions

Although there is some controversy about their long-term effectiveness, behavioral interventions are considered the cornerstone of inpatient treatment for eating problems (Claggett, 1980). The top-priority goal of hospitalization is to help the client regain control of eating behavior. Other psychotherapeutic approaches support this goal, but behavioral treatment is the only way to target specific eating patterns.

The nursing process is readily applicable to behavioral interventions within the overall care of eating problems (Deering & Niziolek, 1988). As youngsters enter the hospital, a specific behavioral outcome can be targeted (e.g., a weight gain of 10 pounds, cessation of vomiting). Other short- and long-term goals must be realistic and consistent with the severity of the problem and the planned length of the hospitalization. Nurses should make it clear to these adolescents that hospitalization will not cure the eating problem. Specific goals can be accomplished, but continued therapy will be required to maintain progress.

A key behavioral outcome for anorexia is usually weight gain. In fact, clients are cognitively unable to respond to other therapeutic interventions after a certain critical level of weight loss (Bruch, 1978). The first step is to develop an individualized behavioral program with a goal weight and an effective set of rewards and consequences. Initially, clients are restricted to the ward to allow for closer supervision. Staff monitor clients in the bathroom to prevent vomiting, especially after meals. Daily weights are taken when the clients are wearing hospital gowns, because they may try to hide heavy objects on their person to falsify results. It is important to maintain an atmosphere of caring rather than punishment. Restrictions should be framed as a way to increase the adolescents' safety until they are able to take better care of themselves. As they gain weight, privileges gradually can be granted. Weight gain is a frightening process for these adolescents, and the nurse's support during this period is vital.

A written contract helps to clarify mutual expectations. The usual requirement is a gain of 2 to 3 pounds of weight per week. A faster weight gain may be psychologically traumatic and physically dangerous, as it does not allow the body time to adjust (Bemis, 1978). Beyond the expectation of weight gain, the stipulations of the behavioral contract should be simple. Detailed contracts that require clients to eat certain amounts of food provide more opportunities for power struggles (Sanger & Cassino, 1984).

If weight loss persists, there may be no alternative but tube feeding or hyperalimentation. These methods should be used as a last resort to prevent death (Maloney & Farrell, 1980). Anti-anxiety drugs may be helpful when the adolescent panics over weight gain, but these drugs should be used only temporarily (Andersen, 1987). Relaxation exercises are often helpful, and the adolescent can continue to use them after leaving the hospital.

Cognitive Interventions

Anorexic and bulimic adolescents have a tendency to underestimate their coping abilities and to exaggerate the consequences of minor variations in their eating patterns. For example, the bulimic adolescent's self-defeating cognitions may perpetuate the binge-purge cycle by undermining any sense of control or progress that the adolescent has. The typical pattern for these adolescents is to overeat, jump to the conclusion that they have failed again, decide that they might as well binge, end up purging, and conclude that they are hopelessly out of control. Depressed feelings about the loss of control then lead to overeating, creating a vicious cycle. Through cognitive restructuring, these adolescents can learn to think more positively and realistically about their capabilities, and they can avoid the vicious cycle by allowing themselves setbacks and giving themselves "permission" to start again.

Burns (1980) identified some typical "cognitive distortions" that can lead to depression and hopelessness. These distortions are easy to identify in adolescents with eating problems. For example, "all-or-nothing thinking" that accepts only perfect performances is common in these adolescents. They believe that they either succeed or fail, that there is no in-between. Nurses can teach them how to combat this kind of distortion by having them: (1) record their automatic thoughts, (2) label the type of distortion, and (3) create rational responses to combat the distortion (Table 24-1). The written records can then be reviewed with the nurse to reinforce the new thought patterns. Using these, together with daily food diaries (Exhibit 24-1), the adolescents can begin to identify binge "triggers," such as negative thoughts, guilt feelings, and reactions to specific events.

Table 24-1 Examples of Cognitive Restructuring

Automatic Thought	Cognitive Distortion	Rational Response
I ate that piece of birthday cake, and my diet is ruined. I might as well binge.	All-or-nothing thinking	It's OK to join a birthday celebration. My decision was reasonable. I'll either cut back on food later today or start my diet again tomorrow.
I should be cured by now. Even though my vomiting is less frequent, I'm not improving fast enough. I should be able to stop immediately.	"Should" statements	I'm imposing an artificial time limit on my recovery by saying what I "should" be able to do. This is a way of punishing myself and not acknowledging my progress. Each step I take is significant.
In group therapy, everyone said I look great and I'm improving. Still, I noticed that Betty's doing better than I am.	Mental filter Disqualifying the positive	I'm dwelling on one negative comparison and ignoring all the great feedback I got from the group. I've got to listen when people tell me good things and try not to let compliments "bounce off me."

Exhibit 24-1 Example of a Food Diary

Wednesday, February 2

A.M.: Woke up and thought about how fat I feel in bed. Exercised. Found old tape measures. My thigh is 21". I've gained 1/2", which at first made me feel horrible. Skipped breakfast.

P.M.: Got through school without eating! Told friends I had eaten my lunch on the bus. I feel better—back in control. Worried about that math test tomorrow. I'm so stupid at math.

Supper time: Mom told me to eat *something* and that's when it started. Went crazy, lost total control, and ate five pieces of bread (buttered!) with dinner. I HATE MYSELF! Binged on cookies after dinner. Then vomited. The guilt is terrible. I felt like I had to eat because Mom cooked a big meal, and I didn't want my family to worry about me. But once I got started . . . . I've got to study for that math test—what a jerk I am! I've got to stop that all-or-nothing thinking. Tomorrow's another day.

Another important cognitive intervention is to educate clients regarding misperceptions related to the bulimia. For example, many adolescents use starvation as a weight control technique and do not realize that it actually triggers bingeing. After starving all day, they feel so hungry and deprived that they end up overeating. If education about the importance of regular meals is not effective, the nurse can review the adolescent's daily food diary and point out the starve-binge pattern. Another common irrational belief is that certain foods are "bad" and must be eliminated from the diet. Adolescents typically try to delete their favorite foods and become discouraged when they are unsuccessful. It is more realistic to integrate these foods into the diet and relabel them as "OK."

Group Interventions

Group therapy may be one of the most effective modalities for intervening with adolescents who have eating problems. The emotional support, the reality testing, and the hope engendered from seeing others improve are important elements of the group experience. Nutrition education and cognitive restructuring may be particularly effective in the group setting, as examples are abundant and reinforcement from peers is available. In fact, group therapy is often viewed as the treatment of choice for bulimia because it provides such a powerful monitoring system and motivation to "abstain."

A number of major issues can be explored in group therapy. Social skills training is helpful for anorexics, who often have trouble establishing close friendships; in the group, they can practice social skills, such as telephoning friends or conversing with boys. Assertiveness training may be helpful for adolescents with bulimia, as they often conform to traditional passive female sex-role stereotypes (Cantelon, Leichner, & Harper, 1986). Their difficulty in acknowledging and expressing anger may be one factor underlying the need to binge and purge. In assertiveness training, clients use role plays, homework assignments, and group exercises to practice new behaviors and explore the fears and anxieties that arise with change. Group therapy is an ideal medium for experimentation because the atmosphere is safe and supportive.

Discomfort with sexuality is common among adolescents with eating disorders and is often explored through group therapy (Oehler & Burns, 1987). Psychoanalysts traditionally have viewed anorexia as a way of denying sexuality, as starving causes the menses to cease and the body to appear more masculine. Anorexics typically either avoid dating or seek relationships that make no sexual demands. Bulimics may be more sexually active, but they also experience guilt and discomfort with their bodies. Group therapy allows for disclosure of fears and experiences, validation by peers, and encouragement of normal sexual behavior.

The discussion of sexuality and sex-role issues in the group may extend to feminist themes and consciousness raising (Boskind-White & White, 1983). It is widely acknowledged that the societal ideal of the thin woman is a key factor in the proliferation of eating problems among adolescents (Schwartz, Thompson, & Johnson, 1982). Adolescents who are struggling to define their identities may feel particularly pressured to conform to rigid societal standards. Group therapy promotes a healthy questioning of values portrayed in the media and in peer groups. Furthermore, since many nurses are young women, they may be particularly effective in modeling self-confidence, assertiveness, and comfort with sexuality.

Discharge Planning and Evaluation

Continued treatment through outpatient care should be planned well before discharge, because a hiatus in treatment frequently leads to relapse. An outpatient team of therapist, nutritionist, and nurse practitioner or physician should be identified and invited to participate in pre-discharge planning conferences. Continuity of care is vital to sustain the progress made during the hospitalization (Deering & Niziolek, 1988).

A discharge contract should be drawn up to specify maximum weight loss permissible to avoid rehospitalization, the frequency of therapist and physician contacts, and any other key aspects of the client's regimen. For some adolescents, it may be helpful to name a case manager to coordinate the activities of the various care-givers and to serve as liaison to the school system. Clinical nurse specialists are ideal case managers because of their experience as coordinators and their knowledge of the physical health problems involved.

As the adolescent prepares to leave the hospital, an evaluation is conducted as part of the nursing process. The nurse and the client may find the outcomes frustrating if unrealistic goals were set. Expectations of a quick cure are certainly unrealistic, as most clinicians agree that eating disorders are difficult to treat, require at least a few years of therapy, and may result in multiple hospitalizations. When reasonable goals are set, however, stepwise progress builds confidence and sustains the hope and motivation of all involved. The evaluation of the nursing care of adolescents with eating disorders should center on the realistic appraisal and revision of goals according to each individual's needs and capabilities.

Nurses also need to evaluate their own reactions to the frequently difficult behaviors of adolescents who have eating disorders. These adolescents may generate intense emotions and countertransference reactions. For example, anorexics commonly use splitting and become manipulative, causing conflicts between staff members. Nurses may feel angry or powerless in the face of this manipulation unless they keep in mind that these youngsters are driven by desperation and fear of losing control. When clients are emaciated, nurses may become anxious that they will die. Rescue fantasies can develop, and there may be an urge to plead with these adolescents to eat, even though this exacerbates the power struggle.

Nurses must support each other so that they can maintain a calm, caring, consistent, and unified approach. Although these adolescents often appear exceptionally competent with perfect grades and diligent performance in other areas of their lives, their self-concepts are fragile and their profound insecurities are well hidden. Nurses who can see beyond their facades and circumvent power struggles will form the most effective relationships.

Individual Psychotherapy

Psychotherapy for eating disorders is an active, goal-directed process. The approaches differ for anorexia and bulimia.

Anorexia

Recognizing that traditional psychoanalytic methods are ineffective in the treatment of anorexia, Bruch (1973) advocated a more directive approach that encourages adolescents to identify and interpret their own thoughts and feelings. In her view, anorexics have a "paralyzing sense of ineffectiveness" that leads them to doubt their own perceptions and to struggle to maintain a facade of control. Passive approaches create a void for these adolescents, who usually deny their problem and often lack insight.

The first task of psychotherapy for anorexia is the establishment of a therapeutic alliance. Most clinicians assume that the main obstacle to establishing an alliance is the anorexic's persistent denial, but it is actually the fact that anorexics do not know how to receive help (Deering, 1987). They are accustomed to taking control of relationships in a counterdependent manner and ignoring their own needs. The nurse's recognition of the adolescent's hidden dependency needs will pave the way to the establishment of a sound therapeutic relationship.

Anorexics usually go through three phases in the development of an alliance: (1) the angry/counterdependent phase, (2) the depressed/needy phase, and (3) the approaching/relating phase (Deering, 1987). In the first phase, they stubbornly resist help and act as if therapy is a farce. Although they usually appear on time for appointments, they cannot acknowledge their need for help. Empathic listening, limit setting, education about the eating disorder, and dialogue on topics other than food are key interventions of this phase. Therapists must actively structure discussions and question these clients about their thoughts and feelings, as long silences cause these adolescents to feel hopeless and abandoned (Levenkron, 1982). The nurse's familiarity with and comfort in treating the physical problems of anorexia inspire confidence and permit more effective education about the symptoms involved.

During the second phase of alliance building, clients become depressed and needy. They begin to recognize their unconscious need for nurturance and more openly express their sad and lonely feelings. Although this phase is difficult, the greater openness fosters the development of a working relationship (Levenkron, 1982; Zeiler, 1982). The adolescents learn how to identify their feelings, express their needs, and ask for help. Because they are not fully capable of eliciting the care that they need, outreach and extra appointments may be necessary, especially with suicidal clients. With clients who have borderline personality disorders, the therapist must be careful not to allow too much regression during this time.

In the final phase, the adolescent clients are better able to approach and relate to the therapist. They recognize their need for help and become more relaxed and reflective in sessions. During this time, the therapist can model more spontaneous styles of relating. The adolescents can plan strategies to overcome their eating difficulty and can begin to take a more active role in their own care. As they improve, they begin to form other meaningful interpersonal relationships outside the therapy.

Most anorexic adolescents have severe ego deficits, and they often require long-term psychotherapy (Zeiler, 1982). The establishment of an alliance is a sign that they have developed more of an observing ego, which facilitates insight and cooperation with therapy (Kieth, 1968). The therapist should become aligned with this observing ego and capitalize on whatever healthy reality testing may be available. Sometimes it helps to ask these adolescents, "What does your healthy side tell you about how to handle that situation?" The therapist may also encourage them to "argue with themselves" over food choices and social dilemmas. Through the process of introjection and identification with the therapist, these clients internalize healthier perceptions of themselves and build ego strengths.

Low self-esteem, body image disturbance, separation-individuation, intimacy, and sexuality are some of the major issues that arise in therapy with anorexic adolescents. It may be difficult to find a balance between these general issues and the more specific eating symptoms. Some therapists rigidly avoid all discussion of eating and weight to maintain a "purer" role as a therapist and to prevent power struggles. Total avoidance of eating issues may be unrealistic and insensitive, however, as these adolescents experience substantial anxiety and emotional distress about their eating patterns. For this reason, eating issues should not monopolize the therapy hour, but they should be allowed some expression.

Although it is controversial, it may even be helpful for outpatient nurse therapists to weight their anorexic clients regularly. This is one way to keep records of their physical status current and to give them feedback when they stop starving themselves and fear that they have gained large amounts of weight. It would seem unfortunate for nurses to avoid physical symptoms and concerns, since this is an area in which they have particular expertise.

Bulimia

Psychotherapy for bulimia involves a greater focus on eating patterns than does psychotherapy for anorexia, especially in the beginning. Until clients bring their bingeing and vomiting under better control, they feel hopeless and discouraged about therapy. Therefore, most treatment programs for bulimia aim for an immediate interruption of binge-purge cycles and place early demands on clients to abstain (Fairburn, 1985). If the therapist sidesteps the eating behavior, therapy can easily drift into endless focus on psychosocial issues with no behavioral change.

As stated earlier, bulimic adolescents usually enter therapy at a point of desperation and are very eager to receive help. Cognitive-behavioral methods capitalize on their motivation and help to structure the early phases of therapy (Fairburn, 1985; Grinc, 1982). The cognitive restructuring methods described earlier can be integrated into the therapy. Behavioral techniques, such as stimulus control (e.g., avoiding the kitchen, limiting the amount of food available, not shopping for food when hungry) may also be helpful (Fairburn, 1985).

The optimal plan may be to require the adolescent to stop all bingeing and vomiting immediately, but this may not be realistic. Setting achievable goals engenders a sense of progress while the adolescent learns that change is possible. Otherwise, the adolescent will push for lofty, unachievable goals and then experience a painful loss of self-confidence, which perpetuates the binge-purge cycle. Proximal subgoals can be developed and revised regularly. For example, an initial goal may be to establish one binge-free day per week or to substitute an activity for a binge-purge cycle. The best strategy is to emphasize a reduction in vomiting, because these clients will not binge if they know they cannot vomit.

Perhaps the most useful behavioral strategy is to substitute pleasurable activities for bingeing. Bulimic patients tend to deprive themselves of enjoyment or feel guilty when they indulge in any sort of fun or relaxation. Their low self-esteem causes them to judge themselves unworthy of pleasure. Bulimics cannot give themselves permission to relax, so they tend not to schedule enjoyable activities. This lack of structure creates boredom, triggering the urge to binge. The therapist may suggest that bulimic clients make a list of activities to replace bingeing. Because it may take some time for clients to become accustomed to allowing themselves these outlets, diaries are used to record guilty feelings.

Once the cognitive-behavioral methods are in place, therapy can shift to a focus on underlying psychosocial issues. For example, dependency is a major issue in therapy with bulimics. Whereas anorexics are typically counterdependent, bulimics are usually more openly needy and lacking in direction. The shame and secrecy associated with bulimic behavior are degrading phenomena that undermine a sense of self-worth. Therapy focuses on helping these adolescents build self-esteem without becoming dependent on the therapist.

The combination of dependency and lack of control make the interpersonal relationships of bulimic adolescents intense and unstable. They tend to have trouble asserting themselves and are sometimes said to "vomit their feelings into the toilet." Because of this, bulimics may be prime targets for victimization (Root, Fallon, & Friedrich, 1986). They may be involved in sexually abusive or battering relationships and are often attracted to boys who undervalue them. A supportive psychotherapeutic relationship that validates the adolescent's positive qualities is essential in order to help them learn to protect themselves from abusive relationships and begin to feel important enough to expect more.

Family Therapy

Nursing interventions for adolescents with eating disorders must extend beyond the individual system to incorporate the family dynamics that perpetuate the symptoms. One of the most central areas of conflict for these families is separation-individuation (Root et al., 1986; Stern, Whitaker, Hagemann, Anderson, & Bargman, 1981). The oft-cited bimodal onset of eating problems at puberty and late adolescence is considered testimony to the link between the symptomatology and struggles with emerging sexuality and autonomy. Families of adolescents with eating disorders often have trouble allowing healthy movement toward independence, and the eating disorder becomes the battleground for power struggles.

In their well-known research with anorexic families, Minuchin, Rosman, and Baker (1978) identified four common characteristics of these "psychosomatic families": (1) enmeshment (i.e., lack of boundaries between family members), (2) overprotectiveness (i.e., difficulty in fostering autonomy), (3) rigidity (i.e., strict adherence to the status quo and difficulty in tolerating change), and (4) lack of conflict resolution (i.e., avoidance of disagreement, glossing over conflict, and detouring conflicts through third parties). In short, the facade of a happy family often masks significant family problems. Frequently, there is a parent-child role reversal with the anorexic controlling and nurturing the parents or functioning as a spouse. This perpetuates the counterdependent, pseudomature style of the anorexic.

Bulimic families seem to have similar problems with separation-individuation. Root and colleagues (1986) described a typology of bulimic families similar to that described by Minuchin and colleagues for anorexic families, except for one additional subtype that they called the "chaotic family." This group of families has more extensive problems, including exceptionally poor boundaries, uncontrolled expression of anger, pseudo-autonomy, inability to express love and affection, unresolved grief and loss, and physical or sexual abuse. Other researchers have corroborated their finding that a high percentage of adolescents with eating disorders have a family history of sexual abuse (Oppenheimer, Howells, Palmer, & Chaloner, 1985).

Family therapy approaches for anorexia and bulimia are similar, except for the more direct parental limit setting required when anorexics are losing weight. Unacknowledged marital problems are a common focus of therapy, as the symptomatic adolescent is often providing a needed distraction from the threat of marital discord. Selvini-Palazzoli (1981) described the "three-way matrimony" that is common in anorexic families. The anorexic child functions as a go-between for the parents, constantly shifting alliances to care for each spouse at the expense of her own adolescent developmental tasks.

Because the marital subsystem is so fluid, the parents have difficulty setting limits and making joint decisions. They may use poor judgment, sabotage the adolescent's progress, or even put the adolescent in danger (Harper, 1983). For example, one couple endorsed their daughter's decision to join the track team and purchased an exercise bicycle for her, despite her extreme and protracted weight loss. The anorexic child quickly learns to manipulate the parents when the limit-setting mechanisms are so ineffective and the parents do not support each other.

Dysfunctional communication patterns are another common problem for these families (Selvini-Palazzoli, 1981). Family members typically disqualify and disconfirm each other's messages. For example, they minimize or discourage anger and other strong emotional responses. In a typically enmeshed style, family members speak for each other on the assumption that they know each other's thoughts and values.

Family therapy involves some restructuring to create clearer boundaries between the parent and child subsystems. For example, Minuchin and colleagues (1978) advocate putting the parents in charge of behavioral weight control programs for anorexics and coaching the parents to work together in decision making and limit setting. Their "family therapy lunch sessions" provided an opportunity to identify problematic family patterns beyond mere struggles over food.

Because of their enmeshment and fear of change, it may be difficult to engage the families of adolescents with eating disorders in therapy. These families may appear to be motivated and cooperative, but the subtle sabotage of change quickly becomes apparent. It is helpful to move slowly and emphasize the family's strengths. For example, these families are usually intact, and they have a strong commitment to the family unit. Validating these strengths may help the therapist to avoid being seen as the threatening outsider who is attempting to "break up the family." At the same time, the therapist must gently support the adolescent's healthy movement toward greater autonomy. This is a difficult process for these children, because they are eager to please and strongly invested in their role as the "good child."

CASE EXAMPLE

Julie, a 14-year-old girl, sought outpatient therapy at the insistence of her family, who were troubled by her continued weight loss. Julie was 5 feet, 6 inches tall and weighed 101 pounds at the time of her first visit. She was wearing heavy, baggy clothes to conceal her figure and to compensate for her constantly low body temperature. Julie was angry and confused because her parents constantly nagged her to eat. She believed that she was much too fat and could not understand why they wanted her to gain more weight. Ever since she had started losing weight, her friends had been complimenting her on her appearance and admiring her willpower.

A nursing assessment revealed that Julie had been bingeing, starving, and purging in fairly consistent cycles since her initial dieting began in the eighth grade, when she weighted 135 pounds. Now she was starving for a few days at a time, bingeing, and then vomiting or using diet pills, laxatives, and excessive exercise to bring her weight back under control. Her parents were unaware of the extreme methods that she was using. A visit to the pediatrician prior to the psychiatric evaluation revealed a weight loss of 35 pounds since her last visit, bradycardia, lanugo, and potassium deficiencies.

Julie's family was puzzled by her weight loss, since they "had always been such a healthy, happy family" and Julie was such a perfect child who "had never given them a day's trouble." They just wanted her to start eating again and get back to normal. Julie's father seemed particularly frustrated, since the answer seemed so simple: "Just eat!"

Outpatient therapy initially focused on the development of a therapeutic alliance with Julie through the discussion of topics other than food. Julie revealed her perfectionistic tendencies and the great pressure that she felt to do well in school so that she could get into a good college. She had always been a "straight A" student, but the new high-school material seemed more difficult for her. In addition, the pressures to wear the right clothes and have the right boyfriend seemed monumental. She did not feel comfortable with boys, yet her friends expected her to at least *want* to go out on dates. Thank goodness, her family was in no rush to have her get involved with boys. They never seemed to like the boys that her older sister dated. Her parents often wished that things could go back to the way they were when the children were small and the family did things together all the time. Julie missed those times, too, and wished that she and her parents could stop arguing about this stupid food issue!

While exploring Julie's concerns, the nurse therapist also monitored her eating behaviors by reviewing weekly food diaries and checking her weight. A gradual increase in weight led to a great deal of anxiety for her. This anxiety was brought under control through cognitive restructuring. (See Table 24-1.)

Periodic family therapy sessions revealed the parents' concerns with their adolescent daughters' increasing autonomy and the parents' tendency to be overprotective. The therapist gently challenged some of the family's rigid rules and helped the girls to begin to assert themselves. As this happened, conflict between the parents intensified, revealing an underlying marital strain. Eventually, a crisis developed; the parents had an argument, and the father came home intoxicated, threatening to move out. Julie began losing weight rapidly, and this precipitated an inpatient admission.

On admission to the hospital, Julie weighed 88 pounds. She was restricted to the ward and immediately began individual, group, and family therapy sessions. Gradually, she gained weight, despite her frequent protests, anxiety attacks, struggles over meals, and secretive vomiting and exercise. The nurses made an effort to connect with her on an emotional level by discussing her fears and concerns about her parents' marriage. She was quick to defend her family, so the nurses were gentle in their approach and often used humor or self-disclosure, telling her about their own experiences as adolescents and the ways in which they coped with family tensions. They also helped Julie to become integrated into the milieu so that she could practice the social skills and assertive behaviors that she was learning in group therapy. Slowly, Julie became more self-confident with her peers and less defensive with the nursing staff. She felt that they were on her side, even though she did not like gaining weight.

When Julie reached her target weight of 95 pounds, she was discharged for further outpatient therapy, and the insights gained from the hospitalization were conveyed to the outpatient nurse therapist in a pre-discharge planning conference. Family members were now more open to therapeutic interventions because they believed that the problem was serious and that they had a role in it. Julie was much more confident that she could build peer relationships outside the hospital, based on her successes with the adolescents in the hospital. She had a more thorough understanding of her starve-binge patterns and her self-defeating thought patterns. She was not cured, but she was moving in the right direction.

Outpatient therapy continued for 2 years. During this time, Julie revealed that her father had sexually abused her. This precipitated another family crisis, which led to the father's beginning court-mandated psychiatric treatment and the parents' entering more intensive marital therapy. Julie was referred to a group for adolescent incest survivors, and she continued her individual and family sessions. Her weight stabilized, and she began to feel more comfortable with her body and her feelings in general. She was able to identify even angry feelings, label them, and connect them with her eating behaviors in her diaries. Slowly, the eating problem faded, and she began to focus more on friendships and school activities.

The family myth of a perfect, loving household had been shattered, but there was a new awareness of how each person *really* felt in both good and bad times of family life. The family had developed enough flexibility for each member to have some independent hopes, desires, and concerns. Julie continued to improve after outpatient therapy ended, although she had some recurrent concerns about her weight. She attended eating disorder self-help group meetings when she was feeling shaky, and she gave herself the option to reenter therapy if the need arose.

RESEARCH

Nursing research on the effectiveness of various behavioral interventions and programs developed for the treatment of eating disorders would make a great contribution to current practice. The studies performed to date have varying degrees of follow-up, different criteria for outcome, and methodological problems that make it difficult to sort out the effects of nonbehavioral aspects of the treatment programs (Halmi, 1985). Most clinicians agree that behavioral intervention is necessary for weight gain, but the specific methods that are most effective remain controversial. Critics cite high post-discharge relapse rates and argue that patients who are forced to gain weight through rigid protocols are bound to rebel when they leave the hospital. The important research question seems to be, how flexible can a program be while still remaining effective? Is it better to have a detailed program that leaves no room for ambiguity about the requirements or to have minimal rules that allow greater client participation in decision making? Because nurses are central figures in the planning and implementation of inpatient behavioral programs, they have important insights on these questions.

Another controversial area that should be studied is the effect of tube feeding and hyperalimentation. There is much debate over how traumatizing versus therapeutic these procedures may be and what their long-term effects are. Nursing research exploring patients' reactions to these intrusive interventions may provide insights into better care for patients who require them.

Other problems that warrant further study include the prevalence of sexual abuse in patients with eating disorders, the effectiveness of mixed versus homogeneous treatment groups for anorexics and bulimics, the applicability of the addictions model to the treatment of eating disorders, and the incidence and characteristics of eating disorders in males. In general, there is much less research on bulimia than on anorexia, even though bulimia is more common. Individual and family therapy approaches for bulimia could benefit from more extensive research.

REFERENCES

Adler, A.G., Walinsky, P., Krall, R.A., & Cho, S.Y. (1980). Death resulting from ipecac syrup poisoning. *Journal of the American Medical Association, 243*, 1927–1928.

Andersen, A.E. (1987). Uses and potential misuses of anti-anxiety agents in the treatment of anorexia nervosa and bulimia nervosa. In P.E. Garfinkel & D.M. Garner (Eds.), *The role of drug treatments for eating disorders* (pp. 59–73). New York: Brunner/Mazel.

Bemis, K.M. (1978). Current approaches to the etiology and treatment of anorexia nervosa. *Psychological Bulletin, 85*(3), 593–617.

Bennett, S.C., Pleak, R., & Silverman, J.A. (1988). Eating disorders in children and adolescents. In C.J. Kestenbaum & D.T. Williams (Eds.), *Handbook of clinical assessment of children and adolescents* (Vol. 2, pp. 938–958). New York: New York University Press.

Boskind-White, M., & White, W.C. (1983). *Bulimarexia: The binge-purge cycle.* New York: W.W. Norton.

Bruch, H. (1973). *Eating disorders: Obesity, anorexia nervosa, and the person within.* New York: Basic Books.

Bruch, H. (1978). *The golden cage: The enigma of anorexia nervosa.* Cambridge, MA: Harvard University Press.

Burns, D. (1980). *Feeling good: The new mood therapy.* New York: New American Library.

Cantelon, C.J., Leichner, P.P., & Harper, D.W. (1986). Sex-role conflict in women with eating disorders. *International Journal of Eating Disorders, 5*(2), 317–323.

Claggett, M.S. (1980). Anorexia nervosa: A behavioral approach. *American Journal of Nursing, 80,* 1471–1472.

Deering, C.G. (1987). Developing a therapeutic alliance with the anorexia nervosa client. *Journal of Psychosocial Nursing, 25*(3), 11–13, 17.

Deering, C.G., & Niziolek, C. (1988). Patients with eating disorders: Promoting continuity of care. *Journal of Psychosocial Nursing, 26*(11), 6–11, 15.

Fairburn, C.G. (1985). Cognitive-behavioral treatment for bulimia. In D.M. Garner & P.E. Garfinkel (Eds.), *Handbook of psychotherapy for anorexia and bulimia* (pp. 160–192). New York: Guilford Press.

Garfinkel, P.E., & Garner, D.M. (1982). *Anorexia nervosa: A multidimensional perspective.* New York: Brunner/Mazel.

Grinc, G.A. (1982). A cognitive-behavioral model for the treatment of chronic vomiting. *Journal of Behavioral Medicine, 5*(1), 135–141.

Halmi, K. (1985). Behavioral management for anorexia nervosa. In D. Garner & P. Garfinkel (Eds.), *Handbook of psychotherapy for anorexia and bulimia* (pp. 147–159). New York: Guilford Press.

Halmi, K.A., & Falk, J.R. (1982). Anorexia nervosa: A study of outcome discriminators in exclusive dieters and bulimics. *Journal of the American Academy of Child Psychiatry, 21*(4), 369–375.

Halmi, K.A., Falk, J.R., & Schwartz, E. (1981). Binge-eating and vomiting: A survey of a college population. *Psychological Medicine, 11,* 697–706.

Harper, G. (1983). Varieties of parenting failure in anorexia nervosa: Protection and parentectomy, revisited. *Journal of the American Academy of Child Psychiatry, 22*(2), 134–139.

Herzog, D.B. (1984). Are anorexic and bulimic patients depressed? *American Journal of Psychiatry, 141,* 1594–1597.

Herzog, D.M., & Brotman, A.W. (1987). Use of tricyclic anti-depressants in anorexia nervosa and bulimia nervosa. In P.E. Garfinkel & D.M. Garner (Eds.), *The role of drug treatments for eating disorders* (pp. 36–58). New York: Brunner/Mazel.

Johnson, C.C., Stuckey, M.K., Lewis, L.D., & Schwartz, D.M. (1982). Bulimia: A descriptive survey of 316 cases. *International Journal of Eating Disorders, 2*(1), 3–16.

Kieth, C.R. (1968). The therapeutic alliance in child psychotherapy. *Journal of the American Academy of Child Psychiatry, 7,* 30–43.

Levenkron, S. (1982). *Treating and overcoming anorexia nervosa.* New York: Warner Books.

Maloney, M.J., & Farrell, M.K. (1980). Treatment of severe weight loss in anorexia nervosa with hyperalimentation and psychotherapy. *American Journal of Psychiatry, 137*(3), 310–314.

Masterson, J.F. (1977). Primary anorexia nervosa in the borderline adolescent: An object relations view. In P. Hartocollis (Ed.), *Borderline personality disorders*. New York: International Universities Press.

Minuchin, S., Rosman, B., & Baker, L. (1978). *Psychosomatic families: Anorexia nervosa in context*. Cambridge: Harvard University Press.

Oehler, J.M., & Burns, J.J. (1987). Anorexia, bulimia, and sexuality: Case study of an adolescent inpatient group. *Archives of Psychiatric Nursing, 1*(3), 163–171.

Oppenheimer, R., Howells, K., Palmer, R.C., & Chaloner, D.A. (1985). Adverse sexual experience in childhood and clinical eating disorders: A preliminary description. *Journal of Psychiatric Research, 19*(203), 357–361.

Pope, H.G., Hudson, J.I., & Yurgelun-Todd, D. (1984a). Anorexia nervosa and bulimia among 300 women shoppers. *American Journal of Psychiatry, 141*, 292–294.

Pope, H.G., Hudson, J.I., & Yurgelun-Todd, D. (1984b). Prevalence of anorexia nervosa and bulimia in three student populations. *International Journal of Eating Disorders, 3*(3), 45–51.

Pyle, R.L., Mitchell, J.R., & Eckert, E.D. (1981). Bulimia: A report of 34 cases. *Journal of Clinical Psychiatry, 42*, 60–64.

Root, M., Fallon, P., & Friedrich, W.N. (1986). *Bulimia: A systems approach to treatment*. New York: W.W. Norton.

Russell, G.F.M. (1985). Anorexia and bulimia nervosa. In M. Rutter & L. Hersov (Eds.), *Child and adolescent psychiatry* (pp. 625–637). London: Blackwell Scientific Publications.

Sanger, E., & Cassino, T. (1984). Eating disorders: Avoiding the power struggle. *American Journal of Nursing, 84*, 31–33.

Schwartz, D.M., Thompson, A.G., & Johnson, C.C. (1982). Anorexia and bulimia: The sociocultural context. *International Journal of Eating Disorders, 1*(3), 20–36.

Selvini-Palazzoli, M. (1981). *Self-starvation*. New York: Jason Aronson.

Stern, S., Whitaker, C., Hagemann, N., Anderson, R., & Bargman, G.J. (1981). Anorexia nervosa: The hospital's role in family treatment. *Family Process, 20*, 395–408.

Zeiler, C.L. (1982). Treatment of ego deficits in anorexia nervosa. *American Journal of Orthopsychiatry, 52*(2), 356–359.

25

Nursing Interventions with Children and Adolescents Experiencing Sexually Aggressive Responses

Ann W. Burgess and Carol R. Hartman

After reading this chapter, the reader will be able to:

1. describe the current theories on juvenile sex offending
2. identify psychiatric nursing interventions for juvenile sex offenders
3. examine the role of the child and adolescent psychiatric nurse clinician in treating and researching juvenile sex offending behavior

All adolescents experience sexual changes that place stress on their ability to adapt and cope. With support and guidance, most adolescents develop a sexual identity with which they are comfortable. When this does not happen, an adolescent may demonstrate problems with sexuality. Such problems may be expressed in a myriad of ways, such as sexual abuse, promiscuity, and sexual inhibitions. Adolescents who exhibit these human responses would benefit from working with psychiatric nurse clinicians, as these professionals are in a key position to assess, diagnose, and plan the nursing care for juveniles with these problems.

THEORETICAL FOUNDATIONS

In searching for the causes of juvenile sex offending, clinicians and researchers have suggested early childhood victimization as one contributing factor (Groth, 1979; Seghorn & Boucher, 1980; Seghorn, Prentky, & Boucher, 1986), although empirically controlled research surveying adult offenders retrospectively does not unequivocally support these assertions (Langevin & Lange, 1983). Deisher, Wenet, Paperny, Clark, and Fehrenbeach (1981), as well as Groth and Loredo (1981), noted that more than half of the incarcerated juvenile offenders studied had themselves been victims of childhood physical and/or sexual abuse, however—a finding that does, indeed, suggest descriptive linkage from abused to abuser.

The mechanisms of transition from victim to victimizer are not yet well understood, but there appear to be four phases in the experience of a sexually abused child that represent critical periods in the child's response and the ultimate outcome. The four phases include (1) pretrauma, (2) trauma encapsulation, (3) disclosure and (4) outcome, and is based on information processing of a trauma model. The model helps explain the impact of trauma and the symptom response (Hartman & Burgess, 1988).

The child's attempts to modify the sensory, perceptual and cognitive alterations that occur during abuse, whether it be physical or sexual, emerge in overt behavioral patterns that specifically reflect the abuse itself. This process, referred to as trauma learning, is characterized by actions that are a replay of the trauma itself. These behaviors can be either direct reenactments of the trauma in which the victim responds to others as if the trauma were ongoing (i.e., the intrusive image or a flashback to being the victim) or repetitions of the traumatic event with the victim vacillating between the behaviors of the victim and the behaviors of the offender. In other words, the repetition replay is a step beyond reenactment in that the victim perceives the experience from the perspective of both the victim and the offender. Repetition characterizes early sexual offending behavior. If the trauma learning process is not disrupted, it is reinforced by the acting-out behavior, and the sexual offending behavior is reinforced by repetition. The distinction between victim and offender becomes blurred, and the victim's identification is almost entirely with the offender (Burgess, Hartman, Howe, Shaw, & McFarland, 1990; Grant, Burgess, Hartman, Shaw, & McFarland, 1989).

Efforts to treat adult sex offenders have been less than optimal when psychiatric nurse clinicians have initially focused on the origins of the behavior rather than on the self-sustaining characteristics of the offending behavior itself. Investigation into the thoughts, feelings, and daydreams of rapists, pedophiles, and sexual murderers reveals an active fantasy life committed to the very crimes that they carry out. This fantasy life is the major affective base for the offender. Pleasure, excitement, and self-fulfillment are rooted in these deviant fantasies. The fact that patterns of reenactment and repetition emerge as a child's effort to master disabling anxiety resulting from sexual abuse suggests that adherence to sexually aggressive acts originates in self-protective efforts. Therefore, it is proposed that, whatever the antecedent insults to the youth that have resulted in sexualized aggression, the construct of the sexualized aggression must be addressed first as the primary motivating factor in the behavior. Initially blaming others for the misbehavior of the juvenile sex offenders adds further confusion to their ability to regulate their behavior. When treatment efforts do not focus on this important reality, the social and family support for the juvenile is diminished.

The earlier the psychiatric nursing assessment and intervention into the trauma learning process, the more successful the interruption of sexually deviant interests. In addition to family treatment, individual treatment must address the reinforcing quality of the sex offense behavior (e.g., the deviant fantasies) and the relationship of that behavior to prior abusive experiences. The linkage of sexually deviant behaviors to efforts of the child to deal with the resonating consequences of the primary abuse cannot be ignored. Rather than singular emphasis on stopping the acting-out behavior, efforts must be made to help the youth make a connection between the abuse, the deviant fantasies, and the offending behavior. From this connection, the juvenile offender can begin to unlink and resolve the sensory, perceptual, and cognitive memory distortions that emerged as defenses against the original abuse.

Psychiatric nursing intervention seems most likely to be successful if undertaken when the offender is a juvenile. The very factor of age, as well as that of gender (most reported sexual offenders are male), act as impediments to that intervention, however. Fundamental to the problem of identifying antecedents to sexually abusive behavior is the fact that those abused are not necessarily consciously aware of their own abuse history (Becker, Cunningham-Rathner, & Kaplan, 1986). Even if they are aware of the sexual abuse, young males are likely to underreport it (Finklehor, 1984; Janus, McCormack, Burgess, & Hartman, 1987; Riskin & Koss, 1987). Consequently, the very population that would benefit most from nursing interventions is the one to which they are most difficult to apply.

EARLY DETECTION AND ASSESSMENT

It is critical for child and adolescent psychiatric nurse clinicians to detect juvenile sex offending behavior early and to perform a careful assessment. The early assessment is to determine whether the youngster is experiencing any sexual activity that is exploitative, repetitive, or deviant. This behavior can be with children, both younger and older. In addition to a general nursing assessment, a TRIADS abuse history and a CARITAS sexual history should be taken.

TRIADS Abuse History

The acronym TRIADS is used to identify critical areas for assessing childhood abuse (Burgess, Hartman, & Kelly, 1990).

> *T*ype of abuse. Was the juvenile physically, sexually, and/or psychologically abused as a child? At what age? What was the dominant type of abuse?
>
> *R*ole relationship. What was the relationship between the child and the offender? Was the abuser a family member (intrafamilial abuse), an acquaintance or authority figure to the child, or a stranger (extrafamilial abuse)?
>
> *I*ntensity. What was the intensity of the abuse in terms of frequency of abusive activities and types of acts performed?

*A*utonomic response. Was the autonomic response hyperarousal or numbing? In the hyperarousal response, there is a history of mood irritability, hyperactivity, explosive fighting; and a drug history of sedatives (e.g., diazepam [Valium], alcohol). In the numbing response, there is a history of aggressing, requiring high risk-taking experiences, constantly seeking "high" experiences; putting themselves and others in dangerous situations; and a drug history of psychoactivating drugs (e.g., amphetamines).

*D*uration. How long did the abuse continue? Was it days, weeks, months, or years?

*S*tyle of abuse. Was the abuse a blitz, spontaneous event, or one or two times? Was the abuse repetitive and patterned in that the juvenile knew when it was to occur? Was the abuse ritualistic or ceremonial, including chants, use of excrement, masks, religion?

Sexual History Taking

The extent of the sexual history should be proportional to the juvenile's needs. The greater the potential for the juvenile's condition to affect his or her sexuality, the greater the need for sexual baseline data. The interview should take place in a quiet, private location with the juvenile in a comfortable position. Because of the sensitivity of the subject, it is better addressed during the later portion of the interview, after the nurse and the client have had a chance to talk for a while. There is no one best place to introduce the topic, but it may seem more appropriate as part of the systems review related to the reproductive system or as part of the social/family history.

As a general tool for identifying sexual problems, Krozy (1980) developed the acronym CARITAS as a reminder of the areas to be covered. (Note that the word *care* is derived from *caritas*.)

*C*oncern. What is the youth's definition of the real or potential concern regarding his or her sexuality? What is the youth's goal?

*A*ttitudes. What attitudes, beliefs, and values are operating? How does the youth feel toward himself or herself, sexual expression, and practices? Specifically explore attitudes toward females, noting rigid biases and hostile attitudes. The adolescent's understanding of what "no" means and the level of value placed on being sexually active.

*R*elationship. What is the type/quality of the client's relationship (e.g., marriage, homosexual, stable)? Who else needs to be involved, and at what point? What actual experiences has the juvenile had with peers, adults, and children, both male and female?

*I*llness. What effect does illness (physical, emotional, surgical, or drug treatment) have on the youth's sexuality?

*T*rust. Does the youth have enough trust in the significant others (e.g., nurse, physician, mate) to be open for help?

*A*wareness. How aware is the youth of the dynamics of sexuality? What is the client's knowledge, and what must the youth (and family) be taught?

*S*ensuality. What techniques, environments, or experiences have improved or hindered sexual expression?

Family Assessment

Areas discussed in a family assessment include the following:

- How did the juvenile learn about sex and reproduction?
- Who was the best teacher in the family or outside of the family?
- Who does he go to when he has questions: peers, family members, teachers?
- Did a family member ever force him to have any type of sexual contact or activity that he did not want?
- Did he ever witness a family member being touched, fondled, or forced to engage in sexual activity to be given certain rewards or privileges?

The task of detecting early juvenile sex offending behavior involves, in part, assisting families in making a decision to disclose a sexually abusive situation within the family. The traditional notion that psychotherapy is effective only when the client voluntarily seeks or agrees to treatment has been persuasively argued in various treatment programs. Such a view ignores the problems in self-regulation presented both by juvenile sex offenders and often by the family constellation.

In juvenile intrafamily abuse cases, family members are caught between two conflicting expectations: the universalistic expectation of the larger society to uphold the rules of the group versus the particularistic expectation to fulfill the obligation to a kinsman, a neighbor, or a fellow member (Parson, 1951). Should family members be loyal to the victim and treat the offender as they would treat any assailant—thinking of their duty as citizens to bring such an offender before the law? Or should they be loyal to the offender and make an exception for him because he is a family member? Clearly, they cannot honor both expectations; they must choose whether to disclose the abuse to outsiders. The choice may be a difficult one.

The family's failure to control the offender sends a mixed and confusing message to the victim and essentially confirms that all types of behavior are acceptable within the confines of the family, but not outside the family. The rights of victimized children can be ignored within the family context for a good number of years before such behavior is identified as wrong and illegal. When the primary interpreter of this complex set of rules is a single mother, her burdens are great. She must not only protect her children, but also provide a value-clarifying environment. If the mother is a young victim of neglect and abuse herself, the problems of child-rearing are intensified.

The family must appreciate and understand their ability to be a positive force for the youth. If the juvenile repeats sexually aggressive acts, the family needs help in holding the youth responsible for his actions so that he can develop his abilities to monitor and restrict his behavior until he is ready to channel his energies into more positive areas.

NURSING DIAGNOSIS

The following nursing diagnoses need to be considered in assessing sexually aggressive problems in juveniles: Altered Motor Behavior, Hyperactivity; Altered Recreational Patterns, Anti-social Reactions; Altered Eating Patterns, such as bingeing; Altered Sleep Arousal Patterns and Nightmares; Altered Cognitive Processes, especially a Capacity for Altered Concentrating. Preoccupation with Fantasy can be an Alteration in Thought Content. In community maintenance, there may be risk taking. In the area of human emotional responses, there are many altered states. Excessive anxiety, fear, guilt, shame, and sadness are particularly important. The area of processing of emotions includes such diagnoses as Altered Feeling Processes of Lability and Mood Swings; Altered Sense of Self; and Altered Sense of Self-esteem (see Appendix B).

NURSING INTERVENTIONS

The overall goal in dealing with an adolescent with sexually aggressive acting-out problems is to stop the criminal behavior.

Providing an Anchor for Safety

The juvenile needs to feel safe before any therapeutic work can begin. There must be rules for personal conduct in all settings—not only in the milieu, but also in recreational, bathing, and sleeping areas. Rules should be negotiated on interpersonal interactions. The psychiatric nurse clinician sets the rules of communication. Some level of confidentiality should be established (e.g., it is safe to talk). Finally, adolescents, must know explicitly that the criminal behavior must stop.

The group setting establishes a social order for rules. It is not for the adolescent to set his or her own rules and act on them; rather, group behavior monitors the social order rules.

The nurse raises the issue of trust in group by eliciting the adolescents' individual criteria for feeling safe in the group. Each member needs to have permission to say, "I don't trust you yet." The nurse needs to create experiences for the adolescents that challenge their criteria for safety. Recreational games can be used to establish trust in the group. For example, having an adolescent fall back and be caught by another adolescent is one exercise that helps establish a feeling of trust.

Building Personal Resources

To begin building their personal resources, adolescents talk about what makes them feel safe individually and in a group, how they comfort themselves (e.g., listening to others, humor, responding to another in a positive way), and what resources they need to feel safe. The psychiatric nurse clinician teaches self-assessment, both negative and positive, using the following areas:

1. behaviors. What are the repetitive behaviors (e.g., sex, aggression, overeating, masturbation)? In the area of sexual acting out, how often does this happen? What triggers it?
2. affect. What are the ranges of emotion (e.g., anger, rage, fear, sadness, depression, suicide, happiness)?
3. sensations. What sensations can they identify (tension, lack of energy, numbness, emptiness, palpitations)?
4. images. What flashes in their mind (e.g., being yelled at, demeaned, hit)?
5. cognitions. What are their presuppositions and beliefs regarding self, others, causes, expectations, and doom?
6. interpersonal relationships. What is the nature of their interpersonal relationships (e.g., bullying, isolation, conflict, argument)?
7. drugs/biology. What health issues are important (e.g., medications, genetic problems)?

When the adolescents understand the sequence of these areas, they can plan strategies. They can determine what resources are needed (e.g., someone to talk to or play cards with when feeling lonely). They can develop an awareness of self-appraisal/monitoring options, identify parts of the self that they like and dislike, and decide what they need to work on. The nurse teaches the youths how to relax and monitor their body reactions. In group, they can role-play anger and relax. This intervention develops their capacity to realize that they can enjoy nonperverted pleasure.

Confronting the Crime

It is essential that the psychiatric nurse clinician accept the youth—but not the criminal behavior. The nurse helps the adolescent recognize that the crime served some personal survival need and acknowledges the difficulty of giving up such behavior. Part of anchoring for safety requires the youth to acknowledge the crime openly and not rationalize it. The goal is to build a system in which there is a sense of self to be healed. Behavior is criticized, not the self.

The nurse must know about the crime, and this knowledge should match the police report. In forensic cases, the juvenile's chart should include such information. Eliminating the secretiveness of the crime (1) builds a sense of self for the adolescent, (2) acknowledges the crime, and (3) emphasizes that the crime was wrong.

There must be both a clear commitment to safety and a clear understanding that, although the criminal behavior is not condoned, the youth can go to someone without fear of reprisal. The approach to the youth must be consistent so the adolescent does not attempt to manipulate the staff. Responsibility is upheld and punishment reduced. The nurse keeps the total treating staff informed of the adolescent's progress.

Once the crime has been detailed individually to the nurse, the youth talks about it in a group setting. Group rules must ensure safety. The adolescent is committed to unlinking the confusion. One helpful group exercise is to draw and discuss the crime scene.

Resurfacing Victimization via the Crime

As previously described, the criminal activity not only is a link to early trauma, but also represents the juvenile's own perpetuating self-behavior. It has its own sensory reward system. The aim of bringing the original victimization to the surface is to decrease the payoff of the crime. There is still a high investment in fantasy and arousal. The exercise works to neutralize the arousal. This process is the trauma encapsulation phase.

It is critical for the juvenile to know that staff members are aware of the criminal behavior. In discussing it with the juvenile, the nurse should:

- detail again the crime. How did he plan the crime? What did he take to the crime scene? What did he do after the crime? What degrading acts occurred during the crime?
- review the crime for feelings. When did those acts happen to him? How did they make him feel? When did he experience those feelings before?
- go back to the adolescent's own victimization; talk about the TRIADS of abuse: physical, psychological, and sexual.
- detail the victimization. How was the adolescent disciplined? How did he learn about sex? If not directly victimized, when was violence or sex witnessed? When was a sense of trust abused?
- trace the linkages. How does the victimization connect to the crime?

This intervention involves traumatic memory work. The nurse takes every detail of the juvenile's rape behavior, from planning to arousal, and associates it to the past. The memory work increases anxiety and is upsetting. The nurse uses group members to dilute the intensity, as well as to implement specific interventions for relaxation and control.

The aim is to desexualize and neutralize the aggression. The nurse can ask whether there is any point at which the adolescent would stop the crime. What would the victim have to do to stop it or escalate it? At this point, an intervention is having the adolescent draw several of his or her victimizations. The drawings access the juvenile's system of retrieval and memory structure and provide data for the nurse to explore.

Processing the Victimization via the Crime

To decrease intensity and arousal from discussing both the crime and the victimization, the psychiatric nurse clinician can use the juvenile's personal resources and daily activities. The intense feelings are best dealt with in group. In this intervention, the psychiatric nurse clinician helps the juvenile to process the information about the crime, the victimization, and ongoing behavior. As daily thoughts and behaviors are changed, the response to trauma as it is stored in memory will change.

The technique of pacing is used. That is, the memories are separated into manageable portions. Otherwise, the youth may balk, because the memories are anxiety-producing.

Enlisting Group Members To Alter Behavior

To manage the anxiety resulting from the traumatic memories, group membership is emphasized. The psychiatric nurse clinician enlists the group to observe the others for such behaviors as eating or sleeping disturbances and depression. As anxiety is increased, negative acting-out behaviors will surface. Group members help each other with anxiety and report back to the group. The question raised in group is, what has it meant to commit such a crime? What daily behaviors are stimulated by thinking of the crime?

Unlinking the Memories and Behaviors

Linking/unlinking takes place through the adolescent's ability to recognize that he or she has alternatives. The transfer of the processed information about the crime and victimization to past memory is the letting go of arousing material. However, what will replace the void? What does the youth want to effect in relationships? In terms of criminal behavior, the reinforcing quality and antecedents of trauma filled the void.

It is necessary to deal with the antecedent sense of injustice that made the youth feel justified in committing the crime. The payoff must be reduced if the criminal behavior is to stop. The adolescent must find alternative ways to get what he wants; when he runs into an obstacle, he must be able to hold his impulse and take a deep breath.

This intervention works on building attachment. The nurse helps the adolescents retrieve and remember experiences in which they felt attached. They need time in the milieu environment to accomplish this. Many adolescents who act out sexually never had positive attachments to anyone.

Terminating Therapy

In the last intervention phase, the nurse brings back to the group the issue of positive attachment and loss. The adolescents may learn to communicate and maintain a sense of self through the positive relationships in the group. There will be a regressive pull that needs to be explicitly discussed in group. Part of the regressive pull is the fear of handling the future day by day. There can be acting out, which should be related to early deprivation and abuse. The nurse acknowledges these links.

In the termination phase, the nurse helps the adolescents build a philosophy of life. This can be part of homework assignments that are then shared in group. This philosophy includes values clarification, right versus wrong, and justice. In the group, these values can be debated. The adolescent must develop the ability to transfer the internalized attachments learned in the group milieu into the outside environments.

Evaluating the Interventions

There are several methods that may be used to evaluate the interventions. The self-report method focuses on symptoms and symptom changes. There are standardized measures of attitudes toward interpersonal violence. There are focused assessments, such as the measurement of sexual arousal to fantasy materials associated with sexual aggression; these are physiological measurements of genital arousal in response to visual and auditory stimuli. In addition, there are observational notes on the type and quality of interpersonal relationships among peers and with older and younger people. Structured situations designed to provoke anger and frustration can be followed up with an exploration of the ways in which the adolescent should deal with these situations cognitively, behaviorally, and interpersonally. These measures can be tailored for nurses working in the milieu or group homes. The outcomes to note are the extinction of sexually aggressive behavior toward others, an increase in positive interpersonal relationships, and positive involvement in work and study.

CASE EXAMPLE

Jim had been certified for trial as an adult at age 14 years, 9 months, following his arrest for breaking into the home of a 21-year-old neighbor, waking her from sleep, brutally raping her, and then attempting to rape her 2-year-old child. Following an uncontested trial, the judge found him guilty. A hearing was held to recommend a treatment plan appropriate for his age and his past history of victimization; the program was to run concurrently with his incarceration.

Background Information

Jim was a small, good-looking male from a poor family with a history of family disorganization, welfare dependency, drug abuse, and psychiatric hospitalization. He was the oldest of his mother's three children, each of whom had a different father. The whereabouts of Jim's father was unknown.

The mother's history followed a pattern remarkably similar to Jim's. She was the oldest of seven siblings and never knew her father. She stated that she never felt loved or appreciated by her mother and that she was jealous of her two younger sisters, whom she believed were her mother's favorites. She had been abused as a child.

The mother was 17 years old when she became pregnant with Jim. In her ninth month of pregnancy, Jim's father broke off the relationship. She cried a great deal, felt alone, and was overwhelmed by the responsibility of motherhood. The pregnancy and delivery were uncomplicated, and Jim weighed 7 pounds, 9 ounces at birth. His mother thought that he "looked like a little girl." Shortly after his birth, the mother began a relationship with another man and became pregnant with her second child. Jim was 17 months old when his brother was born, and he was described as very jealous of his baby brother. His mother reported having difficulty in toilet-training Jim and having to beat him, but that he had been trained before he was one year old.

The mother's paramour was cruel and abused the boys. He also introduced the mother to heroin. She was attracted to him because he was "macho," and it was difficult for her to let go of him. He apparently dominated and controlled her. While under the influence of drugs, she attempted suicide and was subsequently hospitalized for 1 month. During this time, Jim and his brother were placed in foster care. When the mother was discharged from the hospital, she avoided the family, living in isolation for approximately 18 months. She reestablished contact with Jim when he was 6 years old. She has had off-and-on contact with her children, usually avoiding them when on drugs and suffering from agitated depression.

From age 6 to 12, Jim lived in foster care. The foster mother reported that Jim, at age 6, was unable to play with peers, isolated himself in the house, had difficulty in handling aggressive drives, compulsively destroyed toys, was enuretic, and behaved as though he did not have enough to eat. She reported that by age 8, he had begun to act "more normally." Jim did not have any contact with his mother for approximately 3 years, but then he began to call her on the telephone. After Jim began sexual acting-out behavior, he claimed that he was angry with his foster parents for beating him. This accusation was denied by the foster parents.

Jim's history revealed severe behavioral problems at school, such as fighting with his peers and wandering from the classroom. Because of such difficulties, he began outpatient therapy at age 7.

Sexually Aggressive Delinquent Behaviors

The first report of sexualized behavior came from Jim's foster mother when Jim was 10. She had told Jim to go upstairs to change his pants. At the time, a 3-year-old girlfriend of the foster mother's daughter was in the house. Sometime later, the foster mother found Jim and the girl together in the basement, and it appeared that Jim was trying to have sex with the little girl. The girl was still dressed, but, as Jim jumped up, he was pulling up the girl's pants. The girl acted scared, looked for her mother, and said that Jim had said, "Come on; we are going to fuck." Jim later said he was getting ready to "do it."

At age 12, Jim was hospitalized at an inpatient unit for children following an alleged attempted gang rape of a slightly retarded girl at school. It was believed that Jim did not rape the girl, but that he observed the rape. It was the girl's impression that Jim had encouraged the other boys' behavior.

Jim was transferred from the hospital to a state residential facility via an involuntary court commitment. His behavior was described as oppositional, resistant to limits, disruptive during group activities and meetings, and sexually provocative with peers. Furthermore, he refused to accept responsibility for negative acting-out behaviors. Occasionally, restraints were necessary because of his physically assaultive and destructive behaviors.

Psychiatric and Nursing Diagnoses

Jim's condition warranted both a psychiatric diagnosis and a nursing diagnosis to help direct the intervention. The psychiatric diagnoses were:

- Axis I: Post-traumatic stress disorder with the stressor of early childhood physical and sexual abuse
- Axis II: Need to rule out antisocial and narcissistic personality disorder
- Axis III: Bilateral hydrocele
- Axis IV: Moderate to severe stressor of reuniting with mother
- Axis V: Inadequate coping with the characterological defense of splitting

Nursing diagnoses included Potential for Violence, Altered Variations of Sexual Expression; Decision-making Patterns NOS; Judgment Patterns NOS; Ineffective Individual Coping; Defensive Coping; Altered Self-concept, Altered Body Image (see Appendix B).

Treatment

The primary treatment question was, was it too late to assist Jim in correcting the fixed response to his childhood victimization, which was identifying with the aggressor? Failure to treat would allow the rape behavior to continue and to escalate. Jim was developmentally in middle adolescence, but this history and documented pattern of behavior portended a disastrous outcome for him and for others if efforts were not made to reach him at that point. Therefore, the following treatment plan was implemented.

Phase 1

The goal was to contain and control Jim and his sexually aggressive behaviors, and to engage him in socially productive activity. Jim needed a juvenile sex offender program. There were several positive indications for treatment. For example, although he had committed a forcible rape, somehow he had been able to stop his rape behavior with the child through the intervention of the child's mother. The treatment staff believed that Jim might benefit from treatment.

Jim was sent to a juvenile offender residential treatment program that included education, work, social skills, and sensitivity training. The milieu aspect of the residential treatment focused on his day-by-day activities with peers, relationships with authority, schoolwork, and responsibility. In addition, individual counseling focused on establishing an alliance and building trust in a relationship. Such counseling was critical to help Jim begin to establish internal controls. Individual therapy for Jim dealt with the cognitive and behavioral components of impulsive behavior, the childhood victimization, and post-traumatic stress response.

Phase 2

It was speculated that Jim spent a great deal of time preoccupied and distracted by violent, exciting fantasies. A clinician skilled in the area of trauma therapy began to work on eliciting Jim's sexual and aggressive fantasies with the goal of neutralizing their motivational potential for acting out. The fantasies had to be interpreted in terms of their roots in personal pain, loss, and helplessness. The dynamics within the family, such as pervasive jealousy and neglect, supported an attitudinal set in Jim that did not distinguish his actions and their consequences to others or to himself. He constantly and persistently blamed the world for his problems and, thus, felt entitled to act and take what he wanted. No doubt he had little awareness of his own sequence of behavior that led to aggressive and challenging outbursts. Because his rebellious oppositional behavior discharged tension, it had become a goal in itself.

Phase 3

The goal in phase 3 was the psychodynamic unlinking of the aggressive and sexualized exploitative behaviors from memory fragments of early abuse and exploitation. This required detailing all childhood victimization experiences in order to establish a baseline for thoughts, feelings, and behaviors as a victim. Additionally, it was necessary to detail his victim reenactments and repetitions of rape behaviors. At this point, there was direct interpretation of his own victimization.

Jim had numerous fears that had to be explored. He was very preoccupied with his own health and every minor injury to his body. There may have been an underlying anxiety regarding his bilateral hydrocele and the chronic enuresis.

Jim needed to talk of all his deviant sexual patterns. Several deviant patterns were identified, such as the collection of fetish items for masturbation (e.g., panties) and his voyeuristic activities. The greater the number of paraphilias, the more difficult the treatment. He had already assaulted both males and females, young and old.

A key therapy task was the mending of the defensive split between victim and aggressor. Jim needed to reexperience the pain of his own victimization in order to develop empathy for the injury that he had caused to his victims. He had to deal with his memories of the event that resulted in the boys' placement in the foster home. Part of the resurrection of the crisis was the mother's attempt to reunite herself with the boys. Family therapy is critical, as the mother must deal with the manifestations of her own neglect in her children.

Phase 4

This final phase of treatment involved the integration of this work with testing and assurance of Jim's personal control. The goal was for Jim to move into more positive relationships, increase his social skill capacity to take care of himself, and relate to others in a sensitive way.

NURSING RESEARCH AND POLICY

Nursing Research

There is increasing research evidence that adolescents are perpetrating sexual offenses, and concern about the violent juvenile offender is growing (Fagan, Jones, Hartstone, Rudman, & Emerson, 1981). Studies on adult sex offenders indicate that their sexually deviant interests began as juveniles (Abel, Mittleman, & Becker, 1984; Bernard, 1975), are repetitive (Abel, Becker, Mittleman, Cunningham-Rathner, Rouleau, & Murphy, 1987; Burgess, Hazelwood, Rokous, Hartman, & Burgess, 1988), and include multiple paraphilias (Abel et al., 1987; Langevin, 1985; Ressler, Burgess, Douglas, Hartman, & McCormack, 1986). Despite the seriousness of the problem and the need for early intervention to help the adolescent control his or her deviant sexual behavior (Becker et al., 1986), few studies of the characteristics of adolescent sex offenders or of their treatment have been conducted.

Juvenile sex offenders are often hospitalized on psychiatric inpatient units for forensic psychological evaluation. Psychiatric nurses have an opportunity to study this population and contribute to the clinical literature through research. Directions for future nursing research may be in the area of disturbed or deviant sexual patterns, as well as in the treatment of unresolved sexual trauma.

Policy

A strong coordinated alliance between community agencies is essential. The use of the juvenile justice system to intervene positively must be encouraged, because its authority is a powerful incentive for providing external controls, for changing intrafamilial behavior, and stopping the sex offending behavior.

The critical aspect of intervention is linking the family context and system into a program of supportive, corrective responses to the offending juvenile. This will be difficult because of the family's perception of the sexually exploitative behavior of the juvenile as an internal matter. In addition, the family work must be understood as part of a whole contextual approach to juvenile sex offenders that focuses on the motivational structure of the offender. This offender-focused intervention must address not only the sexually deviant behavior, its structure, and the factors that keep it operant, but also the development of countercoping behaviors that offset the antisocial nature of the juvenile and other socially alienating and disengaging patterns.

REFERENCES

Abel, G.G., Becker, J.V., Mittleman, M., Cunningham-Rathner, J., Rouleau, J.L., & Murphy, W.D. (1987). Self-reported sex crimes of nonincarcerated paraphiliacs. *Journal of Interpersonal Violence, 2*, 3–25.

Abel, G.G., Mittleman, M.S., & Becker, J.V. (1984). Sex offenders: Results of assessment and recommendations for treatment. In H. Ben-Aron, S. Hucker, & C. Webster (Eds.), *Clinical criminology: Current concepts* (105–116). Toronto: M&M Graphics.

Becker, J.V., Cunningham-Rathner, J., & Kaplan, M.S. (1986). Adolescent sexual offenders: Demographics, criminal and sexual histories, and recommendations for reducing future offenses. *Journal of Interpersonal Violence, 1*, 431–445.

Bernard, F. (1975). An inquiry among a group of pedophiles. *Journal of Sex Research, 11*, 242–255.

Burgess, A.W., Hartman, C.R., Howe, J.W., Shaw, E., & McFarland, G. (1990). Juvenile murderers and their crime scene drawings. *Journal of Psychosocial Nursing, 28*:26–34.

Burgess, A.W., Hartman, C.R., & Kelley, S.J. (1990). Assessing child abuse: The TRIADS checklist. *Journal of Biopsychosocial Nursing, 28*(4)6–8, 10–14, 40–41.

Burgess, A.W., Hazelwood, R.R., Rokous, F.E., Hartman, C.R., & Burgess, A.G. (1988, January). Serial rapists and their victims: Reenactment and repetition. In R.A. Prentky & V.L. Quinsley (Eds.), *Human sexual aggression: Cultural perspectives* (pp. 277–295). New York: Annals of the New York Academy of Sciences.

Deisher, R.W., Wenet, G., Paperny, D.M., Clark, T.F., & Fehrenbeach, P.A. (1981). *Adolescent sexual offense behavior: The role of the physician.* Unpublished manuscript.

Fagan, J., Jones, S.J., Hartstone, E., Rudman, C., & Emerson, R. (1981). *Background paper for the violent juvenile offender research and development program: Part 1.* Washington, DC: Office of Juvenile Justice and Delinquency Prevention.

Finkelhor, D. (1984). *Child sexual abuse: New theory and research.* New York: Free Press.

Grant, C.A., Burgess, A.W., Hartman, C.R., Shaw, E., & McFarland, G. (1989). Juveniles who murder: Insights for intervention. *Journal of Psychosocial Nursing, 27*(12), 4–11.

Groth, A.N. (1979). Sexual trauma in the life histories of rapists and child molesters. *Victimology, 4,* 1–10.

Groth, A.N., & Loredo, C.M. (1981). Juvenile sexual offenders: Guidelines for assessment. *International Journal of Offender Therapy and Comparative Criminology, 25,* 31–39.

Hartman, C.R., & Burgess, A.W. (1988). Information processing of trauma: Case application of a model. *Journal of Interpersonal Violence, 3*(4), 443–457.

Janus, M.D., McCormack, A., Burgess, A.W., & Hartman, C.R. (1987). *Adolescent runaways.* Lexington, MA: Lexington Books.

Krozy, R. (1980). Human sexuality. In A.W. Burgess (Ed.), *Psychiatric nursing in the hospital and community* (pp. 159–181). Englewood Cliffs, NJ: Prentice-Hall.

Langevin, R. (1985). *Erotic preference, gender identity and aggression in men: New research studies.* Hillsdale, NJ: Lawrence Erlbaum Associates.

Langevin, R., & Lange, R.A. (1983). Psychological treatment of pedophiles. *Behavioral Sciences and the Law, 3,* 403–419.

Parson, T. (1951). *The social system.* New York: Free Press. (Originally published in 1939 as The professions and social structure, *Social Forces, 17,* 457–467).

Ressler, R.K., Burgess, A.W., Douglas, J.E., Hartman, C.R., & McCormack, A. (1986). Murderers who rape and mutilate. *Journal of Interpersonal Violence, 1,* 273–287.

Riskin, L.I., & Koss, M.P. (1987). The sexual abuse of boys. *Journal of Interpersonal Violence, 2*(3), 309–323.

Seghorn, T., & Boucher, R. (1980). Sexual abuse in the childhood as a factor in sexually dangerous criminal offenses. In J.M. Samson (Ed.), *Childhood and sexuality* (pp. 87–95). Montreal: Editions Vivantes.

Seghorn, T., Prentky, R.A., & Boucher, R.J. (1986). Childhood sexual abuse in the lives of sexually aggressive offenders. *Journal of the American Academy of Child and Adolescent Psychiatry, 26*(2), 262–267.

26

Evaluation of Psychiatric Nursing with Children and Adolescents

Christina L. Sieloff Evans

After reading this chapter, the reader will be able to:

1. describe the goal and objectives of the evaluation process
2. identify several types of evaluation
3. describe several of the instruments that can be used in evaluation
4. examine the issues that affect evaluation
5. develop nursing strategies for conducting an evaluation

The nursing process is not finished until the evaluation component has been completed (Langford, 1971), as evaluation modifies each of the prior components of the process (Kah, 1989). Evaluation begins with assessment, proceeds throughout the nursing process, and may continue after a client has been discharged or treatment has been terminated (Barba, Bennett, & Shaw, 1978). In revising an assessment, plan, or interventions with a client, a nurse evaluates the nursing care.

Breeden (1978) defined evaluation as "the process of measuring an object, an activity . . . or an abstraction to determine the extent to which it meets established criteria" (p. 14). From the perspective of psychiatric nursing, Taylor (1986) defined evaluation as "identifying those aspects of care that are indeed helpful to a client and that, therefore, should be continued" (p. 255). Taylor also stated that "all phases of the nursing process may occur simultaneously, and some form of evaluation must take place continuously" (p. 253).

Within the context of the psychiatric and mental health nursing with children and adolescents, evaluation is a process rather than a single act. This process is integrated with the other components of the nursing process and used continuously by a nurse not only to determine the effectiveness of nursing interventions, but also to improve the quality of psychiatric nursing care with the child and adolescent clients.

The Standards of Child and Adolescent Psychiatric and Mental Health Nursing Practice (American Nurses' Association [ANA], 1985) serve as a basis for evaluating the psychiatric nursing of children and adolescents (see Appendix A). These standards provide guidelines for the structure, process, and outcomes that should occur in health care settings where children and adolescents receive psychiatric nursing care.

INTEGRATION OF EVALUATION INTO THE NURSING PROCESS

The evaluation component of the nursing process begins when a nurse initially assesses a client's status and continues as data are reappraised throughout the process. While developing a care plan, a nurse continuously considers, evaluates, and accepts or rejects aspects of the plan in relation to the client. When implementing the plan of care through interventions, a nurse also continuously adjusts interventions as a result of the client's responses to those interventions. Formal evaluation of nursing care, which takes place at the conclusion of the delivery of care to the individual client or family, provides direction for future nursing process activities with subsequent clients. All modifications in the nursing process occur as a result of evaluation.

Within a nurse-client relationship, evaluation provides a mechanism that facilitates communication as a nurse encourages clients to express their perceptions of, and responses to, the nursing care delivered. The nurse then uses the feedback in a self-evaluative process to realistically critique the effectiveness and quality of the care provided.

GOALS AND PURPOSES OF EVALUATION

The primary goal of evaluation in nursing is the improvement of the quality of nursing care in order to meet a client's needs as fully as possible. This goal remains the same, whether the evaluation involves a nurse-client interaction, a nurse-client relationship, or a client's goals. For example, in evaluating a nurse-client interaction, a child psychiatric nurse seeks to ensure that the interaction facilitated the youngster's progress. Both verbal and nonverbal components of the interaction are analyzed to confirm their therapeutic nature. A nurse-client relationship could be evaluated in terms of the presence or absence of transference or countertransference, and whether corrective interventions on the part of the nurse improved the therapeutic focus of the relationship. In evaluating the attainment of goals by a client, a nurse scrutinizes the level of goal attainment to determine if the goals had been appropriately and realistically set. In addition, the nurse determines whether goals were revised as a client's progress warranted.

The specific purposes of an evaluative process are tailored to the particular situation involved. Normally, the purposes of evaluation are:

(1) to conduct a planned critical assessment of [nursing] care, (2) to revise or confirm the plan of care, (3) to conduct a self-assessment,

(4) to review assessment data and nursing diagnosis for accuracy and currency, (5) to review a plan of care for nursing interventions, and (6) to compare [a client's] response to interventions with outcome criteria. (Taylor, 1986, p. 255)

MAJOR TYPES OF EVALUATIONS

Evaluation occurs throughout all phases of the nursing process. Those types of evaluation that can be applied within the context of the nurse-client relationship may focus on: (1) a nurse-client interaction, (2) the nurse-client relationship itself, (3) the client's evaluation of nursing care, (4) the status of a client, (5) a nurse's self-evaluation, and (6) evaluation of a nurse by the nurse's peers.

Nurse-Client Interaction

As the nurse-client interaction is "fundamental to the concept of client-centered care" (Mathews, 1962, p. 154), a nurse-client interaction is a primary context for evaluation. In evaluating a nurse-client interaction, a child psychiatric nurse examines the interaction as an entity to critique his or her verbalizations and nonverbal cues in relation to those of the young client. Did the nurse respond as warranted by the client's cues, or did the nurse respond based on personal or other needs or directions? The nurse also examines the youngster's verbal and nonverbal responses in relation to those of the nurse. Did the nurse's responses create an environment in which the client was free to respond, or did the nurse create a response for the client?

Nurse-Client Relationship

Evaluation of the nurse-client relationship as an entity involves consideration not only of the interactions that make up the relationship, but also of the goals of the relationship and its current status. Are the goals and purposes of the relationship individualized? Did the client participate in their development? Is the relationship progressing therapeutically, or is it changing in response to other needs of the nurse and/or the client? Are the interactions occurring in this phase of the relationship aimed at the achievement of other goals?

A natural time to evaluate a nurse-client relationship is during the termination of that relationship. Termination is an integral part of the relationship and concludes the therapeutic process that the nurse used throughout the relationship. The termination process begins when the nurse and the client begin discharge planning (McCann, 1979).

A nurse may avoid termination for several reasons. If the nurse has not recognized the significance of the nurse-client relationship in the therapeutic process, he or she may not recognize the need to end that relationship. As termination involves emotional processes, the nurse may seek to discount or ignore the need to conclude the relationship. Finally, the nurse responds to the ending of a relationship based on his or her own previous experiences with separation or loss (Campaniello, 1980). If these experiences have been negative or anxiety-producing, the nurse may unconsciously choose to avoid a possible repeat experience. Thus, a nurse must be aware of this potential problem and should seek assistance as needed to address this issue therapeutically with a client.

Client's Evaluation of Nursing Care

The process by which a client gives a critique or review of the nursing care received may involve an informal conversation with the client and family members, or it may be the completion of a more formal client satisfaction survey. Client evaluation is crucial to the accountability of a psychiatric nurse, but it is often overlooked for a variety of reasons. The child and adolescent psychiatric nurse may be uncomfortable requesting a critique of nursing care from a youngster or family members, or using strategies designed to elicit an evaluation from a client in these age ranges. In addition, a nursing department may not provide a mechanism for an objective evaluation.

If the nurse's role is to assist a youngster in the growth process and to facilitate the accomplishment of client goals, however, the nurse must also involve this client in a critique of the care process. Regardless of the client's capabilities, it is important to seek and understand the client's feedback regarding his or her perceptions of the nursing care received. Through this feedback, the nurse can further improve the delivery of care, and the youngster participates in all aspects of the nursing process.

Status of a Client

In evaluating the status of a client, a nurse objectively examines the current status of a client, compares the current status with the client's status on entry into treatment, and determines whether progress has occurred. If it has, the nurse further determines, as much as possible, what has facilitated this progress. If a client's status has not improved or has deteriorated, the nurse is obligated to determine what hindered the growth of the youngster and how this can be changed with future clients. This type of evaluation is also helpful should a youth reenter treatment.

Self-Evaluation by the Nurse

In a self-evaluation, the nurse asks himself or herself, "What characteristics have I brought to the relationship that have helped or hindered the client's growth?" (Cook & Fontaine, 1987, p. 32). Self-evaluation by a nurse is important to clients, as the process encourages the nurse to analyze the delivery of care critically. The nurse can quickly implement adjustments after a personal critique of his or her own nursing behaviors. Clinical supervision can also be very helpful to help a nurse objectively critique his or her delivery of nursing care to a particular client.

Evaluation of a Nurse by Peers

Through the process of examination and critique by peers, a nurse is able to refine skills, strategies, and interventions in a way not possible through any other evaluative process. Helpful suggestions by peers with whom the nurse works often provide insight into areas where growth is needed, but may not be attainable through other techniques.

AIDS TO EVALUATION

Some evaluative aids are tangible, such as instruments that a nurse and client can use. Other aids are created by a nurse and client during the preceding phases of the nurse-client relationship and are used again during evaluation.

Client Goals. The most individualized evaluation aids available to a nurse are the client goals. These may be goals set by the client, the nurse, or (ideally) the client and the nurse in collaboration. In order to be evaluated, each goal should: (1) be measurable, (2) describe a behavior, and (3) have an associated time frame for its attainment. When the outcomes of the delivery of psychiatric nursing care are compared to the initial goals, the success of the nursing interventions can be determined.

Feedback. An invaluable aid to the evaluation of nursing care is feedback. If the evaluation is to be comprehensive, such feedback should be "ongoing and dynamic" (Woody, 1980, p. 74). The child or adolescent, parents, family members, and nursing staff can provide valuable insights into the effectiveness and efficiency of the nursing care. Feedback can provide helpful direction for appropriate revisions in nursing care that may not be apparent to those who are directly providing the care. Milne, Walker, and Bentinck (1985) demonstrated the usefulness of feedback in evaluating the effectiveness of group therapy in a community setting.

Instruments. Several instruments have been developed for use in the evaluation of aspects of psychiatric nursing care, such as the Assessment of Child and Adolescent Functioning (MacNair & McKinney, 1983), the Nurse-Therapist Checklist for Measuring the Effectiveness of Help Given in Therapy with Adolescents (Eggert, 1986), and the Children's Global Assessment Scale (Shaffer, Gould, Brasic, Ambrosini, Fisher, Bird, & Aluwahlia, 1983). A nurse may administer the latter instrument at the beginning of treatment and again at the ending to evaluate a child's progress. Although it is important to determine the reliability and validity of these instruments with specific child and adolescent populations before routinely using them in nursing practice, these instruments can be helpful in gathering data that can then be incorporated into an overall evaluation.

Nursing Rounds. Staff members may evaluate child and adolescent psychiatric nursing care through nursing rounds, reviewing each client's case either formally or informally in order to determine the current status or solve a clinical problem. In grand rounds, informal rounds, milieu meetings, or other meeting formats, nursing staff question and examine the nursing care provided to a specific child or adolescent or in a specific situation. Challenging nursing care situations should be presented to allow for innovative input that can then be used to improve the nursing care delivered.

Standards. As important aids in evaluating the psychiatric nursing care provided to children and adolescents, standards "represent a set of guidelines, a type of measuring stick against which one can line up" (McClure, 1976, p. 27). In this context, standards go beyond minimal guidelines for the existence of a psychiatric agency or basic level of practice. Standards are meant to ensure the delivery of quality care to all clients. For example, the ANA standards of practice (1985) provide process and outcome criteria that can be useful in evaluating psychiatric and mental health nursing care received by individual clients. There is a major difference between the ANA standards and the standards of other reviewing groups (e.g., the Joint Commission on Accreditation of Healthcare Organizations, state departments of mental and public health). The "ANA Standards reflect the optimum to strive for. The other sets of standards reflect the minimum level that can be considered adequate" (McClure, 1976, p. 27).

EVALUATION ISSUES

There are two major groups of issues to be addressed by a child and adolescent psychiatric and mental health nurse in the evaluation process: (1) general issues associated with evaluation, and (2) issues associated with the nursing specialty.

General Issues

Among the general issues to be considered regarding evaluation are: (1) accountability; (2) the who, what, why, when, and how; (3) the impact of culture; and (4) objectivity versus subjectivity. Accountability is "the state of being responsible for . . . actions and being able to explain, define or measure the results of your decision making" (Murray & Huelskoetler, 1983, p. 131). The acceptance of accountability can be considered the hallmark of a profession. Therefore, psychiatric nurses should automatically accept responsibility for their actions and take steps to measure the effectiveness and efficiency of their decision making. It is not a process mandated by external forces, but by the profession itself—"self-regulation entails ethical and moral obligations" (Phaneuf, 1976, p. 5).

The who, what, why, when, and how of evaluation should be determined at the beginning of the evaluative process. Who refers not only to the client, but also to those who should be included in the process and those for whom the evaluation is being conducted. The specific people involved influence the evaluative process. For example, the audience for the evaluation affects the initial establishment of goals (Munro, 1983); if the direct delivery of client care is being evaluated, the goals should be derived from a client's and/or family's perspective.

It is also crucial to define what is being evaluated at the beginning of the process. Otherwise, a nurse may spend time and effort gathering data that are irrelevant to the final evaluation. The data required for evaluation of a nurse-client interaction are different from those required for an evaluation of a nurse-client relationship, for example.

Why an evaluation is conducted refers to the purpose of the evaluation. This purpose also affects the data to be gathered. In addition, it determines the content and format of the final report. In terms of client care, evaluation is conducted to facilitate the progress of the individual child or adolescent.

Factors outside a nurse's control often dictate when an evaluation must be conducted. The setting of a client's discharge date, discharges against medical advice, and the transfer of a client to another unit often occur without input from a nurse. The continual nature of evaluation throughout the nursing process ensures that a client can benefit from evaluation despite an abrupt termination of nursing care.

Finally, how an evaluation is conducted is integrally connected with the who, what, why, and when. It refers to the evaluation's procedure. The actual process of conducting an evaluation, the evaluative strategies used, may direct who must be involved, indicate what data must be gathered, provide answers related to why an evaluation is being conducted, and determine when data should be gathered. The report of the evaluation must be done in terms that the audience, in this case a client, can understand (Wolff, 1986).

The cultures of the evaluator and the client will affect the who, what, why, when, and how. If there is not some understanding of and/or congruence between the two cultures, the outcome of the evaluation will not necessarily reflect the client's true progress.

Absolute objectivity is not attainable, as the analysis of the data is always carried out within the context of the evaluator's framework. It is almost impossible for an individual to eliminate all biases when planning for the evaluation, gathering and analyzing the data, and presenting the final report. It is much more realistic for the evaluator to recognize the potential for bias as the evaluation is conducted and to make every reasonable effort to ensure that biases do not unduly affect the evaluative process.

Issues Specific to Psychiatric and Mental Health Nursing

The evaluation of the psychiatric nursing care of children and adolescents involves such issues as: (1) the therapeutic nursing process, (2) the focus of the evaluation, (3) confidentiality, and (4) language differences.

The involvement of an adult client is important in evaluating psychiatric nursing care, and the involvement of a child or adolescent client is no less important. Clients have a unique perspective on the nursing care delivered. To ignore this in an evaluation, for whatever reasons, is to discount the client and his or her worth. When attempting to increase a youngster's involvement in evaluating the nursing process, a nurse must take into account the developmental level of the client, particularly the client's cognitive skill level. Family members and significant others (e.g., teachers) also have a unique perspective on the nursing care received, and their opinions should also be valued.

The expectations of a client and family regarding nursing care, when compared with the actual outcomes of that care, provide information that can improve a nurse's ability to individualize nursing care in the future. A nurse's expectations of the results of nursing care should also be evaluated routinely as part of the nursing process. Expectations that are too high or too low may create an environment in which family members also have an unrealistic view of a client's potential; furthermore, they may seriously impede a client's progress (Kah, 1989). For example, a child may expect to feel happier after being in the hospital. The nurse may expect the child to express anger more openly. Although these two expectations may be related, the child's developmental level may not support the expression of anger. Instead of feeling more comfortable as a result of nursing care, the child may become increasingly frustrated as the nurse attempts to encourage the child's verbalizations.

Often, the progress of a youngster while receiving psychiatric nursing care is marked by subtle changes in behaviors or verbalizations. If these subtle cues are not detected, an evaluation may suggest that the client has made no progress. By being attuned to these subtle cues, which may appear over an extended period of time (particularly in the case of clients who are receiving residential or long-term care), a nurse is able to evaluate more accurately both the progress of the client and the effectiveness of the nursing care. For example, if a child who had previously expressed anger by hitting anyone who was near one day hits a peer who took a toy away from her—although there were several peers and staff who were closer—the nursing staff may see progress because the child focused on a reason for the anger rather than generalizing the emotion.

The interactions between a nurse and a child or adolescent client present an evaluative challenge. "The nature of an interaction with a client is very difficult to quantify, describe or reproduce" (Kah, 1989, p. 161). The nurse-client interaction is an abstract process that demands acute observational skills for an accurate evaluation. An example of the complex nature of nurse-client interactions can be seen in King's (1981) research to articulate a transaction. It is important to evaluate these interactions, however, as they are the basis for a nurse's therapeutic use of self. If the nurse cannot interact therapeutically with a child or adolescent, the nurse-client relationship will not develop successfully and the client's care will suffer.

In evaluating psychiatric nursing, a nurse must clearly identify the focus of the evaluation. Is the focus the progress of the client or family, or is it the effectiveness of the nursing care delivered? Because it is "frequently impossible for nurses to determine that particular change in client behavior resulted from a specific nursing action or series of actions" (Kah, 1989, p. 160), it is crucial that a nurse clearly understand psychiatric nursing with children and adolescents prior to undertaking an evaluation.

Confidentiality is a key issue in evaluating the psychiatric nursing care of children and adolescents (Faux, Walsh, & Deatrick, 1988). The information gathered in an evaluation of the care of a child or adolescent, and the reporting of that information, should be considered confidential. A client's right to confidentiality must be protected as defined by the policies of the health care facility and the laws of the particular state in which the facility is located. This right also directs who can receive the final reports and what they can do with such information. At the same time, with legal statutes as guidance, others must be protected from potentially violent acts of the client.

Any language differences involved in nurse-client interactions also affect evaluation. Although both nurse and client may speak English, they are not speaking the same level of English. In order to ensure understanding, the nurse must learn the differences in meanings and symbols that a client may use and incorporate this knowledge into the evaluation. In addition, many children and adolescents do not give a nurse direct verbal feedback. In these situations, the nurse should be attuned to nonverbal feedback. If possible, the nurse should confirm this feedback with the client. For example, a child's affect may appear brighter, but the child cannot express this directly. The nurse may say, "You look like you feel better," and wait for the child's response.

STRATEGIES FOR EVALUATIONS

Several evaluative strategies are available to a psychiatric and mental health nurse. The particular strategy chosen depends on: (1) the nurse's philosophical base, (2) the purpose of the evaluation, and (3) the resources available for conducting the evaluation.

A nurse's philosophical base determines what is valued in an evaluation and the conceptual framework in which the evaluation is conducted. This information, in turn, directs the nurse in selecting an evaluative strategy. For example, a nurse working within King's (1981) framework would evaluate the attainment of trans-actions by a nurse and the client, or goal attainment by a client, while a nurse working within Orem's (1985) framework would evaluate the change in the self-care actions.

The purpose of an evaluation is also instrumental in selecting an evaluative strategy. If the purpose is to provide data for a surveying agency, the strategy selected may be different from that selected if the purpose is to evaluate the client's achievement of goals. Often, the culture and climate within the health care setting direct the purpose of an evaluation by stipulating what is valued and what will be rewarded. A nurse then selects a strategy that is consistent with the value structure within which the evaluation will take place.

The resources available to a nurse for conducting an evaluation may frequently determine the selection of an evaluative strategy. If time, funds, and personnel are limited, the strategy selected must be easily carried out by a few people in a short time, perhaps even by the client and family. If greater resources are available, however, a more complex strategy can be selected; for example, the availability of more personnel may make it possible to screen clients for more subtle changes.

Strategies that can be used in evaluation include, but are not limited to, the following: (1) goal attainment strategies; (2) formative or summative strategies; (3) structure, process, and outcome strategies; and (4) systems strategies. These strategies may be combined as long as they are compatible with the nurse's philo-sophical base. For example, both a goal attainment strategy and a systems strategy would be appropriate for a nurse who works within King's (1981) framework.

A goal attainment strategy is based on the goals previously set by a nurse and client and/or family. These "goals are based on priorities of care, establish the criteria for evaluation, and must be observable" (Murray & Huelskoetler, 1983, p. 131). The degree to which the goals have been met determines the success of the nursing care/client progress. For example, if a goal has been set that an adolescent will talk to a nurse when angry rather than hitting the wall, and the adolescent begins to talk to the nurse consistently when angry, progress in this area has been attained. Goals must be measurable, observable, and associated with a time frame in order to be used as evaluative criteria.

Formative or summative evaluation strategies can frequently be used as the for-mat for other evaluative strategies. In formative strategies, evaluation is con-ducted on an ongoing basis during the course of a client's treatment, rather than after a client's discharge. With a summative strategy, evaluation takes place at the conclusion of the nursing process (i.e., on the client's discharge from treatment). It is most appropriate when the full effects of nursing care occur over time, but an evaluation is desired only of the end result. The attainment of long-range goals is appropriately evaluated at the time of the client's discharge, for example.

The use of structure, process, and outcome as bases for evaluation is supported by the format of the ANA standards of practice (1985). Each standard contains structure, process, and outcome criteria that can be used for evaluative purposes. "Each of the components [structure, process, and outcome] requires the use of methods appropriate to it; that is, the methods used should have structure or process or outcome as their primary focus, in full understanding that each of the components influences the other two components" (Phaneuf, 1976, p. 19).

Structure is the "organizational, personnel, and managerial environment in which care is given" (Wolff, 1986, p. 40). Process is "what happens, and in what order" (Bailit, Lewis, Hochheiser, & Bush, 1975, p. 154). Outcome "focuses on the outputs or products of the system" (Litwack, Linc, & Bower, 1985, p. 15). The outputs or products of psychiatric nursing care are changes in client behaviors that the client desires. Peplau (1989) supported the importance of outcome evaluation by noting that "nursing must begin to pinpoint outcomes of nursing interventions in relation to definable phenomena" (p. 27).

Pesut (1989) addressed the differences between focusing on outcomes and focusing on problem solutions. A focus on outcomes emphasizes ways to achieve goals and alternative approaches; a focus on problem solving emphasizes the reasons that a situation has occurred and, often, assigns blame. An emphasis on outcomes rather than problem solving also: "(1) increases efficiency and effectiveness, (2) provides standards for evaluation, and (3) focuses on creative rather than remedial approaches" (p. 28).

The systems approach to evaluation is a holistic approach that fosters a comprehensive view of a client's status. A nurse who conducts a process evaluation is assessing the "dynamic interactions among subsystems" (Litwack et al., 1985, p. 15). An outcome evaluation "focuses on the outputs, or products of the system" (Litwack et al., 1985, p. 15).

RESEARCH

The development and refinement of instruments for the evaluation of psychiatric nursing with children and adolescents require research not only on the reliability and validity of the individual instruments themselves, but also on their reliability and validity with child and adolescent populations. An instrument known to be useful with adult populations cannot automatically be used with the same confidence with younger populations. For example, Mathews (1962) "developed an instrument to measure certain psychological aspects of the nursing-client interaction and to describe its performance" (p. 154)—the Response-to-Patient Inventory. This instrument was "designed to measure a quality of nurse-patient interaction" (p. 154) with adult clients. Prior to implementing it with children, a nurse must examine the instrument to determine if children are able to respond to the instrument as adults do.

Similarly, evaluative strategies appropriate to child and adolescent populations must be developed and refined through research. In their efforts to clarify the facilitative levels of a therapeutic relationship, Aiken and Aiken (1973) identified core dimensions that, they believed, promoted therapeutic relationships: "empathetic understanding, positive regard, genuineness, concreteness and self-exploration" (p. 865). This strategy would focus on evaluating the therapeutic level of the relationship between a nurse and client rather than on goals. Because this research involved adults, however, additional research is needed to determine whether the core dimensions also apply to children and adolescents. Finally, research is needed to evaluate the effectiveness of assessment, nursing diagnoses, planning, and specific nursing interventions with child and adolescent populations who are receiving psychiatric and mental health care.

REFERENCES

Aiken, L., & Aiken, J.L. (1973). A systematic approach to the evaluation of interpersonal relationships. *American Journal of Nursing, 73*(5), 863–867.

American Nurses' Association. (1985). *Standards of child and adolescent psychiatric/mental health nursing practice.* Kansas City, MO: Author.

Bailit, H., Lewis J., Hochheiser, L., & Bush, N. (1975). Assessing the quality of care. *Nursing Outlook, 23*(3), 153–159.

Barba, M., Bennett, B., & Shaw, W.J. (1978). The evaluation of patient care through the use of ANA's standards of nursing practice. *Supervisor Nurse, 9*(1), 42, 45–46, 49–50, 53–54.

Breeden, S.A. (1978). Participative employee evaluation. *Journal of Nursing Administration, 8*(5), 13–19.

Campaniello, J.A. (1980). The process of termination. *Journal of Psychiatric Nursing and Mental Health Services, 18*(2), 29–32.

Cook, J.S., & Fontaine, K.L. (1987). *Essentials of mental health nursing.* Reading, MA: Addison-Wesley.

Eggert, L.L. (1986). The therapeutic process with adolescents. In D.C. Longo & R.A. Williams (Eds.), *Clinical practice in psychosocial nursing* (2nd ed., pp. 281–312). Norwalk, CT: Appleton-Century-Crofts.

Faux, S.A., Walsh, M., & Deatrick, J.A. (1988). Intensive interviewing with children and adolescents. *Western Journal of Nursing Research, 10*(2), 180–194.

Kah, S. (1989). Evaluation. In B.S. Johnson (Ed.), *Psychiatric-mental health nursing: Adaptation and growth* (2nd ed., pp. 158–168). Philadelphia: J.B. Lippincott.

King, I.M. (1981). *A theory for nursing: Systems, concepts, process.* New York: John Wiley & Sons.

Langford, T. (1971). The evaluation of nursing: Necessary and possible. *Supervisor Nurse, 2*(11), 65–66, 68–69, 71, 75.

Litwack, L., Linc, L., & Bower, D. (1985). *Evaluation in nursing: Principles and practice.* New York: National League for Nursing.

MacNair, R.H., & McKinney, E. (1983). *Assessment of child and adolescent functioning: A practitioner's instrument for assessing clients.* Athens, GA: The University of Georgia.

Mathews, B.P. (1962). Measurement of psychological aspects of the nurse-patient relationship. *Nursing Research, 11*(3), 154–162.

McCann, J. (1979). Termination of the psychotherapeutic relationship. *Journal of Psychiatric Nursing and Mental Health Services, 17*(10), 37–46.

McClure, M.L. (1976). ANA standards for nursing services: Considerations in evaluation. *Supervisor Nurse, 7*(8), 27, 30–31.

Milne, D., Walker, J., & Bentinck, V. (1985). The value of feedback. *Nursing Times, 81*(8), 34–36.

Munro, B.H. (1983). A useful model for program evaluation. *Journal of Nursing Administration, 13*(3), 23–26.

Murray, R.B., & Huelskoetler, M.M.W. (1983). *Psychiatric nursing: Giving emotional care.* Englewood Cliffs, NJ: Prentice-Hall.

Orem, D.E. (1985). *Nursing: Concepts of practice* (3rd ed.). New York: McGraw-Hill.

Peplau, H. (1989). Future directions in psychiatric nursing from the perspective of history. *Journal of Psychosocial Nursing and Mental Health Services, 27*(2), 18–28.

Pesut, D.J. (1989). Aim versus blame: Using an outcome specification model. *Journal of Psychosocial Nursing and Mental Health Services, 27*(5), 26–30.

Phaneuf, M.C. (1976). *The nursing audit: Self-regulation in nursing practice* (2nd ed.). New York: Appleton-Century-Crofts.

Shaffer, D., Gould, M.S., Brasic, J., Ambrosini, P., Fisher, P., Bird, H., & Aluwahlia, S. (1983). A children's global assessment scale (CGAS). *Archives of General Psychiatry, 40,* 1228–1231.

Taylor, C.M. (1986). *Mereness' essentials of psychiatric nursing* (12th ed.). St. Louis: C.V. Mosby.

Wolff, E.M. (1986). Systems management: Evaluating nursing departments as a whole. *Journal of Nursing Management, 17*(2), 40–43.

Woody, M.F. (1980). An evaluator's perspective. *Nursing Research, 29*(2), 74–77.

27

Directions in Research of Psychiatric Nursing Care of Children and Adolescents

Mary Lou de Leon Siantz

After reading this chapter, the reader will be able to:

1. define child and adolescent psychiatric and mental health nursing research
2. list historical, current, and evolving trends that are influencing the development of research in child and adolescent psychiatric and mental health nursing
3. describe differences between quantitative and qualitative approaches to nursing research
4. identify ethical considerations in research with children
5. identify ways in which a nurse can develop a research network
6. understand the role of nursing research in social policy

The goal of nursing research is to facilitate the development of clinical nursing interventions that will improve health outcomes and contribute to the optimal delivery of care. The American Nurses' Association (ANA) has stated that

> nursing research develops knowledge about health and the promotions of health over the full life span, care of persons with health problems and disabilities, and nursing actions to enhance the ability of individuals to respond effectively to actual or potential health problems. Nursing research complements biomedical research which is primarily concerned with the cause and treatments of disease (ANA, 1985a, p. 131).

Psychiatric nursing research complements biomedical programs by supporting studies on mental health promotion and prevention, clinical nursing interventions and procedures, delivery methods, and ethical considerations (Merritt, 1986).

Nurse scientists have stated that nursing is the science of caring (McBride, 1988). Nurses have a 24-hour responsibility for patients, providing them with a nonsegmented view of each patient. Nursing in general is concerned with an individual's response to actual or potential health problems. Thus, child psychiatric nurses focus on psychosocial issues with a broad understanding of anatomy and physiology (McBride, 1988). Their interest in physiological issues is based on a holistic concern for each child and his or her psychosocial, spiritual, developmental, and personal needs. Nursing research ensures that the care needs of particularly vulnerable groups, such as children and individuals from diverse cultures, are met in effective and acceptable ways (ANA, 1985a).

According to a National Institute of Mental Health (NIMH) Task Force on Nursing (1987), psychiatric nursing research has three foci: (1) mental health, mental illness, and the prevention of mental illness; (2) persons at risk for mental illness, as well as those who are mentally ill; and (3) mental health services. With respect to mental health and mental illness, nursing research focuses on improving the understanding, treatment, and rehabilitation of the mentally ill; preventing mental illness; and fostering mental health.

Child psychiatric nursing research focuses on the continuous care of children and adolescents who are acutely or chronically mentally ill, those who are at risk for mental illness, and their families (ANA, 1985b). Such research is concerned with therapeutic interventions and environmental modifications that minimize the effects of illness and enhance the ability of children and their families to respond to actual and potential mental health problems (ANA, 1985b). When investigating the delivery of mental health services, nurse researchers are concerned with the design, implementation, and evaluation of new and existing models of service delivery, especially those related to nursing care (NIMH, 1987).

HISTORICAL FACTORS

The potential contribution of child psychiatric nursing research has not always been recognized. Historically, child psychiatric nursing has often been discounted in the child mental health field (McBride, 1988; Pothier, Norbeck, & Laliberte, 1985). The accepted theories of the time concerning the etiology and treatment of disturbed children determined the role that was originally delegated to nursing. Even with the evolvement of knowledge and therapies, child psychiatric nursing did not fare better. It was even separated from the mainstream of nursing (Pothier, 1984).

Opportunities for specialist graduate education by the NIMH indicated a recognition of the potential contribution by nurses. Indeed, the 1950s and 1960s were the golden years for graduate psychiatric and mental health nursing education (Chamberlain, 1983). Even with the onset of the community mental health movement of the 1960s, however, nurses had the potential, but not always the opportunity, to provide services to children (Pothier, 1984).

Yet, few graduate programs to prepare specialists in the field of child psychiatric nursing have developed, with only 12 in existence in the United States by 1988 (Pothier, 1988) and two more planned in 1990. There has also been a decrease in federal, regional, and local funds for services that target children in the United

States (McBride, 1988, 1989). Over time, all these factors have influenced the number of nurses practicing child psychiatric nursing and conducting related research.

CURRENT INFLUENCES

Growing numbers of children, from infants to adolescents, need mental health services now more than ever. It has been estimated that there are more than 62 million children and youths under 18 years of age currently in the United States and that 12% to 15% of these, or 7.5 to 9.5 million children require some type of mental health services (Office of Technology and Assessment [OTA], 1986). Eighty percent of children identified as mentally disturbed receive inappropriate mental health services or none at all (OTA, 1986). Many more children are at risk and in need of preventive services.

Although the scope and types of psychological problems that children experience are broad, data on these problems are difficult to obtain. Clinical studies usually have nonstandardized criteria and vague labels, such as emotional disturbance or clinical maladjustment (Tuma, 1989). Despite such variable criteria, the OTA (1986) found that children experience such mental health problems as faulty life experiences or surface conflicts (80%), neuroses (10%), problems related to physical handicaps (5%), and psychoses or severe mental retardation (5%). It has also been estimated that between 1980 and 2005, the mental health problems of adolescents will increase (OTA, 1986).

Psychiatric nurse researchers have concluded that, although the subspecialty of child psychiatric nursing has struggled for recognition, it is now ready to meet the growing crisis in child mental health (Pothier et al., 1985; Siantz, 1990a). Nurses will succeed by continuing to develop, validate, and evaluate innovative nursing practices through creative research. Ultimately, nursing knowledge is waiting for expansion through systematic studies of the unique phenomena that concern all those practicing in the field of child and adolescent psychiatric and mental health nursing (McBride, 1988; Pothier et al., 1985).

FUTURE TRENDS

With mental, behavioral, and developmental disorders of children and adolescents on the rise, the Institute of Medicine (IOM) recently released a report that documented the critical need for research on children and adolescents with mental, behavioral, and developmental disorders (IOM-NAS, 1989). The report underscored the importance of developing the nation's research capacity to understand and treat the mental disorders of childhood. The National Advisory Mental Health Council (1990) issued a similar report that identified a need for more research on children and adolescent mental illness. Public hearings in Minnesota and California focused on assessing and expanding the public awareness of mental illness among children.

The IOM recommended that a national plan be developed to focus on: (1) the need to encourage and support programmatic research at the frontiers of scientific inquiry, and (2) the need to enhance NIMH's ability to provide sustained leadership in this area. Because the research concerning child and adolescent psychiatric mental health is diverse and complex, it was concluded that the field must move ahead in a broad-based fashion with different research approaches and interdisciplinary perspectives (IOM-NAS, 1989). Such approaches ought to include sensitivity to psychological, social, and biological factors.

As these recent recommendations from the IOM are implemented, there will be new opportunities for child psychiatric nurses in a variety of settings. Child psychiatric nurses with diverse educational preparation will be needed to assist or collaborate on research projects or to direct their own independent research.

Child psychiatric nursing research faces additional challenges as the risk factors that affect the mental health of children continue to proliferate. Poverty is increasing rapidly. One in four children is born into poverty (Gnezda, 1988). Those who survive childhood learn early to cope with the stresses and contingencies of poverty through drugs or sex. An increasing number of school-aged children have teen-aged mothers or come from single-parent families. Many are latchkey children with no one to greet them when they come home from school.

Single parenting is changing the traditional structure of the family. At some point, 59% of children will live with only one parent in a home prone to poverty and stress. One of four children will not graduate from high school (National Resource Center for Children in Poverty, 1988). Teen-age pregnancy especially among 10- to 14-year-olds is increasing (Elliott, 1987). Three of five mothers with preschool children are working full-time; 50% of their children are spending increasing numbers of hours in day care (Kahn & Kammerman, 1988).

Another demographic factor of interest to psychiatric nurses is the changing ethnic minority population. Blacks constitute 11.5% of the total population, with the greatest number 15 years of age or younger. One of three blacks lives in poverty (Department of Health and Human Services [DHHS], 1985).

One of twelve U.S. citizens is Hispanic and children make up more than one-third of the Hispanic population. Furthermore, evidence suggests that the size of this youth group is increasing. It is estimated that by 2023, Hispanics will make up 28% of the U.S. population and will number 99 million. By 2000, the present Hispanic population will double, with more than 10 million children needing mental health care (COSSMHO, 1988).

Among the Indian and Alaskan native populations, children have an alarmingly high incidence of mental health problems. Substance abuse is widespread among Indian children. Adolescents on Indian reservations have a high rate of suicide attempts. The prevalence of child abuse is high on the reservations. All these conditions reflect the serious mental health problems that permeate Indian youth. Currently, mental health resources to combat these problems are minimal (Inouye, 1988).

The number of Asian and Pacific Islanders in the United States increased 120% between 1970 and 1980 (DHHS, 1985). As of 1980, this group numbered 3.7 million and represented 1.6% of the population. The children of Asian and Pacific Islanders have unique mental health needs. Most recently, the influx of Asian refugees has further increased the numbers of Asian children who need mental health services.

The crisis precipitated by acquired immunodeficiency syndrome (AIDS) has created a new host of mental health problems. More than 75% of babies born with AIDS are black or Hispanic (COSSMHO, 1988). Public health experts predict that, by 1991, the number of pediatric AIDS cases will range from 3,000 to 10,000 to 20,000 (Presidential Commission, 1988). Increasing numbers of infants born with AIDS are being abandoned; some are surviving into the preschool years. The number of teen-agers at risk for AIDS, especially runaways, has also increased. Research is needed to develop psychiatric nursing interventions with these children, their mothers, foster parents, and hospital nurses involved in their care (Bishop, 1989).

All these risk factors will continue to affect the mental health status and the incidence of mental illness in U.S. youngsters. Child psychiatric nurse researchers, as well as practicing nurses, need to study and develop interventions that decrease the impact of stress among the culturally, economically, and socially divergent youth (IOM-NAS, 1989). Nurses need to consider the effects that these risk factors have on mental health and mental illness while investigating innovative ways to keep them from overwhelming youngsters and society. Thus, nursing research is needed to establish the reliability and validity of nursing interventions that focus on the prevention, timely detection, and early intervention for mental health problems or mental illness among those children and adolescents at risk (Siantz, 1990a).

RESEARCH TRENDS

Child psychiatric nurses must recognize the importance of integrating their basic science preparation into their research (Drew, 1988). A biopsychosocial model can provide a unique perspective (Christman, 1987). Such a perspective also provides hope for identifying biological markers that indicate systemic change, as skin pigmentation indicates the low levels of the melatonin hormone associated with seasonal affective disorder (Restak, 1989). The influence of biological factors in the development of normal and abnormal behavior and maturation is becoming increasingly apparent (National Advisory Mental Health Council, 1990).

A biological perspective may also help to narrow the gap between nurse researchers who are social scientists and practitioners who are oriented primarily toward providing physical care, giving medications, and managing deviant behavior (McBride, 1989).

Expansion and Testing of Nursing Models

Child psychiatric nurses must continue the development and testing of theories and models that will provide conceptual frameworks for research. The greatest amount of disagreement has occurred around nursing models and theories (Mercer, 1984). These frameworks, which have been used in all areas of nursing practice, education, and research, underscore the growth in the profession and its growing ability to produce research that provides theory for nursing practice (Mercer, 1984).

Psychiatric nurses have frequently dismissed nursing theories because they have been developed by nonpsychiatric nurses (Dashiff, 1988). As professional nurses, child psychiatric nurses must share the profession's commitment to nursing theories. Only through a planned process of testing, revision, modification, and elaboration can theories be changed and expanded so that they become relevant to child psychiatric nursing (Dashiff, 1988). Psychiatric nurses cannot afford to ignore theories developed by nonpsychiatric nurses, as this attitude can only distance the field from the mainstream of nursing.

Gast (1986) undertook a study to expand the self-care theory developed by Orem (1985). According to Orem, the self-care requisites needed to achieve, maintain, or enhance health and well-being are universal, health deviation, and development. Gast defined mental health self-care as "those actions of a person which are directed toward the achievement, maintenance, and enhancement of his/her psychological well-being." Through interviews with child psychiatric clinical nurse specialists, Gast categorized their responses into 14 categories of mental health self-care and developed an inventory that measured mental health self-care among children 8 to 16 years of age. Testing of this inventory is continuing, and this research effort will further explicate Orem's self-care theory.

McBride (1988) commented that psychiatric nursing is beginning a new period of theory development. She contended that the more systematically a particular specialty area is investigated, the more refined the theoretical framework that shapes the research. Norbeck's social support model, for example, is being refined systematically through a series of studies on social support (e.g., Norbeck, Lindsey, & Carrieri, 1981).

In general, nurse researchers have conducted very few studies that test nursing theory. Nursing models have been used primarily as frameworks for nursing research, rather than investigated themselves (Silva, 1986). Nursing theory should be grounded in practice and refined through research, however. Theory should be applied to practice if research is to be more than idle speculation (Dickoff & James, 1968).

Research in Practice and Service Delivery

The reliability and validity of nursing assessment protocols that child psychiatric nurses use in their practice must be studied. This will become even more crucial, as diagnostic classification systems are now being developed (e.g., O'Toole & Loomis, 1989). Along with assessment and classification, nursing interventions for specific diagnostic categories should be validated and standardized.

Nursing interventions that are sensitive to the developmental and cultural needs of infants, preschoolers, school-aged children, and adolescents who are experiencing mental health problems should be studied to establish their reliability and validity. Nurses in clinical practice should consider standardizing their assessment and intervention protocols. A practicing nurse should evaluate what worked, what failed, and why either outcome occurred. Through professional networking, nurses can identify potentially effective interventions for testing.

Research on the Sociotherapeutic Environment

Child psychiatric nurses should investigate which nursing interventions in the sociotherapeutic environment, particularly in an inpatient psychiatric hospital, enhance recovery, mental health growth, and development of children from infancy through adolescence. For example, according to Rowe (1988), the purpose of the sociotherapeutic milieu is to structure a child's daily life experience in a manner that enhances the therapeutic potential of everything that the child experiences. Using attachment theory as a theoretical basis for organizing the sociotherapeutic milieu, Rowe maintained that nursing assessments in the milieu should focus primarily on the child's attachments, development, and internal workings. These assessments should include an examination of the child's use of attachment figures to obtain a sense of security and the effects that the attachment relationship has on later development.

Rowe (1988) described the function of nursing as providing a secure base so that children can explore their internal working models and their relationship with others. Nurses can provide a secure environment through containment, support, and structure (Gunderson, 1978; Rowe, 1988). Containment is the application of external controls when a child's internal controls are not adequate; it provides security by removing the responsibility of self-control from the child when the child is unable to assume that responsibility. Support is the provision of a nurturing, relatively stress-free environment that makes children feel secure. Structure increases security because it clarifies for the child what adaptive behaviors are expected (Rowe, 1988). The reliability and validity of nursing assessments and interventions in the sociotherapeutic environment from this perspective need investigation.

THE SCIENTIFIC METHOD

A nurse who develops, collaborates, or applies research needs to understand the scientific method (Brink & Wood, 1988; Polit & Hungler, 1987). Professional nurses engaged in all aspects of child and adolescent psychiatric nursing, including practice, administration, and education, are responsible for identifying problems that need scientific investigation. Indeed, accountability requires that all child psychiatric nurses not only use research findings in their chosen roles, but also evaluate the findings and methods used in studies (Brink & Wood, 1988).

Choosing a Research Approach

The first step in using the scientific method is to understand the quantitative and qualitative approaches to research, two scientific paradigms that can be used to generate nursing knowledge (Phillips, 1988). The choice between these two approaches is the first design decision that the researcher must make. Each approach has strengths and limitations; each involves different information. They are suited for different types of questions or for different stages of investigation (Porter, 1989).

Nurse researchers debate whether the nature of the study question or the investigator's philosophy of science determines the selection of a qualitative or quantitative approach (DeGroot, 1988). No matter what design approach a researcher chooses, scientific progress depends on both creative ideas and intellectual freedom. Methodological conformity ultimately impedes scientific progress (DeGroot, 1988).

Qualitative Research

Described as the "nonnumerical organization, and interpretation of data in order to discover patterns, themes, forms, examples and qualities identified through field notes, interview transcripts, open-ended questionnaires, journals, diaries, documents, case studies, and other contexts" (Wilson, 1989, p. 454), qualitative research is designed to explore, describe, and interpret processes in their personal and social contexts. This type of research is based on the assumption that it is not possible to study people without describing human experience in detail as it is lived and defined by those living it. This approach emphasizes a subject's reality; it requires a minimum of imposed research structure, because the researcher is trying to understand the experience of the subject. Imposing structure on the research situation by deciding in advance what questions to ask and how to ask them can restrict the portion of the subject's experience that might otherwise be revealed (Duffy, 1987).

Nurse researchers who use qualitative methods value the firsthand descriptions of those who are involved with the phenomenon being studied. In this type of study, a researcher attempts to collect and present a complete and detailed account of findings in order to develop promising leads or ideas (Wilson, 1989). The researcher may organize findings by straight description or by analytic description (Schatzman & Strauss, 1983). In a straight description, the researcher may simply find classes or cases in the data that correspond to categories or classification schemes that have already been identified. Using the stages of psychosocial development of Erickson (1963), for example, a researcher would categorize children according to the description of each stage (e.g., trust versus mistrust, industry versus inferiority). In an analytic description, the researcher tries to develop new classes or categories through an active inspection of the data (Wilson, 1989). For example, May (1983) developed a typology of detachment and involvement styles of first-time fathers.

Qualitative anecdotes can also answer why and how questions associated with quantitative study findings. For example, in a study of the effect of social support on the maternal behavior of Mexican-American migrant farmworkers, an unusually high percentage (100%) of these mothers agreed to participate in the study (Siantz, 1990b). When the mothers were asked at the end of the data collection if they would like to tell the interviewer anything else, they stated that no one had ever asked them about their migration experience during the harvest season. They wanted to share their experiences to help others like themselves. This information was important in understanding the high rate of consent.

In applying the qualitative approach to children, nurses need to familiarize themselves with the various data-gathering techniques available. The first step in a qualitative approach with a child is to understand the child's developmental stage, then choose the most-age appropriate technique. Deatrick and Faux (1989) suggested group and individual indirect observations, multiple interviews in which a variety of play and projective techniques are used, for preschoolers. For school-aged children, they suggested direct and indirect observation of individuals and groups. Single or multiple interviews with individuals or groups are also useful and can be augmented by play. Qualitative techniques that can be used with adolescents include individual and group single interviews and direct observation.

Quantitative Research

The majority of nursing research studies conducted since the 1950s have involved the collection of quantitative or numerical data (Duffy, 1987). A numerical system indicates how much of a critical attribute an object possesses. According to Nunnally (1978), "measurement consists of rules for assigning numbers to objects to represent quantities of attributes" (p. 2).

In measurement procedures, the characteristics of the object, not the object itself, are measured. The measurement procedures constitute the operational definitions of the concepts. The purpose of assigning numbers is to differentiate between persons or objects that possess varying degrees of the critical attributes. If patient A has a lower self-concept than does patient B, patient A should have a lower score on a self-concept measurement scale than does patient B. The critical problem is to ascertain how much lower the score should be to reflect the precise difference.

The process of quantification takes place according to well formulated rules. Whether data are collected through observation, self-report, or some other method, the researcher must specify the conditions and criteria of the numerical values assigned to the abstract characteristic of interest. The researcher must also try to locate measures that are congruent with reality, that is, there must be correspondence between the attribute and its measure (Duffy, 1987).

Quantitative measurement has a number of advantages. For example, it removes the guesswork from the research. An objective measure is one that can be independently verified by other researchers. The numerical results are amenable to analytic procedures in ways the purely qualitative, subjective information is not. Quantitative measures provide reasonably precise information. Instead of describing a child as "rather sad," the researcher can depict the child as depressed, or not depressed, according to a scale. With precision, the researcher's task of differentiation among subjects that possess different degrees of an attribute becomes easier (Polit & Hungler, 1987).

Qualitative versus Quantitative

Child psychiatric nurses need to understand that both approaches have strengths and limitations. Procedures that qualitative researchers use are flexible and exploratory. As the study progresses, the researcher can add or change the types and sources of data collected. The quantitative approach is highly structured and designed to verify predetermined hypotheses with minimal flexibility (Duffy, 1987).

Qualitative data are collected within the context of their natural occurrence. Therefore, any variables that normally influence the data operate without interference. Quantitative data are collected under controlled conditions in order to rule out the possibility that variables not included in the study may explain the hypothesized relationship among the variables (Duffy, 1987).

Qualitative data analysis involves integrating and synthesizing narrative nonnumerical data, such as beliefs, attributes, and symbols (Holm & Llewellyn, 1986). The data have often been obtained through observation methods, interviews, or open-ended questions that are difficult to translate directly into numbers. This process is called content analysis. All unstructured data must undergo content analysis. Categories must be developed from the data that was collected, and each category must be different from all other categories. Furthermore, the categories must be mutually exclusive. For example, in order to identify the nursing interventions that help to decrease a hospitalized adolescent's depression, a nurse may ask recovered teen-agers to recall what the nurse did to make them less depressed. After interviewing a number of adolescents, the nurse would analyze the content of these interviews and identify the categories contained in the interviews.

Quantitative data are analyzed through statistical procedures. Such analyses include a range of procedures from simple to complex and sophisticated methods. Statistical techniques help the researcher to evaluate the outcome of a study objectively and decide if the results are due to chance. Statistical methods make it possible to identify valid generalizations and those that need further investigation (Brink & Wood, 1988).

Ensuring Reliability and Validity

In order to standardize assessment and intervention protocols, nurses need to understand the concepts of reliability and validity. Reliability refers to the stability, consistency, or dependability of a measuring tool (Polit & Hungler, 1987). Validity refers to the degree to which an instrument measures what it was designed to measure (Holm & Llewellyn, 1986). Reliability and validity are not totally independent qualities. An instrument that is not reliable is unlikely to be valid; an instrument cannot validly measure a quality if it is erratic, inconsistent, and inaccurate (Wilson, 1989).

ETHICAL CONSIDERATIONS

The ultimate responsibility for establishing and maintaining ethical practices in research lies with the individual investigator (National Commission, 1977). In conducting research with children, special ethical problems must be considered (National Commission, 1978). These ethical considerations differ from those presented by adult subjects. Ethical guidelines for research with children have been developed by the Society for Research in Child Development (1973).

An individual's autonomy is his or her ability to make decisions freely. A person with diminished autonomy is dependent on others and is, in some respects, not able to deliberate or to act on the basis of deliberation (Veatch & Fry, 1987). Researchers must respect the rights of persons with diminished autonomy, such as children, and protect their right to an informed consent. The principle of autonomy requires that a researcher who works with a child obtain an informed consent from the parent or guardian (Beauchamp & Childress, 1979). An informed consent requires clear, adequate disclosure in language that a person of average intelligence can understand (Siantz, 1988a). The child should also be informed if he or she is at least 7 years of age (Society for Research in Child Development, 1973). The consent must be freely given.

The ethical principle of nonmaleficence should also guide the nurse researcher. This principle requires that the researcher not intend to do harm nor risk harming the subject as a result of the research (Beauchamp & Childress, 1979). It applies to both psychological and physical harm.

The principle of beneficence requires the researcher to take positive steps to help others. Thus, the researcher should prevent harm and remove harmful conditions (Beauchamp & Childress, 1979). A careful analysis of the risks and benefits of the research to the child is, therefore, essential. The principle of justice is based on the assumption that each person is treated fairly and has equal rights (Beauchamp & Childress, 1979).

Each of these principles justifies the need for an informed consent, confidentiality, and an analysis of risks and benefits for the subject (Verzemnieks, 1984). Institutional review boards require researchers to submit their proposals for review by an appointed committee to ensure that these principles have been followed and the rights of the subjects have been protected (National Commission, 1977, 1978). Before any research is undertaken, a proposal must be reviewed by the Institutional Review Board of the participating hospital, university, school, or agency involved. The individual researcher must communicate with these boards, complete their required forms, and secure their approval prior to beginning any study. No matter how young the child, the child's rights supersede the rights of the investigator. Institutional review boards should be established in any setting where children are the subjects of study (Society for Research in Child Development, 1973).

RESEARCH NETWORKS

A nurse can take a variety of actions to help develop an idea. A nurse can collaborate with other nurse researchers to help bridge the gap between practice and research that sometimes occurs. Sometimes it helps to collaborate with those in other disciplines. It is most important not to give up the idea and to realize that research is a slow and deliberate process (Siantz, 1990a).

Nurses who are interested in applying research findings, collaborating, or developing a research problem can help themselves by developing a research network. The first step is to identify other nurses with a common area of interest. These nurses should then set time aside on a regular basis to share ideas, journal articles, or any relevant research material. The next step is for the group to identify a consultant, such as a nurse with research expertise in the area of interest, to meet with the group and help develop the idea further.

A nurse may also find a researcher for collaboration in a research project. In this situation, the nurse is likely to have a clear idea of the research problem that he or she wants to investigate. The working environment may provide access to an established researcher in the field.

A nurse may also try to develop linkages with schools of nursing. Faculty members with established areas of research expertise and interests may be willing to consult or collaborate with the nurse. Ultimately, a nurse interested in research must understand that research is not a solitary process. At every step, a collegial relationship is important—especially for the novice.

Research can be time-consuming and hard work. A clinician may find that scholarly pursuits compete with patient care demands. Developing a research team may be one way to share the "burden" (Haller, 1989). Care should be taken not to involve so many individuals that the planning becomes cumbersome and slow, however.

In considering whether to undertake a research project, a nurse must also consider the amount of money that will be required to execute the study. Potential sources of funding range from federal grants to regional, state, and local funding. Professional organizations, such as the American Nurses Federation and Sigma Theta Tau, provide opportunities for qualified nurses to conduct pilot studies. Private foundations also provide money for specific areas.

The National Institute of Mental Health is a potential funding resource for nursing research. As members of one of the four core mental health disciplines, child psychiatric nurses should take advantage of the research opportunities available at the NIMH (McBride & Friedenberg, 1989, NIMH, 1990). The NIMH uses a range of funding resources in its extramural programs, including small grants, regular conference grants, and small business innovations research grants (McBride & Friedenberg, 1989). The development of child psychiatric and mental health nursing research will depend largely on the extent to which nurses take the initiative in making their interests known, identifying potential funding resources, and then taking advantage of their opportunities.

SOCIAL POLICY IMPLICATIONS

The importance of research to the growth and development of knowledge in child and adolescent psychiatric and mental health nursing cannot be overstated. Research is vital not only to the development of the specialty, but also to the population that it serves: children, adolescents, and their families. Knowledge based on the findings of child and adolescent psychiatric nurses can also be used to help formulate social policy that will affect the mental health and development of children and adolescents.

Policy makers do not have the expertise that child and adolescent psychiatric nurse clinicians, administrators, educators, and scholars have acquired through practice and research. Thus, nurses are in a unique position to communicate clearly to policy makers through their publications and expert legislative testimony what youngsters need to maintain health and prevent mental illness in a variety of settings. Child and adolescent psychiatric and mental health nursing research will provide the hard facts that nurses need to advocate on behalf of children, adolescents, and their families.

REFERENCES

American Nurses' Association. (1985a). *Directions for nursing research: Toward the twenty-first century*. Kansas City, MO: Author.

American Nurses' Association. (1985b). *Nursing: A social policy statement*. Kansas City, MO: Author.

Beauchamp, T., & Childress, J. (1979). *Principles of biomedical ethics*. New York: Oxford University Press.

Bishop, S. (1989). The psychiatric nursing shortage and the HIV epidemic: A call to action (Editorial). *Journal of Child and Adolescent Psychiatric and Mental Health Nursing, 2*(1), 1.

Brink, P., & Wood, M. (1988). *Basic steps in planning nursing research from question to proposal*. Boston: Jones and Bartlett.

Chamberlain, J. (1983). The role of the federal government in the development of psychiatric nursing. *Journal of Psychiatric Nursing, 21*(4), 11–17.

Christman, L. (1987). Psychiatric nurses and the practice of psychotherapy: Current status and future possibilities. *American Journal of Psychotherapy, 41*, 384–390.

COSSMHO (The National Coalition of Hispanic Health Services Organizations). (1988). *Delivering preventive health care to Hispanics: A manual for providers*. Washington, DC: Author.

Dashiff, C. (1988). Theory development in psychiatric mental health nursing: An analysis of Orem's theory. *Archives of Psychiatric Nursing, 2*(6), 366–372.

Deatrick, J., & Faux, S. (1989). Conducting qualitative studies with children and adolescents. In J.M. Morse (Ed.), *Qualitative nursing research: A contemporary dialogue* (pp. 185–203). Gaithersburg, MD: Aspen Publishers.

DeGroot, H. (1988). Scientific inquiry in nursing: A model for a new age. *American Nursing Science, 10*, 1–21.

Department of Health and Human Services. (1985, January). *Report of the Secretary's Task Force on Black and Minority Health* (Vol. 6).

Dickoff, J., & James, P. (1968). A theory of theories. *Nursing Research, 17*, 197–203.

Drew, B. (1988). Devaluation of biological knowledge. *Image: Journal of Nursing Scholarship, 20*, 25–27.

Duffy, M. (1987). Methodological triangulation: A vehicle for merging quantitative and qualitative research methods. *Image: Journal of Nursing Scholarship, 19*, 130–133.

Elliott, J. (1987, October). *Maternal and child health*. Paper presented at the Invitational Maternal Child Nursing Conference sponsored by the University of Oregon School of Nursing and Division of Maternal Child Health. Washington, DC.

Erickson, E. (1963). *Childhood and society* (2nd ed.). New York: W.W. Norton.

Gast, H. (1986, October). Developing an inventory to measure mental health self-care in children. *Psychiatric Mental Health Nursing: Proceedings of a Conference Defining the Discipline for the Year 2000*. Co-sponsored by Society for Education and Research in Psychiatric-Mental Health Nursing, The Psychiatric Nursing Education Program Division of Education and Service Systems Liaison and the National Institute of Mental Health.

Gnezda, T. (1988). Economic implications of child care and early childhood education policy. Unpublished manuscript. Center for Children in Poverty, New York.

Gunderson, J. (1978). Defining the therapeutic processes in psychiatric milieu. *Psychiatry, 41,* 327–335.

Haller, K. (1989). Building a research team. *MCN: The American Journal of Maternal Child Nursing, 14*(4), 296.

Holm, K., & Llewellyn, J. (1986). *Nursing research for nursing practice.* Philadelphia: W.B. Saunders.

Inouye, D. (1988). Children's mental health issues. *American Psychologist, 10*(43), 813–816.

Institute of Medicine-National Academy of Science. (1989). *Research on children and adolescents with mental, behavioral, and developmental disorders: Mobilizing a national initiative* (Publication No. IOM-89-07). Washington, DC: National Academy Press.

Kahn, A., & Kammerman, S. (1988, April 21). Testimony prepared for Hearing of Subcommittee on Human Resources, Committee on Education and Labor. Testimony presented to the U.S. House of Representatives, Subcommittee on Human Resources, Hearing on Child Care.

May, K. (1982). The phases of father involvement in pregnancy. *Nursing Research, 31,* 337–342.

McBride, A. (1988). Coming of age. *Archives of Psychiatric Nursing, 2*(2), 57–64.

McBride, A. (1989, October 19). *Psychiatric nursing in the 1990's.* Paper presented at the Biological Psychiatry and the Future of Psychiatric Nursing conference sponsored by the Mental Health and Alcohol Nursing Service of the Clinical Center, National Institute of Health.

McBride, A., & Friedenberg, E. (1989). Research opportunities at the National Institute of Mental Health. *Image: Journal of Nursing Scholarship, 21*(4), 251–253.

Mercer, R. (1984). Nursing research: The bridge to excellence in practice. *Image: Journal of Nursing Scholarship, 16*(2), 47–51.

Merritt, D. (1986). The National Center for Nursing Research. *Image: Journal of Nursing Scholarship, 18,* 84–85.

National Advisory Mental Health Council. (1989). *A national plan for research on child and adolescent mental disorders: A report to Congress.* Rockville, MD: NIMH, Alcohol, Drug Abuse, and Mental Health Administration, & Department of Health and Human Services.

National Advisory Mental Health Council. (1990). *A national plan for research on child and adolescent mental disorders: A report to Congress.* National Institute of Mental Health, Alcohol, Drug Abuse, and Mental Health Administration, Department of Health and Human Services.

National Commission for the Protection of Human Subjects of Biomedical and Behavioral Research. (1977). *Research involving children* (DHEW Publication No. (05) 77-0005). Washington, DC: U.S. Government Printing Office.

National Commission for the Protection of Human Subjects of Biomedical and Behavioral Research. (1978). *The Belmont Report: Ethical principles and guidelines for the protection of human subjects of research* (Vol. 1, DHEW Publication No. (05) 78-0013). Washington, DC: U.S. Government Printing Office.

National Institute of Mental Health (1987, September). *Report of the Task Force on Nursing.* Rockville, MD: Author.

National Institute of Mental Health (1990). *Implementation of the National Plan for Research on Child and Adolescent Mental Disorders.* Program Announcement, US Department of Health and Human Services, Public Health Service, Alcohol, Drug Abuse, and Mental Health Administration. Rockville, MD: Author.

National Resource Center for Children in Poverty. (1988, June). *Early childhood education and childcare.* Panel on Early Childhood Education and Childcare, Columbia University, New York.

Norbeck, J., Lindsey, A., & Carrieri, V. (1981). The development of an instrument to measure social support. *Nursing Research, 30,* 264–269.

Nunnally, J. (1978). *Psychometric theory.* New York: McGraw-Hill.

Office of Technology and Assessment. (1986). *Children's mental health: Problems and services. A background paper* (OTA-BP-H-33). Washington, DC: U.S. Government Printing Office.

Orem, D. (1985). *Nursing concepts of practice* (2nd ed.). New York: McGraw-Hill.

O'Toole, A.W., & Loomis, M.E. (1989). Revision of the phenomena of concern for psychiatric-mental health nursing. *Archives of Psychiatric Nursing, 3*(5), 288–309.

Phillips, J. (1988). The reality of nursing research. *Nursing Science Quarterly, 1*(2), 48–49.

Polit, D., & Hungler, B. (1987). *Nursing research principles and methods.* St. Louis: J.B. Lippincott.

Porter, E. (1989). The qualitative-quantitative dualism. *Image: Journal of Nursing Scholarship, 21*(2), 98–102.

Pothier, P. (1984). Child psychiatric nursing. *Journal of Psychosocial Nursing, 3*(22), 11–21.

Pothier, P. (1988). Graduate preparation in child and adolescent psychiatric mental health nursing. *Archives of Psychiatric Nursing, 2*(3), 170–172.

Pothier, P., Norbeck, J., & Laliberte, M. (1985). Child psychiatric nursing: The gap between need and utilization. *Journal of Psychosocial Nursing, 23*(7), 18–23.

Presidential Commission on the Human Immunodeficiency Virus Epidemic. (1988). *Report of the Presidential Commission on the Human Immunodeficiency Virus Epidemic.*

Restak, R. (1989). The brain, depression and the immune system. *Journal of Clinical Psychiatry, 50*(5) (suppl.), 23–25.

Rowe, J. (1988). Attachment theory and milieu treatment. *Journal of Child and Adolescent Psychiatric and Mental Health Nursing, 1*(2), 66–71.

Schatzman, L., & Strauss, A. (1983). *Field research.* Englewood Cliffs, NJ: Prentice-Hall.

Siantz, M. (1988a). Children's rights and parental rights: A historical and legal/ethical analysis. *Journal of Child and Adolescent Psychiatric and Mental Health Nursing, 1*(1), 14–17.

Siantz, M. (1988b). Defining informed consent. *American Journal of Maternal Child Nursing, 13*(2), 94.

Siantz, M. (1990a). Commentary: Trends and directions in child psychiatric nursing. *Journal of Child and Adolescent Psychiatric and Mental Health Nursing, 3*(2), 65–68.

Siantz, M. (1990b). Maternal acceptance/rejection of Mexican-American migrant mothers. *Psychology of Women Quarterly, 14*(2), 245–254.

Silva, M. (1986). Research testing nursing theory: State of the art. *Advances in Nursing Science, 96,* 1–11.

Society for Research in Child Development. (1973). Ethical standards for research with children. *Newsletter,* 3–5.

Tuma, J. (1989). Mental health services for children. *American Psychologist, 44*(2), 188–199.

Veatch, R., & Fry, S. (1987). *Case studies in nursing ethics.* Philadelphia: J.B. Lippincott.

Verzemnieks, I. (1984). Ethical issues related to pediatric care. *Nursing Clinics of North America, 19*(2), 319–329.

Wilson, H. (1989). *Research in nursing.* Menlo Park, CA: Addison-Wesley.

Appendix A

ANA Standards of Child and Adolescent Psychiatric and Mental Health Nursing Practice

Professional Practice Standards

Standard I. Theory. The nurse applies appropriate, scientifically sound theory as a basis for nursing practice decisions.

Standard II. Assessment. The nurse systematically collects, records, and analyzes data that are comprehensive and accurate.

Standard III. Diagnosis. The nurse, in expressing conclusions supported by recorded assessment and current scientific premises, uses nursing diagnoses and/or standard classifications of mental disorders for childhood and adolescence.

Standard IV. Planning. The nurse develops a nursing care plan with specific goals and interventions delineating nursing actions unique to the needs of each child or adolescent, as well as those of the family and other relevant interactive social systems.

Standard V. Intervention. The nurse intervenes as guided by the nursing care plan to implement nursing actions that promote, maintain, or restore physical and mental health, prevent illness, effect rehabilitation in childhood and adolescence, and restore developmental progression.

Standard V-A. Intervention: Therapeutic Environment. The nurse provides, structures, and maintains a therapeutic environment in collaboration with the child or adolescent, the family, and other health care providers.

---

*Standards V-D and X apply only to the clinical specialist in child and adolescent psychiatric and mental health nursing.

Source: From *Standards of Child and Adolescent Psychiatric and Mental Health Nursing Practice* by American Nurses' Association, 1985, Kansas City, MO: American Nurses' Association. Copyright 1985 by American Nurses' Association. Reprinted by permission.

Standard V-B. Intervention: Activities of Daily Living. The nurse uses the activities of daily living in a goal-directed way to foster the physical and mental well-being of the child or adolescent and family.

Standard V-C. Intervention: Psychotherapeutic Interventions. The nurse uses psychotherapeutic interventions to assist children or adolescents and families to develop, improve, or regain their adaptive functioning, to promote health, prevent illness, and facilitate rehabilitation.

Standard V-D.* Intervention: Psychotherapy.* The child and adolescent psychiatric and mental health specialist uses advanced clinical expertise to function as a psychotherapist for the child or adolescent and family and accepts professional accountability for nursing practice.

Standard V-E. Intervention: Health Teaching and Anticipatory Guidance. The nurse assists the child or adolescent and family to achieve more satisfying and productive patterns of living through health teaching and anticipatory guidance.

Standard V-F. Intervention: Somatic Therapies. The nurse uses knowledge of somatic therapies with the child or adolescent and family to enhance therapeutic interventions.

Standard VI. Evaluation. The nurse evaluates the response of the child or adolescent and family to nursing actions in order to revise the data base, nursing diagnoses, and nursing care plan.

Professional Performance Standards

Standard VII. Quality Assurance. The nurse participates in peer review and other means of evaluation to assure quality of nursing care provided for children and adolescents and their families.

Standard VIII. Continuing Education. The nurse assumes responsibility for continuing education and professional development and contributes to the professional growth of others studying childrens' and adolescents' mental health.

Standard IX. Interdisciplinary Collaboration. The nurse collaborates with other health care providers in assessing, planning, implementing, and evaluating programs and other activities related to child and adolescent psychiatric and mental health nursing.

Standard X. Use of Community Health Systems.* The nurse participates with other members of the community in assessing, planning, implementing, and evaluating mental health services and community systems that attend to primary, secondary, and tertiary prevention of mental disorders in children and adolescents.

Standard XI. Research. The nurse contributes to nursing and the child and adolescent psychiatric and mental health field through innovations in theory and practice and participation in research, and communicates these contributions.

Appendix B

Classification of Human Responses of Concern for Psychiatric Mental Health Nursing Practice

1. HUMAN RESPONSE PATTERNS IN ACTIVITY PROCESSES

1.1   *Motor Behavior*

    1.1.1   Potential for Alteration

        *1.1.1.1   Activity Intolerance

        1.1.1.2

    1.1.2   Altered Motor Behavior

        *1.1.2.1   Activity Intolerance

        1.1.2.2   Bizarre Motor Behavior

        1.1.2.3   Catatonia

        1.1.2.4   Disorganized Motor Behavior

        *1.1.2.5   Fatigue

        1.1.2.6   Hyperactivity

        1.1.2.7   Hypoactivity

        1.1.2.8   Psychomotor Agitation

        1.1.2.9   Psychomotor Retardation

        1.1.2.10   Restlessness

    1.1.99   Motor Behavior Not Otherwise Specified (NOS)

1.2   *Recreation Patterns*

    1.2.1   Potential for Alteration

        1.2.1.1

        1.2.1.2

    1.2.2   Altered Recreation Patterns

        1.2.2.1   Age Inappropriate Recreation

        1.2.2.2   Anti-Social Recreation

---

*Approved NANDA Diagnoses

Source: From "Revision of the Phenomena of Concern for Psychiatric Mental Health Nursing" by A.W. O'Toole & M.E. Loomis, 1989, *Archives of Psychiatric Nursing, 5*, pp. 292–299. Copyright 1989 by W.B. Saunders. Reprinted by permission.

	*5.1.2.1	Post-trauma Response		
	*5.1.2.2	Rape Trauma Syndrome		
	*5.1.2.3	Compound Reaction		
	*5.1.2.4	Silent Reaction		
	5.1.99	Abuse Response Patterns NOS		

5.2   *Communication Processes*
    5.2.1   Potential for Alteration
   *5.2.2   Altered Communication Processes
          5.2.2.1   Altered Nonverbal Communication
       *5.2.2.2   Altered Verbal Communication
               5.2.2.2.1   Aphasia
               5.2.2.2.2   Bizarre Content
               5.2.2.2.3   Confabulation
               5.2.2.2.4   Echolalia
               5.2.2.2.5   Incoherent
               5.2.2.2.6   Mute
               5.2.2.2.7   Neologisms
               5.2.2.2.8   Nonsense/Word Salad
               5.2.2.2.9   Stuttering
    5.2.99   Communication Processes NOS

5.3   *Conduct/Impulse Processes*
    5.3.1   Potential for Alteration
         *5.3.1.1   Potential for Violence
         5.3.1.2   Suicidal Ideation
    5.3.2   Altered Conduct/Impulse Processes
         5.3.2.1   Accident Prone
         5.3.2.2   Aggressive/Violent Behavior Toward Environment
         5.3.2.3   Delinquency
         5.3.2.4   Lying
         5.3.2.5   Physical Aggression Toward Others
         5.3.2.6   Physical Aggression Toward Self
               5.3.2.6.1   Suicide Attempt(s)
         5.3.2.7   Promiscuity
         5.3.2.8   Running Away
         5.3.2.9   Substance Abuse
         5.3.2.10 Truancy
         5.3.2.11 Vandalism
         5.3.2.12 Verbal Aggression Toward Others
    5.3.99   Conduct/Impulse Processes NOS

5.4   *Family Processes*
    5.4.1   Potential for Alteration

6. HUMAN RESPONSE PATTERNS IN PERCEPTION PROCESSES

6.1   *Attention*
    6.1.1   Potential for Alteration
    6.1.2   Altered Attention
          6.1.2.1   Hyperalertness
          6.1.2.2   Inattention
          6.1.2.3   Selective Attention
    6.1.99   Attention Patterns NOS

6.2   *Comfort*
    6.2.1   Potential for Alteration
   *6.2.2   Altered Comfort Patterns
          6.2.2.1   Discomfort
          6.2.2.2   Distress
       *6.2.2.3   Pain
                6.2.2.3.1   Acute Pain
             *6.2.2.3.2   Chronic Pain
    6.2.99   Comfort Patterns NOS

6.3   *Self Concept*
    6.3.1   Potential for Alteration
    6.3.2   Altered Self Concept
       *6.3.2.1   Altered Body Image
       *6.3.2.2   Altered Personal Identity
       *6.3.2.3   Altered Self Esteem
            *6.3.2.3.1   Chronic Low Self Esteem
            *6.3.2.3.2   Situational Low Self Esteem
        6.3.2.4   Altered Sexual Identity
            6.3.2.4.1   Altered Gender Identity
    6.3.3   Undeveloped Self Concept
    6.3.99   Self Concept Patterns NOS

6.4   *Sensory Perception*
    6.4.1.   Potential for Alteration
   *6.4.2   Altered Sensory Perception
        6.4.2.1   Hallucinations
            *6.4.2.1.1   Auditory
            *6.4.2.1.2   Gustatory
            *6.4.2.1.3   Kinesthetic
            *6.4.2.1.4   Olfactory
            *6.4.2.1.5   Tactile
            *6.4.2.1.6   Visual
        6.4.2.2   Illusions
    6.4.99   Sensory Perception Processes NOS

7. HUMAN RESPONSE PATTERNS IN PHYSIOLOGICAL PROCESSES

7.1   Circulation
    7.1.1   Potential for Alteration
          7.1.1.1   Fluid Volume Deficit
    7.1.2   Altered Circulation
          7.1.2.1   Altered Cardiac Circulation
              *7.1.2.1.1   Decreased Cardiac Output
          7.1.2.2   Altered Vascular Circulation
              *7.1.2.2.1   Altered Fluid Volume
              *7.1.2.2.2   Fluid Volume Excess
              *7.1.2.2.3   Tissue Perfusion
                  *7.1.2.2.3.1   Peripheral
                  *7.1.2.2.3.2   Renal
    7.1.99   Altered Circulation Processes NOS
7.2   Elimination
    7.2.1   Potential for Alteration
    7.2.2   Altered Elimination Processes
          *7.2.2.1   Altered Bowel Elimination
              *7.2.2.1.1   Constipation
                  *7.2.2.1.1.1   Colonic
                  *7.2.2.1.1.2   Perceived
              *7.2.2.1.2   Diarrhea
              7.2.2.1.3   Encopresis
              *7.2.2.1.4   Incontinence
          *7.2.2.2   Altered Urinary Elimination
              7.2.2.2.1   Enuresis
              *7.2.2.2.2   Incontinence
                  *7.2.2.2.2.1   Functional
                  *7.2.2.2.2.2   Reflex
                  *7.2.2.2.2.3   Stress
                  *7.2.2.2.2.4   Total
                  *7.2.2.2.2.5   Urge
              *7.2.2.2.3   Retention
          7.2.2.3   Altered Skin Elimination
    7.2.99   Elimination Processes NOS
7.3   Endocrine/Metabolic Processes
    7.3.1   Potential for Alteration
    7.3.2   Altered Endocrine/Metabolic Processes
          *7.3.2.1   Altered Growth and Development
          7.3.2.2   Altered Hormone Regulation
              7.3.2.2.1   Premenstrual Stress Syndrome
          7.3.99   Endocrine/Metabolic Processes NOS

7.10.2.1	Altered Immune Response	
	7.10.2.1.1	Infection
7.10.2.2	Altered Body Temperature	
	*7.10.2.2.1	Hyperthermia
	*7.10.2.2.2	Hypothermia
	*7.10.2.2.3	Ineffective Thermoregulation

7.10.99 Physical Regulation Processes NOS

8. HUMAN RESPONSE PATTERNS IN VALUATION PROCESSES

8.1   *Meaningfulness*

8.1.1   Potential for Alteration
*8.1.2   Altered Meaningfulness
     8.1.2.1   Helplessness
     *8.1.2.2   Hopelessness
     8.1.2.3   Loneliness
     *8.1.2.4   Powerlessness
8.1.99   Meaningfulness Patterns NOS

8.2   *Spirituality*

8.2.1   Potential for Alteration
8.2.2   Altered Spirituality
     8.2.2.1   Spiritual Despair
     *8.2.2.2   Spiritual Distress
8.2.99   Spirituality Patterns NOS

8.3   *Values*

8.3.1   Potential for Alteration
8.3.2   Altered Values
     8.3.2.1   Conflict With Social Order
     8.3.2.2   Inability to Internalize Values
     8.3.2.3   Unclear Values
8.3.99   Value Patterns NOS

Index